Still the Promised City?

ROGER WALDINGER

Still the Promised City?

AFRICAN-AMERICANS AND NEW IMMIGRANTS IN POSTINDUSTRIAL NEW YORK

HARVARD UNIVERSITY PRESS

Cambridge, Massachusetts, and London, England

for Max

Copyright © 1996 by the President and Fellows of Harvard College
All rights reserved
Printed in the United States of America
Second printing, 1999

First Harvard University Press paperback edition, 1999

Library of Congress Cataloging-in-Publication Data

Waldinger, Roger David.
    Still the promised city? : African-Americans and new immigrants
in postindustrial New York / Roger Waldinger.
        p.   cm.
    Includes bibliographical references and index.
    ISBN 0-674-83861-0 (cloth)
    ISBN 0-674-00072-2 (pbk.)
    1. Afro-Americans—New York (N.Y.)—Economic conditions.
2. Afro-Americans—Employment—New York (N.Y.)
3. Immigrants—Employment—New York (N.Y.)   4. New York
(N.Y.)—Economic conditions.
I. Title.
F128.9.N3W32   1996
330.9747'1'00896073—dc20

95-43335
Rev.

Contents

Acknowledgments

Few books begin with a bow to municipal bureaucrats, but that's where first thanks for this book belong, since the ideas that appear in the following pages derive from a report I wrote over a decade ago, with my friend and colleague Thomas Bailey, for a then obscure, now defunct branch of New York City's government. At the time, Tom and I were just emerging from that ritual known as the dissertation; coming up for air, we stumbled on the debate about cities' changing economies and their minority population base. We were taken aback to learn that most scholars saw the roots of minority economic distress in the disappearance of low-skilled jobs, since the immigrants whom we had been studying were converging on New York in growing numbers and seemed to have no trouble finding work, low skills and other handicaps notwithstanding. New York's economy, we concluded after some review of the relevant statistics and studies, retained plenty of entry-level jobs; the problem was that too few of them went to native-born, black Americans.

For the next several years, we contented ourselves with punching holes in the conventional wisdom, using new sources of data and more elaborate techniques. Much to our surprise, those efforts met with some success; eventually, we concluded that we might indeed have the making of a book, realizing full well that a successful book would have to do more than say that the other guy is wrong. This book represents the culmination of our early attempts to describe the new urban reality and explain its unexpected shape.

As matters turned out, I ended up writing that book alone. Though we had great fun working together, Tom's interests in technological change and educational reform led him elsewhere before we had a chance to make substantial progress. Chapter 7 is largely drawn from a paper that we coauthored; early drafts of the second and third sections of Chapter 1 were also written in tandem. For better or (more likely) worse, responsibility for the rest of the book lies in my hands alone. Fortunately, I have been able to count on Tom's continuing interest in this project and on his wise and skeptical reactions to my ideas. For that, and for his continuing friendship, I am deeply grateful.

I began work on this book while on the faculty of the City College of the City University of New York. The proletarian Harvard of yore has taken a considerable beating in recent years, and I am glad to say that CCNY deserves a far better reputation and fate. I found it to be a stimulating environment and an exciting place in which to teach. It was also a school that supported its junior faculty, without which help I would never have gotten started on a project such as this. Special thanks are due to Steven Goldberg, my former chairman; Arline McCord, then dean of the Division of Social Sciences; and Jeffrey Rosen, her successor; they allowed me to leverage a grant from the Robert Wagner Institute of Public Policy, then headed by Professor Asher Arian of the CUNY Graduate Center, so that I could gain a semester's release from teaching. They also permitted me to take a year's sabbatical leave, during which time I conducted most of the field research on which I report in the pages to follow.

I had the good fortune to spend the academic years of 1989–1991 at Columbia University's Eisenhower Center for the Conservation of Human Resources, directed by Eli Ginzberg. A leader in research on health and employment policy for five decades and more, Eli is also an expert on New York and its ever-changing people; his confidence in me and his support of this project were a source of great encouragement, and I am delighted to be able to thank him in public. Thanks also are due to the staff of the center, in particular Charles Frederick, and to Meg Koppell and Rob Smith, who provided invaluable research assistance. My colleague Greta Gilbertson worked with me on a number of projects, one of which, never completed, nonetheless provided data on which I report in Chapter 8.

I completed this book three thousand miles away from New York, on the sociology faculty at UCLA. The move to UCLA had many benefits, fringe and otherwise: it forced me to stop researching and start writing; more important, it allowed me to join a community of like-minded scholars. I am especially grateful to my colleagues Mehdi Bo-zorgmehr, Rogers Brubaker, Ivan Light, David Lopez, Ruth Milkman, and Jeffrey Prager, who too often found themselves importuned to read part of this book and always answered yes. UCLA also attracts a group of extraordinarily talented graduate students, and it is my good luck that some of them were interested in this project. I thank Michael Lichter, with whom I have worked closely for the past few years and to whom much of the credit for the techniques used in the analysis of niches belongs. Michael did a heroic job in preparing the runs from the Censuses of Population; Hiromi Ono was kind enough to take over from Michael when he got busy with another project. When the book was completed, Nelson Lim took on the responsibility of preparing a final manuscript; in addition to his superb technical work, he also gave me a searching critique of Chapter 1, which I have tried my best to answer. Deborah Ho, an outstanding UCLA undergraduate, has somehow had the patience to put up with me, taking care of sundry bibliographic questions and making sure that my office didn't come to a crashing halt.

Many friends and colleagues read portions of this book; unfortunately space precludes my mentioning all their names here. But since they know who they are, I am delighted to acknowledge their help and to tell them that community does indeed exist in the academic world and that it has made a great difference in this case. Thanks also go to Michael Aronson, my editor at Harvard University Press, who saw merit in this book and quickly shepherded it along; to the three anonymous readers who assessed the manuscript for the press and gave it careful, helpful reviews; and to Elizabeth Hurwit, to whom I am in great debt for her meticulous copyediting.

I also wish to express my gratitude to a number of institutions for their financial help: I was supported by several PSC-CUNY Faculty Research Grants; by grants from the UCLA Academic Senate; and by grants from the Ford Foundation and the U.S. Department of Labor to the Eisenhower Center for the Conservation of Human Resources.

Portions of Chapter 6 appeared originally as "The Continuing Significance of Race: Racial Conflict and Racial Discrimination in Construction," *Politics & Society* 19, no. 3: 291–324, copyright © 1991 by Sage Publications. Reprinted by permission of Sage Publications, Inc.

My deepest thanks go to the members of my family. My parents and my grandmother have always been a great source of encouragement. They have also helped by example. My father's unending struggle to continue writing and researching, notwithstanding the ravages of Parkinson's Disease, represents a model of commitment to the scholarly enterprise to which I can only aspire and never expect to attain. My wife, Hilary, not only tolerated my years of nattering about this book and the time it consumed; she was also willing to lend her good grammatical and stylistic sense to helping improve the text. My daughter, Miriam, showed great timing by arriving just before I finished the manuscript; her sweet presence has been a source of great joy ever since. My son, Max, was often good enough to let his father write in peace. But he usually had a better idea in mind—like playing computer games, going swimming, or heading to the creek to catch crayfish—and of course he was right. For that reason, and for countless others, I dedicate this book to him with all my love.

1 | The New Urban Reality

New York's brush with fiscal insolvency in the mid-1970s signaled the end for the old industrial cities of the United States. Its revival in the 1980s heralded the emergence of the nation's largest cities as world service centers. The smokestack cities of the industrial heartland unfortunately have no replacement for their run-of-the-mill production activities, steadily eroding under the twin impact of computerization and foreign competition. But in the largest urban agglomerations—Chicago, Los Angeles, Philadelphia, and, especially, New York—the advent of a postindustrial economy has triggered a new phase of growth. The key activities of the new economy—information processing, the coordination of large organizations, and the management of volatile financial markets—are overwhelmingly urban-based. And their dynamism has yanked these largest cities out of the economic torpor into which they had sunk.

The new urban vitality notwithstanding, cities remain deeply troubled—perhaps more so than before. The paradox of urban plenty is that comparatively few of the city's residents have been able to enjoy the fruits of growth. The number of poor people living in central cities has not fallen but risen, and dramatically so. Instead of arresting social dislocation, the economic turnaround has exacerbated the urban social problems identified thirty years ago. Though right and left differ on social policy responses, both camps agree that a sizable segment of the poor has been lopped off into an "urban underclass"—persistently poor and with no connection to legitimate ways of making a living.[1]

Demography is the subtext to the contemporary tale of urban woe.

"Back to the city" has been the catchword of the new urban profes-sionals—today's huddled masses, piled up in neighborhoods in and around the downtown business centers. But the influx of this much maligned gentry never matched the attention it received in the press. The tide of people flowing cityward remains what it has been for the past forty years: America's big cities attract mainly nonwhites. First came blacks, displaced from the technological backwaters of the agrarian South. Then came a wave of immigrants from the labor-surplus areas of the developing world: today's urban newcomers are arriving in numbers that rival the great migrations of a century ago.[2]

Thus the city of services is also a "majority minority" city. But how does this population base fit into the urban economy of today?

The received academic wisdom maintains that there is no fit at all. The industrial city grew because it possessed labor, and what it demanded of its labor was willing hands and strong muscles—not diplomas or technical expertise. But in the city of information pro-cessing and the transaction of high-level business deals, these qual-ities count no more. The equation between the city's economic func-tion and its population base has no place for the unlettered, no matter how willing. The decline of the industrial city has left minorities high and dry.[3]

But a dissenting interpretation, now sufficiently repeated to have become a conventional wisdom, tells a different tale. Modern urban development simultaneously generates high-level professional and managerial jobs and a proliferation of low-skilled, low-income "ser-vice" jobs. The polarized metropolis leaves minorities far from use-less; instead, they serve as the new drawers of water and hewers of wood. In this version, it is not the poor who depend on the rich for their beneficence or for jobs and income to trickle down. Rather, the rich need the poor—to provide low-cost services, to maintain the city's underbelly, and to prop up what remains of the depressed man-ufacturing sector.[4]

In this book I argue that both stories—however intuitively appealing they may be separately or together—have it wrong. Neither metaphor, of polarization or of dislocation, captures the impact of the post-industrial urban transformation.[5] At root, both depict faceless, imper-sonal structures inexorably performing their actions on an inert urban mass. Not subjected to analysis, the structures are instead taken for granted, abstracted from any historical context, and divorced from the specific interests and forces that might have given them shape. Conflict and politics do not enter into these accounts of the making of the postindustrial economic world. Passing over dominant groups and their interests, these rival stories treat the new polyglot working and middle classes as an undifferentiated mass, helplessly playing out the scripts written for them by history.

But no *deus ex machina* determines which people get jobs, how they do so, and whether they then move ahead. The mechanisms of matching and mobility are social arrangements, shaped by the historical contexts in which they have grown up and subject to change—not simply as a result of pressures from the impersonal forces of the world economy, but in response to the actions of contending parties in specific societies and places. This book places the people and groups that have made, maintained, and changed the structures of today's postindustrial urban economy at the very center of the discussion.

My interpretation of the new urban reality will be developed in a single, sustained argument in the pages that follow. In briefest compass, the argument reads like this: The story of ethnics in America's cities is a collective search for mobility, in which the succession of one migrant wave after another alternatively stabilizes and disrupts the labor queue. In a market economy, employers allocate jobs to the most desirable workers they can recruit; but each market economy bears the imprint of the social structure in which it is embedded. In a race-conscious society like the United States, employers rank entire groups of people in terms of their ethnic and racial characteristics. All things being equal, members of the core cultural group stand at the top, followed by others.

The instability of America's capitalist economy subjects the labor queue's ordering to change. Growth pulls the topmost group up the totem pole; lower-ranking groups then seize the chance to move up the pecking order; in their wake, they leave behind vacancies at the bottom, which employers fill by recruiting workers from outside the economy—namely, migrants. The structure of the labor queue goes unchallenged as long as these newest arrivals are content to work in the bottom-level jobs for which they were initially recruited. But the economic orientations of the newcomers inevitably change, and when they do, complementarity is likely to be replaced by competition—which fans continuing ethnic strife over access to good jobs.

Competition between newcomers and insiders takes the form of conflict over the ethnic niche. Although migrants start at the bottom, they enter the economy under the auspices of friends or kin, which means that they begin with connections. Networks funnel the new-comers into specialized economic activities: as newcomers flow into the workplaces where earlier settlers have already gotten established, ethnic concentrations, or niches, gradually develop. The path up from the bottom involves finding a good niche and dominating it—which means that good jobs are reserved for insiders, leaving the next wave of outsiders excluded. Thus, the search by an earlier migrant group for labor market shelters eventuates in barriers that the next round of arrivals must confront.

Of course, economic life in America's cities is not all conflict. In some cases, the queue process simply pulls insider groups up the totem pole, leading them to abandon niches that a new group of out-siders can take over. In other instances, conditions in the niche un-dergo relative deterioration, in which case the barriers to outsiders get relaxed. These conditions ensure that ethnics in the labor market are sometimes noncompeting, segmented groups. But the scarcity of good jobs relative to the surplus of job seekers guarantees that competition never disappears.

Thus, the structures that African-Americans and new immigrants confront result from America's serial incorporation of outsider groups and from those groups' attempts to create protective economic shel-ters. The continuous recourse to migration as a source of low-level labor, so characteristic of the United States, has made ethnicity the crucial and enduring mechanism that sorts groups of categorically dif-ferent workers into an identifiably distinct set of jobs. For this reason, the ethnic division of labor stands as the central division of labor in the cities of twentieth-century America; the fates of new immi-grants and African-Americans are bound up in its making and remak-ing.

New York City is the prism through which I develop this argument in full. As America's first postindustrial place, New York is a critical case for any explanation of urban change and its impact. I mean "first" in the sense of arriving at postindustrialism before its urban rivals and in the sense of having moved further toward the advanced service economy than any other principal urban center. New York also ex-emplifies the new melting pot—heated to full boil. New York is not only a minority majority city. It is also the Mecca for the newest immigrants, just as it has been throughout the history of the United States. Nowhere else does one find quite so complex an ethnic mosaic. Consequently, no other city provides as good a platform for studying how ethnic group resources and strategies interact with structural changes to shape ethnic group fates.

This book recounts the transformation of New York's ethnic division of labor since midcentury, a story I tell in two parts. One details how the very instability of the labor queue and the ethnic division of labor it engenders create opportunities for outsiders and newcomers. The second shows how these pieces of the pie have been divided up.

The conventional wisdom attributes urban disaster to the loss of white city residents. In fact, the outflow of white New Yorkers is what has given newcomers their chance. During economic downturns, whites fled the city faster than the rate of decline. And when the economy reheated, the outward seepage of whites slowed down but never stopped.

Over the years, the disproportionately declining white presence produced a ladder effect, creating empty spaces for newcomers up and down—though mainly down—the economic totem pole. Reflecting the influence of *prior* migration histories, the impact of white population decline rippled through New York's diversified economic complex in an uneven way. With the exception of those in construction and a few other skilled trades, New York's white ethnic proletariat disappeared after 1970, though a myriad of blue-collar jobs remained. Consequently, ethnic succession generated opportunities both in declining industries, where the rate of white outflows often outpaced the rate of job erosion, and in growth industries, where whites poured out of bottom-level positions even as demand for low-skilled workers increased. New York's small-business sector experienced the same round of musical chairs: newcomers moved in as white ethnics abandoned petty retailing, garment contracting, and other less remunerative business lines. A similar sequence of events occurred in many parts of the public sector, especially after 1975, when whites left municipal service for better opportunities elsewhere.

Since succession provides the backdrop for the economic stories of new immigrant and African-American New Yorkers, the central question concerns who got which jobs and why. In the 1970s and 1980s, black New Yorkers built up and consolidated the niche they had earlier established in government work. Public sector employment offered numerous advantages, including easier access to jobs and an employer that provided better, more equitable treatment. But convergence on government employment had the corollary effect of heightening the skill thresholds of the chief black economic base.

To be sure, connections helped in gaining access to municipal jobs; and my case studies show that black civil servants networked as much as anyone else. However, civil service positions held promise only to those members of the community with the skills, experience, and credentials that government required—qualities not shared by the many African-American New Yorkers who have found themselves at economic risk.

Of course, work in the bowels of New York's economy could have been a possibility. Yet the data and the case studies demonstrate a steady erosion of African-Americans' *share* of the large number of remaining, low-skilled jobs—even as the *number* of low-level jobs held by minorities, native and immigrant, steadily grew. The African-American concentrations of old, from the most menial occupations in domestic service to later clusters like garment or hotel work, largely faded away. And African-Americans simultaneously failed to make headway in those low-skilled sectors where competition with whites had previously kept them locked out.

The immigrants, by contrast, responded to ethnic succession in ways that expanded their economic base. Initially, the match between their aspirations and broader labor market dynamics created openings that the newcomers could fill. On the one hand, the immigrants' social origins predisposed them to embrace jobs that native New Yorkers would no longer accept; meager as they appeared to New Yorkers, the paychecks in the city's garment, restaurant, or retail sectors looked good in comparison to the going rate in Santo Domingo, Hong Kong, or Kingston. On the other hand, the city's factory sector was suffering a hemorrhage of older, native workers that outpaced the leakage of jobs, leading employers to take on new hands.

The initial portals into New York's economy channeled the newcomers into bottom-level jobs. The links between the workplace and the immigrant community helped convert these positions into platforms for upward movement. Immigrants were simply tied to others who would help them, right from the start. The connections among newcomers and settlers provided an informal structure to immigrant economic life; that structure, in turn, furnished explicit and implicit signposts of economic information and mechanisms of support that helped ethnics acquire skills and move ahead through business and other means.

In the end, new immigrant and African-American New Yorkers shaped their own fates by creating distinctive ethnic economic niches.

But history had much to do with where each group could find a place. Looking over their shoulders toward conditions in the societies from which they have just departed, migrants move into industrial economies at the very bottom, taking up the jobs that natives will no longer do. While today's immigrants follow this traditional pattern, African-Americans, by contrast, are the migrants of a generation ago. The earlier pattern of rejections and successes shapes their searches of today, foreclosing options that immigrants, with their very different experiences and orientations, will pursue. Unlike the immigrants, African-Americans aspire to the rewards and positions enjoyed by whites. But the niches that African-Americans have carved out require skills that the least-educated members of that community simply don't have; African-American networks no longer provide connections to these more accessible jobs; and relative to the newcomers, employers find unskilled African-Americans to be much less satisfactory recruits. As for better-skilled African-Americans, they often compete with whites on unequal terrain, since past and present discrimination in housing and schools makes African-American workers less well prepared than whites. In this way, the mismatch between the aspirations of the *partly* disadvantaged and the requirements of the jobs to which they aspire provides the spark for persistent economic racial conflict between blacks and whites.

By contrast, immigrants have moved into noncompeting positions, taking over jobs that whites have deserted in their move up the occupational pecking order. Once the immigrants gain a lock on low-level jobs, ethnic connections funnel a steady stream of newcomers, excluding black New Yorkers who are not members of the same ethnic club.

Thus, the advent of a majority minority economy marks the emergence of a new division of labor, in which the various groups of new New Yorkers play distinct economic roles. Niche creation by African-Americans and immigrants has evolved into a mutually exclusive carving up of the pie: in carving out a place in the ethnic division of labor, the two groups effectively open or foreclose opportunities for each other. As in the past, control over good jobs and desired resources is subject to contest. Thus, the various components of New York's polyglot working and middle classes follow the example of their predecessors, continuing in, and reinvigorating, the pattern of interethnic economic competition that long characterized the city's white ethnic groups.

I detail this story in the chapters to follow. The rest of this introductory chapter returns to the conventional accounts of urban economic change, before elaborating on the alternative perspective I briefly presented above. The next three chapters will trace out the argument in numbers. Chapter 2 tells the story of New York's economic and demographic transformations, examining its re-peopling, through vast internal and international migration flows, and its postindustrial transition. Chapters 3 and 4 explore the impact of these simultaneous shifts, revealing the birth of a new ethnic division of labor in the aftermath of New York's decisive economic change.

The remaining chapters consist of a series of case studies documenting the processes of ethnic niche creation and maintenance. Chapter 5 focuses on two entry-level industries, garments and hotels, that have provided mobility paths for immigrants but not for African-Americans. Chapter 6 examines the construction industry—an ethnic niche par excellence, but one from which African-Americans have been largely excluded despite their constant efforts to contest barriers to access. Chapter 7 moves on to the public sector, showing how and why African-Americans have penetrated so deeply into the state employment system. Chapter 8 discusses small business, a prime example of new immigrant mobilization of informal resources and African-American inability to successfully do the same. Chapter 9 then reviews the argument and sketches out its implications for the future.[6]

In this book I have been deliberately eclectic in choosing methodologies. Unlike most of my counterparts in the social sciences, I am not wedded to any methodological approach. Ultimately I plead pragmatism, in a quest for methodological strategies that work; my conclusion is that different methodologies are best for different questions.

Finally, a word on the sources on which this book is based. While Chapters 2 through 4 make much use of the public use samples from the 1940, 1950, 1970, 1980, and 1990 Censuses of Population, the entire book relies on a combination of material: in-depth interviews, extensive consultation of primary and secondary sources, as well as long-time, close-up observations of the industries and sectors I discuss.[7] Notes to specific chapters provide details on the sources, and I discuss the field work in an appendix to the book. But ultimately, and importantly, the book is the product of more than a decade's research on New York and its people and industries. It is the particular knowledge I have gained in the process, leavened with theory, that gives this book its strength.

A Skills Mismatch?

The mismatch thesis occupies the place of honor in the literature on urban poverty. The city was once a place where low-skilled new-comers could get a job and slowly start the climb up the occupational ladder. The advent of the postindustrial economy, argue mismatch proponents, undermined the city's historic role as staging ground of upward mobility.

The mismatch hypothesis first emerged as part of the structural unemployment controversy of the late 1950s and early 1960s. Analysts concerned by a then sluggish economy and fearful of an impending technological revolution fingered skill inadequacies as the source of employment dislocation. Whether the effects of the 1964 tax cut disproved the structural unemployment thesis, as some Keynesians argued, or not, the low unemployment rate of the late 1960s eclipsed the controversy as well as the fears of technological displacement. At the same time, the public policy agenda changed, with worries about the fate of blue-collar workers eclipsed by the preoccupation with race. In this context, the mismatch discussion took a new twist and began to focus on the problems of black workers.

More than two decades after this reformulation, the basics of the mismatch argument remain unchanged. It still emphasizes manufacturing's decline but now connects this shift to sinking black economic fortunes. As Frank Levy noted in his volume on income inequality in the 1980 Census Monograph series:

> Between 1950 and 1960 New York . . . had sustained its population through high birthrates and significant in-migration from rural areas. Many of the in-migrants were black, and over the decade the proportion of blacks in the city's population rose from 10 to 15 percent. The in-migrants were coming in search of higher incomes, and in these early postwar years the cities could accommodate them. Cities had both cheap housing, and most important, manufacturing jobs . . . Because of these jobs, cities could still serve as a place for rural migrants to get a start.[8]

But what was true in the late 1950s rapidly changed. Developments in technology and communications, argued John Kasarda, decimated the "traditional goods-processing industries that once constituted the economic backbone of cities, and provided entry-level employment for lesser-skilled African-Americans." In return for the eroding factory sector, cities gained a new economy dominated by "knowledge-intensive white-collar service industries that typically required education beyond high school and therefore precluded most poorly employed inner city minorities from obtaining employment."[9] Thus, on the demand side, the "very jobs that in the past attracted and socially upgraded waves of disadvantaged persons . . . were disappearing"; on the supply side, the number of "minority residents who lack the education for employment in the new information-processing industries [was] increasing."[10] In part, the burgeoning ranks of low-skilled workers reflected the advent of African-American baby boomers; in part, it resulted from the renewal of mass immigration and the arrival of poorly schooled newcomers. But whatever the precise source of demographic change, it boded ill for urban America and its future.

And so, over the past thirty years demand and supply factors fell out of sync; in Kasarda's words, the "conflicting residential and employment base changes . . . placed the demographics and economics of our cities on a collision course."[11] As we approach the year 2000, these woes take on a particularly aggravated form since the unfolding economic landscape will offer far fewer low-skilled opportunities than ever before. In the words of the scenario spinners at the Hudson Institute, "very few new jobs will be created for those who cannot read, follow directions, and use mathematics." Fast-track growth is predicted for jobs that require much higher education, although the bulk of employment will remain in less demanding positions like those filled by cooks, secretaries, and cashiers. But even these lower-level "workers will be expected to read and understand directions, add and subtract, and be able to speak and think clearly."[12]

Put demand and supply trends together and you have an "impending U.S. jobs 'disaster.' "[13] With the entire work force straining to keep up with enhanced job requirements, those minority workers who start out behind are unlikely to make up the gap. The Hudson Institute offers the following dim forecast:

> Given the historic patterns of behavior by employers, it is . . . reasonable to expect that they will bid up the wages of the relatively smaller numbers of white labor force entrants, seek to substitute capital for labor in many service occupations, and/or move job sites to the faster growing, more youthful parts of the country, or perhaps the world. Blacks, and particularly black men, are those most likely to be put at risk if such strategies dominate.[14]

That the mismatch hypothesis has survived a quarter-century of intellectual twists and turns is testimony to its intuitive appeal, as well as the impact of repetition and the prestige of its proponents. But the mismatch hypothesis offers a particular, if not to say curious, interpretation of minority employment problems. A close look at those particularities highlights its deficiencies.

First, the mismatch hypothesis has a definite political twist. It blames not discriminating whites but rather the loss of central city manufacturing jobs and the failures of the educational system. To be sure, mismatch proponents do not deny that discrimination persists, though they claim its main effect results from the continuing legacy of bad deeds done in the past. They assert, moreover, that the significance of discrimination, like that of race, is on the decline. Twenty-five years ago the Kerner Commission argued that "racial discrimination is undoubtedly the *second* major reason why the Negro has been unable to escape from poverty."[15] The contemporary literature is rarely so explicit in its causal ordering, but the failure of the literature on mismatch to more than mention discrimination speaks volumes.[16]

If discrimination has lost its force, what explains the peculiar industrial and occupational distribution of blacks? Blacks, as I shall note throughout this book, are concentrated in a handful of sectors, not dispersed throughout the economy. The puzzle, from the skills mismatch point of view, is that the African-American economic niches do not happen to coincide with the principal clusters of low-skilled jobs. Take the case of construction. Construction workers learn their skills on the job, as in the past; educational levels are very low, relative to the urban average; and these are jobs that men are particularly likely to seek. But construction is an industry from which blacks continue to be excluded. Nationwide, the proportion of blacks employed in the industry is well below parity. And construction is just a special case of skilled blue-collar work: here is a domain, relatively low educational levels notwithstanding, in which blacks have much less than a fair share.

While mismatch proponents have no doubt about the source of the problem, they are not so consistent about the population at risk. In its early formulations, the theory centered on black migrants from the South. But black migrants were not the most seriously troubled. Indeed, a number of studies using the 1970 census showed that even controlling for age and education, black migrants from the South living in northern cities had higher incomes, lower incidence of poverty, lower unemployment, and less frequent reliance on welfare than northern-born blacks.[17]

Two decades after the great black migration north, one no longer hears about the specific disabilities of black newcomers. Instead, cities are home to a new cohort of arrivals, this time immigrants from overseas. This latest batch of newcomers fits awkwardly with the basic framework, but mismatch proponents do what they can with this inconvenient fact. As of now, the population mismatched with the urban economy has become an undifferentiated aggregate of everyone not classified by the government as white.

This approach simply will not do: the mismatch hypothesis stands at odds with the immigrant phenomenon itself. If indeed urban employers are hiring none but the highly educated, then why have the leading postindustrial centers also emerged as the principal settlements of the new immigrant population? The key problem, first highlighted by the comparisons among northern- and southern-born blacks, is that labor market outcomes vary in ways that are not explicable in terms of differences in schooling and educational skills. In the largest U.S. cities, the employment of immigrant Hispanics has grown while the employment of native blacks has declined. Yet schooling levels among immigrant Hispanics are most out of sync with those of the rest of the labor force and way below African-Americans', whose educational standing has steadily improved.[18]

A closer look at the employment patterns of immigrants raises even more questions about the basic mismatch assumption. Immigrants were far more dependent on manufacturing than were African-Americans in 1970—a time when the central city goods production base was almost intact. If the decline of manufacturing is to blame for the employment problems of African-Americans, then why has the economic base of immigrants not blown apart? And since no one argues that educational requirements are a barrier to African-American employment in manufacturing, why were immigrants and not African-Americans able to make substantial gains in factory jobs?

This line of questioning leads to another observation: manufacturing was not particularly important for the economic fate of blacks. Black New Yorkers were already underrepresented in manufacturing as of 1970, and in the years since then they have shifted even further away from goods production jobs. In fact, the move out of manufacturing is consistent with the overall evolution of African-American employment, which, as I shall establish in Chapters 3 and 4, has changed in ways that reduce exposure to the job loss resulting from industrial decline. Consequently, the concentrations established by 1980 should have left African-Americans well positioned to experience the changes of the 1980s. That African-American economic opportunities have *not* substantially widened suggests that there is more to the game than being in the right industrial place at the right time.

As I noted earlier, the mismatch equation really has two sides: the supposedly fast-changing requirements of jobs and the slowly evolving schooling levels of blacks. Everyone "knows" that urban jobs demand more and more education; hence, mismatch proponents have not lingered overly long on establishing this fact. What everyone knows, however turns out to not quite be the case. Skill requirements have indeed gone up, but only to a modest degree. Consequently, people with modest levels of schooling have continued to fill a surprising number of jobs. In 1990, for example, persons with twelve years or less of schooling held close to half (44 percent) of all New York City jobs.[19] In general, the tendency toward skill deepening has also slowed substantially since 1960. Ever since then, however, the job picture for blacks has become increasingly grim.[20]

If mismatch proponents move quickly over the question of changing educational requirements, they never stop to examine their assumption about the schooling levels among blacks. Anyone familiar with the educational history of blacks will find irony in the argument that economic problems have been aggravated because schooling performance has gotten *worse.* The historical record, entirely obscured in contemporary debates, attests to tremendous progress against extraordinary obstacles: prohibitions against teaching reading and writing during slavery; not just separate, but woefully underfunded schools in the postbellum South; and the highly segregated, overcrowded systems that greeted the migrants when they came north. As bad as urban schools may be today, the educational environment of African-American schoolchildren never had any good old days.[21]

The crucial issue, therefore, involves the pace and extent of change. Have disparities between blacks and whites in educational attainment narrowed or increased? More important, have blacks kept up with the educational requirements of urban employers—whose work force, as I have noted, is hardly lily white?

Nationwide, over the past twenty years African-Americans have made substantial, if still incomplete, strides toward catching up with whites. At least two indicators provide strong evidence of a diminishing gap. School enrollment rates among college-aged youth tell us about trends among those likely to acquire the up-to-date skills that employers supposedly want; on this count, the increase from 1970 to 1990 among blacks aged 18–24 was substantial and considerably greater than that among comparably aged whites. By contrast, high school dropout rates help identify the size of the population most likely to be hurt by heightened job requirements; here too, as Christopher Jencks has noted, with the dropout rate among blacks falling since 1970, the story is more encouraging among blacks than among whites.[22]

Thus, the skills mismatch rests on a series of widely accepted "facts" that closer examination reveals to be untrue. Blacks never made it into the factory sector in such numbers that manufacturing's later decline would be a disaster. And the schooling story is far more complicated than the simplistic mismatch contentions, with plenty of evidence that blacks are less behind than they were ten, not to speak of twenty, years ago.

A Dual City?

Inaccurate in depicting blacks, the mismatch theory also has nothing to say about the new immigrants who have flocked to the largest post-industrial cities. The puzzle is why the new immigrants converged on the largest urban centers at precisely the time when so many of the traditional routes of immigrant economic mobility have presumably been blocked.[23]

The best-known answer to this question contends that the growth of producer services—finance, insurance, engineering, law, management consulting—has polarized the cities of high finance. The shift to producer services does indeed breed new jobs requiring high levels of education, as the mismatch hypothesis asserts. But critics of the American economy maintain that the growth of services also involves a process of economic restructuring. Service growth at the top simultaneously generates jobs for chambermaids and waiters, investment bankers and lawyers, while positions in between these extremes are slowly but steadily reduced. Restructuring also results in a deployment of new labor force groups, attracting immigrants from overseas to fill the expanded bottom-level jobs.

The coming of the hourglass economy thus creates the demand for immigrant labor. But the relationship between cities and immigrants works both ways: the arrival of the immigrants helps explain why the past two decades have seen an "urban renaissance." On the one hand, the influx of foreign-born workers has given the comatose manufacturing sector a new lease on life. Immigrants, so the story goes, have been a more pliable labor force, and so factory employers have not been obliged to keep wages at parity with national norms. In contrast to nationals, immigrant workers can also be deployed in more flexible ways, thereby giving urban manufacturers the scope to customize production and place greater reliance on subcontracting. As yet another plus, urban manufacturers can also draw on a large, vulnerable population of illegal immigrants. Their presence has given new meaning to the word exploitation, making "the new immigrant sweatshop . . . [a] major U.S. central city employment growth sector in the past decade."[24]

Immigration has also propelled the service economy along. According to Saskia Sassen, who has researched New York:

> Immigration can be seen as a significant labor supplier for the vast infrastructure of low-wage jobs underlying specialized services, and the high-income life-styles of its employees. Messenger services, French hand laundries, restaurants, gourmet food stores, repair and domestic services—these are just a few examples of the vast array of low-wage jobs needed for the operation of the specialized service sector and its employees. Immigrants represent a desirable labor supply because they are relatively cheap, reliable, willing to work on odd shifts, and safe.[25]

The immigrant presence also facilitates the continued expansion of the labor supply for newly created professional and managerial jobs. As Bennett Harrison and Barry Bluestone argue, "the provision of . . . services to the office workers becomes *the* major economic activity for the rest of the city." In their view, "the high cost of living in cities containing corporate headquarters requires that professional households include more than one wage earner in order to sustain a middle-class life style. This, in turn, forces this new aristocracy to consume more and more of the services that workers in an earlier generation would have produced for themselves."[26] By furnishing the "large cohort of restaurant workers, laundry workers, dog walkers, residential construction workers, and the like,"[27] immigrants lower the costs of keeping a high-skilled labor force in place. Were it not for the foreign-born, the advanced service sectors in New York or Los Angeles would have to pay their highly skilled workers even more and thus lose out in the broader competitive game.

The contrast between restructuring and mismatch hypotheses shows that the virtues of one are the vices of the other. The restructuring hypothesis offers a plausible explanation of the immigrant arrival to the postindustrial city. Because proponents of the restructuring hypothesis do not even mention the economic problems of blacks, however, they beg the question of why all the new low-level jobs went to immigrants and not blacks. Amazingly enough, at a time when the specter of displaced, unemployed blacks looms so large in the mismatch hypothesis, the restructuring hypothesis has returned blacks to their old place as "invisible men."

Clearly any adequate account of the urban postindustrial change has to explain the new ethnic division of labor. But the restructuring hypothesis is not weak on this count alone; it also falls short on strictly factual grounds.

Consider the key contention about the changing *structure* of jobs and skills. Evidence that polarization is under way comes from Bureau of Labor Statistics projections of the absolute *number* of new jobs created between now and the turn of the century. Much has been made of the large number of jobs in low-skilled occupations that are expected to be added to the economy by the turn of the century. Of the ten occupations that will require the largest number of new workers, two—registered nurses and primary school teachers—necessitate college degrees. All of the others—janitors, cashiers, truck drivers, and the like—involve skills that can be picked up on the job with little, if any, schoolroom knowledge. But this pattern is largely an artifact of the occupational classification system itself. Low-skilled jobs tend to be less differentiated than higher-skilled jobs; one finds many highly discrete occupational categories at the top of the job hierarchy, in comparison to the situation at the bottom, where a relatively small group of categories lump together large groups of workers. Consequently, regrouping the occupational data presents a different picture of the trajectory of change. Once one reorganizes the occupations into broad categories (executive, administrative, managerial; professional; and so forth), it turns out that the occupations that grew at above-average rates between 1975 and 1990 were the broad occupational groups with above-average educational levels. Projections indicate that those same occupational categories are likely to grow fastest between 1990 and 2005, whereas jobs with generally low educational levels, while remaining quite numerous, will continue to decline.[28]

The figures just presented cover the U.S. economy as a whole. But what about the major urban centers? Occupational polarization mischaracterizes the job trajectory in New York. Although the number of jobs eroded during the bad days of the 1970s, some occupations did grow: professionals increased by 16.5 percent, managers were up 27 percent, and service workers gained an additional 5.8 percent. Meanwhile, all of the blue-collar occupations shrank. The growing tilt toward services explains part of this story, but only part. Within every sector—whether manufacturing or transport, retail or business services—the mix of occupations underwent considerable change, yielding a trend toward occupational upgrading, not polarization. The proportion of workers employed in all blue-collar occupations (craft, operative, laborer, and service) substantially declined in every sector except professional service. Good times in the 1980s breathed life back into some previously declining occupations, but the overall shape of change remained the same. Employment in professional, managerial, and sales jobs grew by about a third in each area in the course of the decade; together, the three occupations accounted for 95 percent of all the new jobs added during the 1980s.

Thus, despite tales of the growth in the number of janitors and fast-food workers, data on occupational change and projected occupational growth for the country as a whole and for New York fail to provide any support for the notion that low-skilled jobs are proliferating. Given this trend, how can the arrival of new immigrants be explained?

An immigrant-absorbing and generally growing service sector would be a possibility, but here again the polarization view leads us further off the track. Surprisingly, the traditional immigrant employing industries have continued as the shock absorbers for the latest immigrant inflow. Manufacturing and retail remain overwhelmingly the chief immigrant concentrations. As for the service side, there is only one sector in which the foreign-born are greatly overrepresented—that old immigrant standby, personal services. Those sectors comprising the "new" urban economy—finance, insurance, real estate, business services, professional services—rank below the average in their reliance on immigrant labor. Moreover, the trends since 1970 provide little evidence that the advanced service industries are becoming more immigrant-dependent.

Thus, the polarization hypothesis has the story about changing urban economies wrong. It also fails to account for the other side of the equation—immigrants. Though much is made of the exploitability of a large, illegal immigrant labor pool, this point cannot be pushed too far. The illegal immigration numbers game has now been played out: we know that the guesstimates from the early days widely inflated the size of the undocumented population. The number of illegal immigrants—about 3.5 million as of the late 1980s—is greatly overshadowed by the number of new legal immigrant residents and citizens. Similarly, the view that illegal immigrants are significantly more vulnerable than their legal counterparts can no longer be sustained. A decade and a half of research on illegal aliens has shown that their economic, demographic, and human capital characteristics differ little from those of legal immigrants of similar ethnic backgrounds. According to a 1989 U.S. Department of Labor report, "in many instances, illegal status does not lead to significantly lower earnings, nor does it appear to impede mobility substantially."[29] In other words, there are fewer illegal immigrants than conventional accounts once suggested, and they are doing better—or not quite as badly—as one might have thought. Compared to Los Angeles, the destination overwhelmingly favored by illegal immigrants, New York has exercised a modest attraction for unauthorized migration—which makes it still more doubtful that the influx of an especially vulnerable labor force explains New York's rebound from economic collapse.

The Ethnic Division of Labor Transformed

If the prevailing accounts of the impact of the postindustrial urban economy do not hold up, what alternative might there be? The answer is an explanation that provides a single consistent story for African-Americans *and* for immigrants. I begin with a model of how jobs are allocated among ethnic groups.

THE ETHNIC QUEUE

The simplest model assumes that in a race-conscious society like ours, entire groups of people are *ordered* in terms of desirability for preferred jobs, with skill-relevant characteristics serving as additional weights. At each level of relevant skill, members of the core cultural group stand at the top of the ranking, followed by others. Under these conditions, job growth at the top of the hierarchy principally benefits the topmost ranked group; as members of this group ascend the totem pole and fill these new positions, jobs lower down the ladder open up for everyone else. Conversely, should the overall economy, or even particular sectors, turn down, the average position of the core cultural group will drop, pushing all others still further down.

Access to jobs also depends on the shape of the queue—that is, the relative sizes of groups. For our purposes, the critical development occurs when the relative size of the core cultural group declines—either as a result of an economic expansion that absorbs the existing labor force or as a consequence of out-migration. Changes in the shape of the queue trigger upward movement for those with positions lower down. But these shifts also create shortages in low-paying, low-status jobs where former incumbents have seized the chance to move toward better-paying, more prestigious positions. With employers limited in their ability to raise wages or substitute capital for labor, groups external to the labor market—migrants, whether native or foreign—move into the economy, entering the queue at the very bottom.

Whereas employers rank groups of workers in terms of their desirability, groups of workers rank jobs in terms of the relevant resources that jobs can provide. Rankings are also subject to change: erosion in a job's relative pay, prestige, or security may trigger its abandonment by members of the core cultural group, which in turn creates opportunities for lower-down groups, whose opportunities are more constricted. Of greater importance to us are the changes that occur in the rankings of migrants and their children. Differences in origin between natives and migrants yield disparate rankings, with migrants accepting jobs that natives will reject. Since preferences evolve with exposure to prevailing wage and status norms, differences between migrant and native rankings diminish over time; the children of the migrants are likely to operate with the same ranking system as natives.[30]

This model of the ethnic queue moves us beyond mismatch and polarization hypotheses. First, it helps us identify the sources of opportunity within an otherwise unfavorable economic environment. Second, it allows us to link the process of serial migrant labor movements into the urban economy to a cycle of complementary and competitive relationships between old-timer and newcomer groups, and thus to place the changing ethnic division of labor in historical perspective.

OPPORTUNITY AND THE ETHNIC QUEUE

Because changes in the shape of the queue will reallocate jobs among ethnic groups, the crucial factor involves the pacing of demographic relative to economic shifts. Although urban economies shifted steadily from goods to services throughout the postwar period, their demography changed at an even more rapid pace. Whites, who compose the preferred group, have been a steadily diminishing component of the population base. In cases of economic decline, as in New York in the 1970s, the white outflow greatly exceeded the erosion of jobs. And when economic growth turned New York around, as it did during the 1980s, the size of the white population did not keep pace with the increase in jobs.

Moreover, New York's economy has always been distinguished by its reliance on migrants, whether foreign or native, to fill low-level jobs. Industries in the "secondary sector," like retailing or restaurants, have traditionally been havens of employment for immigrants and their children. But that tradition has bred a chronic dependence on outside sources of new recruits, because workers' preferences have evolved with exposure to prevailing economic norms. Whereas migrants accept jobs that natives reject, the migrants' children share the natives' ranking system. Thus, as the second and later generations of European immigrants have entered the labor market, they have dropped out of the effective labor supply feeding into the secondary sector.[31] This process of cycling through industries and sectors has bred an additional demand for replacement labor—beyond that generated by compositional changes alone.

This model provides an adequate prediction of how changes in the number and characteristics of white workers will affect the gross opportunities for new immigrants and for African-Americans. It does not tell us how the jobs vacated by departing whites will be allocated among the contending, successor groups. Here, the queuing metaphor leads us awry, with its suggestion that both jobs and groups are ranked in a stable, orderly way, with top-ranked groups moving into higher-ranked jobs, and so on down the line.

This image of orderly succession stands at variance from reality because ethnic ties serve as a basic mechanism for sorting workers among jobs. Groups are funneled into special places in the labor market—which I shall call niches—and then maintain those specializations, albeit at varying rates of persistence, over time.[32] Thus, when ethnic succession occurs, it upsets an already established ethnic division of labor. And the fundamental *structuring* role of ethnicity means that compositional shifts simply create the circumstances under which the ethnic order in the labor market can be transformed.

How the ethnic division of labor arises and changes are the issues to which I turn below.

THE MAKING OF THE IMMIGRANT NICHE

We can think about the making of an immigrant niche as a two-stage process. First comes a phase of specialization in which placements are affected by skill, linguistic factors, or predispositions. Historians have argued that in the early to mid-nineteenth century migrants had far greater opportunities to transfer a skill directly into urban American economies than at any time since.[33] And yet premigration skills still affect the match between newcomers and employers. Greeks from the province of Kastoria, where a traditional apprenticeship in fur making is common, tend to enter the fur industry; Israelis move into diamonds, a traditional Jewish business centered in New York, Tel Aviv, and Brussels; Indians from Gujarat, previously traders, become small store owners; and West Indians, many of whom have had exposure to mechanical crafts in oil fields, sugar refineries, or shipyards, find work in construction.

Language facility may similarly be a barrier to, or a facilitator of, specialization. English-language ability has steered immigrants from the anglophone Caribbean into health care, where the importance of interpersonal communication has been an impediment to immigrants that are not native speakers. By contrast, Koreans arrive with professional degrees, but, because they are poor English speakers and lack appropriate credentials or licenses, turn to retailing.

Groups may also be predisposed toward certain types of work; the fact that migrants are people in a stage of transition has an especially important influence on the types of jobs they pick up. Not yet certain whether they will settle down for good or return home, still evaluating conditions in terms of lower-quality employment back home, immigrants are likely to be favorably disposed toward low-level, low-status jobs. And that favorable evaluation extends even to jobs in declining industries where the prospects for long-term employment are poor.[34]

Whatever the precise mix of factors that determine the initial placements, occupational closure quickly sets in; this process represents the second stage. Networks of information and support are bounded by ethnic ties. Newcomers move and settle down under the auspices of friends, kin, and "friends of friends." When looking for work the new arrivals may prefer an environment in which at least some faces are familiar; they may feel uncomfortable with, or be ineligible for, the institutionalized means of labor market support; and they are likely to find that personal contacts prove the most efficient way of finding a place to work. Thus, later arrivals pile up in those fields where the first settlers established an early beachhead.[35]

More important, the predilections of immigrants match the preferences of employers, who try to reproduce the characteristics of the workers they already have. Recruiting among the relatives and friends of incumbents is the cheapest way of finding help; it greatly increases the quantity and quality of information about the relevant characteristics of a prospective recruit; and since it brings new workers into an environment where they are surrounded by people who know them, network hiring provides an additional mechanism for maintaining control. Over time, hiring opportunities can become detached from the open market, being rationed instead to insiders' referrals as part of a quid pro quo between incumbents and employers.[36]

FROM IMMIGRANT TO ETHNIC NICHE

What happens after the initial immigrant niche is put in place? The answer depends, in part, on the nature of the niche itself. If the niche provides rewarding employment or mechanisms for expanding a group's economic base, specializations are likely to persist. Niches often vary by industry, with different industries holding out distinctive pathways for getting ahead. In a small-business industry, like retailing or construction, one succeeds by starting out on one's own. By contrast, where large organizations prevail, one moves up by getting more schooling, picking up a certification, acquiring seniority, or some combination of the three. Whatever the particulars of the employment context, acquiring industry-relevant contacts, information, and know-how can take place on the job in an almost costless way. By the same token, moving beyond the ethnic niche imposes considerable costs.

The structure of rewards among economic specializations varies, as does the potential for niche expansion. As already noted, time often changes the match between a group and its original niche. Immigrants, looking back at the conditions they left behind, are willing to start out at the bottom of the pecking ladder; their children, however, want a good deal more, looking askance at those very same jobs. The advent of the second generation, therefore, is a momentous event, though not so much, as some social scientists have suggested, because the second generation accepts the cultural patterns of natives. Far more important are the aspirations of the second generation, which in contrast to their parents' now extend to the economic goals and standards of natives. Moreover, job predispositions are rarely abstract preferences; rather, they are informed by understandings about the probability that movement down one economic branch or the other will lead to failure or success. If group A experienced discrimination in industry B, and has reason to think that some level of discrimination there will persist, job seekers from group A have good reason to look for work in other fields. This same assessment of opportunities and constraints might create a preference for those types of work where exclusionary barriers exercise the least effect.

Thus, members of the second generation may move on to different jobs. Do they shift as a group? Or do they scatter, moving outward as they filter upward from the ethnic niche, as the conventional thinking suggests? The argument for the latter view rests on its assumptions about why the first generation concentrated in the first place. To the extent that concentration is explained by lack of skills and education, and seen as a source of disadvantage, then rising levels of education and growing similarity with the core cultural group imply that upward mobility goes hand in hand with dispersion out of the immigrant niche.

Skill deficiencies are only one of the factors in my account of the first-generation niche, however. I place much greater weight on the role of ethnic networks and their impact on the actions of both workers and employers. Consequently, my view suggests a different scenario, in which the continuing importance of ethnic networks shapes a group's employment distribution into the second, and later, generations. Just as with the first generation, the second generation's search for advancement takes on a *collective* form. Starting out from an immigrant niche, the second generation is already embedded in a cluster of interlocking organizations, networks, and activities. Not only do these commonalities shape aspirations, they also create the organizational framework for the rapid diffusion of information and innovations. Thus, the social organization of the second generation serves as a mechanism for channeling people into the labor market; once a favorable niche develops, informal recruitment patterns can quickly funnel in new hires.

THE ADVANTAGES OF THE ETHNIC NICHE

The process of niche formation turns ethnic disadvantage to good account, enabling social outsiders to compensate for the background deficits of their groups and the discrimination they encounter. The networks that span ethnic communities constitute a source of "social capital," providing social structures that facilitate action, in this case, the search for jobs and the acquisition of skills and other resources needed to move up the economic ladder.[37] Networks among ethnic incumbents and job seekers allow for rapid transmission of information about openings from workplaces to the communities. And the networks provide better information within workplaces, reducing the risks associated with initial hiring. Once in place, ethnic hiring networks are self-reproducing, since each new employee recruits others from his or her own group.

While the development of an ethnic niche provides a group with privileged access to jobs, one classic example—that of small business—suggests that it can do far more. Ethnic businesses emerge as a consequence of the formation of ethnic communities, with their sheltered markets and networks of mutual support. Individual firms may die off at an appalling rate, but business activity offers a route to expansion into higher profit and more dynamic lines. Retailers evolve into wholesalers; construction firms learn how to develop real estate; garment contractors gain the capital, expertise, and contacts to design and merchandise their own clothing. As the ethnic niche expands and diversifies, the opportunities for related ethnic suppliers and customers also grow.

With an expanding business sector comes both a mechanism for the effective transmission of skill and a catalyst for the entrepreneurial drive. From the standpoint of ethnic workers, the opportunity to acquire managerial skills through a stint of employment in immigrant firms both compensates for low pay and provides a motivation to learn a variety of different jobs. Employers who hire co-ethnics gain a reliable work force with an interest in skill acquisition—attributes that diminish the total labor bill and make for greater flexibility. Thus, a growing ethnic economy creates a virtuous circle: business success gives rise to a distinctive motivational structure, breeding a community-wide orientation toward small business and encouraging the acquisition of skills within a stable, commonly accepted framework.[38]

Sociologist Suzanne Model coined the concept of "hierarchically organized niches" to denote ethnic economic concentrations in which employees not only work among their co-ethnics but are hired and overseen by co-ethnic owners and managers.[39] These characteristics usually define the ethnic economy; they can also be found in the public sector. Along with small business, the civil service forms the other classic ethnic niche, even though it is governed by seemingly opposite principles. Moving into civil service has been an ethnic mobility strategy for over one hundred years, and not just because ethnic networks increase a group's access to jobs. Once in place, groups of ethnic workers repeatedly engage in bargaining games that shelter them from competition and exclude opportunities for promotion from all but insiders. Thus, the public sector comes under group pressures that make it a protected, self-regulating enclave. And that trait increases its attraction for stigmatized groups that fare poorly in the private market.

JOB COMPETITION

I have depicted niche formation as the unintended result of activities of which people are only partly aware. But once the niche is in place, different dynamics occur. The higher the level of concentration in the niche, the more frequent and more intense the interaction among group members. These interactions make them feel that they belong to a group. If the niche is one of the salient traits that group members share, it also helps define who they are. As a result, members pay greater attention to the boundaries of the niche and the characteristics of those who can and cannot cross those boundaries. As the niche strengthens group identity, it sharpens the distinction between insiders and outsiders.[40]

Once established, the niche also takes on properties that make it difficult for outsiders to get in the door. A variety of factors incline ethnics toward working with others of their own kind whenever they can. Fearful that outsiders might undercut wages, workers prefer to train co-ethnic neophytes whom they trust; anxious about the reliability and performance of job applicants who walk in off the street, employers prefer to hire the friends and relatives of their key workers; concerned that a vendor might not deliver on time, or that a customer might delay in paying the bill, business owners look for known entities with track records of successful dealings with others. In effect, membership in an ethnic community serves as an index of trust in an economic transaction, telling co-ethnic actors that one can rely on another. The web of contacts within a community works in the same direction; the history of prior exchanges with members of an ethnic network provides a baseline against which future behavior can be assessed. Since relations among co-ethnics are likely to be many-sided rather than specialized, community effects go beyond their informational value, engendering both codes of conduct and the mechanisms for sanctioning those who violate norms.

The trust extended from one member of a community to another, though both efficient and efficacious, is not available to everyone. Outsiders lack the traits, histories, and relational ties conducive to collaboration or trust; on these grounds alone, rational considerations lead insiders toward economic exchanges with their own.

Since employers and employees in the niche tend to arrive at agreement over hiring practices and promotional rules, past practices operate with a similar, exclusionary effect. To be sure, the parties often fight with one another over the content of the rules. But the quarrels rarely get out of hand: in hierarchically organized niches, such as the civil service, managers and workers often come from the same group and identify with one another. In other cases, where higher management and the rank and file have little in common, the line managers who make key personnel decisions generally share the views, and often the origins, of the important workers with whom they interact.[41]

Thus, over time, hiring practices and promotional rules get adapted to the needs of incumbent groups. Often, the entry criteria demand more exacting skills than the jobs require. As long as insiders and the members of their network furnish a steady stream of qualified applicants, however, employers have no incentive to relax their hiring criteria to ease the way in for outsiders. Once in place, the rules change slowly; the weight of tradition stands in their favor, sustaining incumbents' belief in the fairness of rules and the rule-making process.

All this is important because the labor market is not always home to a game of ethnic musical chairs, in which some groups move one rung up the ladder, allowing newcomers to take up the vacated rung. Although the queue metaphor suggests movement without friction, the structural properties of the labor queue can shift or stabilize in ways that either forestall or promote ethnic conflict over jobs.

Recall that outsider groups enter the economy in response to labor shortages and then gravitate toward the tier of labor-scarce jobs, remaining in that ambit as long as their (low) economic orientations match the (low) requirements and perquisites of the jobs. What happens next generally follows one of several scenarios. In the succession scenario, the shape of the labor queue can change if later economic expansion further tightens the supply of established groups, pulling the low-ranked group up the totem pole. In the leapfrogging scenario, the characteristics of the low-rank group—in particular, its schooling levels—substantially improve, making the group more desirable to employers and thereby reordering its position in the labor queue. In the persistence scenario, the preferences of the low-rank group remain unchanged, in which case its tolerance for low-level work stays more or less the same.

But one can also imagine a sequence of events ending in conflict, in which the preferences of low-rank groups change more quickly and more extensively than either the order or the shape of the labor queue. In this case, the ambitions of outsiders extend to higher-level jobs to which established groups remain firmly attached. But the allocation procedures exclude all those who do not meet hiring criteria, which have previously evolved in ways that fit the preferences of incumbents. Under these circumstances, competition becomes overt and leads to ethnic conflict, as newcomers seek to alter hiring and promotion rules and incumbents try to maintain the structures that have protected their group's jobs.

As the advent of ethnic conflict threatens the order of the queue, outcomes will depend on the resource-mobilization capacity of outsider and insider groups and on their ability to use those resources to effect changes in recruitment and promotional structures. Power makes such a difference because niches are ultimately not that easy to control. Employers may have a preference for hiring one of their own or may yield to the "tastes" of their employees. They can never totally ignore, however, the potential cost savings made possible by recruiting outside the niche or the desirability of gaining skills that the in-group cannot provide. Similarly, unions might block the front door that gives access to a trade; but the presence of ethnic entrepreneurs, who hire and train their co-ethnics, provides a back door through which a corps of skilled workers can be built.[42] In the public sector, particular groups may control information about openings and exams but they cannot prevent the competitive exam process from allowing skilled outsiders to gain entrée.

There is more to job competition than the human or social capital of insider and outsider groups. Groups' resource-bearing capacities in the political realm often count for a great deal: shifts in the relative balance of *political* power between incumbents and outsiders can lead to policy changes that alter recruitment practices, opening up defended, previously closed ethnic niches. While political pressure can make a difference, the range of exposure to political forces varies with the characteristics of labor market arrangements. Government's instruments will be most effective in those segments of the economy where hiring and recruitment practices are most institutionalized, and thus most susceptible to internal and external monitoring. By contrast, political intervention will carry much less weight in small-firm sectors, which mainly rely on informal recruitment mechanisms.

DISCRIMINATION

This account of job competition provides an explanation of the activation, persistence, and possible decline of discrimination; because it stands at variance with established economic and sociological views, a comparison with the alternative, better-known accounts deserves attention. In economics, the most powerful statement explains the behavior of discriminators as a manifestation of their "tastes": thus, whites have a distaste for working with blacks.[43] The economists' assumptions about whites' preferences have been subject to criticism on several grounds—don't whites really want to maintain social distance? aren't they principally concerned with preserving status differences relative to blacks? But the most damaging criticism is simply that by assuming distinctive preferences, the economists beg the question at hand, namely, what causes whites' peculiar tastes?[44] As the ethnic order becomes more complex, the import of this failure becomes increasingly grave, since whites seem to have a much stronger distaste for blacks than they do for the various foreign-born groups who are just as visibly identifiable.

But let us assume that whites do indeed have such a strong distaste for working alongside blacks; what difference would it make? White employers with a "taste for discrimination" would pay a premium to hire mainly white crews, deducting the costs of the psychic discomforts they must endure from the wages of any blacks they engage. Like any other preference, the taste for discrimination is not equally shared by all white employers; those employers who experience less psychic pain from proximity to blacks should be happy to hire an entirely black crew at bargain rates. In a competitive market, the lowest-cost, nondiscriminating producer would inevitably compel the discriminators to either swallow their distastes and hire more blacks or else go out of business.

By definition, the economic model thus predicts declining discrimination. The problem, of course, is that persistent discrimination is what requires explanation. Moreover, the economists' approach focuses almost entirely on wages, whereas occupational segregation and access to employment lie at the heart of black-white disparities.

Sociologists, by contrast, are wont to explain discrimination as the reaction of "high-priced" labor to competition from "lower-priced" competitors, as can be seen in William J. Wilson's highly influential book *The Declining Significance of Race.*[45] In this account, black migrants entered the north as low-price labor: willing to work at rates below those acceptable to whites, blacks were used by employers in their efforts to "undercut the white labor force by hiring cheaper labor." These attempts fanned whites' antagonism toward blacks and efforts at either excluding African-Americans outright or else confining them to low-level jobs. As the American state expanded its role in regulating industrial and race relations from the New Deal on, the potential for wage competition between blacks and whites steadily diminished. With whites no longer having to fear displacement from low-priced blacks, they lost their motivation to discriminate.

The conventional economic approach predicts declining discrimination without, however, accounting for what activates discrimination in the first place. The conventional sociological framework goes one step better in addressing the question of motivation but, likewise, forecasts discrimination's decline. Unlike the economists' approach, the job-competition perspective provides an answer to the question of motivation; unlike the sociologists' approach, it also tells us why discrimination might persist.

The economists are certainly right in thinking that discrimination is in part a matter of tastes; as I contended above, however, those tastes are not exogenous but rather a consequence of the development of an ethnic niche. Moreover, the motivation to maintain boundaries around the niche does not just emanate from an abstract desire to be with others of one's own kind (or even to maintain social distance from some stigmatized other); rather, it derives from the process of serial migrant labor market incorporation, which in turn spurs the cycle of complementary and competitive relationships between old-timer and newcomer groups.

The instability of capitalist economies leads to a recurrent recourse to outsider groups, who enter the queue at the bottom, where they work in complementarity to higher-ranked insiders. But the initial situation of complementarity lasts only as long as the economic orientations of the two groups diverge; once the aspirations and orientations of the two groups converge, job competition ensues. Under these circumstances, a combination of economic and noneconomic factors impel insider groups to prevent outsiders from gaining access to the niche. The influx of a stigmatized other threatens the overall standing of the group's niche—itself often recently won. More important, incumbents in a good niche have a scarce commodity to protect. Even in the best of times, good jobs attract a surplus of applicants, which tells us that there are never enough truly desirable positions. The exclusion of outsiders keeps competition in check, serving the needs of incumbents while also preserving a resource for future cohorts of insiders not yet admitted to the niche. Finally, competition activates cultural and ideological sources of group affinity and exclusiveness, since incumbents' sense of group identity is embedded in stable networks and patterns of hiring, recruitment, and mobility.

BLACK-WHITE ANTAGONISM

Thus, discrimination can be seen as the consequence of job competition, with the niche taking the form of a kind of group property. Though perhaps Balkanized, the labor market is not yet the Balkans, with each group pitted against the next. On the contrary, as one black skilled-trades worker pointed out to me: "When the white workers are in the room, it's fuckin' guinea this, stinking kike that, polack this. When I come into the room, they're all white."

This statement pungently crystallizes the intellectual puzzle of why so much more antagonism characterizes the encounters between whites and blacks than those among the plethora of culturally distinctive, visibly identifiable groups that joust with one another over economically desirable slots.

The answer to that puzzle, I suggest, has several parts. First, race is a particularly convenient marker, with slightly more subtle ethnic criteria providing more difficult, and therefore more costly, means around which to organize exclusion. Second, in the American context race is far more than a marker: it is a characteristic suffused with meaning, adding an extraeconomic dimension to the entry of blacks into a dominant white niche. Third, conflict has been crucial to blacks' efforts to move into dominant white niches, and far more so than has been true for other outsider groups.

The persistence and intensity of black-white conflict reflects, in part, the mismatch between black economic ambitions and the thresholds needed to enter the jobs to which blacks aspire. Whereas African-American migrants accepted jobs that whites would no longer do, the migrants' children and grandchildren have sought positions in niches which whites have not left. In this quest, African-Americans resemble other outsider groups who began as migrants at the bottom. But earlier groups of outsiders like Italians or Jews, as well as contemporary counterparts like Chinese, Koreans, and even Jamaicans or Dominicans, have had access to resources—education, skills, capital, and most important, assistance from their co-ethnics—that have helped them find alternate routes into defended niches and improve their bargaining position with incumbent groups. Lacking these resources, African-Americans have been more likely than other outsider groups to pursue a directly competitive strategy for entering a niche. That strategy, in turn, has heightened the defensive orientations of whites, intensifying their concern with boundary maintenance and markers, and breeding a cycle of escalating conflict.

SLICING THE PIE

Thus far, I have tried to explain why ethnic groups develop economic specializations and how those specializations evolve. But the problem is still more complex, because I need to provide an account of how the same opportunity—the vacancies created by the diminishing presence of whites—has had such different effects on immigrants and on African-Americans.

The answer lies in the framework developed above. A group's *prior* place in the ethnic division of labor exercises a crucial influence on its chances of benefiting from the opportunities that arise from succession. To inherit the positions abandoned by departing whites, one needs a recruitment network already in place. Since hiring works with a built-in bias toward incumbents, recruitment into an industry can become a self-feeding process; consequently, replacement processes will work to the advantages of those groups that most easily and quickly produce new recruits.

Timing also influences the outcome. When ethnic succession stirred up New York's ethnic division of labor, history had put African-Americans and new immigrants in different places. At the high tide of black migration to New York, whites were still solidly entrenched in the city's working class; even low-level, traditionally immigrant industries retained whites within their effective labor supply; in more skilled, manual jobs, whites maintained virtually complete control. In contrast to the circumstances under which the post-1965 immigrants entered the economy, African-Americans encountered a situation in which white ethnic incumbents held on to all but the bottom-most positions; the strength of these network-based tendencies toward social closure narrowed the scope of black employment and shaped their pattern of job concentration.

By the time compositional changes in the 1970s and 1980s produced widespread vacancies, African-Americans had developed alternative feeding points into the economy. These black niches were shaped by previous experience. Sectors that provided more and better opportunities gained a heavier flow of recruits. Where, by contrast, discrimination continued to prevail, the potential supply of African-American workers dwindled. Although the transitional nature of the migration experience had conditioned earlier cohorts of black workers to accept jobs in the traditional immigrant industries, the children and grandchildren of the southern migrants had taken on aspirations that precluded this type of work. Consequently, employers turned to immigrants to fill the vacancies created by the massive outflow of whites. Once a small cluster of "seedbed" immigrants implanted itself, networks among newcomers and settlers quickly directed new arrivals into the appropriate places in the job market. Given employers' preference for hiring through networks—and the ability of employees to pressure their bosses to do so—information about job openings rarely penetrated outside the groups that concentrated in a particular trade. As the newcomers built up their niches, they limited entry to members of the club. Thus, history became crucial in understanding who got which pieces of New York's pie and why.

2 | People and Jobs

The huddled masses that moved through Ellis Island arrived at a thriving factory town. But industrial New York passed its zenith well before midcentury; by the postwar years, the shape of the city's economic future could already be discerned. Even as yesterday's industrial base ceded place to tomorrow's office complex, the city's role as a staging ground for legions of newcomers continued as before. This chapter traces New York's simultaneous economic and demographic transformations as a prelude to the studies of ethnic New Yorkers and their changing roles in the city's evolving economy that appear in the chapters to follow.

An Economy in Change

Though its export base was still heavily manufacturing-oriented in the 1950s, New York shifted from goods to services earlier than did the rest of the United States. Goods production activities warranted two volumes in the celebrated New York Metropolitan Region Study, with the title of one of the books, *One-tenth of a Nation*, succinctly expressing manufacturing's importance. The size of New York's factory sector may have impressed scholars, but as early as 1950 there were already proportionally fewer New Yorkers working in manufacturing than in the nation as a whole. The proportion then grew steadily smaller: whereas the local economy boomed in the 1950s and 1960s, manufacturing fared less well. The city's mix of manufacturing industries spelled problems for those manufacturers who were still trying to make it in New York. The labor-intensive industries that made up the cornerstones of the local manufacturing sector—apparel, electronics, and other forms of light manufacture—found themselves under severe wage pressure. Not surprisingly, factory jobs started to leak out of the city in the early 1950s, with the erosion continuing until the late 1960s, when the nation's superheated economic environment kept New York's old and obsolescent plant in demand. Harbor-related activities—the other major, and even older, component of New York's blue-collar export base—also suffered decline. The city's labor costs were high, its docks outdated, its loading and unloading facilities impossible. Many port activities moved to other locations in the region—particularly, New Jersey—but the movement of jobs and people westward and eastward took a good chunk of shipping and other transportation activities in tow.[1]

However dismal the situation for manufacturing or harbor jobs, New York did better than many other older cities—where manufacturing decline led to population loss as early as the 1950s. In the case of New York, two growth trends offset the impact of a dwindling factory sector. First, the city's white-collar corporate complex boomed. Changes in technology brought new jobs in communications (television) and transport (air); a robust economy led to growth in advertising; the merger mania of the 1960s and the expansion of government regulation meant additional work for New York's corporate offices; and the burst of economic growth in the 1960s spurred a buildup of jobs on Wall Street. Thus, expansion of the white-collar private sector took up part of the slack created by manufacturing's decline. The expanding rolls of government employees did the rest of the job. Local government responded to a welter of pressures, including growing demands by civil rights groups and municipal unions. Political conditions—an expansive federal treasury and a weakened constituency of revenue-providing groups like small businesses and homeowners—made adding more bodies to government payrolls a convenient response to the tumult in the streets.[2]

New York's economy reached its apogee in 1969; thereafter the decline was brutal and swift. President Nixon's attempt to curb inflation sparked a minor recession in 1969; for New York City, however, the downswing produced major job losses. The rest of the nation soon pulled out of the doldrums, but jobs continued to seep out of New York. The 1970s marked the passage to a new stage of intensified interregional and international competition, in which capital became

increasingly mobile and a revolution in communications and technology accelerated the relocation of jobs from high- to lower-cost
areas. Under the impact of this change, New York's manufacturing
complex—with its antiquated and inefficient infrastructure, outdated
plant, and high-cost labor—could no longer compete. The 1970s also
brought bad times to the once vibrant white-collar sector. Wall Street
went from bull market to bear market as falling stock market prices
reflected the weakening U.S. economy and the squeeze on large corporate profits. To cut costs, securities firms sought to reduce their
back-office operations, filled mainly with low-level clerical function-
aries. This process marked the first phase of office automation, and it
hastened the winnowing-out process. Further job losses occurred as
large corporations moved their headquarters out to the suburbs—an
increasingly frequent event in the 1970s. The weakening of export
sectors brought inevitable decline to local economy industries, hitting
the city's enormous wholesaling and retailing complex with particular
force.[3]

At the time, New York's collapse appeared to spell the end for the
old, industrial cities. Not only were the northern cities caught in a
seemingly unending spiral of decline; their dwindling fortunes seemed
to reflect a broader "power shift," in which people and resources were
moving from these older centers of wealth and population to the
South. Kirkpatrick Sale first spotted the emerging trend. In Sale's
view, the new growth poles of the economy—agribusiness, defense
industries, advanced technology, oil and natural gas production, real
estate and construction, and tourism and leisure—had become concentrated in the states of the "southern rim," causing a massive shift
of people and power.[4] A number of more academic treatments later
substantiated Sale's somewhat anecdotal account, documenting the
simultaneous ascent of sunbelt cities and decline of northern urban
areas.[5]

But then in 1977 New York's eroding economy suddenly turned
around. For the next ten years—until Black October's stock market
crash of 1987—the economic growth machine kept on steadily
churning out new jobs. Although the precise causes of New York's
economic revival are still a matter of debate, the doomsayers clearly
misinterpreted the nature of the earlier regional change and over-
looked the persistent sources of economic strength.[6]

Even before the city arose from its deathbed, economist Robert
Cohen noted that the sunbelt's newly improved fortunes did not con-

note a *power* shift. Instead, "the traditional locations of corporate control functions"—foreign sales by multinational corporations, research and development expenditures, international banking, loans to large corporations, and business services—remained where they had always been.[7] The dominant actors were firms based in the older metropolitan areas at the top of the urban hierarchy. Moreover, new forms of urban agglomeration bound businesses together. Corporate headquarters could leave New York City, as they did in the 1970s, but they could not do without the corporate headquarters complex they left behind. The linkages among corporate headquarters, corporate service firms (banks; law, accounting, and security firms; advertising agencies and other business services), and ancillary business services rooted these components of the corporate headquarters complex in New York.[8]

Two key developments created these new sources of urban agglomeration: the shift to services and globalization. Production in the U.S. economy has changed, "with financial, business, and information services becoming increasingly important inputs to the economy's processes of production."[9] Needs for information services have grown steadily and fast—in fact, faster than the rest of the economy. This intensifying demand for information services worked to the advantage of New York and other large cities: with its already large buildup of information services, New York was ideally positioned to benefit from the rapid growth of this demand in the 1980s.

Globalization yielded similar effects. Internationally oriented business is both more complex and more uncertain. Large corporations that have developed heavy foreign involvements find themselves more, not less, dependent on their external providers of business services. These services increasingly fall to a cluster of firms that are disproportionately based in the largest diversified urban centers. And the dominant business service firms have also capitalized on their existing expertise and resources, moving more quickly than their competitors to exploit emerging global markets.[10]

Changes in the economic environment led to impressive local economic growth *and* tighter links to New York. Paradoxically, the geographical spread of routinized manufacturing and information-processing activities increased the need for centralizing key control activities. As a result, New York, along with Tokyo, London, and Frankfurt, emerged as one of a handful of "global information hubs," characterized by dense and sophisticated telecommunications networks. The efficiency and effectiveness of information flows into and out of the city reinforced New York's competitive edge as a location for information-oriented global functions. While telecommunications "allowed the decisions and ideas generated in the city to be electronically distributed around the world through advanced communications technology," they did not eliminate the need for proximity in information services.[11] On the contrary, internationally oriented businesses continued to depend on frequent, and interorganizational, face-to-face contacts at high levels.[12] They also put a premium on access to a large pool of highly specialized talent. Thus, New York retained a strong hold on the growing information services sector.

For much of the 1980s, service growth pumped the local economy's prime. Between 1977 and 1987, the information industries added 206,516 jobs—or almost two-thirds of all new jobs generated during those years. The payroll contribution was even higher—a not surprising consequence of the booming financial markets, sharply rising increases in educational requirements, and a burgeoning demand for specialists, particularly in finance but in other fields as well. The strength of the information industries in turn spilled over into other fields. In contrast to the lackluster seventies, construction boomed: Manhattan alone gained more than 53 million square feet of new office space between 1981 and 1990, an increase of more than 25 percent over the 1980 level.[13] Retailing, which had sagged badly with the loss in population and buying power during the seventies, also encountered much better days.

But manufacturing continued to be a loser. Throughout the 1980s, the city's garment makers chanted a mournful tune. To some extent, manufacturing fell victim to its neighbors' successes. The low-rent loft districts in midtown Manhattan attracted advertisers or publishers, pushed out of their more prestigious addresses by expanding law firms or foreign banks but still capable of paying a more handsome rent than a hard-pressed clothing factory.[14] But the real threat to New York's production activity came from those who could make clothing more efficiently—as did the big clothing producers down south—or more cheaply, like the factories of Hong Kong, China, and Thailand. Garment manufacturing dwindled steadily during the 1980s: by the end of the decade employment in the city's garment complex fell below the 100,000 mark. For the same reasons, no manufacturing industry but printing—which was buoyed by Wall Street's need for near-instant turnaround of prospectuses and legal documents—escaped apparel's unfortunate fate.

Whereas government had just averted collapse in the fiscal crisis of the mid-1970s, the much better times of the 1980s led to considerable growth. As in every other locale, New York City's government found the pressure to increase city payrolls irresistible. Faced with the need to restore basic services that had been cut during the years of fiscal stringency, as well as to provide services for new problems—homelessness, crack, AIDS—that arose during the 1980s, government's payroll steadily expanded. By 1990, the size of the local government payroll had virtually returned to the level enjoyed before the fiscal house collapsed in 1975.

The Postindustrial Structure of Jobs and Skills

Thus, New York's transformation from factory to office complex changed what people did; Figure 2.1 tells that story in numbers. While New York alternated between bust and boom in the seventies and eighties, the overall direction of industrial change remained the same. In 1970, just over 20 percent of employed New York City residents made a living in manufacturing. Twenty years later, the factory sector's share had shrunk by almost half; financial services (FIRE, meaning finance, insurance, and real estate) employed as many people as manufacturing; and three times as many people worked in the various services, put together, as were to be found in factory jobs. Virtually unchanged, however, was the adjunct but still crucial role of the public sector, which accounted for just under a fifth of the jobs generated during the 1980s.

The shift from goods to services also meant a different mix of jobs. The garment industry's woes led to fewer sewing machine operators; the financial sector's expansion spawned more opportunities for brokers, programmers, and the like. These two examples fit right into the pattern shown in Figure 2.2. Notwithstanding claims about polarization, the numbers reveal a clear trend toward a proliferation of higher-level positions and a relative decline for just about every other kind of job. To be sure, many lower-level categories stabilized or even grew during the prosperous 1980s. But even the building boom of the 1980s, which produced a sizable increase of craft workers, did not reverse the relative erosion of blue-collar jobs. By 1990, professional and managerial jobs together employed as many New York City residents as all blue-collar categories combined.

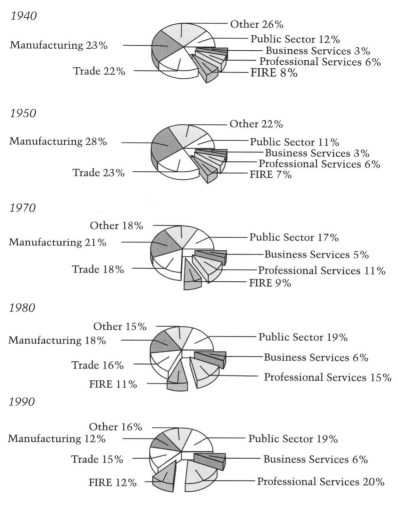

Figure 2.1 Distribution of employed New Yorkers aged 25–64, by sector, 1940–1990. (*Source:* Census of Population, 1940–1990.)

Occupational and industrial shifts went hand in glove: New Yorkers changed what they did; and industries underwent significant changes in the types of jobs they maintained. Virtually each industry recapitulated the basic pattern: over time, the higher-level, white-collar ratio rose. In finance, for example, the impact of capital deepening, computerization, and shedding of back-office operations to suburbs appeared in a diminishing portion of clerical workers. Even manufac-

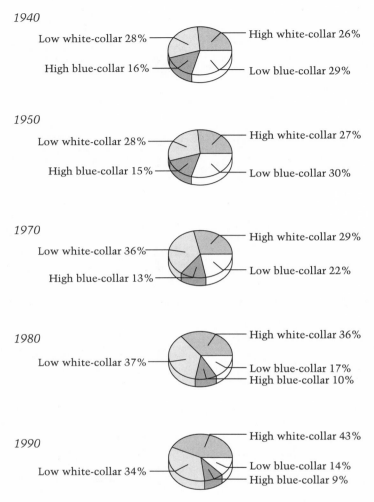

1940

Low white-collar 28% — High white-collar 26%

High blue-collar 16% — Low blue-collar 29%

1950

Low white-collar 28% — High white-collar 27%

High blue-collar 15% — Low blue-collar 30%

1970

Low white-collar 36% — High white-collar 29%

High blue-collar 13% — Low blue-collar 22%

1980

High white-collar 36%

Low white-collar 37% — Low blue-collar 17%
High blue-collar 10%

1990

High white-collar 43%

Low white-collar 34% — Low blue-collar 14%
High blue-collar 9%

Figure 2.2   Distribution of employed New Yorkers aged 25–64, by type of occupation, 1940–1990. (*Source:* Census of Population, 1940–1990.)

turing saw the blue-collar presence dwindle, since the factory jobs fled faster than did the administrative or front-office activities. Thus, shifts in the mix of occupations interacted with shifts in the mix of industries to move New York even faster along the trajectory of post-industrial change.

The new basis of New York's economic strength required workers with different types of training than those the city's economy had needed in years gone by. Processing, creating, and transmitting information involves higher-level intellectual skills acquired through years of schooling. As the demand for workers with higher skills intensified, the educational structure of the work force also changed. The role of workers with little schooling sharply contracted. In 1970, three-quarters of the city's workers had not gone beyond the high school degree; by 1990, that proportion had fallen to just under a half. Every sector experienced the declining need for less-educated workers. Of course, the advanced services led the trend toward heavier use of better-educated workers. But even construction or personal services, industries that had traditionally placed little weight on formal educational credentials, employed significantly more workers with higher education by 1990.

This brief sketch of New York's recent economic history highlights the question with which I began this book. Unlike the Detroits or Clevelands of the country, New York successfully managed the transition from the old to the new economy—but at a price. The traditional industries that absorbed low-skilled newcomers went into irreversible decline. The new sources of economic strength demanded skills that relatively few immigrants or native minorities possessed. But if the urban economic environment became so unfavorable, why did the immigrants continue moving cityward? And since both immigrants and native minorities confronted the same economy, why were their economic fates so sharply contrasting? Before we start to answer these questions, we must look at the demographic changes that simultaneously transformed New York.

A People in Flux

Ethnic change has been a constant in New York, from the early nineteenth century to the dawn of the twenty-first. Then, Irish peasants fled the potato famine to work in the city's domestic quarters and docks; today, the newcomers include refugees looking for political security as well as those who simply want a better life. From past to present, New York has seen an endless cycling through of one group after another. The cumulative impact of this incessant churning left a decisive mark in the 1980s when New Yorkers of European origin became a numerical minority. Like so many other major metropolises, New York is now a majority minority city.

In this simple quantitative sense, New York resembles its other urban counterparts. Yet it remains qualitatively, and fundamentally, distinct. Elsewhere, the advent of a majority minority city results from two opposing migratory waves: the influx of displaced black sharecroppers from the South, peaking in the 1960s; and the suburban seepage of the white population, which took off in the 1950s and has continued, unceasingly, ever since.

The people of New York also changed for just these reasons. But there is a third factor that propelled New York's demographic shift: a three-decade-long wave of immigration that brought roughly eighty thousand newcomers a year—many from Third World countries that previously had little or no presence in New York at all.[15] Immigration multiplied the number of New Yorkers of non-European origin and also made them far more diverse. The immigrants differ from one another, as well as from the native minority groups with whom they are classified in official statistical counts. Those differences do not simply reflect variations in national origins but also extend to the social structure of life in New York.

The Crosscurrents of Internal Migration

Even in New York, change takes time. The transformation of the city's population occurred in two phases, one of which originated at the turn of the twentieth century, the second of which began in the mid-1960s.

"Six great groups entered the city two by two," wrote Nathan Glazer and Daniel Patrick Moynihan just before the new immigration began: Irish and Germans in the mid-nineteenth century, Jews and Italians during the decades just before and after 1900, and African-Americans and Puerto Ricans from World War I on.[16] While New York's African-American community predated all of the other "great groups," relatively few blacks made their home in New York until well into the twentieth century. In 1890, the black share of the population was 1.6 percent—just about what it had been on the eve of the Civil War. But in the 1890s the South started losing blacks from out-migration, and that loss quickly translated into New York's gain. By 1920, New York was home to 150,000 black residents—who, though only 3 percent of the city's population, made New York the largest urban concentration of blacks in the country.[17] In the next twenty years, as European immigration faltered and then stopped, and bad conditions in the rural South provided additional reasons to leave, the number of black New Yorkers tripled. Postwar prosperity and a new wave of mechanization in the South launched a final, massive flow northward. By 1950, the African-American population numbered 748,000—almost double the 1940 levels. Twenty years later, when the census counted an additional 920,000 black New Yorkers, the migration from the South had virtually come to a halt.[18] By 1970, newcomers were just a scattering—barely 2 percent—among a population that was already more than half New York–born.[19]

Puerto Ricans, the last of Glazer and Moynihan's "great groups," have a more limited history in New York. Lawrence Chenault, the first scholar of the city's Puerto Rican community, estimated that there were 500 Puerto Ricans living in New York in 1910.[20] A steadily growing exodus from this new possession of the United States boosted the total to 45,000 over the next twenty years. The movement to New York continued steadily during the 1930s, came to a complete halt during the war years, and then took off with the introduction of air service to San Juan. But the migration progressed erratically. Migration rates from Puerto Rico to New York more than doubled in the 1950s, rising from an average annual inflow of 18,700 persons between 1940 and 1950, to 41,200 between 1950 and 1960. Yet in the 1960s, for reasons that are still poorly understood, the flow dropped to a level slightly smaller than that recorded during the late 1940s. Thus, between 1950 and 1970 New York's Puerto Rican population rose from 246,000 to 847,000, with recent migrants accounting for less than 8 percent of the population five years or older by the latter date.[21]

While blacks and Puerto Ricans converged on New York in growing numbers, whites moved out. Net out-migration of whites started in the 1940s—before the suburbs became filled with tract housing and the highways necessary to convey the new suburbanites back and forth from the city. As governments at various levels encouraged investment in housing and built roads at a dizzying pace, new residential vistas opened up for the city's massive corps of white-collar workers: increasingly, they opted for a suburban lifestyle centered on owner-occupied, single-family housing in a low-density setting. Some of the demand for single-family homes could be satisfied within the boundaries of the five boroughs; Queens and Staten Island, in particular, had enough cheap, vacant land to support a massive wave of suburban-style construction. Ultimately, the suburban push could be met only in underdeveloped communities within commuting distance of the city's principal concentrations of employment. Since the region already possessed a comprehensive and relatively high quality transit system with lines that fed into Manhattan, and then gained an extensive, similarly oriented, roadway network, growing numbers of middle-class families could live outside but still work downtown. And so they did. Net out-migration of whites leapt up to almost a million in the 1950s and continued at the same level during the next decade.[22]

Thus, from the 1940s through the 1960s two demographic crosscurrents swept through New York: the outward tide of whites and the inward flow of African-Americans and Puerto Ricans. In the 1970s, bad times deprived New York of its historic magnetic attraction. White New Yorkers accelerated their departure to greener pastures in the suburbs and beyond, in reaction to the bleak economic situation. Native black and Puerto Rican migration to New York withered as well. While local factors weakened the city's pull on internal migrants, the New York pattern mirrored trends nationwide. The 1970s marked a turnaround in the historic exodus of African-Americans from the South. For the first time since World War I, the cities of the North—New York included, of course—lost their attraction; the South, which had previously been gaining white migrants as its economy boomed, now became a net recipient of black migration as well. As for Puerto Ricans, the flagging of their migration in the 1960s turned out to presage the shape of things to come. Embedded in a pattern of circular moves back and forth from the island, and discouraged by the decline of the industries that had absorbed the original migration wave, the surplus of Puerto Rican newcomers over return migrants dried up.[23] Outflows greatly exceeded inflows for all groups of native-born New Yorkers between 1975 and 1980. As an indicator of how far the trends of the past had been reversed, African-Americans recorded the highest levels of net out-migration of all.

The Advent of the New Immigrants

Just when New York could no longer retain its native population, it reverted to its role as an immigrant mecca. The new immigrants began flocking to New York even before the liberalization of U.S. immigration laws in 1965. Their arrival has been the principal driving force of demographic and ethnic change in New York ever since—and will be for the foreseeable future.

THE NEW IMMIGRATION TO THE UNITED STATES
Immigration revived with the passage of the Hart-Celler Act in 1965. The 1965 reform transformed the immigration system with a few bold

strokes. First, it abolished the old country-of-origin quotas, which allotted small quotas to southern and Eastern Europe, and still smaller—almost prohibitively small—quotas to Asia. Second, it established two principal criteria for admission to the United States: family ties to citizens or permanent residents, and possession of scarce and wanted skills. Third, it increased the total number of immigrants to be admitted to the United States.[24]

The system established by the 1965 reforms essentially remains in place to this day, despite constant debate and continuous overhauling. But the Hart-Celler Act spawned changes that were entirely different from the plans of the advocates of reform. The legislation was principally intended to benefit Eastern and southern Europeans—the groups hardest hit by the nativist legislation of the 1920s. By the 1960s, however, workers from Italy or Yugoslavia had fallen out of the orbit of trans-Atlantic migration. Instead, the newcomers who took advantage of the newly liberalized system came from Asia, Latin America, and the circum-Caribbean.

In 1965 no one expected the burgeoning of Asian immigration. The reforms tilted the new system toward immigrants with kinship ties to permanent residents or citizens. Since there had been so little Asian immigration in the previous fifty years, how could Asian newcomers find settlers with whom to seek reunification? As it turned out, kinship connections were helpful but not essential. The 1965 reforms also created opportunities for immigrants whose skills—as engineers, doctors, nurses, pharmacists—were in short supply. Along with students already living in the United States and with easy access to American employers, these professionals made up the first wave of new Asian immigrants—creating the basis for the kinship migration of less well-educated relatives. Thus, by the 1980s Asia had emerged as the number two source area, accounting for 37 percent of all the immigrants who moved to the United States during these years.[25]

The growth of migration from Latin America and the circum-Caribbean followed a different trajectory. The professional route allowed Asian migration to follow a sudden growth curve. For example, between 1940 and 1960 fewer than 400 Indians moved to the United States each year; in the 1960s the flow ratcheted up to 2,700 per annum, and then increased steadily till it reached the 25,000-per-year mark in the 1980s.[26] By contrast, migration from such countries as Jamaica, Colombia, and the Dominican Republic had already swelled to more than a trickle by the time immigration reform occurred. These pioneering immigrants established beachheads in the economy that encouraged newcomers to try their luck as well. As Eugenia Georges recounts in her reconstruction of the history of migration from one small Dominican village to New York: "However small in number, the earliest migrants, all of whom settled in New York, were nonetheless important for the immediate example they provided to future migrants. They demonstrated that migration was feasible. Once the next wave of Piñeros began to arrive in New York, these pioneers provided many with a place to stay, with orientation, and with other forms of assistance."[27] Once the new legislation created a more favorable environment for Western Hemisphere immigration, newcomers found settlements already in place, thanks to the efforts of these pioneers.

Immigrants passed through the front door opened by the 1965 reforms in a variety of ways. In addition, many of those who could not enter through the front door came in through the back: the existence of established migrant communities and networks that funneled new arrivals to the labor and housing markets allowed undocumented immigrants to enter and work in the United States without legal authorization. Just how many have done so has long been a matter of dispute, with wildly disparate estimates and guesstimates, ranging from 2 to 12 million, a stock in trade in the undocumented immigration debate. More recently, demographers have settled on a methodology for "counting the uncountable," which has in turn yielded estimates on which much of the immigration research community can agree. This methodology pointed to an undocumented population of about 2 to 4 million residing in the United States as of 1980, of whom over half had come from Mexico.[28]

A desire to stem undocumented immigration dominated immigration policy debates ever since enactment of the Hart-Celler Act; with the passage of the Immigration Reform and Control Act of 1986, known as IRCA, Congress attempted to close the back door and control this unauthorized flow. IRCA had two major provisions: an amnesty for undocumented immigrants who had resided continuously in the United States since January 1, 1982; and sanctions against the employers of illegal immigrants. The bill established a twelve-month period, from May 4, 1987, to May 5, 1988, during which eligible undocumented immigrants could apply for legalization. In IRCA undocumented immigrants found at best a "cautious welcome," as Susan Gonzalez Baker concluded, with countless bureaucratic hurdles and anxiety-provoking administrative rules littering their path to amnesty.[29] In the end, 1.76 million persons were legalized under IRCA's general amnesty, though perhaps as many as 1 million persons who were eligible for amnesty chose not to go that route.[30]

As expected, amnesty did diminish the pool of undocumented immigrants. Although Congress designed sanctions and more stringent border controls in the wake of IRCA to curb future undocumented flows, the available evidence suggests that despite some initial success, these efforts ultimately failed to curb the flow. Unauthorized migration clearly persists, yielding a net increment of 300,000 undocumented entrants each year.[31] The best estimates indicate that the total number of undocumented residents grew by over 50 percent between 1980 and 1992.[32]

NEW YORK'S NEW IMMIGRANTS

What Ellis Island was to earlier immigrant cohorts, Kennedy Airport is to the current immigrant wave. Its economic travails notwithstanding, New York remains the new immigrants' choice location. Immigrants flocked to New York when the city's economy prospered, as it did during the 1960s and most of the 1980s. And they also came, in unexpected numbers, when the city's economy flagged.

Even before the Hart-Celler Act inaugurated the fourth immigration wave, New York welcomed a sizable immigrant flow. But once the new law took effect, as Figure 2.3 shows, the immigrant influx took off. Between 1966 and 1979 over 1 million legal immigrants established their first residence in New York City. Data gaps, due to the virtual collapse of record-keeping procedures in the Immigration and Naturalization Service, afflict the record for 1980 and 1981. Fortunately, data are available for the rest of the 1980s, indicating that the city's booming economy attracted the largest immigrant influx since the immigration laws were changed in 1965.[33]

The arrival of so many newcomers gradually altered the city's demography. New York always retained more of an immigrant presence than America's other big cities, but by 1960, its foreign-born population was an aging, slowly diminishing mass; throughout the 1960s, the losses due to deaths and out-migration among the old-timers offset the influx of the post-1965 arrivals. The immigrant comeback did not show up until the 1980 census: by then, not only were the foreign-born numbers bigger, but their make-up had greatly changed, tilting away from Europe and toward the Third World.

Number of   New York as
legal   % of U.S.
immigrants

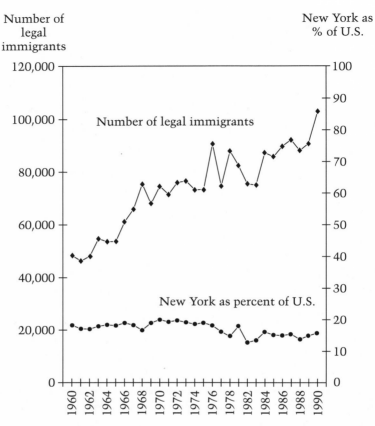

Figure 2.3   Legal immigration to New York City, 1960–1990. Immigration
levels for 1988–1990 exclude persons legalized under 1986 Immigration
Reform and Control Act. (*Sources:* Immigration levels for U.S.: *Statistical
Yearbook of the Immigration and Naturalization Service,* annual volumes.
N.Y.C. immigration levels, 1960–1979, *ibid.*; 1982–1990: City of New York,
Dept. of City Planning.)

The 1990 census recorded a further burgeoning of immigrant ranks:
2 million strong, the new New Yorkers from abroad accounted for 28
percent of the city's population. As Figure 2.4 demonstrates, the non-
European post-1965 arrivals clearly dominated the immigrant ranks,
not only among the most recent immigrants but among the foreign-
born population as a whole.

New York is an immigrant city like no other in two distinct ways.
First, as noted above, it receives more newcomers than any other
urban center. Second, it attracts a different mix of immigrants.

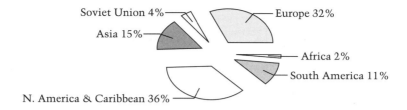

Immigrated prior to 1980

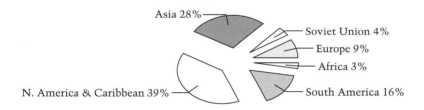

Immigrated between 1980 and 1990

Figure 2.4   Origins of all foreign-born New Yorkers, 1990. (*Source:* Census of Population, 1990.)

THE CARIBBEAN CONNECTION

More than any other factor, the Caribbean connection feeds newcomers into New York. Caribbean immigrants have New York roots that stretch back well before passage of the Hart-Celler Act. Sizable numbers of black immigrants from the then British crown colonies in the West Indies arrived in New York before 1930; by 1930, there were 55,754 black immigrant New Yorkers, more than a sixth of the city's black population.[34] The depression encouraged many of these immigrants to return home; the stagnant economy, followed by war and then new legislative restrictions on colonial immigrants, greatly stemmed the flow. Nevertheless, the earlier migration left in place a base of kinship connections that were reactivated once the Hart-Celler Act reopened the front door.[35]

The new Caribbean migration has taken off from this earlier migration experience but has developed in different ways. In the early 1960s, political events—notably the rise of Fidel Castro in Cuba and the fall of the Dominican dictator Trujillo—sparked the first sizable Caribbean flows. The Cuban influx quickly tapered off, with Miami becoming the nation's Cuban capital and Union City, New Jersey, attracting many of the refugees who chose not to relocate again. But Dominicans continued to converge on New York, in two parallel tracks. A steadily growing population moved into New York through the front door: by the late 1980s, almost one-sixth of the new, legal immigrant arrivals to New York came from the Dominican Republic. At the same time, a burgeoning traffic of persons arrived on non-immigrant visas—163,000 in 1989, up from less than 5,000 in 1960.[36] Though some of these nonimmigrants came and went quickly, others lingered, moved into the labor market, and often stayed for good.[37]

While the Dominicans top the list of migrants from the Caribbean, the entire circum-Caribbean has been involved in the post-1965 wave. Migration from countries with earlier outflows, like Jamaica, Trinidad, and Barbados, has been renewed at the same time as new sources have come on stream. In the 1980s, Haitians accounted for 6 percent of the decade's legal arrivals; Guyanese—a group whose presence has gone undetected by social scientists and journalists alike—ranked even higher, with almost 8 percent of the decade's legal immigrant arrivals. By 1990, one out of every three immigrant New Yorkers was Caribbean-born.[38]

THE NEW ASIANS

In New York up until the mid-1960s, Asian mainly meant Chinese: though distant from the main centers of the West Coast, New York was home to a growing Chinese population in the first two postwar decades, most of which was native-born. After the barriers to Asian immigration fell, Chinese immigration to the United States shot up, moving from a little under 5,000 in 1965, to 25,000 in 1967, to almost 50,000 a year during the 1980s. New York became the chief recipient of this burgeoning population flow: now home to the largest Chinese community in the country, New York attracts as many overseas Chinese as San Francisco, Los Angeles, Oakland, Honolulu, and Seattle combined. Once in New York, the newcomers first reinvigorated the small aging community in Chinatown, which more than tripled in numbers between 1960 and 1980, and later spilled over into new areas of settlement in Brooklyn and Queens.

The Chinese are now only one component of a rapidly growing, diverse Asian population. Indians, Koreans, Filipinos, and others—who thirty years ago counted small, almost invisible communities dominated by students and a handful of businessmen and professionals—have established a visible presence. Although it generally ranks behind West Coast cities as a starting point for these other Asian groups, New York still attracts a sizable, steady flow of newcomers from all over Asia. The 1990 census shows that Asians constituted 20 percent of the city's foreign-born population.

NEWCOMERS FROM THE OLD WORLD—EUROPEANS
European immigration to New York never stopped; it just slowed down. In the 1930s, the city was host to a large influx of Jewish refugees from Germany, Austria, and other parts of Europe; after the war, the survivors of concentration camps and other "displaced persons"—both Jewish and gentile—arrived in numbers sufficient to revive waning immigrant organizations for still another generation.[39] The 1965 reforms sparked a sudden burst of movement from southern and Eastern Europe, but as economic conditions improved, especially in Italy and Greece, these migrations quickly tailed off. Then an old source of immigrants suddenly came back on stream: responding to internal and external pressures, the Soviet Union opened the doors to Jewish emigration. In the course of the 1970s, about 35,000 Soviet Jewish refugees moved to New York.[40]

Soviet doors shut in the late 1970s, allowing only a trickle to leave for Israel or the United States, until the mid-1980s, when the refugee flow resumed, this time on a far more massive scale than before.[41] While over 11,000 Soviets made it to New York in the 1980s, other events in Eastern Europe—most notably, the repression of the Solidarity movement in Poland—added to the steady flow of refugees seeking haven in New York.[42] Finally, bad times in one of the earliest countries to send emigrants—Ireland—reactivated this long-dormant source. The new Irish immigrants first came as tourists, extending their sojourn to work in construction or as baby-sitters and waitresses. But as with other illegal immigrations, connections to kin and to employers were soon established, with the result that legal Irish immigration began to climb in the late 1980s.[43]

New York differs from other principal immigrant-receiving areas in several important respects, as a comparison with Los Angeles will attest. Despite the image of Los Angeles as the nation's most diverse metropolis, the key to understanding its immigrant base is the proximity of the border. In 1990, more than half of the post-1965 adult immigrants to Los Angeles came from three countries alone, Mexico, El Salvador, and Guatemala, with Mexico accounting for the great bulk of this group. For many of these newcomers, entry into the United States occurred through the back door—which is why Los Angeles accounted for a third of all the undocumented immigrants counted in the 1980 census and roughly the same proportion of the population who legalized under IRCA.

The new New Yorkers tend not to come from the same countries as the new Angelenos: some of New York's most important new immigrant groups—Dominicans, Jamaicans, Haitians, Guyanese—are rarely found in Los Angeles. More important, New York's new immigrant population is extraordinarily diverse. Dominicans composed the single largest post-1965 group counted in the 1990 census—and they accounted for just over 13 percent of the new immigrant arrivals. Chinese were the next largest, with 9.7 percent, followed by Jamaicans, with just over 6 percent; no other foreign country accounts for more than 5 percent of the new immigrant arrivals.

Of course, geography matters to New York as well as to Los Angeles: the Caribbean acts as New York's most important source area. But the Caribbean is itself extraordinarily variegated, culturally, linguistically, and ethnically: New York's three most important Caribbean source countries (the Dominican Republic, Jamaica, and Haiti) each represent distinct cultural systems. Geography has also kept undocumented migration relatively contained. The 1980 census found that New York was home to just over 10 percent of the undocumented population; just over 5 percent of the legalizees lived in New York; and about 40 percent of those had overstayed nonimmigrant visas, as opposed to 11 percent in Los Angeles.[44] Though net undocumented numbers continued to grow after 1980, notwithstanding the effects of the amnesty granted in mid-decade, New York's share of the nation's undocumented population in the early 1990s remained roughly what it had been a decade before.[45]

Demographic Consequences

Immigration has both accelerated and transformed the postwar pattern of demographic change. In terms of numbers, New York's population decline decisively turned around during the 1980s. In 1990, the city was home to 7.3 million people, roughly 250,000 persons above the 1980 level. Furthermore, almost all of the population gained by the New York region was concentrated in New York City, representing a dramatic reversal of a more than fifty-year-old trend.

In terms of demographics, the white, non-Hispanic share of New York's population continued to shrink. Although the economic boom of the 1980s reduced the imbalance between out- and in-migration flows, New York's somewhat greater attraction to whites was still too modest to offset the impact of low birth rates and high mortality rates among whites. Hence, by 1990 the white share of the population had fallen to 43 percent.

The diminishing white presence transformed the "minority" population into the numerical majority; at the same time, immigration made New York's "minorities" far more diverse than ever before. Creole- and English-speaking immigrants form a growing share of the black population, which continues to lose natives drawn to other states and localities. High rates of immigration have brought Hispanics close to blacks as the largest of New York's minority groups, while also diminishing the relative weight of Puerto Ricans among this expanding Hispanic population. And large foreign inflows from Asia have made Asians the most rapidly growing group, albeit one that has built on a relatively small population base.

"New" New Yorkers in a New Economy

The changing configuration of the city's economy affected the new New Yorkers in increasingly diverse ways. Notwithstanding the turbulence of the 1960s, the economic view from the end of that decade suggested that the latest waves of entrants—at the time, African-Americans and Puerto Ricans—were moving into the economy in ways that paralleled the experience of earlier, European groups. The boom times of the 1960s had steadily pushed the nonwhite unemployment rate down; by 1970, joblessness among African-American and Puerto Rican New Yorkers was well below the average for blacks and Hispanics nationwide, and was only marginally higher in comparison to the pattern for whites.[46] Similarly, high labor force participation rates among African-American and Hispanic men and among African-American women seemed to indicate strong attachment to the job market, not discouragement. Only among Puerto Rican women was there evidence of a diminishing role in paid employment.

Finally, as Emanuel Tobier has pointed out, "the real income of the city's black households increased substantially" during the 1960s.[47]

For African-Americans and Puerto Ricans, the onset of bad times in the 1970s largely undid the gains of the 1960s. Job growth ceased: by 1980, employment for both groups had fallen below the level recorded ten years earlier. Bleak economic prospects led to displacement and discouragement: by 1980, barely two-thirds of prime-age African-American males were employed. Unemployment reached more than twice the level experienced by whites. And many African-American men had simply given up trying to find work: more than a quarter

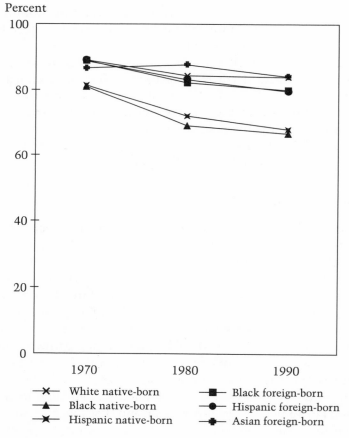

Figure 2.5   Employment rates of men aged 25–64 in six ethnic groups, 1970–1990. (*Source:* Census of Population, 1970–1990.)

reported not being in the labor force at all. Black women did fare better, increasing employment even in the face of economic distress. But white women made much more sizable gains and experienced joblessness to a lesser degree.

Good times in the 1980s brought little improvement (see Figure 2.5): African-American employment grew, but not in sufficient quantity; the losses suffered by African-American men were never restored. By 1990, the employment scene was even more dismal than it had been a decade before: one-third of African-American males still did not have a job and unemployment rates for African-American males were now

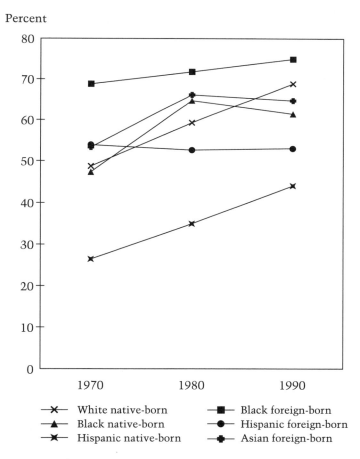

Figure 2.6   Employment rates of women aged 25–64 in six ethnic groups, 1970–1990. (*Source:* Census of Population, 1970–1990.)

almost three times the level among whites. Nor did an avalanche of office jobs do much for the employment situation of African-American women, who continued to experience far more unemployment than their white counterparts (see Figure 2.6).

But while African-Americans saw their base in the local job market erode, the employment of immigrants steadily expanded. The city's foreign-born residents grabbed sizable chunks of additional jobs in years of contraction and years of growth alike. And the liabilities of the newcomers, many with limited English-language proficiency and little knowledge of the local labor market or its institutions, did not seem to significantly hurt their employability. While so many black men fell out of the labor market during the 1970s, the employment rates of immigrant men held virtually constant with those of whites. What had been relatively modest disparities in labor force activity between African-American and immigrant men in 1970 widened and stayed large. Since job holding among black immigrants remained relatively high, with employment rates for black immigrant women rising and well above native whites', it seems unlikely that the economic problems of African-Americans can be reduced to a matter of race. Employers may well have preferred whites to the city's foreign-born, visibly identifiable immigrants, but these new minorities still found plenty of jobs. Thus, the analytic puzzle concerns why African-American and immigrant fates diverged; that is the question to which we now turn.

3 | The Ethnic Division of Labor Transformed

The story of New York since midcentury, as Chapter 2 shows, is the making of the city of services and the implantation of its majority minority population base. In this chapter and in the next, I ask how, if at all, these two components fit together.

The conventional answer is that they don't. As to why population and economy are increasingly out of sync, mismatch advocates offer an explanation that emphasizes changes in economic structure and the lagging adaptation of the new New Yorkers to the requirements of the city's employers. In this view, manufacturing decline and service growth are the crucial transformative factors. Minorities' exposure to industrial decline and their exclusion from the sources of growth force them to the margins of the labor market, and eventually out of the market altogether.

These contentions are put to the test in this chapter and found wanting. First, I discover a series of unexpected findings. African-Americans' participation in the labor market has certainly declined since midcentury but not for the reasons adduced by mismatch theory: relative to other minority groups, African-Americans have been at low risk of displacement by structural change. Immigrants have been the biggest job winners in recent decades; and yet these newcomers have consistently been at risk, given their overconcentration in declining jobs. Moreover, African-Americans and new immigrants occupy unanticipated positions in the economy: black New Yorkers have shifted into jobs requiring higher levels of education. By contrast, immigrants have generally expanded their employment by adding jobs in low-skilled sectors.

Having raised sufficient doubts about the accepted wisdom, I then go on to develop an alternative account of these deviant observations. The second part of this chapter builds on the arguments developed in Chapter 1 to uncover the sources of opportunity for African-American and immigrant New Yorkers.

Making Sense of the Numbers

Before moving on to the data, a few words are warranted—first, on the population I analyze; then, on the way I categorize the groups in question; and last, on my approach to the numbers. All of the quantitative data reported in this book apply to prime-age adults, aged 25 to 64, living in New York City. Limiting the analysis to adults simplifies matters, since youth behave differently from their elders, and inter-ethnic variations among youth often take a distinctive form.[1]

Similar considerations affect my approach to ethnic classification. Immigration, past and present, has given New York an extraordinarily variegated demographic base, indeed one so diverse as to make reality almost too complex to analyze as a coherent whole. In this chapter I abstract from the city's historically specific ethnic groups, reorganizing the population into four ethnonational groups—whites, blacks, Hispanics, Asians—and then dividing each group (Asians excepted on the grounds of small numbers) into native and foreign components.[2] As with all abstractions, this classification scheme involves some distortion of reality, without, however, doing significant harm. The commonalities among the specific groups assembled under each synthetic category—for example, the West Indian population that constitutes the largest block of "foreign blacks," or the Spanish-speakers from the circum-Caribbean that predominate among the "foreign Hispanics"—considerably exceed their differences. Reducing the many components of New York's population base to a handful of groups yields significant advantages, both in tractability and in an increased ability to make sense of the totality of ethnic change.

In approaching the numbers, I use a basic conceptual tool called the "index of representation." This simple device measures over- or underconcentration in an industry or occupation. If a group's index in an industry is one, then its share of the industry is at parity with its share of the economy overall. A score greater than one for any given industry indicates that a group is overrepresented in an industry; if the score falls below one, then the group is underrepresented.³

The index of representation is particularly helpful for two reasons. First, both mismatch and polarization are essentially hypotheses about concentrations in particular sectors and the consequences of those concentrations. Second, my own argument casts the development of economic concentrations, or niches, as the principal mechanisms by which ethnic groups move into and up the economy. I define a niche as an industry in which a group's share is at least 1.5 times its share of the total economy. Because niches are easiest to establish in small industries that have little weight on a group's overall employment picture, I classify industries as niches only if they employ a minimum of a thousand people.⁴

The index helps to examine a group's position in the economy at any one point in time. But the crux of the argument has to do with change. Given the conceptual thrust of the mismatch approach, I am interested in how a group's position in the economy at one time affected its position at another. I want some measure of the effect of the group's distribution among all industries, as well as a measure of the effect of a group's concentration in particular industries. Mismatch proponents essentially assume that industry position determines all later outcomes: if a group is too dependent on an industry set for decline, then bad fortunes at a later time are virtually guaranteed. But this framework is far too simplistic. Clearly, other factors affect the employment position of a group. If a group can increase its share of an industry, then it can gain jobs even if the industry undergoes substantial decline. Shifts in a group's size are yet another complicating factor. If the number of people in a group diminishes faster than the economy declines, or remains stable when the economy is growing, then some portion of the job decline will be due to a "population effect"—independent of whatever is happening in particular industries.

To sort out the effect of these different factors and their contributions to ethnic employment change during each of the intercensal periods from 1940 to 1990, I use a technique known as shift-share analysis. The details of shift-share analysis are somewhat complex and a full explication, along with details of the calculations, is presented in Appendix 1 to this book. But the basic elements are summarized easily enough. As I use it, shift-share analysis breaks down employment change into four components of theoretical interest:

1. *The growth effect:* the amount of job change that would have

taken place *if* a group's employment in each industry had changed at exactly the same rate as the local economy.

2. *The industry effect:* the difference between the growth rate of an industry and the total growth rate of the area. Thus, if an industry changed at the same rate and in the same direction as the local economy, the industry effect would be zero. The *net industry effect* is a measure of the impact of the overall industry distribution. Negative net industry effects indicate a pattern of earlier concentration in absolutely or relatively declining industries; positive net industry effects indicate concentration in growth sectors. The net industry effect provides an estimate of the gains or losses at the end of one intercensal period that are directly attributable to the industry distribution at the beginning of that period.

3. *The population effect:* the impact of a change in the size of a group relative to the overall population. If a group's population changed at the same rate and in the same direction as the local economy, the population effect would be zero. Negative population effects indicate diminishing relative size; positive population effects indicate growing relative size. A key issue will be the contrasting impact of the population effect, on the one hand, and the industry and growth effects, on the other.

4. *The shift:* the difference between the actual change and the total change attributable to the above effects. The shift represents those overall or industry-specific changes in a group's employment that are *not* associated with changes in the economy, in industries, or in a group's population size.

Added together, these four components equal the total employment change experienced during each of the intercensal periods I examine.

The Mismatch: An Empirical Critique

As revealed in Chapter 2, the mismatch hypothesis is right on at least one count: its analysis of the change in the skills structure of the urban economy. Just as the theory contends, traditional entry-level jobs in manufacturing and elsewhere have suffered a severe erosion. Notwithstanding the contentions about polarization, there is no evidence that the growth of higher-level jobs has been paralleled by a burgeoning of positions at the bottom of the economy.

The fact that mismatch provides a reasonable description of what has happened to the urban economy may explain why it has survived so long as the principal explanation of the economic problems of urban minorities. Clearly, the economy has changed in ways that are unfavorable to people with lower levels of skill. And when compared to whites, the skill level of African-Americans, as measured in terms of education acquired, continues to lag behind. Thus, it makes perfect sense to argue that the decline of manufacturing *must* have been devastating for African-Americans.

But what must be true just isn't so. As I shall demonstrate, mismatch fails, both as description and as prediction. Ironically, its intuitive plausibility lies at the source of its vulnerability: once one questions its root assumptions, some surprising patterns emerge.

THE GHETTO'S GOLDEN DAYS?

Chronologically, the mismatch story begins in the halcyon days of the postwar boom, when manufacturing industries extended their welcome to African-Americans. The timing of African-American movement into manufacturing could not have been worse, with concentration in the factory sector occurring in the Indian summer of the urban-industrial complex. Consequently, the postwar period proved unlike the earlier black experience in American cities, when "former sharecroppers and agricultural workers became proletarians earning their living from wages in a primarily industrial labor market," as historian Michael Katz writes.[5] Although the shift to services created growth in postindustrial activities, employment opportunities for low-skilled minority residents withered once manufacturing jobs began to seep out of the city. As John Kasarda has put it, "it did an African-American high school dropout in the South Bronx little good to learn that the old footwear factory that closed near his home was replaced by a gleaming new Manhattan office tower, just a short bus ride away."[6] With "the disappearance of industrial jobs," writes Katz, "the African-American experience is one of *deproletarianization*."[7]

Thus, the mismatch hypothesis places manufacturing decline at the heart of African-American employment problems. But that scenario assumes that African-Americans first penetrated the factory sector in large numbers. A look at the historical record, however, reveals that in New York, the much-vaunted African-American proletariat enjoyed a stunted and short-lived existence.

Black New Yorkers found themselves confined to the peripheries of the city's economy until World War II. At the turn of the century, African-Americans found work mainly in domestic labor, with 90 percent of black women and 55 percent of black men working in personal service occupations. African-Americans' confinement to domestic service represented, in part, the unfavorable terms of competition with European immigrants, who had evicted them from the trades where they had previously been accepted. The continued expansion of New York's economy slowly opened doors in a few manufacturing industries; the shutoff of immigration during World War I, and its permanent demise after 1924, further accelerated dispersion

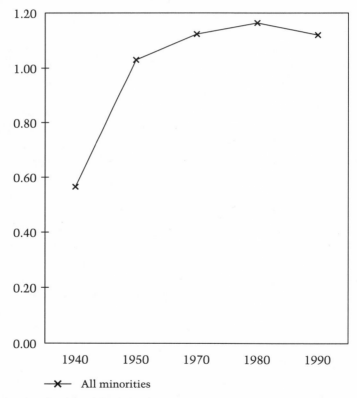

—✕— All minorities

Figure 3.1   Index of ethnic representation in manufacturing, for employed persons aged 25–64 in all minorities, 1940–1990. Index of representation = group's share of manufacturing employment ÷ group's share of total employment. (*Source:* Census of Population, 1940–1990.)

into other fields, as we shall see in greater detail in Chapters 4 and 5. But the depression largely put an end to these gains. In 1940, 42 percent of employed black New Yorkers were still engaged in domestic service. Even at that late date, when almost 70 percent of black New Yorkers worked in industries where their share of the industry was at least 1.5 times as great as their share of the economy overall, there were only three small manufacturing industries, employing a total of 1,800 African-American workers, that could be similarly classified as African-American ethnic niches.

With the advent of World War II doors to other jobs were finally unlocked; blacks made large employment gains in manufacturing, in particular. Yet, unlike those in Chicago or Detroit, African-American gains in New York's goods-producing sector proved short-lived. Lacking auto factories or steel mills, New York's factory sector was a concentration of low-wage jobs; as we shall see in later chapters, white workers remained ensconced in the better-paying, more skilled positions, while African-Americans more readily secured opportunities in the service sector (for example, health care) and in government.

Even during the brief period when black New Yorkers found a substantial berth in manufacturing, they never established a significant employment concentration or niche. African-American representation in manufacturing increased notably during the 1940s, but as Figures 3.1, 3.2, and 3.3 show, the 1950 census found African-Americans underrepresented in manufacturing, at a level well below parity. From then on, African-American representation in manufacturing steadily dwindled, until by 1990 the circle was almost closed, with representation levels approaching the level experienced on the eve of World War II. African-Americans entered the 1990s the *least* dependent on manufacturing jobs of all New York's ethnic groups.

Just how narrowly black New Yorkers penetrated into the factory sector emerges from a more disaggregated look. African-Americans carved out a few niches in manufacturing in the aftermath of the postwar boom and ensuing labor shortage. But even in 1950, when half of black New Yorkers worked in industries that could be classified as niches, the manufacturing niches accounted for barely 4 percent of total employment. Thereafter, African-American employment in niches slowly stabilized at around the one-third level. But the manufacturing niches virtually disappeared. In 1990, there was but one manufacturing industry in which the African-American

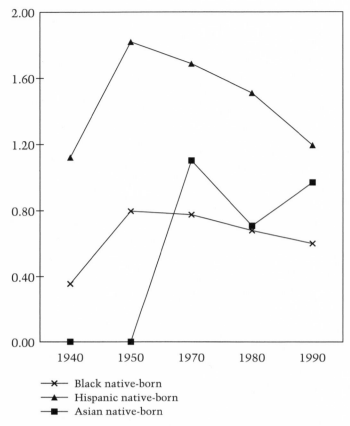

Figure 3.2   Index of ethnic representation in manufacturing, for employed native New Yorkers aged 25–64, 1940–1990. Index of representation = group's share of manufacturing employment ÷ group's share of total employment. (*Source:* Census of Population, 1940–1990.)

share was at least 1.5 times their share of the economy—accounting for less than a quarter of one percent of total African-American employment.

If the underrepresentation of black New Yorkers in manufacturing implied low exposure to the factory sector's decline, the same could not be said for Hispanic or Asian immigrants. Manufacturing was already a key source of employment for the small population of Hispanic immigrants from the Caribbean and Latin America living in New York in 1940. With representation levels in manufacturing far

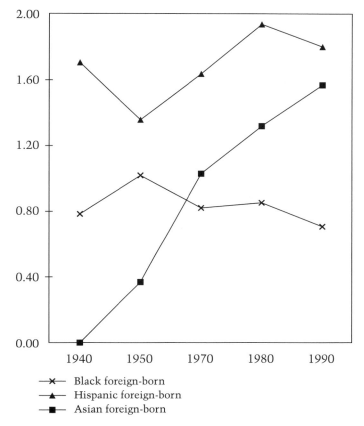

Figure 3.3   Index of ethnic representation in manufacturing, for employed foreign-born New Yorkers aged 25–64, 1940–1990. Index of representation = group's share of manufacturing employment ÷ group's share of total employment. (*Source:* Census of Population, 1940–1990.)

exceeding blacks' as of 1940, Hispanic immigrants continued to build their concentration in the factory sector for the rest of the century. Asians had no presence in manufacturing as of midcentury, but they subsequently found a foothold.

The disaggregated view underlines manufacturing's centrality for both of these immigrant groups. In 1970, 1 in every 5 immigrant Hispanics worked in a manufacturing industry that could be classified as a niche, as opposed to 3 of every 100 African-Americans— even though one-third of black New Yorkers worked in an industry that could be considered a niche. In 1970, when the Asian niches were to be found mainly in the services, a sizable niche had been developed in the vulnerable apparel industry, which was only to grow in size and importance over the next two decades.

Thus, in 1970, just when the factory sector was about to take a terrible beating, a disproportionate number of Asian and Hispanic immigrants' jobs depended directly on the fortunes of New York's hard-pressed manufacturers. If the basic mismatch contention is right, the new immigrants entered the postindustrial transition poised for disaster.

FROM FEAST TO FAMINE?

Having invoked a mythical past, mismatch accounts go on to construct a scenario of change in which the city loses its capacity to absorb new labor market entrants as its industrial base erodes: "The momentous economic transformations that have *undermined the manufacturing base* of central-city economies . . . [have left] behind what is for [minorities] an economic wasteland."[8]

In this view, the shift to services "has translated into massive job destruction in the very sectors that have traditionally supplied the brunt of employment to the minority poor."[9] The factory jobs of old have largely been replaced, and these new jobs are "the kind that are least accessible to the urban poor, who seldom possess the educational credentials, social skills, and cultural capital required by such positions."[10]

Contentions about an "economic wasteland" notwithstanding, postindustrial New York retains significant absorptive capacity: as of 1990, the majority minority city had a majority minority economy as well. The retrospective view exposes two diverging trends: the steady, uninterrupted, and massive decline of white employment, starting from 1950 and continuing over the next four decades; and the continuous expansion of the once small minority employment base until it outstripped white employment in 1990 (see Figure 3.4).

Aggregating as it does groups with distinct backgrounds and experiences, the category "minority" obscures crucial differences between African-American and new immigrant New Yorkers. In the years 1940–1970 sizable increases occurred in African-American employment (as can be seen by calculating from percentages shown in Figure 3.5). Job growth then turned sluggish, but the immigrant job base burgeoned. Neither bad times nor boom times seemed to close the gap: African-Americans lost jobs during the 1970s and made only a

Number, in millions

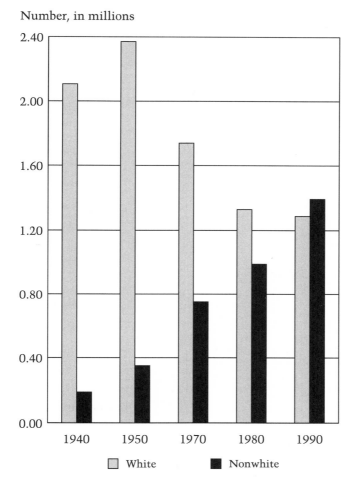

Figure 3.4 Ethnic composition of employed New Yorkers, 1940–1990.
"Nonwhites" include employed native and foreign-born African-Americans,
Hispanics, and Asians, aged 25–64. "Whites" include employed native and
foreign-born non-Hispanic whites, aged 25–64. (*Source:* Census of
Population, 1940–1990.)

modest recovery in the 1980s, unlike the immigrants who scored big
job gains in both decades. The contrasting trends among immigrant
and native blacks are particularly telling, underlining the distinctiveness of the African-American employment experience.

A close look at the manufacturing story similarly fails to provide

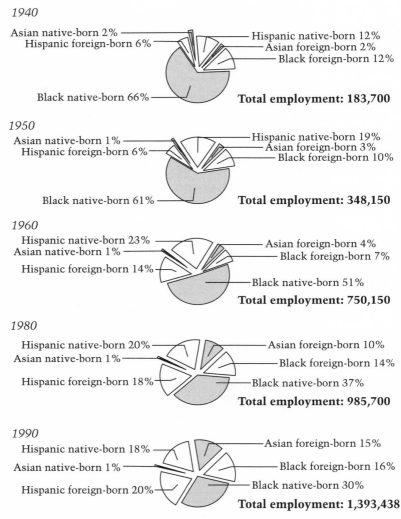

1940
Asian native-born 2%
Hispanic foreign-born 6%
Hispanic native-born 12%
Asian foreign-born 2%
Black foreign-born 12%
Black native-born 66%
Total employment: 183,700

1950
Asian native-born 1%
Hispanic foreign-born 6%
Hispanic native-born 19%
Asian foreign-born 3%
Black foreign-born 10%
Black native-born 61%
Total employment: 348,150

1960
Hispanic native-born 23%
Asian native-born 1%
Hispanic foreign-born 14%
Asian foreign-born 4%
Black foreign-born 7%
Black native-born 51%
Total employment: 750,150

1980
Hispanic native-born 20%
Asian native-born 1%
Hispanic foreign-born 18%
Asian foreign-born 10%
Black foreign-born 14%
Black native-born 37%
Total employment: 985,700

1990
Hispanic native-born 18%
Asian native-born 1%
Hispanic foreign-born 20%
Asian foreign-born 15%
Black foreign-born 16%
Black native-born 30%
Total employment: 1,393,438

Figure 3.5   Ethnic makeup of minority workers aged 25–64, 1940–1990.
(*Source:* Census of Population, 1940–1990.)

comfort for the mismatch view that factory job erosion has devastated the minority employment base. While the net decline in manufacturing employment is not open to doubt, manufacturing was by no means as barren of minority job opportunities as mismatch proponents suggest. Total minority employment in manufacturing virtually doubled between 1950 and 1980, after which it declined by almost 16

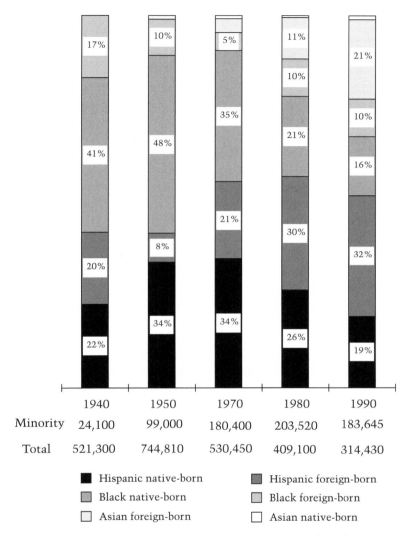

Figure 3.6   Minority employment in manufacturing, among all workers aged 25–64, 1940–1990. (*Source:* Census of Population, 1940–1990.)

percent (Figure 3.6). But again, an attempt to take apart the category of minority reveals diverging interethnic trends. Black New Yorkers made substantial, if limited, gains in manufacturing up to 1970; thereafter, the African-American job base in goods production eroded badly. By contrast, non-European immigrants generally racked up factory job gains throughout the same period. Even during the 1980s, when the manufacturing sector shrunk smaller and smaller, the immigrant Asian presence kept on expanding: by 1990, Asians significantly outnumbered African-Americans in goods production. Thus, as in the economy as a whole, sizable job opportunities opened up for minorities in the declining manufacturing sector. And the pattern of job gain consistently varied among minority groups—suggesting that more is involved here than a simple sorting by skills.

Not only is the doomsday scenario wrong: the intellectual reasoning behind it receives little, if any, support. Mismatch proponents argue that "massive job losses in the very industries in which urban minorities were concentrated" put them badly at risk.[11] Shift-share analysis is designed to assess precisely this contention. As I noted above, the industry effect measures the extent of employment change attributable to growth or decline in any particular industry; when the effects for all industries are added together, we see the net industry effect. This is our measure of how severely groups were at risk, telling us to what extent job change was due to prior concentration in declining or growing industries. If the mismatch scenario is correct, African-Americans' net exposure to industrial decline should have increased over the entire period in question, with positive or neutral scores in the early years (indicating placement in growth industries) giving way to sharply negative scores (indicating concentration in industries that were to decline).

Figure 3.7, which displays the net industry effects, shows that the "at-risk" factor for African-Americans changed in ways that contradict the mismatch hypothesis. Sharply negative for the 1940s, the industry effect turned in the opposite direction, diminishing but remaining negative over the 1950–1970 period. By the 1970s, however, black New Yorkers crossed the threshold to a slight positive industry effect, a pattern sustained during the next decade. Over the long term, then, black New Yorkers moved out of their historical concentrations in declining sectors, developing a job mix that reduced their exposure to the downside of New York's postindustrial transformation.

The immigrant comparison provides no single contrast. Black immigrants, though beginning in an unfavorable position, quickly shifted to jobs in expanding industries; by 1980, they were the best positioned to benefit from the subsequent proliferation of service jobs. Other groups followed quite different trajectories. Native Hispanics began in a cluster of declining industries and stayed there for

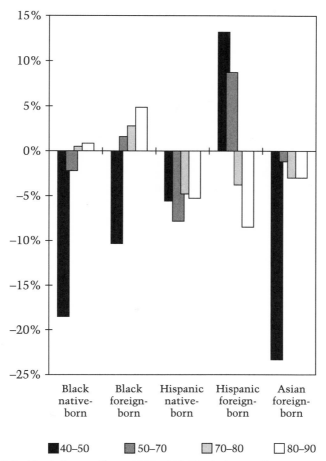

Figure 3.7   Net industry effects, 1940–1990. Net industry effect = predicted percentage change in net employment at the end of the intercensal period, based on the industry distribution at the beginning of the period. (*Source:* Census of Population, 1940–1990.)

the entire fifty-year period. By contrast, immigrant Hispanics steadily moved from a less to a more exposed position. Concentrated in expanding sectors in 1950, immigrant Hispanics displayed a strongly negative industry effect in 1970. Yet, in this case a "bad" position was followed by extraordinary job gains over the next ten years. Still more exposed to job loss in 1980, Hispanic immigrants nonetheless added close to 100,000 jobs in the next decade. Asian immigrants similarly began with an industry mix that left them highly at risk as they were crowded into the retail and service sectors. While Asian immigrant exposure to industrial decline diminished as employment diversified, the net industry effects exhibit a persistent concentration in declining industries—and yet no other group matched the Asian record of job growth in either the 1970s or the 1980s.

The shift-share analysis implicitly questions the last mismatch contention—that the growth industries proved impenetrable to minorities; a closer look at the data brings this point home. The long-term trend involves steady minority gain in the advanced services, in this case an improvement shared by African-Americans and new immigrants. In 1990, almost 250,000 native and immigrant minority workers were employed by private sector firms in the advanced services—finance, business, and professional services—representing an increase of almost sixfold relative to 1970 levels. These gains boosted minority representation as well, though by 1990 the minority job base in advanced services still fell short of parity. But black immigrants developed an early concentration in the professional services (mainly private sector health care institutions); they retained this sector of overrepresentation through 1990, by which time they also reached parity in business services. A comparison with manufacturing puts matters into perspective: while African-Americans made slower headway in finance than in the other advanced services, by 1990 they had a considerably larger presence, both absolutely and relatively, in banks and insurance companies than in the declining factory sector.[12]

Thus, the trajectory of New York's shift from industry to services stands at variance with the basic mismatch claims. The postindustrial experience is one of continuity, not rupture, with the past: New York's economy has remained a staging ground for newcomers, notwithstanding the irreversible decline of its manufacturing base. On the one hand, the new sources of job growth proved permeable to the newest New Yorkers. On the other hand, factory job loss had a limited, if any, dislocating effect. Beginning the postindustrial era already marginal to the factory sector, African-Americans had relatively little to lose from its decline. By contrast, immigrants have generally had greater exposure to industrial decline and yet their employment has continued to grow.

THE SCHOOLING-JOBS MISUNDERSTANDING

"The growth of white-collar jobs in the cities," writes Isabel Sawhill in the *Public Interest*, "means that more urban jobs require more education."[13] Indeed the trend lies just in that direction: in New York City, for example, the number of jobs filled by people who had not finished high school dropped by almost 60 percent from 1940 to 1970, and then halved again in the following twenty years. From this point, it is a simple jump to the conclusion that lack of higher-level schooling is what keeps African-Americans from getting the newly created urban jobs.

But consideration of supply-side conditions introduces several complicating factors. A decline in the supply of low-skilled labor might offset the impact of diminishing needs for low-skilled help. Even if the work force as a whole lagged behind employers in acquiring higher skills, individual groups might improve their schooling levels at a faster than average rate. While groups that did well would increase their attractiveness to employers, their move up the pecking order would diminish the competition among those less-skilled workers left behind—assuming, of course, that no additional infusions of low-skilled labor ensued.

During the years from 1940 to 1970 the employment of workers with little skill massively eroded, but job prospects for the very low skilled actually improved.[14] As Figure 3.8 shows, the ratio of low-skilled persons to low-skilled jobs fell between 1940 and 1970—just as one would expect, given the rapid educational upgrading of the city's work force and the diminishing presence of workers from the old immigration, who had arrived in the United States with little, if any education. Things changed for the worse after 1970, but not because of any shift in employers' requirements: if anything, the number of low-skilled jobs declined at a slightly slower rate than before. Rather, the new immigrants began converging on New York, producing an upswing in the ratio of low-schooled workers chasing after the remaining low-level jobs.

But note that this shift had its greatest effect on the bottommost jobs. In contrast to the experience of their less-educated peers, New Yorkers with a high school degree found that their competitive situation stayed more or less the same after 1970: then, as in 1990, there were about one and a half persons with a high school degree for every job held by a high school graduate. That distinction matters a good deal for the issue at hand, since it is precisely in the category of high school graduates that African-Americans have pulled ahead of the other groups competing for lower-level jobs.

Moreover, the ethnic choices available to the employers of low-

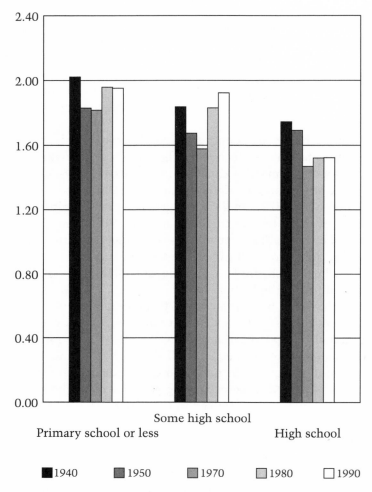

Figure 3.8   Ratio of low-skilled persons to low-skilled jobs, 1940–1990.
(*Source:* Census of Population, 1940–1990.)

skilled labor also shifted dramatically in the years after 1970 and in ways that should have benefited native blacks, if labor market sorting were all a matter of skills. Until then, employers of low-level help still had access to a labor force that was mainly white; as we shall see in the chapters to follow, those white workers enjoyed preferential treatment when it came to hiring; they also did best when employers decided who would move into those skilled positions for which little or no formal schooling was required. After 1970, the number of low-skilled white workers dropped precipitously, with the result that opportunities for their minority counterparts actually improved. Notwithstanding the oft-repeated contention that "the bottom fell out in urban industrial demand for [the] poorly-educated" after 1970,[15] job holding among minority New Yorkers with a high school degree increased by almost 60 percent between 1970 and 1990, while employment among those with less than a high school degree essentially held steady. One need also recall that the postindustrial city retains ample needs for the services of the poorly schooled; in 1990, almost half of all employed New Yorkers had a high school degree or less.

Still, one could argue (along with one prominent analyst) that "low levels of education and literacy . . . put ghetto residents at the end of the hiring queue."[16] Indeed, African-Americans steadily lost out in the scramble for low-skilled jobs, which instead have gone to the latest arrivals to New York. But if skill deficiencies account for a group's order on the hiring queue, Table 3.1 shows that educational shifts among black New Yorkers have moved them well beyond the bottommost place on that line. This table provides a comparative perspective on how the various New Yorkers measure up against one another on the skills criterion, since it gives the odds that members of one group will fall into a particular educational category, as opposed to members of all other groups. Compared to all other New Yorkers, African-Americans became progressively less likely to fall into the lowest-skilled category and increasingly more likely to fall into middle- to higher-level categories, with the most notable increase occurring in the "some college" category. Recasting the statistics in more readily comprehensible terms, Table 3.1 tells us that in 1970, there were three African-Americans with some college education for every four other New Yorkers with the same level of education. By 1990, the ratio had flipped, yielding four African-Americans with some college education, for every three other New Yorkers who had also attended college short of a final degree.[17] By contrast, native and immigrant Hispanics were twice as likely as other New Yorkers to report educational attainment below the high school degree as of 1990. Between 1970 and 1990, the odds of falling into the lowest category increased among native Hispanics and among *all* the immigrant groups—exactly opposite the trend among African-Americans. And the educational profile among African-Americans makes them an almost perfect match for the city's black immigrants—who have maintained high employment rates even as the African-American employment base has eroded.

Table 3.1 Comparative educational attainment, ethnic New Yorkers, 1970–1990
(odds of group falling into educational category compared to all other New Yorkers)

	1970	1980	1990
Native-born blacks			
Less than high school	1.23	1.20	1.09
High school	1.04	1.17	1.27
Some college	0.74	1.13	1.29
College	0.30	0.38	0.48
Foreign-born blacks			
Less than high school	1.22	1.71	2.03
High school	0.85	0.77	0.88
Some college	0.21	0.34	0.52
College	1.51	0.65	0.56
Native-born Hispanics			
Less than high school	1.74	2.00	2.02
High school	0.56	0.77	0.96
Some college	0.30	0.65	0.87
College	0.11	0.22	0.29
Foreign-born Hispanics			
Less than high school	1.00	0.96	1.11
High school	1.16	1.16	1.11
Some college	1.08	1.36	1.30
College	0.52	0.57	0.55
Foreign-born Asians			
Less than high school	0.99	0.94	1.10
High school	0.47	0.59	0.75
Some college	0.97	0.89	0.75
College	2.48	1.89	1.36

Source: Census of Population, 1970, 1980, 1990.
Note: Data for all adults aged 25–64, employed and not employed.

Thus, African-Americans have been much less educationally deficient than mismatch proponents suggest; not surprisingly, therefore, the labor market configuration for black New Yorkers has evolved from a concentration in low-skilled positions to one that reflects the skill composition of the overall economy. Figures 3.9 and 3.10 plot the correlation between average levels of education in an industry, weighted for industry size, and the percentage of an ethnic group employed in that industry. At midcentury, black New Yorkers were en-

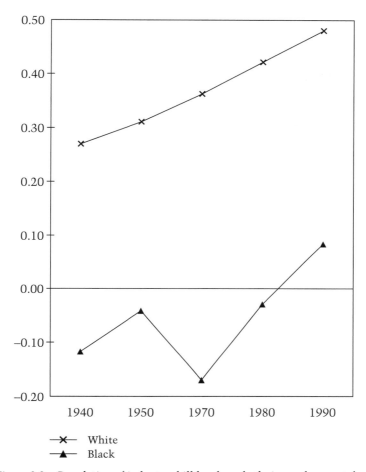

Figure 3.9   Correlation of industry skill levels and ethnic employment, for employed native-born New Yorkers aged 25–64, 1940–1990. (*Source:* Census of Population, 1940–1990.)

sconced in industries that demanded little schooling of their incumbents—even relative to the low educational requirements of the time. By 1990, however, in an economy where the average worker had four and a quarter more years of schooling than did his or her counterpart a half-century before, the previously negative correlation between educational levels and African-American employment disappeared. In effect, African-Americans had become neutrally positioned relative to the skill requirements of the postindustrial economy, clustering in

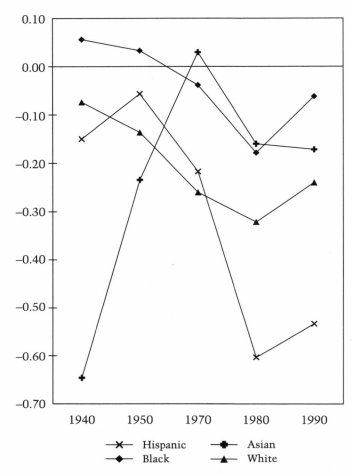

Figure 3.10   Correlation of industry skill levels and ethnic employment, for employed foreign-born New Yorkers aged 25–64, 1940–1990. (*Source:* Census of Population, 1940–1990.)

jobs that required either a high school degree or some college education.

By contrast, the evolving labor market configuration for immigrants bears the traces of their skill gap. Negative—and for two of the groups, increasingly negative—correlations define the relationship between immigrants and the skill requirements of the industries in which they are employed. The correlation for immigrant Hispanics stands out as extraordinarily strong, reminding us that this group's economic base has grown through expansion at the bottom of the economy. Immigrant Asians have largely followed the same path, offset somewhat by the infusion of more educated immigrants and their entry into higher-skilled jobs.

ISN'T THE MISMATCH A PROBLEM OF BLACK MEN?

Perhaps the mismatch hypothesis can be saved after all. At root, mismatch proponents make an argument about African-American men, supposedly the most dependent on manufacturing jobs. The erosion of the factory sector, the argument goes, should have been doubly devastating for men. Not only was employment lost, but the jobs that disappeared were sources of good pay, rewarding workers of relatively little schooling at levels with which replacement opportunities in services could never compete.

But the manufacturing-mismatch explanation, as applied to men, runs into all the problems encountered before. Most important, production jobs always eluded African-American men. Though African-American men established a few clusters in the factory sector that were sufficiently dense to classify as niches, these manufacturing concentrations never counted for much in the total African-American employment picture. In 1970, when manufacturing employment among African-American men reached its all time high, not even 6 out of every 100 black male New Yorkers worked in manufacturing industries that could be classified as niches. Even then, the densest concentrations of African-American men were to be found in the public sector, whose importance as an employer of black males has only grown as the black manufacturing concentrations have virtually disappeared.

The picture at a more aggregated level looks the same: African-American employment in manufacturing never reached parity, unlike the situation among other groups of minority men, who have been overrepresented in the factory sector since 1970 or before. Although black New Yorkers diminished their dependence on production jobs after 1970 while immigrants tended to deepen their manufacturing concentrations, job growth trajectories diverged. The 1980s brought virtually no recovery to African-American men, hard hit during the 1970s. By contrast, immigrant employment stayed on a sharply upward curve during both periods, increasing fourfold among black immigrant men and sixfold among Asian immigrant men between 1970 and 1990. Nor do educational deficiencies appear to distinguish African-American men, as native black–native white skill gaps have shrunk over the past century.

If the comparison to immigrants shows that the manufacturing mismatch does not tell why African-American men have increasingly fallen into economic trouble, it does suggest some different lines of explanation. Whereas immigrant men were *more* exposed than African-Americans to manufacturing's decline, they also made greater headway into other more stable, if low-skilled, sectors. In 1970, for example, the retail sector employed almost 27,000 native black men and just over 10,000 immigrant Hispanic men; twenty years later, the tables had turned, with more than 35,000 immigrant Hispanics in retail and fewer than 15,000 native blacks. Whether one changes the contrast group to another one of the immigrant populations or moves through the low-skill sectors, the pattern of reversal of fortune reappears with but one exception—the public sector, which, by 1990, employed more than three times as many African-American men as manufacturing. But understanding disparate rates of movement into the city's persisting low-skilled sectors raises questions about the ways in which jobs get allocated to specific groups—and these are issues that the mismatch framework simply does not address.

Polarization: A Brief, Critical Review

The polarization hypothesis occupies less space in this chapter's empirical critique. As established in Chapter 2, the basic polarization claims do not match the underlying occupational and skill trends. Since the polarization hypothesis gets the story of economic change wrong, it seems unlikely to do better in explaining the pattern of minority job change. Hence, only a brief review is in order.

The key contention concerns the relationship between services and the pattern of immigrant job growth: the new sources of growth in the advanced services generate low-level jobs, which in turn, provide the launching pad for the expansion of immigrant employment. This story is afflicted by two problems, one related to the underlying analytic framework, and the second involving its empirical applicability. At the conceptual level, the difficulty is how to find insight into intergroup differences in an approach that emphasizes structural changes that should affect seemingly similar groups in like fashion. The empirical side makes that question particularly vexing, since employment in the advanced services seems to define the immigrant economic role only in the singular case of foreign-born blacks. Even here the specifics bear little evidence of a link between immigration and the new sources of economic dynamism in finance, consulting, law, or any of the other producer services: the crucial niches have developed in both the public and private components of three health care industries, together employing 20 percent of the city's immigrant black workers.

The immigrant Hispanic and Asian cases further compound the empirical problems. Both groups gained employment by adding to early concentrations established in the declining manufacturing sector, becoming more, not less, overrepresented in the factory sector from mid-century on. As for the advanced services, both groups saw numbers increase as hiring opportunities expanded along with the postindustrial shift. Representation levels, however, *diminished* after 1970, indicating that, relative to population size, the immigrant share of advanced service jobs dwindled as service employment grew. Rather than the advanced services, retail (that old immigrant standby) provided a crucial platform for employment expansion—allowing for massive increases in job holding while preexisting concentrations were either maintained, as in the Asian case, or built up, as among the immigrant Hispanics. A more disaggregated view highlights the disconnection between immigrant employment from New York's new sources of economic growth: while 45 percent of immigrant Hispanics and 39 percent of immigrant Asians worked in industries that could be classified as niches in 1990, not a single producer service industry appeared on this list.

A New Ethnic Division of Labor

The data reviewed so far tell a simple, though startlingly new story: History cannot be escaped, and the economic trajectories of New York's minorities bear the distinctive imprint of their past. Manufacturing decline has had relatively little impact on the economic fate of New York's African-Americans, largely because they never made it into manufacturing in great numbers in the first place. In a sense, black New Yorkers have successfully adapted to the city's postindustrial transformation—sharply upgrading their skills, narrowing the educational gap that has always distinguished them from native whites, and moving away from sectors affected by the tides of economic decline. That shift into the middle ranges of the economy is consistent with views that emphasize the growing internal stratification of the African-American population. But black New Yorkers' evolving position in the labor market is hard to reconcile with the mismatch scenario—especially since immigrants, with skill levels that are often lower and rarely higher than their African-American counterparts, have massively expanded their economic base. The immigrant phenomenon violates the basic tenets of the mismatch approach, especially since the newcomers' route to job growth has involved taking over less-skilled jobs, many of which are found in declining industries. Here again, we detect the influence of history, as early immigrant concentrations provided a platform for subsequent building up of employment.

If our collection of deviant observations tells us that New York's postindustrial economy is inextricably bound up with its new population base, it leaves two broad questions unanswered. First, what are the sources of opportunities for both established groups and new arrivals? Second, how and why have economic trajectories among New York's ethnic groups diverged? The rest of this chapter answers the first of these questions. Chapter 4 traces out the transformation of New York's ethnic division of labor and examines its consequences.

In search of the sources of opportunities, I begin with the point first made in Chapter 1: because native white workers stand at the top of the hiring queue, any relative decline in the size of the white population can create vacancies for which the replacement workers are more likely to be nonwhites. In this scenario, compositional changes can offset the impact of structural shifts, creating *more* job openings for minorities despite manufacturing decline or even erosion in the aggregate citywide economic base.

We have already seen one indicator of compositional change. Native white New Yorkers have held a steadily shrinking share of the job pie ever since midcentury: in bad times, white employment dropped by far more than did employment for the city overall; in good times, native whites registered just a slight fraction of net job gains. Looking at population shifts relative to changes in the economy provides another, mor telling indicator of compositional change: it portrays changes in the shape of the hiring queue from which employers can draw. To see how the shape of the hiring queue evolved, look at Figure 3.11. There we see the estimated population change for whites from 1940 to 1990, had their numbers grown or declined in proportion to the changes in employment for the period, contrasted with their ac-

Number, in millions

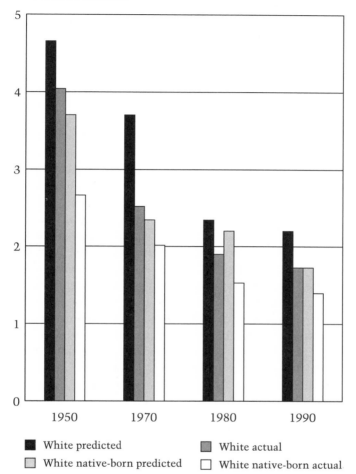

Figure 3.11   Actual and predicted levels of white population aged 25–64 in New York City, 1940–1990. Predicted population = population size at the beginning of intercensal period × (1 + proportional change in employment over intercensal period, persons 25–64 only). (*Source:* Census of Population, 1940–1990.)

tual population shifts. The figure displays straightforward trends: in bad and in good times, the availability of employers' preferred group— native whites—declined. But the better measure compares population change to changes in the size of the economy, since the latter determines the length of the hiring queue.

For our purposes, the years from 1970 to 1990 bracket the period that counts. Had white population decline been proportional to job erosion during the crisis years of the 1970s, New York would have lost 174,000 prime-age whites; instead, an additional 619,000 whites left the city for the suburbs and still greener pastures further afield. The city's economy boomed during the 1980s, but good times only slowed the outward seepage, without yielding any net addition to the diminishing white population base. Had white population shifts in the 1980s been proportional to the job gains of the period, the city would have gained an additional 308,000 whites; instead, it endured a net loss of 168,000 whites. These figures tell us that population shifts altered the shape of the hiring queue, providing opportunities for new-comers to move up the job ladder—if only for the reason that em-ployers had fewer choices from among whom to hire.

Because native whites left New York's economy at a continuing and disproportionate rate, their exodus created a demand for replace-ments—in substantial numbers. Manufacturing, the linchpin sector for the whole mismatch debate, nicely illustrates the impact of native white decline. Though manufacturing has been on the decline since midcentury, the downward spiral among native white factory workers has taken an even faster course. The factors contributing to this dis-proportionate loss in white manufacturing employment vary from decade to decade; however, a careful look at one crucial period—the years 1970–1980—highlights the surprising dynamics at work.

As can be seen in Figure 3.12, New York's economic decline—what I have generically labeled the "growth effect" for the purposes of shift-share analysis—contributed about 18,000 of the approximately 110,000 jobs that native whites lost in manufacturing during these years. The factory sector did still worse than the economy overall; consequently, sectoral decline—in shift-share terms, the "industry ef-fect"—made for the loss of an additional 42,000 jobs. Remembering that the different components of change have to sum up to the total, absolute change for the period, a look at Figure 3.12 reveals that the growth and industry effects account for little more than one half of all the manufacturing jobs lost by native whites' during these years. Many additional jobs were lost due to the population effect: by 1980, there were fewer whites whom manufacturing employers could re-cruit than had been available in 1970. Since some of the remaining native whites left manufacturing in search of better prospects else-where, Figure 3.12 also shows a negative "shift" out of the factory sector. Together, whites lost almost 50,000 jobs owing to the popu-

Number of workers

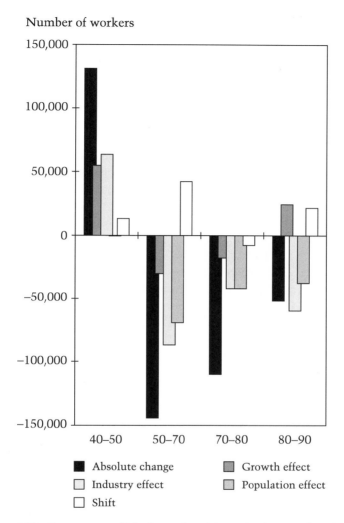

Figure 3.12   Components of job change for white native-born workers in manufacturing, 1940–1990. Absolute change = growth effect + industry effect + population effect + shift. (*Source:* Census of Population, 1940–1990.)

lation effect and to the shift; that sum gives us the size of employers' "replacement demand" in the manufacturing sector during the crucial 1970s. In the 1980s, by contrast, native whites shifted into manufacturing, after controlling for growth, industry, and population effects. Nonetheless, white losses exceeded the effects attributable to economic changes (growth plus industry) alone by about 16,000 jobs, providing an estimate of the extent of replacement demand in the factory sector.

Thus, for most of the postwar period, the white exodus from manufacturing created vacancies for replacements, allowing minority and immigrant workers to build up a job base even while the factory sector declined. Were replacement only a manufacturing story, succession processes like these would have yielded limited opportunities for the new New Yorkers of the past forty years. In comparison to other cities, New York had an already smallish factory sector as of midcentury. And the sector's overall decline puts a natural limit on the potential for minority job growth through replacement—with the decline in minority manufacturing employment in the 1980s suggesting that this natural limit has already been reached.

The replacement story is in fact writ large, however, and its prevalence can be traced to two sources. The first involves the extraordinary transformation of the skill structure of New York's remaining white workers, a change that can be summed up in just a few numbers. On the low-skilled side, the proportion of native white workers with less than a high school degree tumbled from 59 to just under 7 percent in the fifty years following 1940; on the high-skilled side, the proportion of native white workers with four years of college or more rose from 11 to 48 percent.

The second source of succession comes from the lag between white skill shifts and changing skill requirements in the economy overall. New York's economy has maintained a strong, if declining, demand for low-skilled workers ever since midcentury, as we have already seen. The number of native whites filling those low-skilled jobs, however, has tumbled at a disproportionate rate.

A slightly modified version of the shift-share analysis used above highlights the dual impact of white population decline and skill changes on succession processes. In this case, rather than aggregating jobs by major industry sector, I aggregate them according to educational level—less than high school, high school, and so on (Figures 3.13 through 3.16). Thus, the "category effect" indicates the impact of a change in the number of jobs at a particular schooling level at any point in time. Since low-skilled jobs have been steadily eroding, category effects for jobs requiring less than a high school degree have been negative for every period that I examine. But in Figure 3.13 the bar representing the category effect is a good deal smaller than the bar for

Number of workers

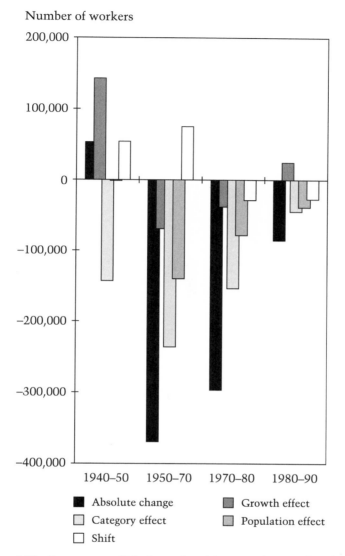

Figure 3.13   Components of job change for white native-born workers in jobs requiring less than a high school degree, 1940–1990. (*Source:* Census of Population, 1940–1990.)

Number of workers

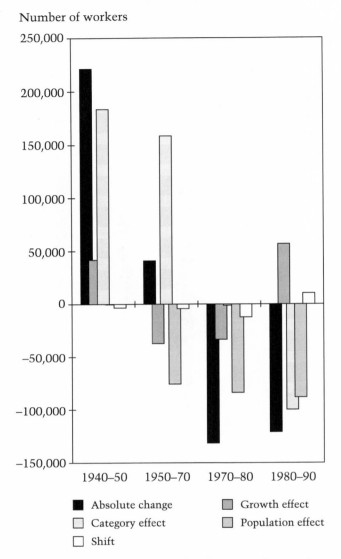

Figure 3.14   Components of job change for white native-born workers in jobs requiring a high school degree, 1940–1990. (*Source:* Census of Population, 1940–1990.)

Number of workers

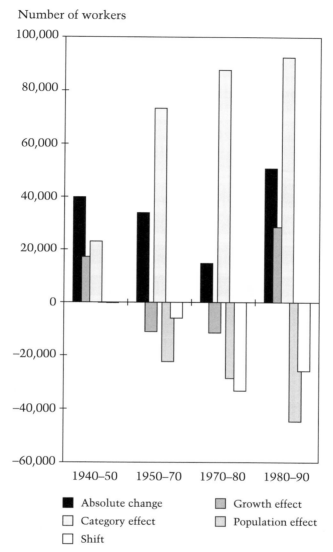

Figure 3.15   Components of job change for white native-born workers in jobs requiring some college education, 1940–1990. (*Source:* Census of Population, 1940–1990.)

Number of workers

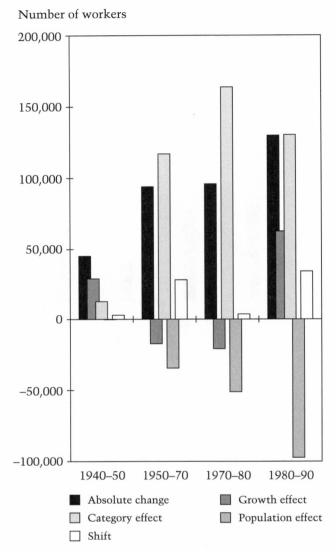

Figure 3.16   Components of job change for white native-born workers in jobs requiring a college degree or more, 1940–1990. (*Source:* Census of Population, 1940–1990.)

absolute change for every period since 1950: this contrast tells us that native whites have been losing low-skilled jobs at a rate that's disproportional to the total decline in low-skilled employment. As in the manufacturing case, part of the disparity can be attributed to the effects of diminished population size: all things being equal, fewer and fewer whites have been available to staff the remaining low-skilled positions. But all things have not been equal, since the upgrading of whites' educational levels has outpaced the upgrading of skill requirements in the economy overall. Despite variations from period to period, we see sizable losses due to shift—indicating sharply eroded white shares of the lowest-skilled jobs, even after adjusting for population decline.

Focusing on the crucial years between 1970 and 1990 illuminates the dynamics that rearranged labor market outcomes. Jobs for New Yorkers with less than a high school degree employed 297,000 fewer native whites in 1980 than they had a decade before. Roughly 38,000 of these jobs disappeared because of economic decline; the erosion of the low-skilled base wiped out another 153,000. All the remaining losses resulted from the changing availability of low-skilled whites. As already seen, native whites seeped out of New York's labor market during the 1970s; this population effect produced a loss of almost 78,000 jobs. Even after adjusting for population size, the 1980 data reveal relatively fewer whites working in low-skilled jobs than had been the case a decade before: consequently, the shift accounted for a loss of over 28,000 jobs. Added together, the shift and the population effect give us the size of replacement demand, yielding over 106,000 vacancies that can be ascribed only to the consequences of ethnic succession. The story for the 1980s reads much the same, with one exception: the replacement process worked with even greater effect. While native white employment in the low-skilled sector declined by over 85,000, the buoyant state of the city's economy slowed the decline of jobs requiring little schooling: growth and category effects combined caused a loss of only 20,000 jobs. All of the remaining decline can be attributed to the diminishing size of the white population base, on the one hand, and to the reduced availability of those white workers who remained in the city, on the other. Since employers needed replacements for low-skilled whites who could no longer be found, splitting up the components of white job change explains the previously unaccountable: namely, why minorities could make sizable job gains in low-skilled jobs and in sectors undergoing severe decline.

Increasing white concentration in knowledge-intensive jobs has compensated for whites' diminishing presence in low-skilled positions. If whites' gains matched up to employers' growing needs for higher-skilled workers, then the size of the columns measuring absolute changes and category effects would be equal. Figures 3.14 and 3.15 show that absolute changes were almost always smaller than category effects, indicating that native whites rarely absorbed the potential gains resulting from increased demands for high-skilled workers. Although native whites increased their employment in jobs requiring some college education during the seventies and eighties, their gains were too small to keep up with growth in this category, reflected in the negative shifts

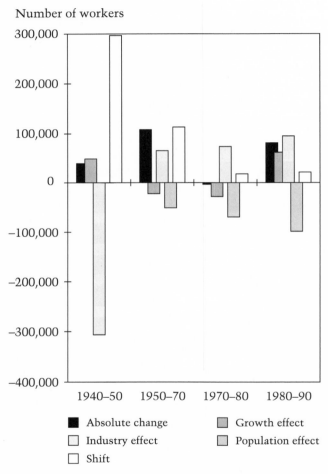

Figure 3.17   Components of job change for white native-born workers in the advanced services, 1940–1990. "Advanced services" includes private sector finance, insurance, real estate, business services, and professional services. Absolute change = growth effect + industry effect + population effect + shift. (*Source:* Census of Population, 1940–1990.)

presented in Figure 3.15. The shift-share analysis even points to some compositional change among the most educated laborers, as native white gains fell short of the increases attributable to the growing demand for college-educated workers during the 1970s, as seen in Figure 3.16.

The same pattern emerges when we examine employment changes in the most knowledge-intensive of the growth sectors, professional services, business services, and FIRE. In this case, we find the flip side of the manufacturing story: there, the losses among whites were relatively greater than the sector's decline; here, whites generally added jobs, but not in numbers that were proportional to the sector's expansion. In fact, during the pivotal 1970s, native whites actually lost jobs in advanced services, even as the advanced service sectors expanded; consequently, almost 50,000 jobs opened up owing to the shortfall in the native white labor supply. In the next decade, native whites streamed into the advanced services, but still not in sufficient quantities to meet employers' demands. As can be seen from Figure 3.17, the sum of the growth and industry effects towered over the employment gains that native whites made during the 1980s; for the most part, that disparity translated into vacancies, which employers sought to fill with workers from New York's expanding minority population base.

Thus, in the growth sectors, compositional change created demand, not so much for replacement of white workers as for complements; in this way, compositional change expanded the scope of job opportunities that could be captured by minority workers.

But the question of *who* got the jobs vacated by whites, whether in declining or expanding sectors, is not a simple matter at all. As I argued in Chapter 1, the process of ethnic succession in the postindustrial city does not involve an orderly march up the hiring queue. Education obviously influences an individual's ability to attain a particular job, but other, powerful, contextual factors sort groups into different and distant positions in economic space. Just how and why sorting occurs is a matter to which I shall attend in the chapters that report on the case studies. The next step is to examine the trajectories followed by African-Americans, new immigrants, and white ethnics as they have responded to the pressures of ethnic competition and industrial change. As we shall see in the next chapter, ethnic adaptation has taken the route of economic specialization. Consequently, the components of New York's polyglot working population play distinctive economic roles, with African-Americans and various new immigrants becoming more, not less, different over time.

4 | The Making and Remaking of the Ethnic Niche

I concluded the last chapter by describing how the white population that stood at the head of employers' hiring queue shifted in size and composition, creating vacancies at lower rungs of the occupational structure which less-preferred groups could fill. But to leave our account there is to leave it half told. Compositional change opened up possibilities for advancement throughout New York's industrial complex. Yet, the various components of the city's polyglot working and middle classes each converged on particular industries and sectors, establishing trajectories that squarely differentiated one from another.

Multiple patterns of economic adaptation indicate that the responses to replacement demand did not follow automatically from the mechanical adjustment of the hiring queue. As I argued in Chapter 1, the hiring queue itself is a historical construct, socially constituted by the self-interested and often contested actions of ethnically diverse employer and worker groups. Consequently, the queue changes in contingent ways, with both opportunities and options linked to the historically specific experiences of a succession of insider and outsider groups.

Thus, the transformation of New York's ethnic division of labor over the past half-century is equally the history of African-Americans and new immigrants and of the European ethnic groups that arrived earlier. I tell that history by focusing on six groups—Jews, Italians, African-Americans, West Indians, Chinese, and Dominicans, the first three consisting of native-born New Yorkers, the latter three constituting the largest ethnic components of the new black, Asian, and Hispanic immigrant populations, respectively.[1] The shift from the more abstract ethnic classification system of the previous chapter inevitably makes this account somewhat incomplete. But I have a different goal in this chapter, that of delineating the trajectories of change, which requires a greater degree of concreteness and specificity than before. Though my choice inevitably excludes the entire cast of characters, the ethnic groups on which this chapter focuses are clearly the central *dramatis personae* of the story I wish to tell.

The framework developed in Chapter 1, where I argued that the incorporation of ethnics into New York's economy involves a continuing convergence on some set of economic specializations, provides an analytic structure for the capsule histories that follow. In this chapter, I trace the development, transformation and, in some cases, attenuation of the ethnic niche, detailing the location of those niches, their structural characteristics, and the degree to which the pattern of economic concentration has distinguished each group's position, relative to the others. As in the previous chapter, I define a niche as an industry, employing at least one thousand people, in which a group's representation is at least 150 percent of its share of total employment. Since the state plays an important role in niche formation, not just as an agent that can reinforce or open up niches but as a locus of niches as well, I further cross-classify the usual categories, separating private from public sector employment within an industry.

But there is more to my account of the ethnic niche than the claim that concentration is a salient and persistent trait of ethnic economic life in New York. Remember that the conventional wisdom tells us that clustering is a transient phenomenon, waning rapidly after the first generation, and all for the better—since diffusion is the way that ethnics move up and get ahead. By contrast, I maintain that niches may provide a protected environment—not just an orbit of jobs to which ethnics of any group may have privileged access, but also an arena in which they are treated more favorably than in jobs of lower ethnic density. Concretely, that contention means that ethnics employed in niches may do better than their counterparts who work in industries of lower ethnic density—even after controlling for background characteristics. It also implies that niches may offer more equitable terms of compensation, so that ethnics will come closer to the rewards of comparable native whites, again after controlling for background differences. Thus, in this chapter, I assess the consequences of

Table 4.1 Niche characteristics for native-born Jews, 1940–1990

	Characteristics of niches				Percentage of niche employment			
	Employed in niche	Female	Mean years of schooling	Mean earnings	Public sector	Self-employment	Manufacturing	Managerial/ professional/ technical
1940	56%	27%	11.5	$13,778	20%	15%	29%	31%
1950	51%	23%	12.2	$21,487	22%	26%	8%	44%
1970	45%	42%	13.6	$38,170	31%	18%	5%	46%
1980	41%	50%	16.0	$31,945	26%	19%	2%	69%
1990	49%	52%	16.3	$47,497	20%	22%	8%	78%

Source: Census of Population, 1940–1990; data for employed persons aged 25–64.

Note: Jews defined as children of Russian-born parents, 1940–1970; persons of Russian ancestry, 1980, 1990; 1940 data for wage and salary earnings only; all earnings in 1990 dollars.

clustering in niches for each group's overall economic adaptation by comparing earnings inside and outside niches, before and after controlling for background characteristics. As I move from group to group, I also contrast earnings inside and outside the niches with the experience of a common reference group of native whites, first looking at the raw gap, and then using a statistical procedure that gives the members of each group the same rewards as comparable members of the reference group.[2]

Jews

Although the Jewish presence in New York extends far back, almost to the city's founding, Jews did not become an important, visible element in the city's economic life until the mass migration from Russia began in the 1880s. The Russian Jews established an economic base concentrated in a limited, and highly distinctive, set of industries almost immediately upon their arrival. Since then, the Jewish niches have evolved considerably, with old concentrations falling off and new ones developing. Yet niche concentration remains an enduring characteristic of Jewish economic life in New York (Table 4.1).

The turn-of-the-century arrivals from Russia came just when the demand for factory-made clothing began to surge. Garments, as I shall recount in somewhat greater detail in Chapter 5, became the premier Jewish trade, a home for Yiddish-speaking proletarians and a launching pad for fledgling entrepreneurs.[3] At the start, the immigrants clustered in an incredibly dense settlement at the edge of the factory and warehouse district where they worked. Concentration provided further stimulus to a legion of petty traders. Jews dominated the army of ethnic street merchants, who were in turn avid customers of Jewish wholesalers and retailers, who, by successfully competing with department stores, provided employment to a large, overwhelmingly Jewish work force.[4]

The Jews' concentration in commerce and clothing manufacture defined their initial place in the ethnic division of labor. Jewish specializations barely overlapped with the Irish; domestic service and general labor were rarities among Jews, but common Irish pursuits; by the same token, tailoring and retailing, whether as merchant or peddler, were far more likely to engage Jews than Irish.

The insularity of the Jewish ethnic economy, as in the case of clothing, kept head-to-head competition with non-Jews to a minimum; even where Jews and non-Jews were active in the same field, as in construction and real estate, connections to co-ethnic workers and clients helped Jews sidestep competitive obstacles.[5]

The advent of the second generation consolidated the original concentrations while also fostering attempts to move beyond the ethnic economy. The relatively rapid educational progress of younger immigrants and of the immigrants' children prepared them to work outside the ethnic economy, but gentile employers rarely hired Jews. One study, completed just before the Great Depression, found that the doors of New York's large, corporate organizations—"railroads, banks, insurance companies, lawyers' offices, brokerage houses, the New York Stock Exchange, hotels . . . and the home offices of large corporations of the first rank"—were infrequently opened to Jews.[6] The surge into the schools, and through the schools into the professions, met with resistance from the older, largely Protestant population that dominated these institutions. By the 1920s, numerous private universities and colleges, as well as medical schools and law schools, had implemented quotas on Jewish admission.

In the 1930s, the advent of the depression, combined with the continuing, indeed exacerbated, effects of discrimination outside the ethnic economy, led many second-generation Jews to seek an alternative in public employment. Though the quest for government jobs, and in particular teaching positions, had started earlier, the straitened circumstances of the 1930s accelerated this search. Dentists applied for jobs as chemists in the city's health department, lawyers took the exam for policemen, those with Ph.D.'s sought out work as high school teachers.[7] The quality and quantity of Jews vying for government employment increased; changes in the structure of government employment led to a rapid increase in Jewish employment in the public sector and, with it, growing conflict with other white ethnic groups (as we shall see in Chapter 7).

Thus, the coming of age of the second generation brought a paradoxical change. While the U.S.-born Jews continued to occupy a distinctive place in New York's economy, just like their parents, the second generation developed an economic configuration of its own. On the eve of World War II, just over half of second-generation Jewish New Yorkers worked in industries that could be classified as Jewish niches. Apparel ranked first among the second-generation niches, but it now served as a base for white-collar employment and was to be drained of most of its Jewish workers once prosperity returned after the war.[8] Government accounted for almost one out of every five niche jobs; the other Jewish niches were scattered over a wide range of manufacturing and retail trades. Overall, these second-generation concentrations provided ample scope for mobility: 31 percent of the Jews employed in niches worked in professional and managerial jobs, a higher figure than for those outside these niches, and that disparity would only grow in years to come.

Despite the fall of discriminatory barriers in the postwar years, just under a half of Jewish New Yorkers still worked in ethnic concentrations by 1970.[9] Those concentrations retained more than a trace of the earlier pattern, with a variety of retail and wholesale niches supporting one-fifth of niche employment. Jews' rapid movement into the professions made its mark on the ethnic niche as well: by 1970, higher education, legal services, accounting, and physicians offices were Jewish niches as well. But the defining characteristic of the Jewish niches was the importance of public sector employment, accounting for almost 31 percent of niche jobs. Reliance on government reduced the insularity of the Jewish niches, as blacks increasingly penetrated into the public sector. Government consequently became a flash point of black-Jewish conflict, as the two groups contended over access to jobs and the rules of civil service promotion.

By 1990, Jews had entirely transformed their niche all the while retaining a distinctive economic role. Though even more concentrated then they had been in 1970, Jewish New Yorkers had largely shed their traditional economic base, retaining only a handful of small clusters in trade.[10] In all respects but one, the Jewish niches of the late twentieth century had an utterly postindustrial cast, with education, legal services, publishing, advertising, public relations, and theaters topping the list. The persistently high rate of self-employment remained the strongest link to the past: more than one out of every five niche jobs involved independent work. These new, postindustrial niches served as concentrations of particularly well paid jobs. In a twist on the usual assumption that links economic status with diffusion out of ethnic economic specializations, Jews in niches earned more than those employed in industries with lower levels of Jewish concentration. As Table 4.2 shows, these advantages disappeared after controlling for background characteristics, largely because the human capital characteristics of Jews in their industrial concentrations were so exceptionally high. And though the industries of Jewish concentration treated Jews better than comparable native whites, the reward structure was favorable for Jews whether in industries of Jewish density or not.

A brief look at some of the traditional Jewish niches reveals how firmly they were cast by the wayside and with what effect. The Jewish petite bourgeoisie proved long-lived, enduring in sizable numbers up to the early 1970s, as I shall recount in Chapter 8. Its disappearance created vacancies into which new immigrant entrepreneurs rapidly and successfully moved. By the last quarter of the twentieth century, the once ubiquitous Jewish shopkeeper had faded from the scene: the storekeepers' sons and daughters had better things to do than mind a shop; and their parents, old, tired, and scared of crime, were eager to sell out to new groups of immigrant entrepreneurs. By 1990, Jews were heavily overrepresented among self-employed doctors, dentists, and engineers but virtually absent from the ranks of those petty entrepre-

Table 4.2 Comparative earnings in ethnic niches, 1990

| | Niche v. non-niche | | Group v. native whites | | | |
| | | | Niche | | Non-niche | |
	Raw	W/controls	Raw	Adjusted	Raw	Adjusted
Men						
Jews	110%	99%	111%	103%	118%	107%
Italians	115%	118%	73%	91%	88%	98%
African-Americans	116%	109%	73%	85%	51%	72%
West Indians	93%	93%	56%	85%	53%	77%
Chinese	57%	68%	41%	56%	53%	79%
Dominicans	80%	82%	45%	74%	43%	92%
Women						
Jews	109%	103%	110%	104%	109%	101%
Italians	104%	113%	70%	89%	80%	92%
African-Americans	105%	105%	82%	91%	68%	81%
West Indians	102%	103%	69%	88%	62%	80%
Chinese	48%	69%	38%	65%	67%	94%
Dominicans	70%	80%	42%	84%	49%	97%

Source: Census of Population, 1990; data for employed persons aged 25–64.

Note: Comparison group defined as non-Jewish, non-Italian, native-born whites. First comparison (niche v. non-niche) holds characteristics constant and estimates impact of employment in niche. Second comparison (group v. native whites as defined above) holds industry distribution constant, retains groups' characteristics, but gives groups the same rewards as native whites. For complete explanation, see note 2 to this chapter.

neurs who made their living in trade. Light manufacturing underwent a similar Jewish exodus; collectively, the Jewish withdrawal from New York's traditional small business sectors provided a chance for a legion of immigrants, and not just Koreans. At the end, as at the beginning, of the twentieth century, newcomers dominated the ranks of New York's petite bourgeoisie.

Though more persistent than in retail or apparel, the Jewish presence in the public sector is becoming a thing of the past. Working as a city engineer or accountant used to be a Jewish pastime; now these occupations engage far many more Patels than Cohens. Only in teaching and in higher education do the traditional Jewish concentrations remain in force. And here, as demonstrated in the affair of Leonard Jeffries—the former chair of black studies at City College, who rails against the college's "head Jew" and the "kabala" of supposedly controlling Jewish faculty—the manifestations of earlier competitive patterns persist.

Thus, the old Jewish concentrations are mainly gone, but a distinctive Jewish role in New York's economy lives on. Unlike the older ethnic economy, the Jewish pursuits of the late twentieth century are detached from the dynamics of interethnic competition that characterized earlier periods. But the emergence of postindustrial Jewish ethnic niches offers strong testimony to the continued intertwining of ethnicity and economics and to the enduring importance of social networks as carriers of information and mechanisms of economic facilitation. As we shall see in the Italian case to follow, ethnic trajectories do not always follow the same path. Yet the Jewish and Italian experiences are alike in two crucial ways: both groups established long-lasting strangleholds over entry portals and mobility ladders; and both gave up traditional economic pursuits at century's end, expanding opportunities for outsiders.

Italians

Along with the Jews, peasant migrants from southern Italy dominated the waves of newcomers who streamed into New York in the years between 1880 and 1920. The Italian migration picked up steam later than did the outflow of Jews from the Russian pale. But by the time Congress closed the doors to immigration in 1924, Italian New Yorkers outnumbered their Jewish counterparts; the numerical weight of the Italian first- and second-generation populations would be felt in the city's economy for decades to come.

Unlike the Jews, who brought with them experience in trade and greater exposure to urban economies and the skills they required, the Italians were agriculturalists, with little in their background that would favor rapid movement up the economic ladder. Petty trade beckoned to many, and at the turn of the century, Italians were heavily overrepresented among the ranks of the city's legions of peddlers. Artisanal skills allowed some to enter crafts; barbering, tailoring, and boot and shoe repair soon gained substantial Italian contingents. But the great bulk of Italian newcomers had few alternatives to the most menial of occupations: men worked as laborers in the city's booming building industry or as longshoremen on the docks; women sewed in sweatshops or at home. Despite starting out at the very bottom, some Italians moved up to skilled or low-white-collar ranks by the mid-1920s. For the bulk of the population, however, the climb up the totem pole was slow and arduous. By 1931, almost a third of Italian-born men still worked as common laborers and another 10 percent found themselves engaged in some trade related to construction—activities that left Italians vulnerable to the depression's exactions.[11] In the mid-1930s, a study by the New York Welfare Council found that "almost twice as many of the youth of Italian parentage as of the other foreign stock has fathers whose usual occupation was in unskilled labor."[12] Though outdistancing their parents, the emerging second generation still encountered severe barriers. In the mid-1920s, more than a quarter of native-born Italian men labored in unskilled jobs; a decade later, in the midst of the depression, one out of five Italian youth lived on relief, in contrast to a shade over one in ten among Jews.[13] As with their parents, low educational levels slowed the progress of the second generation; though the legacy of Italian culture may not have been as constraining as earlier social scientists have thought, there is no question that schooling levels among New York–born Italians were relatively slow to rise.[14]

Thus, the Italians entered New York as a proletarian population and remained so for several decades, despite the presence of an entrepreneurial nucleus based in petty trade.[15] On the eve of World War II eight out of ten Italian immigrants still found themselves engaged in blue-collar occupations, as did seven out ten among the second generation. Networks had channeled these first- and second-generation Italians into discrete segments of New York's economy, though they were not quite as heavily niched as the Jews (Table 4.3). But the more important contrast lay in the circumstances of employment: Italians found themselves clustered in industries and occupations where they were bossed and directed by others. "There was fierce conflict," reports anthropologist Robert Orsi, "between Italians and the longer-established Irish who controlled the distribution of work and served as foremen and supervisors in Harlem's industries."[16] Irish-Italian conflict was equally endemic on the docks, where the Irish had long ruled; competition between the two groups played no small role in the persistence of the shape-up and the debility of the longshore union. In other industries—bedding, painting, and especially garments—Italians workers found themselves dependent on Jewish contractors and manufacturers.[17] In the 1930s, as Italians felt the unending bite of the depression, their resentment against their Jewish bosses (and union leaders) grew increasingly strong. A 1938 report prepared for the American Jewish Committee found "racial hatred spreading" among Italian tailors and "many openly anti-Semitic elements" among Italian building craftsmen.[18]

The census data buttress these historical accounts. The Italian niches lay scattered among a swath of manufacturing and retail industries. Few provided meaningful top-level opportunities—in the case of apparel, the largest Italian niche of the time, barely 4 percent of the industry's second-generation Italians worked in managerial or professional jobs. However, the presence of an Italian mayor, Fiorello LaGuardia, at the city's helm and administrative changes that loosened the Irish stranglehold on government jobs helped Italians move into the city's bureaucracy: 14 percent of Italians employed in ethnic niches worked on the public payrolls, though generally in poorly paid jobs.

World War II's advent and the prosperity of the postwar years slowly pulled Italians up the labor queue but not out of the ethnic niche. The 1950 census provides indicators of modest change: printing and publishing, a concentration of skilled, male jobs, replaced apparel as the largest Italian niche. Government now provided an expanded Italian berth, though one that was still modest by Jewish or Irish standards. But in general, the Italian economic niches of midcentury differed little from the niches that had been carved out before the war.

Three out of every ten second-generation Italians still worked in an ethnic niche in 1970; by then, the ethnic niche had evolved into a concentration of skilled but almost exclusively blue-collar jobs.[19] Ap-

Table 4.3 Niche characteristics for native-born Italians, 1940–1990

	Characteristics of niches				Percentage of niche employment			
	Employed in niche	Female	Mean years of schooling	Mean earnings	Public sector	Self-employment	Manufacturing	Managerial/professional/technical
1940	45%	35%	8.6	$ 8,670	14%	7%	58%	8%
1950	26%	15%	9.5	$15,748	12%	11%	43%	13%
1970	32%	28%	9.9	$25,575	18%	11%	35%	9%
1980	14%	14%	11.9	$27,964	38%	8%	2%	10%
1990	17%	37%	13.3	$38,545	7%	8%	3%	29%

Source: Census of Population, 1940–1990; data for employed persons aged 25–64.

Note: Italians defined as children of Italian-born parents, 1940–1970; persons of Italian ancestry, 1980, 1990; 1940 data for wage and salary earnings only; all earnings in 1990 dollars.

parel topped the list of Italian concentrations, pointing to the persistence of the ethnic pattern established at the turn of the century and the industry's continued dependence on its traditional labor force. The influence of the past could be detected in other niches as well—construction, retail groceries, wholesale food, bakeries, and barber shops all ranked as Italian niches. The most dramatic shift involved the heightened Italian presence on government payrolls, as civil servants accounted for close to a third of Italians in ethnic niches. But unlike the Jews, who worked for government as teachers, college professors, and accountants, the Italian civil servants clustered in the post office, in sanitation, and in transportation.

By the last quarter of the twentieth century, however, Italian New Yorkers had entered the "twilight of ethnicity," as Richard Alba has argued, and ethnicity's fading influence can be detected in the utterly transformed role that Italians play in New York's postindustrial economy.[20] In 1990 the once flourishing niche was but a shadow of its former self, with less than one fifth of Italian New Yorkers working in industries that could be classified as ethnic niches. While some of the remaining niches—trucking, bus driving, and sanitation—provided a link to the Italian New York of the past, other clusters connected to the postindustrial present. One single postindustrial concentration—the securities industries—accounted for more than a quarter of employment in the 1990 concentrations.

A transformed educational profile explains why Italians have become players of a different kind: in 1990, 30 percent of New Yorkers of Italian ancestry had received four years of college or more—four times the rate reported in 1970. Greater schooling detached Italians from their traditional concentrations: by 1990, the Italian seamstress, twenty years earlier the mainstay of the garment industry, had virtually disappeared, replaced by technical and professional workers, as evidenced by the largely female, Italian niches that appeared in doctors' and dentists' offices. Education simultaneously propelled Italians into the upper ranges of the economy: management and the professions engaged almost 40 percent of New Yorkers of Italian ancestry in 1990. Still, traces of Italian disadvantage remain: even in its reduced state, the niche provides better-paying jobs than the other industries in which Italian density is not quite so high. And wherever Italians work, they neither do as well as other native whites nor, when background characteristics are controlled, receive comparable rewards.

The story of Italian New Yorkers and their economic niches contrasts with the experience of their Jewish counterparts. Unlike the Jews, the Italians established a proletarian presence in New York's economy, gradually moving up the blue-collar job ladder and settling into well-paying, skilled positions by midcentury. Business played a more important role in the Jewish trajectory, which took Jews on a more rapid path into the middle class. When at last the Italians moved into the upper reaches of New York's economy, the size of their ethnic niches drastically declined—quite unlike the situation among Jews, whose niches have simply been reconfigured to fit their upper-middle-class skills and resources.

If the Italians no longer occupy a distinctive position in New York's economy, they still play an important role, as 9 percent of employed New Yorkers reported Italian ancestry in 1990. Their proletarian persistence through the immediate postwar decades helps account for the bottlenecks experienced by blacks and Puerto Ricans in their search for good jobs in the city's factory complex. By contrast, the Italian ascent *out* of the working class in the late twentieth century provides part of the explanation for the expanding economic role of the city's minority and immigrant working class.

African-Americans

The advent of World War II caught black New Yorkers still reeling from the effects of the depression. The 1940 census counted 17 percent of black men and 14 percent of black women as jobless, and of those who worked, four out of ten gave personal service as their type of employment. African-Americans' concentration in domestic service had exposed them to the rudest of the depression's severe blows: servants' wages had declined badly during the 1930s, with a surplus of domestic help leading to the appearance of "slave markets" throughout New York City.[21] Service engaged most black New Yorkers in public as well as private employments: aside from construction laborers doing emergency work on government payrolls, only a scattering of tiny African-American clusters fell into the goods-producing category. In addition to private household work, African-American service niches appeared in laundering, hotels, and taxi service. Only in the postal service—an image of things to come—did black New Yorkers have a shelter from the ravages of the depression and the specter of discrimination.[22]

The advent of World War II changed things, but not as quickly nor as dramatically as is often thought. Industries that had previously closed their doors to black workers were forced by labor shortages to change their hiring practices; as they did so, African-American concentrations in their traditional clusters declined. By 1950, black New Yorkers were no longer as tightly squeezed into a small number of industries as had been the case a decade earlier. And they enjoyed expanded opportunities in manufacturing and in the public sector as well.

Personal services lost little of their importance, however—one out of every five African-American workers was in domestic work or laundering in 1950, and household workers were even more likely to be African-American than had been the case ten years before. Though headway had been made into manufacturing, the record hardly looks outstanding: in 1950, manufacturing employed just 6 percent of black New Yorkers at work in an ethnic niche, and not a single one of the African-American clusters was linked to the sectors—apparel, electronics, and printing—that formed the core of the city's then robust manufacturing complex. African-Americans made more progress in the railroads, a preexisting niche where wartime shortages had done much to increase black employment. But supply constraints had pulled blacks into railroads without also pulling them up the job ladder: as the New York State Commission against Discrimination found in a survey later in the decade, almost 80 percent of black railroad workers were engaged in just seven occupations that employed only 14 percent of their white counterparts.[23] Of greater importance than either factory or railroad jobs were the expanded concentrations in the public sector: by 1950, there were African-American niches in public hospitals and transportation, in addition to the post office. These public sector concentrations already kept more African-Americans at work than did all of the manufacturing sector. They also provided significant employment opportunities to African-American men.

Thus, contrary to the conventional view, New York never developed an African-American proletariat of any significance. Chapters 5 and 6 provide a detailed accounting of the barriers to proletarianization in two critical cases, apparel and construction, but the lineaments of the argument can be outlined now. The route into goods production had too many barriers for black New Yorkers to build their economic base in the traditional way. The construction case shows that white ethnics held on to the best manual jobs, notwithstanding strenuous black efforts to overcome these impediments. But the building trades was by no means the only such case. While the printing industry served as a sizable stronghold of high-wage employment in the fifties, its concentration in New York did not redound to the benefit of African-Americans. To get into the skilled jobs one needed to become an apprentice, and the apprentices in turn came from the ranks of the industry's unskilled workers. As these occupations were filled through recommendations from workers already in the trade, blacks were effectively excluded from the printing crafts, as the New York State Commission against Discrimination noted in its report of 1960.[24] The few blacks who made it into the apprentice programs—in 1963 there were only 42 blacks and Puerto Ricans among the 600 typographical apprentices—often dropped out in discouragement over the long stint required in low-paid apprentice jobs.[25]

The apparel case sheds further light on the peculiar mix of disincentives that deterred African-Americans from heading into manufacturing. As in printing, Jewish and Italian workers remained firmly ensconced in the skilled and better-paying jobs, and blacks had little chance of dislodging these incumbents. Over time, the industry's low position in the wage hierarchy eventually came to discourage African-Americans from seeking out entry-level opportunities.

The largest of New York's manufacturing industries, apparel was hardly unique. As the 1950s progressed, the city's factory sector fell under increasingly severe competitive pressure. As the decade neared its end, low wages and sweatshop conditions became a scandal; the city government was forced to set up a special commission on the conditions of low-wage workers and the issue of a local minimum wage became a political hot potato. While goods production did not prove to be alluring, the expanding service and public sectors beckoned. The case of hospitals, the single largest employer of African-Americans, provides a key to understanding how black New Yorkers carved out their place in the ethnic division of labor. Even as manufacturing employment dwindled, New York's hospital sector developed after World War II into "a giant sponge soaking up surplus, unskilled labor."[26] Blacks had worked in hospitals before the war, but always in the company of other European ethnics scrounging for work in the bowels of New York's crowded labor market. Hospital workers were "very much like the cooks, laundresses, charwomen, and kitchen help that you will find wherever you go. They include Negroes, Irish, Italians, Poles," noted one journalist writing in the middle of the depression.[27] Good times in the 1950s rescued the white ethnics, which meant that hospitals leaned even more heavily on blacks and Puerto Ricans. The occupational structure made it particularly easy for African-American workers to find a berth in health care, as the hospital sector shifted toward greater reliance on low-level workers during the war and the following fifteen years. With annual turnover well above the 50 percent level, the hospitals were always hiring.

The combination of strong demand and few competing groups led to a rapid buildup of low-skilled African-American hospital labor. African-American employment grew in just the manner described in Chapter 1, with established African-American employees sponsoring newcomers and recruitment frequently occurring through "familial chain migration patterns," as in this example from Leon Fink and Brian Greenberg's book on the hospital workers' union: "Mae Harrison, widowed in her early twenties, left the farm country near Greenville, South Carolina, in 1952 to join her mother in New York and through a friend got a job as a nurse's aid at Beth Israel Hospital."[28]

By 1970, blacks and Hispanics made up 80 percent of the hospital service and maintenance work force in the voluntary hospital sector and 60 percent of the total work force in the municipal hospitals.[29] The 1970 census indicates that private and public hospitals then ranked first and second, respectively, among African-American niches, together employing 8 percent of native black New Yorkers.

Fink and Greenberg tell the story of workers in New York's voluntary hospitals, and in so doing miss out on the most fateful labor market development—African-Americans' massive shift into the public sector, a trend that marked the health sector and many other fields as well. Black New Yorkers had only a fleeting concentration in the voluntary hospitals: by 1980, this category no longer ranked as an African-American niche; it similarly failed to appear on the 1990 list, even though the category of public sector hospitals maintained its status as the single largest black niche. By the latter date, six of the ten largest African-American niches, together employing one of every five black New Yorkers, were to be found in the public sector.

The movement into government employment was fueled by the same factor that sped African-Americans' entry into health care: ethnic succession, occurring first in lower-level jobs but later expanding throughout the government hierarchy, created vacancies into which blacks could slip without much competition from whites. Government also proved to be an employer that treated blacks with greater

Table 4.4 Niche characteristics for African-Americans, 1940–1990

	Characteristics of niches				Percentage of niche employment			
	Employed in niche	Female	Mean years of schooling	Mean earnings	Public sector	Self-employment	Manufacturing	Managerial/ professional/ technical
1940	69%	47%	7.5	$ 6,493	17%	2%	3%	6%
1950	43%	54%	8.3	$10,047	23%	2%	6%	3%
1970	43%	48%	10.3	$18,643	36%	2%	6%	11%
1980	34%	58%	11.9	$20,043	70%	1%	2%	20%
1990	37%	58%	13.2	$26,001	75%	1%	1%	27%

Source: Census of Population, 1940–1990; data for employed persons aged 25–64.

Note: African-Americans defined as native-born black persons, by race; 1940 data for wage and salary earnings only; all earnings in 1990 dollars.

fairness than they encountered in the private sector, in part because blacks' votes spoke louder than their wallets, and in part because the buildup of black employment created networks that supported entry and upward movement. As Peter Eisinger discovered from a survey of upper-tier employees in the city's Human Resources Administration, "high-level black civil servants are far more likely to have grown up in working- and lower-class families than in solidly middle-class families" and were also more likely to be of lower-class origin than were their white counterparts.[30] Of course, blacks met resistance from entrenched white ethnic civil servants, which they countered with political mobilization—a strategy that yielded considerable, though uneven success, as I shall demonstrate in Chapter 7.

Thus, in the fifty years between 1940 and 1990 a profound transformation occurred in the economic positions filled by black New Yorkers. On the eve of World War II, as Table 4.4 shows, African-Americans were tightly clustered in a handful of niches, mainly in personal services, where they found employment at the very bottom of the job ladder. By 1950, concentration diminished significantly, reflecting the equalizing effect of World War II and the postwar boom. While a new set of niches, dominated by civil, not personal service, evolved in the years that followed, levels of concentration did not significantly decline. By 1990, 37 percent of African-American New Yorkers worked in industries where the concentration of blacks was at least 50 percent higher than their share of the economy; civil servants constituted eight of every ten African-Americans employed in these African-American niches. Put in a slightly different perspective, 28 percent of all employed African-Americans worked in African-American public sector niches; another 9 percent worked in other areas of the public sector where the concentration of black New Yorkers was not quite as high.

The formation of a black niche in the public sector has generated significant economic benefits. By definition, it has also yielded a diminishing African-American presence in the private sector; where the African-American employment base has declined, so too have the opportunities for access to contacts, networks, and job-training opportunities diminished. Black New Yorkers have picked up employment in advanced service sectors, like finance or professional services. But the local economy industries, with their lower skill thresholds reveal a different pattern: though African-Americans used to concentrate here they do no longer.

Perhaps the most notable change is the virtual disappearance of the African-American domestic worker: in 1990, less than 3 percent of black New Yorkers worked in personal services, a far cry from the 40 percent level recorded in 1940. In a sense, the decline from domestic service represents an escape from the most menial type of dead-end employment. Yet, domestic work also provides a berth for workers utterly lacking the skills that a postindustrial society demands; in this respect, the fact that in 1990 all other groups, with the exception of native whites, maintained heavier concentrations in personal services deserves some note.

Domestic household work does not stand as an isolated example. The changing division of labor in hotels—a concentration of low-skilled but reasonably paid jobs—shows the same erosion of African-American employment alongside the expansion of immigrant job holding. The personal service story is writ large in retail, always one of New York's biggest, most vibrant industries. Retail never provided a truly open door to African-Americans. Retail means selling, and selling involves interpersonal contact: for a long time, the racist preferences of white New Yorkers kept blacks out of positions involving contact with a mainly white clientele.[31] The irony is that the African-American presence in retailing has stopped growing, indeed suffering relative decline, even as the clientele of the city's customer base has become increasingly nonwhite and as white distaste for interaction with black salespersons has surely diminished. Though consistently underrepresented in retail and in sales jobs for the past half-century, black New Yorkers did increase their penetration between 1950 and 1970. Progress then ceased: African-Americans saw their retail employment tumble significantly, while picking up only a few thousand jobs in sales. By 1990, African-American representation in the retail sector, with its concentration of low- to medium-skilled jobs, had fallen below 1950 levels!

To understand why African-Americans have fallen out of retailing, consider Thomas Bailey's book on New York's restaurant industry. Restaurants, along with household service, hotels, and laundries, had long been a traditional area of black concentration. But racism assured that black workers rarely made it to the "front of the house"; rather, they worked in the kitchen or in service jobs like porter or busboy. The kitchen offers a starting point to the greenest unskilled worker; with its hierarchy of jobs extending from dishwasher to cook, it also provides a ladder of upward movement. Moving up, however, usually means shifting from one restaurant to another, an uncertain endeavor unless one is bound up with a strong ethnic network tying workers to owners, as often characterizes immigrants. The incentive to move up in the kitchen is constrained by the limited returns to investment in cooking skills: all things being equal, a young worker would do better establishing a career in some other field. In any case, access to kitchen jobs cannot compensate for the barriers in the front of the house, where white preferences for social and physical distance from blacks have kept African-Americans underrepresented in waiting jobs, with consequences that Bailey details: "Black waiters in New York restaurants were rare. Several managers said that they preferred not to hire black waiters. Two asserted that customers complained if there were too many blacks working in the dining room. Most native-born black men in the survey were working in middle- to upper-level kitchen jobs."[32] Exclusion from waiting jobs makes the structure of restaurant opportunities far more unattractive to African-Americans than to the immigrants or native whites for whom the portals to the front of the house are always open. As Bailey notes, waiters tend to make more money than any other nonmanagerial restaurant employees, a handful of highly skilled chefs excepted. Waiting also provides informal instruction in the skills needed to run a restaurant, which is why Bailey found that "when owners of full-service restaurants draw their managers from their employees, they almost always do so from among waiters and bartenders." Given the combination of opportunities for training and savings, it is no surprise that "most restauranteurs who worked their way up had at least some waiting experience."[33]

With opportunities constricted, African-Americans have faded out of restaurants. Restaurants employed proportionately more blacks than did retail a half-century ago; since then, African-American restaurant employment has been on a downward curve. In 1990, black New Yorkers' representation in New York's kitchens and dining rooms had sunk to .35, leaving African-Americans with just over 5 percent of restaurant industry jobs.

The evolving structure of African-American employment also helps illuminate a long-standing scholarly dispute over the absence of a black business class. Government breeds bureaucrats, not entrepreneurs. As African-Americans have come to cluster in government, the self-employment rate among those in African-American niches has also declined: for all practical purposes, no self-employed African-Americans were to be found in the 1990 black economic niches. Some black New Yorkers did engage in independent business activities outside the black niches. But the size of the African-American business class, paltry in 1940, remained so in 1990.

The sources of such severe African-American underrepresentation in business are surely various, and I will explore the matter at greater length in Chapter 8. But there is little doubt that the structure of African-American employment itself constitutes one of the most formidable barriers to business growth. With little African-American employment in the small business industries, and therefore few opportunities to effect the contacts and gain the skills needed to make a business grow, it can be no surprise that the ranks of African-American entrepreneurs have been thinly filled.

If the movement into government has not been without costs, it has yielded significant benefits as well. The African-American push for public sector jobs can be understood only as a rational search for opportunity in a constrained environment: relative to the alternative, government has offered African-Americans easier access to employment and surer chances of moving up the job ladder.

As black New Yorkers have moved from the private to the public sector, the structural characteristics of their niches have changed as well. By 1990, the African-American niches mainly consisted of middle-tier jobs, providing access to full-time work, better earning chances, diminished exposure to discrimination, and increased employment at managerial or professional levels. To be sure, some of the African-American niches, like the post office, the mass transit system, and the telephone company, resembled factories in shape: though reasonably well-paid, African-American employees, like the rest of their counterparts, were compressed into a narrow tier of low-level jobs. Elsewhere there were ample managerial opportunities, of which African-Americans availed themselves with considerable success: 42 percent of the black New Yorkers employed in the city's hospitals, to take the example of the largest African-American niche, worked at the managerial, professional, or technical level. Regardless of industry, the entry thresholds to the African-American niches ranked reasonably high, in part because many of the niches have been built up in large bureaucratic institutions that have far more stringent hiring criteria and mechanisms than do small employers in retail or service. With but one small exception, the average schooling of African-American workers in the thirty-seven African-American niches exceeded the high school level in every case.

If New York's African-American niches turn out to be a concentration of relatively high-skilled jobs, one reason is that government offers a particularly supportive environment to black professionals and managers. African-American professionals and managers fare better in the public than in the private sector, in quite striking contrast to their white counterparts. More important, perhaps, government substantially reduces the effects of race: after adjustments for background factors, the earnings of African-American and white female government workers stand at parity, and African-American male civil servants rank not too far below their white counterparts. Thus, the best-educated black New Yorkers experience the rewards of private and public sector employment in substantially different ways.

Movement up the ladder and into the public sector has changed the terms of comparison between African-American and white employment concentrations, as Table 4.5 reveals. In 1940, native blacks were pretty much confined to lower-tier jobs, wherever they were employed; for women, moreover, jobs in the African-American niche compared unfavorably to those outside.

Table 4.5 Comparative earnings in the African-American niche, 1940–1990

| | Niche v. non-niche | | Group v. native whites | | | |
| | | | Niche | | Non-niche | |
	Raw	W/controls	Raw	Adjusted	Raw	Adjusted
Men						
1940	99%	89%	48%	52%	53%	68%
1950	107%	108%	59%	68%	59%	69%
1970	102%	101%	73%	79%	58%	76%
1980	115%	108%	79%	85%	61%	77%
1990	116%	109%	73%	85%	51%	72%
Women						
1940	75%	85%	34%	56%	63%	78%
1950	95%	95%	67%	82%	66%	89%
1970	93%	100%	76%	86%	75%	85%
1980	104%	104%	81%	88%	79%	89%
1990	105%	105%	82%	91%	68%	81%

Source: Census of Population, 1940–1990, data for employed persons aged 25–64.

Note: Comparison of black earnings inside and outside niches holds characteristics constant and estimates impact of employment in niche; black/white comparison holds industry distribution constant and gives blacks whites' rewards. For complete explanation, see note 2 to this chapter.

The niche that African-Americans carved out for themselves over the next fifty years yielded several concrete, observable economic benefits: its jobs increasingly paid better than did those outside the niche; and it provided reduced exposure to discrimination, though by no means eliminating the gap between blacks and whites. To some extent the superiority of niche employment stemmed from the characteristics of the jobs themselves: by and large, niche jobs required higher levels of education than did those outside the niche. Consequently, adjusting for background factors reduces the advantages yielded by working in the niche. Yet even when one compares African-Americans with equal amounts of education or experience, calculations from the 1990 census indicate that men in the niche enjoyed a $2,358 advantage in annual earnings over their non-niche counterparts. Women in the niche did better as well, with those working in the industries of African-American concentration making $1,144 more than those who worked outside the niche. And these 1990 levels reflect considerable improvement in real earning power, as can be seen from Table 4.4.

The niche also reduced the force of discrimination. In 1990, black New Yorkers earned significantly less than native whites, whether they worked in African-American niches or not. Differences in the backgrounds of African-Americans and whites account for some of this disparity: whites tend to have more experience and more education than African-Americans, factors that increase earnings, regardless of race. Even if we control for background characteristics between African-Americans and whites and just vary rewards, whites still earn more than African-Americans. But as Table 4.5 shows, the reward structure in the industries of African-American concentration tends to be relatively equitable: if African-American men were rewarded in the same way as comparable whites, the earnings of African-American men would move from 73 to 85 percent of the white male average. Outside the niche, by contrast, the same statistical procedure changes the African-American average from 51 to 72 percent of the white average—pointing to a much larger gap in rewards for comparable whites and African-Americans. African-American women also find a similarly sheltered environment in the niche, doing even better, relative to white women, than do men.

Looking over the past half-century, the course of African-American progress in New York has taken a paradoxical turn. The shape of this shift can be seen in Table 4.6, which displays changes in the index of

Table 4.6 Index of industrial dissimilarity: African-Americans, 1940–1990

	Jews	Italians	West Indians	Dominicans	Chinese
1940	65	58	—	—	—
1950	35	52	—	—	—
1970	41	36	37	55	72
1980	39	29	29	54	59
1990	39	29	25	49	53

Source: Census of Population, 1940–1990.

Note: Computations not done for West Indians, Dominicans, and Chinese because of insufficient numbers in 1940 and 1950; for group definitions, see note 1 to this chapter.

dissimilarity, with scores indicating the percentage of African-Americans who would have to change industries in order to have the same distribution as a comparison group. On the one hand, the record indicates significant movement away from the earlier situation of isolation in the economy's periphery. As African-Americans escaped from their confinement to low-level service work, their segregation from New York's largest European ethnic groups dropped sharply from its prewar height. On the other hand, a new role in the division of labor appears to have crystallized with the growth of the postindustrial economy. In this situation, African-Americans find themselves as separated—if not more so—from the newest New Yorkers as from those of European origin. And as African-American employment has increasingly become concentrated in the public sector, the African-American position in the ethnic division of labor has also stabilized.

Thus, African-Americans' search for opportunity has left an uneven yield. Their quest for better jobs has taken them into the public sector, where indeed they have found significant rewards. Broadly speaking, the advantage of the public sector takes two forms: more equitable treatment, as noted above, and shelter from the buffeting winds of economic change. Unlike the mass of New York's workers, African-American workers in the industries that form the African-American niche saw real wages hold fast during the troubled 1970s; with the resumption of growth in the 1980s, paychecks in the African-American niche increased in real value as well. The consolidation of an African-American niche largely based in middle-range government jobs is not an entirely happy tale, however. The virtues of government work are also its vices: they are good jobs that attract competitive applicants, which leaves less-qualified black New Yorkers out in the cold. The public's payrolls also have proportionately fewer places for the truly low skilled than do the African-American concentrations of old, reducing the advantages of network hiring for those African-American New Yorkers who need it the most. In the end, the path of black progress has led to a specialized economic role in which African-Americans find themselves detached from the private sector activities where they were previously engaged and where the newest New Yorkers now prevail.

West Indians

Although English- and Creole-speaking migrants from the Caribbean are a major presence among the post-1965 newcomers, these groups can boast a continuous history in New York dating back to the early 1900s. The status of Caribbean New Yorkers has long held a fascination for social scientists: as blacks who are also immigrants, they provide a natural case study in the relative importance of race as compared to ethnicity. For one group of social scientists, the West Indian experience in New York testifies to the limits of race: these accounts have emphasized West Indians' upward mobility, prominence in politics, and supposed prowess as petty entrepreneurs.[34] The historical record clearly provides some support for this view, but most scholars of the more recent experience have been skeptical, finding that Caribbean immigrants generally share the economic fate—and disadvantages—of their native black counterparts.[35]

But whatever the resolution of this controversy—and it seems unlikely to fade—there can be little question that black immigrants have succeeded in expanding their economic presence in New York at a time when African-Americans have seen their economic role diminish. While that one single fact suggests that race is not uniquely determining, more interesting is the way in which the Caribbean base has grown. Unlike the Chinese and the Dominicans, whose path into New York's economy involved taking over the traditional immigrant reserves, the West Indians have added jobs by adapting to New York's postindustrial economy.

The contemporary West Indian niches, however, bear little resemblance to the concentrations that West Indians established earlier in the century. The Caribbean entrepreneurial spirit impressed many observers of the pre–World War II community, in particular, its preeminent student, Ira DeA. Reid, who made much of the nascent West Indian business sector.[36] But the truth is a bit more complex. On the one hand, the black business sector was badly stunted, for foreigners and native-born alike. On the other hand, the West Indians did notably better than their native-born counterparts and were twice as likely to be self-employed. Real estate, especially, proved a more fruitful avenue of growth: raising capital through rotating credit associations they had imported with them from the islands, Caribbean immigrants engaged in considerable property speculation, with the result that real estate had emerged as a small, but still significant, Caribbean niche by the eve of World War II.[37] They also made some progress in the professions, for example medicine, thanks to the selectivity of the migration and the growing black consumer market. But the rank and file Caribbean New Yorker shared the fate of his or her native black counterpart. In 1940, domestic service and laundering ranked as the top two West Indian niches, employing one out of every five Caribbean New Yorkers. During the war years, a sizable number of West Indians not only emigrated but also developed new areas of specialization: by 1950, apparel, the railroads, and the subways had emerged as West Indian niches, together employing a little over a fifth of the city's West Indians; another 11 percent of the West Indian work force still worked in domestic service and laundries.

Although restrictive U.S. immigration laws choked off Caribbean migration after 1952, the outflows quickly resumed once the Hart-Celler Act reopened the doors in 1965.[38] This time, the newcomers found a new way into New York's economy, one that took them into the health sector. As with African-Americans, West Indians benefited from twin changes on the supply and demand sides: prosperity depleted the white presence in lower-paid hospital positions; and increased demand for health services led to expanded payrolls. The newcomers also built on a nucleus that the earlier immigrants had developed, as Fink and Greenberg's interviews with pioneer members of District 1199, New York's hospital workers' union, make clear.[39] Several additional factors spurred the influx into health care: nurses became increasingly difficult to find, a problem that afflicted hospitals nationwide but took an aggravated form in New York. The new immigration law made hiring from abroad the easiest, quickest way to fill nursing vacancies. And with an English-speaking, literate, and well-trained population for whom opportunities were either declining

Table 4.7 Niche characteristics for West Indians, 1970–1990

| | Characteristics of niches | | | | Percentage of niche employment | | | |
	Employed in niche	Female	Mean years of schooling	Mean earnings	Public sector	Self-employment	Manufacturing	Managerial/ professional/ technical
1970	50%	67%	10.3	$18,593	11%	4%	8%	23%
1980	40%	74%	11.4	$17,411	21%	1%	3%	25%
1990	34%	73%	12.1	$21,629	20%	4%	2%	27%

Source: Census of Population, 1970–1990; data for employed persons aged 25–64.
Note: All earnings in 1990 dollars.

or growing too slowly, the West Indies quickly became the area of choice: about one-third of the legal Jamaican immigrants classified as professionals between 1962 and 1972 were nurses.[40] Thus, by 1970, hospitals emerged as the premier West Indian niche, both in the public sector, where African-Americans predominated, and more importantly in the voluntary and private sector.

Over the next twenty years, as the migration continued and the ranks of West Indian jobholders quadrupled, hospitals provided a viable platform, for employment expansion and for diffusion into other health specialties. By 1990, three health specialties—hospitals, nursing homes, and health services—had developed into Caribbean niches, together providing employment to 22 percent of Caribbean New Yorkers.

As with other immigrant groups, the relative importance of the niche diminished as West Indian numbers grew. In 1970, 50 percent of working Caribbean New Yorkers made their living in one of the industries that could be classified as Caribbean niches; by 1990, 34 percent of the vastly expanded Caribbean labor force worked in the industries that made up the Caribbean niche (Table 4.7). Diffusion out of the niche took two principal routes: into government employment and into the financial sector. In both cases, literacy, English-language proficiency, and relatively high educational backgrounds—the same characteristics that had propelled West Indians into health care—eased the way into these emerging fields. Despite diffusion out of the niche, the concentrations that the West Indians established stood them in good stead. Health care—the key area of concentration—provided not just jobs but relatively good jobs: 41 percent of the West Indian hospital employees worked in professional, managerial, or technical positions. And unlike the African-American clusters, the West Indian concentrations were open to workers with lower skills: in 1990, average years of schooling exceeded the twelfth-grade level in only three of the ten largest Caribbean concentrations.

But the case of the Caribbean niche shows that all that glitters is not gold. With 44 percent of West Indian women working in ethnic concentrations, but only 20 percent of West Indian men, the Caribbean niche is essentially a concentration of women's jobs, a statement that holds true for no other group under consideration in this chapter. Moreover, the West Indian niche appears not to alter the structure of rewards, unlike the African-American concentrations. Although African-Americans and West Indians earn less than native whites in their respective niches, as can be seen in Table 4.2, the gap is a good deal greater in the West Indian case. And the industries in which West Indians have clustered appear to offer a less equitable environment, in contrast to the African-American niches. Giving men employed in niches the same rewards as otherwise comparable whites has a much greater impact on West Indians than on African-Americans, which tells us that the terms of compensation in West Indian niches remain badly tilted in favor of whites.

In the end, however, the configuration of jobs both within and outside the West Indian niche has provided Caribbean immigrants with a viable route into New York's postindustrial economy. Notwithstanding the rapid infusion of newcomers with little prior exposure to the needs of New York's employers, West Indians maintained a high employment rate throughout the years of expanded immigration; health care and other Caribbean niches gave a particular edge to West Indian women, who currently enjoy the highest employment rates of all the groups surveyed in this chapter. As the revival of economic growth in the 1980s improved earnings prospects for New Yorkers both native and foreign-born, real earnings among West Indian immigrants improved as well. And thus, the story of Caribbean New Yorkers and their economic niches provides a new twist on the lively and continuing debate over race and the scope for ethnic choice. Caribbean immigrants have carved out a piece of New York's economy quite distinct from that occupied by native black New Yorkers, with the importance of ethnic niches indicating the continued centrality of immigrant ties.

Chinese

Of all the new immigrant groups, the Chinese have the oldest history of settlement in New York; though the new immigration represents a significant departure from the older community with its roots in the nineteenth century, the new Chinese New Yorkers nonetheless built on the foundations established by their predecessors.

New York's Chinatown, located on the Lower East Side of Manhattan, where countless immigrants have settled, grew rapidly in the late nineteenth century, as Chinese sought out less hostile environments away from California. By 1900, there were 6,321 Chinese in New York City, up from approximately 500 in 1873. Natural growth and renewed immigration after World War II gradually boosted the

Chinese population to 33,000 in 1960. Prohibited from working in a wide variety of professional and nonprofessional occupations until the 1940s, Chinese New Yorkers only gradually abandoned the ethnic economy. In 1960, 40 percent of employed Chinese New Yorkers engaged in trade, most presumably in restaurants, and another 25 percent made their livelihood in the laundry business. Similarly, Chinatown remained an important population center, retaining just under a third of the city's Chinese population by 1960.

The advent of the new immigration at once transformed and reinvigorated the old ethnic economy. In 1960, Shein-woo Kung had identified 380 Chinese businesses in Chinatown;[41] three decades later, a vastly expanded Chinatown was now home to almost 3,000 Chinese concerns. Whereas the ethnic economy had largely been a center of retail and wholesale trade, the new Chinatown boasted a far more diversified structure, with retail and wholesale trade and services accounting for about two-thirds of Chinese businesses, and manufacturing composing another fifth.[42] The vitality of the service and retail sectors bears testimony to the impact of population growth, which relegated white tourist trade, an economic mainstay during the first half of the century, to second place behind the wants of local ethnic consumers.

While the ethnic trade replaced the tourist trade as a source of retail business, the growth of restaurants took over from the dying laundry business, which had dwindled from as many as 4,000 hand laundries in the 1930s to roughly 1,000 as of 1983.[43] Behind the restaurant boom lay the convergence of supply and demand factors: the influx of immigrants allowed Chinese restaurants to offer a relatively inexpensive meal, just when American lifestyle changes led to a taste for more exotic foods and greater spending on meals made in restaurants, rather than at home. By 1992, the New York Chinese Business Directory listed just over 400 Chinese restaurants in Manhattan, with nearly 300 more scattered throughout Queens, Brooklyn, the Bronx, and Staten Island.

An unlikely source—New York's declining garment trade—provided another impetus to growth. Just a handful of shops eking out an existence in the early 1960s, the Chinese garment sector burgeoned into a major complex of over 450 factories employing almost 18,000 workers in 1990—a story I will detail in Chapters 5 and 8.

Thus by the 1990s, New York, now home to the nation's largest Chinese concentration, boasted a vigorous Chinese ethnic economy.

As the chief emporium for the region's Chinese population, China-town has had a magnetic attraction for ethnic businesses, pushing commercial rents higher than in any other business area, save the most prestigious downtown locations.[44] Eager to capture the crowds attracted by the area's agglomeration of businesses, merchants crowded into any available space. By the late 1980s, Vietnamese and Chinese were setting up "mini-malls" in ground-floor lofts, crowding as many as forty merchants selling low-cost jewelry, sportswear, electronic products, and prepared foods into a space previously occupied by a single store.[45] Meanwhile, armies of peddlers selling batteries and audio tapes, scarves, T-shirts, and food of every description spilled over onto the sidewalks. Elsewhere in the city, the development of satellite Chinatowns in Queens and in Brooklyn galvanized the growth of Chinese businesses selling to a strictly ethnic clientele.

Population growth also spurred proliferation of new businesses and diversification into new business lines. As Alejandro Portes and Min Zhou have pointed out, "services that rely on an ethnic clientele, such as accounting, insurance, real estate agencies, doctors and herbalists, barber and beauty shops, and jewelry stores . . . experienced tremendous growth" since the onset of the new immigration.[46] Similarly, the vigorous expansion of the Chinese restaurant and garment industries had a synergistic effect on each other—with the mass of garment workers commuting into Chinatown each day turning out to be avid customers of the area's restaurants—while also generating expansion in ancillary fields.[47] The 1992 New York Chinese Business Directory, for example, listed twenty-four restaurant equipment suppliers, fifty-five restaurant suppliers, sixteen sewing machine dealers, eight sauce manufacturers, and five thread suppliers. The census indicates that, by 1990, wholesale apparel and miscellaneous manufacturing had evolved into concentrations for the immigrant Chinese, testifying to the tendency for niches to spill over into related trades.

Thus, in the quarter-century after the advent of the new immigration, Chinese economic niches grew, diversified, and consolidated. True, relative concentration in niches diminished between 1970 and 1990, reflecting the internal diversity of the Chinese newcomers to New York. Though the city attracted a disproportionately proletarian migration, mainly reflecting Hong Kong and mainland origins, substantial numbers of well-educated Chinese also gravitated to New York. The higher-skilled arrivals found numerous portals of entry throughout the economy. In general, the professional services offered substantial employment chances for upper-tier Chinese. Almost half of the Chinese who moved out of niches found managerial and professional occupations, where, however, the terms of their compensation fell considerably below the treatment received by native whites.

But the ethnic economy, where 50 percent of Chinese New Yorkers worked in 1990, remains the phenomenon of interest because it offered extraordinary employment opportunities to newcomers with few of the traits needed to secure a berth in New York's postindustrial world. In 1990, two trades, restaurants and apparel, alone provided jobs for just over a third of the immigrant Chinese. Both industries had the virtue of requiring little in the way of formal education: in 1990, the average Chinese garment worker had just under eight years of schooling, the average Chinese restaurant worker just under nine.

Apparel and restaurants, however, shared the defect of low wages. In some respects, conditions in the Chinese niches deteriorated even as those clusters grew: average earnings in constant dollars diminished considerably between 1970 and 1990, as Table 4.8 shows. The Chinese niches are the lowest-paying of all the ethnic concentrations reviewed in this chapter; average 1990 earnings in the Chinese niches barely equaled half the average in the industries of African-American concentration.

Further comparisons darken the picture still more. In 1990, Chinese men employed in ethnic niches made 57 percent as much as their counterparts in industries of lower Chinese density (see Table 4.2); women in the niche did even worse. Since the niche is a refuge for the newest arrivals and the poorest educated, adjustments for background characteristics improved the comparison, but not by much: men and women in the niche still fared worse than their statistical counterparts working in industries of lower Chinese concentration. When the focus switches to comparisons between Chinese and white workers within the same industries, niche industries remain more disadvantageous than employments outside the niche. The industries of Chinese concentration treat comparable white and Chinese men more equitably than do those industries where the Chinese presence is not so dense. But equity is small consolation given remuneration levels—which remain abysmally low.

Yet, the advantages of the particular ethnic economy that the Chinese have carved out should not be dismissed out of hand. Though the real earnings of Chinese workers employed in ethnic niches took a bath during the 1970s—a trend that occurred in virtually all but the

Table 4.8 Niche characteristics for Chinese, 1970–1990

	Characteristics of niches			Percentage of niche employment			
	Employed in niche	Female	Mean years of schooling	Mean earnings	Public sector	Self-employment	Manufacturing	Managerial/ professional/ technical
1970	79%	31%	8.2	$17,756	4%	18%	29%	19%
1980	61%	46%	8.1	$11,116	2%	9%	47%	10%
1990	50%	47%	8.8	$13,173	1%	9%	47%	10%

Source: Census of Population, 1970–1990; data for employed persons aged 25–64.
Note: All earnings in 1990 dollars.

healthiest sectors during these years of New York's economic decline—real wages turned back up during the 1980s. More important,
perhaps, the particular structure of the Chinese ethnic economy, and
the role played by gender in sorting workers among jobs, make ethnic
employment a viable strategy, not just for getting started but for mod-
estly moving ahead. The key factor is that the ethnic economy provides jobs for men and women, with the former concentrated in restaurants and the latter clustered in garments. Both industries also
accommodate workers—younger people, older immigrants—who do
not often make it through hiring doors outside the ethnic economy.
Consequently, the ethnic economy allows Chinese immigrants to re-
constitute the family-wage economy of the late nineteenth and early
twentieth centuries: when pooled together, couples' earnings, and occasionally those of children and older relatives, lift the families of
ethnic economy workers out of poverty. In 1990, 70 percent of the
households in which employees of any one of the Chinese niche industries lived reported incomes 150 percent or more above the poverty
level. These data converge with other indicators of Chinese progress.
Notwithstanding Chinatown's growth, the majority of Chinese New
Yorkers have now moved to middle- and lower-middle-class areas in
Queens and Brooklyn.[48] Ethnic economy workers are a bit less likely
to live outside Chinatown, but the spread of garment shops to the new
Chinese neighborhoods indicates that even the lowest-level workers
are dispersing as well.[49] Along with the move beyond Chinatown has
come the acquisition of homes—yet another sign that New York's
proletarian Chinese population is moving ahead.[50]

Thus, as the Chinese case shows, the old ways of making it in New
York have not disappeared, the advent of the postindustrial economy
and its skill-intensive employers notwithstanding. In this instance,
ethnic succession opened the portals to traditional immigrant industries; with an ethnic nucleus in place—long established in the restaurant case, emergent in the garment case—new arrivals were quickly
funneled into a thriving ethnic economy.

While Chinese New Yorkers diffused into other sectors, even as
the ethnic economy burgeoned, the more skilled newcomers remained linked to the niche and its key industries in important ways.
Even the better-educated immigrants tended to bunch up together:
the 1990 census shows that engineering services had become a niche
for these high-skilled immigrants, albeit one that they shared with
many other groups. Outside the ethnic concentrations, the Chinese

also made much of the opportunities to work on their own. And unlike other, high-skilled Asian groups, such as Indians, the Chinese stayed city-bound, establishing middle-class Chinatowns in which the incomes of the higher earners were kept circulating within the ethnic economy.[51]

As we have seen, that economy had employment aplenty; it offered fewer opportunities to earn well. But the abundance of jobs, made accessible through the ties of ethnicity, seems to have put Chinese on the road toward reproducing the success, and sharing the travails, of New York's earlier immigrants.

Dominicans

Newcomers from the Dominican Republic constitute the single largest nationality in New York's incredibly mixed population of post-1965 arrivals. The burgeoning of New York's Dominican community represents a new turn for immigrant New York, as Dominicans, unlike either the Chinese or their anglophone neighbors from the Caribbean, did not establish a significant presence in New York until after 1960. Statistics from the immigration service do trace a slight trickle of Dominican newcomers through the 1950s. Even these newcomers undoubtedly built on the footsteps of earlier pioneers, as in the case of Sherri Grasmuck and Patricia Pessar's pseudonymous village "Juan Pablo," where the first native emigrated to the United States in 1941, "followed by a handful of other young men who departed in the forties and fifties."[52] But until well past midcentury two factors—the high cost of migration and travel restrictions imposed by the Trujillo regime—kept the migration stream small and restricted to those with both capital and privileged connections to the regime.

Trujillo's assassination in 1961 marks the true beginning of mass Dominican migration to New York. With Trujillo's death came the demise of his emigration restrictions; U.S. consular officials, concerned about left-wing turbulence on the island, also made it much easier for potential exiles to leave.[53] Dominicans with the financial resources needed to secure visas for travel or residence in the United States now found their path relatively unimpeded. U.S.-bound migration jumped sixfold from 1960 to 1962; for the rest of the 1960s, about 8,700 Dominican immigrants, accompanied by a much larger number of tourists, came to the United States each year. Right from the start, the great majority of these arrivals converged on New York. Despite its growing size, the Dominican flow remained extraordinarily New York–centered: 6 out of every 10 Dominicans who immigrated to the United States between 1982 and 1989 moved to New York City.

As with other new arrivals, the Dominican immigrants of the 1960s depended on earlier settlers; a single seedbed immigrant, anthropologist Eugenia Georges discovered, later "found union jobs for over a dozen later arrivals in the large New York hotel in which he worked for fifteen years."[54] More important was the legacy of an earlier wave of Spanish-speaking immigrants from Puerto Rico, who had become heavily ensconced in garments, restaurants, hotels, and a variety of light manufacturing and retail trades. These industries, as Glenn Hendricks noted in the very first monograph on Dominican immigrants, had already adapted themselves to "Puerto Rican workers and worked out organizational patterns, including bilingual supervisors or mediators between managers and employees"; hence, a changeover to a different set of Hispanic workers posed few adjustment difficulties.[55] Employers may also have been more favorably inclined toward Hispanic workers as militancy among black workers increased during the turbulent 1960s, as one study suggests.[56] But the key factor was simply the naturally high rate of turnover prevailing throughout New York's low-wage sector: in effect, employers were always hiring, which gave the edge to any group with a disproportionately high application rate. One garment employer told me the following story of how his shop gained an immigrant Hispanic work force—a story that seems to apply to many of the other immigrant-penetrated industries as well: "In the 1960s my shop was mainly black and Puerto Rican with a sprinkling of older Jews and Italians. Then one day I woke up and I found that I didn't have any more people from Puerto Rico. The only remaining black is my cutter. And the rest of my workers come from the Dominican Republic, with a bunch from Ecuador, El Salvador, and Chile."

Whatever the exact mechanisms by which Dominicans penetrated New York's declining low-skill sector, the census statistics pinpoint a highly concentrated group. By 1970, just over a quarter of Dominicans worked in apparel and restaurants, both of which could be classified as niches. As with the other groups, over the next twenty years Dominicans moved out of their niches—but at a gradual pace. By 1990, industries that could be classified as niches employed more than half of a greatly expanded Dominican work force (Table 4.9).

The Dominican case again underscores the particularities of immigrant adaptation and incorporation into New York's economy. The

Table 4.9 Niche characteristics for Dominicans, 1970–1990

| | Characteristics of niches | | | | Percentage of niche employment | | | |
	Employed in niche	Female	Mean years of schooling	Mean earnings	Public sector	Self-employment	Manufacturing	Managerial/professional/technical
1970	65%	48%	7.8	$13,992	2%	3%	73%	2%
1980	65%	49%	7.9	$12,121	0%	3%	63%	5%
1990	55%	45%	9.1	$14,333	2%	10%	37%	4%

Source: Census of Population, 1970–1990; data for employed persons aged 25–64.
Note: All earnings in 1990 dollars.

Dominicans have little public sector employment, unlike African-Americans, and only one small cluster of government work that would classify as an ethnic niche. They overlap with West Indians only in hotels and private household work, and lack any concentrated presence in the health sector. Apparel and laundries rank as points of intersection with the Chinese, but the other Dominican concentrations—auto repair, services to buildings, miscellaneous manufacturing, and retail and wholesale groceries—have not seen any sizable Chinese penetration.

But if the Dominicans have found a singular economic role, their experience can best be understood as yet another variation on the immigrant pattern already described. The persistence of industries requiring rudimentary skills, like apparel or building services, secures continuing paths into the bottom of the economy: in 1990, average schooling levels among Dominicans sank below the eleventh-grade level in each of their top ten ethnic concentrations. Low-skilled industries generally provide low wages, and that remains true in the Dominican case, where average earnings fall into the basement, well below the levels recorded in either the African-American or West Indian concentrations. In real terms, compensation has essentially remained stagnant over the past twenty years—yet another point of difference between Dominicans, on the one hand, and West Indians and African-Americans, on the other. Dominicans in ethnic niches do less well than those employed in industries with lower Dominican concentrations, a disparity that persists even after controlling for differences in background characteristics. The wage gap is large wherever Dominicans are employed; relative to native whites, Dominicans do poorly, whether in industries of high Dominican density or low. As in the Chinese case, Dominicans find somewhat more equitable treatment in those industries where they cluster—but this trend tells us only that the Dominicans have converged on low-paying industries where comparable whites also earn miserable wages.

Thus, Dominican niches deliver jobs but not employment of very high quality. Moreover, Dominicans may already be cycling out of the most menial positions into which they gravitated when the migration was young. Some of New York's immigrant entrepreneurs have tapped into a newer, more pliable labor force of immigrants from Mexico and Central America, as we shall see in Chapter 8. And Dominicans themselves have apparently joined the trend: Luis Guarnizo's interviews with Dominican entrepreneurs in Washington Heights underline their growing reliance on newly arrived Mexicans eager for jobs of any sort. The conversation Guarnizo reports with a large Dominican garment manufacturer, who contends that "Dominicans are less willing to accept hard work at low wages,"[57] is certainly consistent with census data indicating that Dominican employment rates have fallen steadily since 1970, with the situation among women, among whom less than half are employed, appearing increasingly alarming. Moreover, diffusion outside the niche appears to be occurring more slowly for Dominicans than for other groups. Those Dominicans working outside the niche make a good deal less than their West Indian or Chinese counterparts, who tend to arrive with somewhat higher levels of education.

These materials suggest that the Dominican experience in New York is yet another case of immigrants recruited to fill vacancies in dead-end jobs, who drop out of the labor market as aspirations rise and as they realize they have blundered into a trap allowing no mobility. Yet, the ledger does provide evidence for a somewhat more optimistic view. Dominicans working outside the niche have increasingly penetrated the public sector and gained a growing number of managerial and professional jobs, though the record still indicates modest progress on both counts. Beyond the ethnic concentrations, Dominicans frequently find themselves in a unionized environment—an attribute with uniformly beneficial consequences for wages, and often for benefits as well.[58]

Participation in the city's manufacturing and service complex in turn feeds back into an increasingly vibrant, neighborhood-based ethnic economy. With one out of every ten Dominicans in ethnic niches working on their own account, self-employment has become an increasingly significant dimension to the Dominican economic role. Census data point to the newfound importance of business, reflected in rising self-employment rates and in the niches that have emerged in retail and wholesale groceries and auto repair.[59] The same picture emerges from surveys and ethnographic research conducted in Dominican residential concentrations in the Washington Heights area of northern Manhattan, the Jackson Heights and Corona sections of Queens, and the Sunset Park neighborhood in Brooklyn. Resembling Chinatown and its new satellites in Queens and Brooklyn, the Dominican neighborhoods serve as extraordinarily buoyant commercial centers, jam-packed with retail and service businesses. Guarnizo estimates that 1,500 to 2,000 visible Dominican-owned stores operate in the chief shopping streets of Washington Heights alone.[60] As they have developed, the neighborhood ethnic economies have evolved into export platforms for entrepreneurial expansion into Puerto Rican and other neighborhoods populated by other groups of Hispanic origin. As in the Chinese case, the job-generating capacity of the ethnic niche provides a conduit to a modest, though low, standard of living. In 1990, 63 percent of the households of Dominican workers employed in ethnic niches had incomes that exceeded 150 percent of the poverty level.

In the end, the Dominicans' role in the New York economy is too new and still too unsettled to permit unambiguous conclusions about their fate. One thing is clear: visibly identifiable and among the less-educated of New York's newcomer groups, Dominicans have established a large and growing place in the city's economy. That role firmly implants them in New York's traditionally immigrant sectors. As in the past, that segment of the economy is dominated by low-paying industries with limited options for mobility. Yet, these industries allow immigrants to get ahead through small business, an activity in which the newcomers' ability to mobilize and pool community resources makes a considerable difference. Thus, with the right combination of entrepreneurship and gradual movement into the public sector and into the middle layers of the economy, Dominicans might climb up New York's pecking order. But the immigrants' low skills, and the constraints of the distinctive sectors into which they have moved, could also provide the ingredients for a much unhappier story. Which outcome will prevail only time will tell.

This survey of the economic life of New York's ethnic groups reflects at once constancy and change. Notwithstanding contentions that ethnic ties are carryovers from earlier social orders, bound to wither under the corrosive effects of industrialization and technological change, ethnicity remains no less central today to the ordering of New York's labor market than it was a half-century ago. Older patterns of distinction have lost some of their distinctiveness, but they have hardly faded away. Meanwhile, the resurgence of immigration has introduced new dimensions of complexity, establishing clear lines of demarcation among the new New Yorkers.

The ethnic ordering of New York's labor market can be characterized along the horizontal and vertical dimensions of specialization and rank. At the horizontal dimension, Jews and Chinese define the spectrum, with Jews at one end of the continuum and Chinese, closely shadowed by Dominicans, at the other. These groups, as Figure 4.1 makes clear, occupy the most distinctive economic roles: Jews are highly niched and heavily ensconced in postindustrial sectors; traditional immigrant trades in manufacturing and various local economy industries occupy Chinese and Dominicans to a disproportionate extent. Italians stand at the center of the continuum: they rub shoulders with Jews in postindustrial activities, while overlapping with African-Americans and West Indians in remaining Italian niches like sanitation, as well as in sectors like construction or health services, where Italian concentrations do not reach niche levels.

As to African-Americans, they have changed but have not escaped their singular role in New York's segmented system. Even the largely black, anglophone West Indian population, the only group to follow the tracks of African-Americans into the public sector in significant numbers, occupies a distinctive economic position. In an ironic measure of progress, African-Americans find themselves more separated from the new immigrants from Asia or Latin America than they do

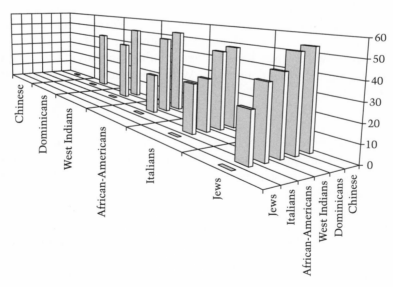

Figure 4.1   Index of industrial dissimilarity among ethnic groups, 1990.
(*Source:* Census of Population, 1990.)

from the older groups of European origin, with whom they have contended for the past half-century. The distance that separates black New Yorkers from Asian and Latin immigrants also represents the lengths that African-Americans have traversed in their shift out of declining sectors, with their concentrations of low-skilled jobs.

The postindustrial pattern of specialization also comprises a system of inequality, as can be seen from Figure 4.2. At the top of the hierarchy stand the Jews: although the Jewish niches are to be found in

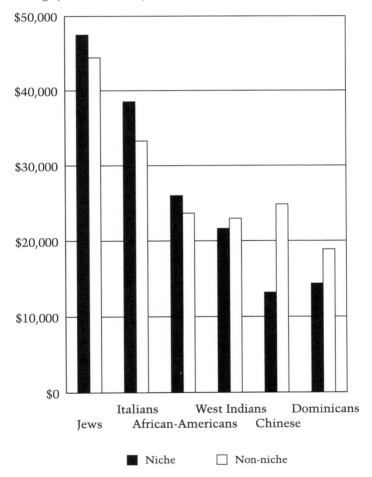

Earnings (in 1990 dollars)

Figure 4.2 Earnings inside and outside the ethnic niche, 1990. (*Source:* Census of Population, 1990.)

New York's best-paying industries, Jews do better than others wherever they are employed. Dominicans fill up the bottommost rungs,
falling into niches that have yet to develop significant earning power
and otherwise remaining trapped in low-paid jobs. Italians still lag
behind Jews, while surpassing all others. The positions occupied by
African-Americans place them at middling levels, though as with Italians and Jews, the industries of black concentration provide superior
rewards. The West Indians neighbor close by, ensconced in a concentration that provides jobs mainly for women. As to the Chinese, their
position is dragged down by the relatively low earnings of immigrants
employed in ethnic niches; on average, those immigrants who have
diffused into the broader economy do about as well as native blacks.

Although we can specify the two-dimensional position that ethnic
groups occupy at one any time, we should not forget that the ethnic
division of labor is also a process, characterized by continuing, if
sometimes intermittent, struggle for place. As the city's older residents of European origin have stepped into new positions, they have
distanced themselves from their old niches, into which the new immigrants have moved. By contrast, better-educated and -skilled black
New Yorkers find themselves in close occupational proximity to
white workers of various ethnic stripes, with whom, however, they
have not yet caught up. Thus, while New York's segmented system
separates the newest arrivals from the city's established groups, reducing the potential for intergroup conflict, it also keeps African-
Americans rubbing shoulders with white ethnics. In this case, familiarity often breeds strife, as we shall see.

5 | Who Gets the "Lousy" Jobs?

Creating and exchanging information, not interacting with machines, is now the "fundamental fact about work in the post-industrial society," writes the theorist Daniel Bell. But if communication represents the shape of things to come, the emergent postindustrial economies of today have not yet dispensed with jobs that involve toil and travail. There are still floors to scrubbed, beds to be made, clothes to be sewn, and grocery stores to be run. In this chapter I look at two classic bottom-level industries—garments and hotels—and ask who does the dirty work in America's postindustrial cities?

Employers answer the question this way:

> I find that whereas there are fewer blacks in the factory, the office staff has become black and Puerto Rican. This has been the normal progression: the parents work in the factories, and the kids look for white-collar jobs. In the office, we get young Hispanics and blacks who are second generation and have never set foot in a factory. (manager of a belt factory)

> The foreign-born are a very important source of labor. Years ago people at the bottom of the ladder were Germans and Irish. They moved up and were replaced by black Americans who are now being replaced by Hispanics, blacks from the Caribbeans, and Asians. We still have many older Puerto Ricans, but we have few younger Puerto Rican applicants. It's a replacement process, as other workers move up the ladder. (manager of a large business hotel)

A look at the census confirms these accounts. Black New Yorkers made their first major move beyond domestic work by finding jobs in the garment industry: in 1950, African-Americans composed almost 10 percent of the city's clothing workers, playing a considerably more important role in garments than they did in the city's economy overall. But while the African-American presence in New York's economy then burgeoned, it leveled out in the clothing shops. By 1990, when Asian and Hispanic immigrants had virtually replaced the Jewish and Italian old-timers, native black workers retained but a small corner of the industry's jobs. So go the numbers in hotels, and in the myriad of other light manufacturing and private service industries that form the economy of the "other New York."

If interviews and census data tell a story of musical chairs, with the departure of white ethnics leaving empty seats for replacements, then why did immigrants, and not native blacks, take over these classic entry-level jobs? "Wrong attitudes" is one answer, offered by the likes of Charles Murray or Lawrence Mead, with the implication that blacks balk at this type of work. But placing the blame on attitudes oversimplifies the situation, since preferences are just one of a variety of factors that sort workers out among jobs. Even if we accept the assertion that only newcomers will take up the tasks that natives disdain, the historical facts tell us that African-Americans once clustered in these jobs, indeed not so long ago. If African-Americans have the "wrong attitudes," why did they first concentrate in these industries, only gradually to withdraw?

The possibility that immigrants have pushed African-Americans out might also explain the results of this latest round of musical chairs. But the argument for head-to-head competition implies a certain sequence of events: first black employment, then the entry of immigrants, next declining jobs for African-Americans—a sequence that clashes with the facts. It also implies an association of immigrants with lower wages, which in the hotel case, where good wage data can be found, turns out not to be the case.

What follows is a rather different view of the events. The argument, building on the job-competition model developed in Chapter 1 and fleshed out through these two case studies, contends that the source of the transient black presence lies in a complex of interacting sociological and economic factors. Though labor shortages pulled African-Americans into these low-level industries, they ran into competition with white workers, keeping the potential for advancement down. With weak incentives for continued attachment, African-American tolerance levels diminished over time, making them less tractable labor—especially as better alternatives came along. When the window of opportunity finally opened—as white ethnics finally filtered out of these jobs—immigrants had entered the queue behind African-Americans. The ready availability of immigrant labor made for the quick implantation of immigrant networks. From then on, connections among immigrant veterans and newcomers had a multiplier effect, freezing out others. Thus, the job-competition view brings back whites into the story of who has succeeded in developing a niche and recasts this story in terms of the historically contingent circumstances under which outsider groups enter the system.

Garments: Through the Factory's Revolving Door

Cutthroat capitalism has long reigned supreme in apparel—an industry with many small firms and few barriers to new entrants, where today's successful firm is often tomorrow's failure. Wages make up a high percentage of any firm's total costs. And since wages are far more variable than the other key factors, wage slashing by potential competitors is a sufficiently potent threat to keep all firms in line. Usually too small to train and promote in-house, apparel firms recruit skilled help from outside. Smallness means few promotional opportunities—which weakens any worker's attachment to any single establishment. Other factors—the industry's susceptibility to seasonal and cyclical shifts in demand and the frequency with which firms go in and out of business—keep workers moving in and out of the industry and from one employer to another.

Thus, the industry veers not just toward cutthroat capitalism but toward a disorganized capitalism. Here a variety of factors step in to provide some structure. A myriad of product and price specializations curb competition. The industry's major union—the International Ladies' Garment Workers' Union (ILGWU)—strives to take labor out of competition by standardizing labor costs, a goal it achieved with greatest success forty years back. Most important, ethnic connections—among employers of various sorts, between employers and workers, and among workers—channel the flow of information and workers, placing people in such a way that positions in the industry also demarcate the boundaries of an ethnic group.

The importance of ethnicity means that the rag trade presents newcomers with a segmented system, in which the order of a group's entry into the industry largely circumscribes its role. But those roles have also been intermittently contested, mainly because the industry's tendency to exhaust its traditional labor supply has forced it to recruit new, outsider groups. Interethnic conflict is bound up with the specific conditions under which groups have entered and progressed through the industry.

Russian Jews got in at the start. Mass migration from Russia began in the late nineteenth century, just when the demand for factory-made clothing began to surge. Many had been tailors in the old country, and though most had worked with needle and thread, they quickly adapted to machine production. Garments became the Jewish trade, and it soon attracted countless "greenhorn tailors" who had previously made their livelihoods in different pursuits but now found it profitable to claim expertise in the needle trades. The industry was equally prompt in adapting itself to the newcomers. The emergence of the contractor was the key development: an immigrant himself, the contractor housed his factory in the same tenements where the immigrants lived, recruiting labor among his *landsleit* or fellow "hometowners." These connections helped the contractor hold on to his labor force during the industry's wild seasonal fluctuations. As long as immigration continued to provide a steady flow of new arrivals too bewildered and too dependent to look for work elsewhere, the contractor could be assured of maximum productivity.

With a massive labor force in place, other factors made New York the nation's clothing manufacturing capital. As the industry expanded, the opportunities for mobility through the Jewish ethnic economy multiplied. Through rags, some greenhorns found riches: the sweatshop workers who moved to contracting and then to manufacturing, or possibly to careers in retailing, filled the newly formed ranks of New York's "alrightniks." Those who remained tied to the world of the shops built the needle trades unions, where Jewish immigrants and their descendants have remained dominant, even to this day.

But no sooner was it made then the ethnic economy was transformed. The Jews moved ahead quickly, and rapid Jewish social mobility led to a dwindling Jewish working class. Italians, arriving in large numbers at a slightly later date, moved in behind. But coming in later meant that they also found the ethnic structure of the industry in place. Thus, they began as workers for Jewish owners, gradually moving up into contracting but rarely penetrating into retailing or designing functions. Though basically harmonious, the Jewish-Italian encounter did not proceed without distress. The Italians proved somewhat difficult to unionize: a population of peasants, they accepted conditions that the somewhat better-settled Jews would refuse and lacked the latter's revolutionary fervor to boot. But the garment workers' union learned how to appeal to the Italians, who also had leaders who discovered how to shape the *paesani* into union loyalists. The sequence of events forced the Italians to enter the union as junior partners, however. On the shop floor, ethnic turbulence persisted, especially in the 1930s, when the depression made for particularly bad blood. By the eve of World War II, when the garment industry supported almost as many Jews as it did Italians, Jews were five times more likely to be bosses. By contrast, the Italians were almost twice as likely to be found among the sewers' ranks. The remaining Jewish garment workers resented the Italians' primacy and the consequent shift in influence; the Italians chafed at the dominance of the Jews. But strain was managed, with Jewish-Italian competition never leading to overt conflict.[1]

INTO THE FACTORIES

Blacks had a well-established role in the domestic production of clothing at the turn of the century, but they missed out on the transition to factory work.[2] The huge immigrant influx crowded them out of the industry; with labor more than abundant, employers had no need to activate other sources of supply. World War I altered these circumstances, but the war led to only modest gains, which quickly dissipated with the resumption of immigration and the industry's plunge into a downward cycle. Not until the mid-1920s, when the imposition of tight immigration controls significantly reduced the supply of immigrant labor, did employers begin to hire blacks in significant numbers.[3] Although the depression pushed blacks down the hiring queue, it did not force them out of the niche they had established among low-end dress employers.

The advent of World War II provided the decisive change. Even before Pearl Harbor, employers could no longer fill their lowest-skill, entry-level jobs, leading them to immediately waive existing barriers to hiring blacks. Needle trade shops that had hired only Italian speakers, for example, bowed to the force of circumstances and took on outsiders.[4] As the war dragged on, hiring slots opened up for all comers willing to start at the minimum wage, and government made

Table 5.1 Ethnic employment in the apparel industry, 1940–1990

	Total	Whites		Hispanics		Blacks		Asians	
		Native	Foreign	Native	Foreign	Native	Foreign	Native	Foreign
Employment									
1940	153,900	50,700	94,800	1,400	1,900	2,900	2,200	—	—
1950	213,840	77,550	98,010	12,870	1,980	20,130	3,300	—	—
1970	113,700	42,400	27,400	14,000	12,150	11,500	1,650	100	4,350
1980	98,960	23,360	16,260	13,500	20,700	6,480	3,520	340	14,640
1990	64,245	10,388	6,396	5,029	14,547	2,706	3,092	309	21,393
Index of representation									
1940		0.61	1.64	0.98	2.38	0.35	1.38	—	—
1950		0.62	1.62	2.45	1.18	1.18	1.22	—	—
1970		0.66	1.78	1.77	2.48	0.66	0.74	0.34	3.09
1980		0.51	1.55	1.52	2.68	0.42	0.61	0.90	3.57
1990		0.41	1.17	0.85	2.15	0.27	0.59	0.78	4.26

Source: Census of Population, 1940–1990.

Note: Index of representation = share of group in category ÷ share of group in total economy.

active efforts to recruit new workers. By 1940, half of the industry's new workers were nonwhite.[5]

The result of wartime mobilization can be seen in Table 5.1, which traces patterns of ethnic concentration in garments from 1940 to 1990. Badly underrepresented among the ranks of garment workers in 1940, African-Americans moved above parity a decade later, when just over 20,000 African-Americans worked in New York's clothing shops. Thereafter, native black employment plunged, erasing the concentration that had briefly been established. By 1970, there were only 11,500 native blacks working in garments; by 1990, the number had dropped to less than 3,000, leaving African-Americans severely underrepresented in an industry in which they had once played a prominent role.

That role was always circumscribed, even in the days when African-Americans loomed larger in the industry's employment picture. From the outset, blacks gained employment in the lowest-paying, least desirable jobs. While employers' straitened circumstances during World War I pulled black women into the shops, a 1919 study found them at work in the dirty, monotonous, poorer-paying jobs, requiring a minimum of skills, that white women refused to take.[6] By the 1930s, when the black employment base had grown, it had not substantially been upgraded: the black clusters remained at the low end of the dress trade, in children's garments, and in undergarments—especially in week-work shops, where the pace of work was less grinding and the opportunities for earnings correspondingly fewer. After 1940, black employment expanded in lines like skirts or snowsuits, where employers had done away with the artisan-like method in which each worker constructed a full garment, using a quasi–assembly-line organization instead.[7] Men did even less well than women, concentrating in ancillary jobs like shipping clerk or "push-boy," jostling racks of clothing and textiles through the garment center's crowded streets.

Notwithstanding blacks' brief, confined appearance, conflict—with white coworkers, employers, and union officials—suffused their experience in the industry. New York's garment employers did little to actively foment antagonism toward blacks, and in this respect they differed from their counterparts in the other centers of garment production. In Chicago, employers first recruited blacks as strikebreakers in 1917; working in tandem with officials of the National Urban League, they resorted to the same tactic in 1921, in 1927, and again in the early 1930s.[8] In Philadelphia, blacks moved into the garment shops in 1921 in just the same way.[9] Despite an occasional suggestion in the contemporary literature that New York's garment bosses similarly recruited blacks as cheap labor to *replace* incumbent white workers, the bulk of the evidence indicates otherwise.[10] Blacks never played the role of strikebreakers in New York's garment shops; and in contrast to the situation elsewhere, the garment workers' union established close working relationships with the National Urban League, prior to the 1930s. Consequently, the ebb and flow of black employment in New York's garment shops corresponded to the ups and downs of the hiring queue: blacks were hired during periods of shortage—World War I, the late 1920s, the 1940s—and let go during periods of slack. Indeed, the greatest hiring spurt occurred when the industry experienced its most severe shortage—during World War II— conditions that also allowed the ILGWU to exercise its greatest control over labor cost competition.

ON THE PERIPHERY

Nonetheless, interethnic tensions circumscribed the contours of mobility. Whereas blacks were easily absorbed into entry-level positions, skilled jobs proved far more difficult to permeate, for reasons that reveal the interpenetration of ethnicity and economics in this trade. "Going partners" is how the old-timers describe the ways in which garment workers gained their skills. An employer explained: "In the old days . . . I used to get operators through the families. I would locate a daughter next to her mother. End of my responsibility. The daughter was not on the payroll. When the mother felt that the daughter could do the work herself, then I put her on the payroll. With this arrangement I was just obligated to pay piece rates. The [union] business agents would wink at the practice." Going partners saved the employer the expense of training a worker who could pick up and leave the next day for his competitor's firm. In an industry where busy seasons threatened to pull in operators who would then scramble for work during slow seasons when jobs got scarce, partnering also assuaged workers' concerns about competition, rationing chances within established networks and keeping out newcomers who might work below the accustomed norms.

But the industry's reliance on going partners closed doors to newcomers who did not belong to the club. As in other trades, employers were constantly on the lookout for more docile workers, as one scholar noted.[11] In contrast to their counterparts elsewhere, garment bosses had limited incentives and also fewer opportunities to foist outsiders upon their incumbent workers, notwithstanding the potential to be gained from a more passive, indebted employee. Concern about losing an investment in a worker's skill was certainly one factor inclining employers toward the partner system that the workers, in any case, preferred. But incumbents' resistance to the idea of introducing outsiders proved a far more formidable obstacle. The industry paid its workers by results and the piece-rate system bred conservatism. On the one hand, established workers anxiously sought to hoard the best jobs for themselves and fought among one another when the division of work seemed unfair. "In every instance where personal or social hostility [between black and white garment workers] had been evident," the Consumers' League discovered in 1919, "piece work had prevailed."[12] On the other hand, incumbents regarded outsiders with "suspicion and distrust," worrying that the influx of blacks would "eventually degrade working conditions" and push down rates.[13] As the sociologist Irving R. Stuart noted, "the lower standards of the Negroes and the Spanish-speaking workers led the other workers to fear that they would be able to accept inadequate wages and working conditions which had been built up over many years." Dependent on operators who would work hard to deliver styles before they became obsolete, employers had to be on the edge of desperation before antagonizing their core group of workers.

Thus, black workers' inability to get training from experienced machinists kept them from entering the more skilled trades, as the Consumers' League found just after World War I. More than twenty years later, when Stuart observed that hostility toward blacks had grown with the increase in their numbers, the same barriers blocked the road to skilled work:

> [Union officials] unanimously expressed the belief that Negroes could not be expected to advance, even if they had the incentive to do so, because of the lack of workers willing to sponsor Negroes for training as sewing machine operators in the shops. All Business Agents, in one form or another, suggested that workers in the trade believed it would result in a loss of social standing if they sponsored a Negro newcomer to the craft. Furthermore, even if a newcomer came from a non-union shop, with some practical experience in the craft, some form of assistance was necessary because the pace of an incentive wage shop was vastly different from the speed demanded of a worker in a weekly wage shop. Without some form of assistance and the good will of the other

workers, the possibility that a stranger would be able to successfully complete the necessary 35 hour trial period was doubtful.[14]

The ILGWU's adaptation to the earlier patterns of interethnic conflict—the creation of separate Jewish and Italian locals—raised yet another barrier to movement into higher-skilled, better-paying jobs. The first to feel the pinch from the declining supply of white ethnic labor, the large Jewish dressmakers' Local 22 was also the first to take in outsiders: it organized nearly four thousand black dress workers in one fell swoop in 1933. But the old-timers were fearful of the newcomers and reluctant to extend them the goodwill and cooperation that lubricated the acquisition of skills. Meanwhile, the most skilled, and best-paying jobs lay in territory organized by the Italian dressmakers' Local 89—which accepted Italians only. Though these owners were theoretically free to hire whom they wished, practical considerations, as noted above, generally tied their hands. During World War II, for example, a black member of Local 22 who found herself banned from a better-paying job, controlled by Local 89, petitioned New York State's fledgling Commission against Discrimination for redress. Despite the commission's ruling in this worker's favor, the strictures against non-Italian members remained fully in place.[15]

In the end, as a union official noted in 1953, "the best jobs (were) . . . hard for the newcomers to get," producing a " 'job ceiling' . . . set just above the semi-skilled level."[16] By the mid-1950s, job erosion in the high-skilled and well-paid dress and coat trades further diminished opportunities, though as one study found, young white workers were still far more likely to find jobs in these more desirable trades than their black or Puerto Rican counterparts.[17] Blocked from the industry's best positions, minority workers flooded into the low-paid, low-end branches of the trade, like skirts or undergarments, that flourished during the postwar years.

If black women found the route to skilled work tough going, they nevertheless advanced beyond the industry's most unskilled jobs; black men, however, fared still worse. The industry's huge army of female workers, many of them young, had always been prone to instability, with high turnover rates keeping hiring doors perpetually open.[18] While churning created new vacancies, pushing employers further down the labor queue for women, the expansion of New York's white-collar sector began producing opportunities for women with high school educations in increasing numbers from the 1920s on, the likes of which did not redound to their male counterparts.[19] But men were far more likely to retain lifelong attachments to the industry. More important, skilled men's occupations continued to draw young Jewish or Italian recruits at a time when women from these same groups were seeking better prospects elsewhere. In 1947, for example, the cloak pressers' local reported 600 new members, "nearly 70 percent of [them] . . . the sons or relatives of older members."[20] Three years later, when the pressers observed "a younger element steadily streaming into the local," newcomers constituted a quarter of the local's members.[21] A former ILGWU official, writing about the skirt industry in 1957, noted the contrast between the situation among the mainly female sewing machine operators—"where the shortage of labor has been a major factor preventing discrimination"—and the operations in cutting and pressing, which "have a reservoir of young American-born men in their ranks, and, not being troubled by any shortage of labor, have not needed many new workers."[22] Indeed, the cutters' manager told a journalist in the late 1950s, "Every day, some member comes in and wants to get his son or son-in-law into the trade, so we try to get him a job." As of 1958, the cutters' local counted more than 500 sons and sons-in-law among its 8,300-person membership.[23]

Thus, competition with skilled white ethnics shunted black men into the industry's least desirable jobs, as shipping clerks, helpers or, most commonly, push-boys.[24] In most situations, even low-skilled jobs like these would provide a chance for newcomers to prove themselves to their employers, learn the rudiments of skilled work, and gradually move up the ladder. But as with the best women's jobs in the cloak and dress trades, a peculiar mix of custom and contract meant that access to jobs hinged on connections. In the coat pressers' local, newcomers needed formal clearance as well as an insider who would teach them the trade. "To protect . . . new workers," reported Local 35 to the ILGWU's 1947 convention, the pressers "require all learner-applicants to receive permits from the membership committee while their 'sponsors' must obligate themselves to teach the applicants properly during the work-season."[25] The dress pressers were more flexible, allowing employers to take a talented shipping clerk and train him on the pressing machine. But even though shipping clerks and pressers made up separate divisions of the same local, only one minority shipping clerk, conceded the dress pressers' leader, had ever leaped across the occupational divide.[26] And at the apogee of the skill hierarchy, where anyone who approached the cutting table fell into the jurisdiction of the cutters' local, neither a formal nor an informal program regulated the entry of newcomers to the trade. Instead, "the good offices" of the cutters' local were enlisted to "have a young man learn the trade." The cutters' manager gave the following explanation of how this system worked:

> Let us say a father wishes his son to become a cutter. He comes up to me. I am a member of the union for 25 years. The boy doesn't want to go to school. I want him to learn to be a cutter. We will try to get an employer to get him to teach him the trade, so I try . . . I have to call a meeting of my cutters in the shop and explain to them that we have permitted this young man to learn the trade, and I appeal to them to teach him the trade, because they are the ones who will teach him the trade. We have no school. He has to learn the trade at the cutting table.[27]

Not surprisingly, then, the industry's traditional ethnic groups retained dominance over the skilled positions. By the early 1960s, according to the ILGWU's own efforts at an internal ethnic census, blacks composed about 10 percent of the members in one of the lower-skilled trades, and Hispanics another 40 percent.[28] The more skilled dressmakers, then 43,000 strong, included roughly 3,000 black members along with 4,500 to 5,000 "Spanish" members, leaving a minority share of less than 20 percent.[29] But for all practical purposes, the very best jobs remained off-limits to members of the newer groups: despite the ILGWU's best efforts to identify minority members, it could find only 103 blacks and 149 Puerto Ricans and Spanish speakers among the 7,500 unionized cutters.[30]

OUT OF THE FACTORIES

The high point of black employment came at the twilight of the industry's heyday in New York. After World War II, competitive conditions shifted, eroding the city's employment base and confronting remaining employers with severe pressure on wages.[31] Conditions of decline set the stage for a more antagonistic relationship between blacks and whites. "Racial prejudice . . . is by no means absent from the shops, all observers testify," wrote Will Herberg, the former education director of the dressmakers' local, in 1953: "Some years ago, Jewish workers were prone to accuse the 'Italians' of 'taking away' their work; today, both Jews and Italians tend to look askance at the newcomers for the same reason. Reports of business agents and an examination of grievance board cases indicate that ethnic prejudice often combines with competitive rancor and personal grudges."[32] Behind the fear of work being "taken away" lay contention over the proper division of work: since the earnings in a piece-rate industry like garments reflect productivity, declining conditions led workers to fight "over the bundle"—that is, the job on which one could make out the best.

Faced with this newly adverse competitive environment, the ILGWU adopted a strategy of wage restraint to save jobs in New York.[33] Whatever this policy's merits, it clashed with the changing economic orientations of the industry's rank and file. Job growth during the late 1940s and 1950s concentrated in less-skilled apparel lines like skirts or snowsuits. Although "the upsurge in production resulted in a new demand for thousands of new workers," as Roy Helfgott noted in the late 1950s, blacks were not available "in sufficient number to fill the demand for labor." Helfgott suggested that "with full employment, wages in the garment industry at the lower levels were not particularly attractive to Negroes."[34] Moreover, younger people seemed particularly likely to "avoid employment in the apparel industry," as researchers studying the graduates of the city's High School of Fashion Industries found.[35] Likewise, a 1960 Harvard University study reported that: "The complaint of a shortage of workers has been expressed in our interviews by the representatives of practically every branch of the garment complex . . . The industries, at their going wage rates, have generally had trouble recruiting native youths, white or Negro."[36]

If the wage situation discouraged new applicants, it proved far more distressing for those workers already in the trade; stagnant wages, combined with the intersection of the union and its new minority members, made for particularly bad blood. Black and Puerto Rican members clustered at the low-paid, low-skilled ends of the industry, where they bore the brunt of the ILGWU's "go-slow" stance toward employers. The union's policies were aggravated by its sharply hierarchical policies, which kept almost all power in the hands of its white, mainly Jewish leaders.[37]

The changing mood of the minority rank and file, which shifted during the late 1950s, only made matters worse. Employers in the very bottom tier of New York's light manufacturing sector, often linked to if not officially belonging to the garment complex, had sought refuge from the pressures of wage competition by recruiting black and Puerto Rican workers and shackling them with meaningless wage agreements secured from corrupt unions. But in the late 1950s, a sudden upsurge of militancy undid these protective devices, as wildcat strikes—spearheaded by minority workers—broke out in the leather, pocketbook, and novelty trades.[38] The same wave of discontent spread to the garment trades: as an indicator of the disgruntled state of the minority rank and file, the Association of Catholic Trade Unionists received sixty shop complaints in 1958 against the ILGWU, mainly from its black and Puerto Rican members.[39] More powerful expressions of discontent arose as well, with minority workers protesting against the union's failure to adequately represent their interests, pulling wildcat strikes, and seeking help from other unions.[40] The ILGWU's performance was particularly dismal in the one area where black men concentrated most heavily: the push-boys and shipping clerks fell into the jurisdiction of a corrupt local that turned a blind eye when unionized employers kept workers off the union rolls.[41]

Racial conflict moved from the shop floor to the public arena in the early 1960s, when black and Puerto Rican organizations pushed for a new, higher citywide minimum wage, only to be opposed by the ILGWU.[42] These two sides subsequently squared off when civil rights and antipoverty organizations attempted to gain federal funds to train minority sewing machine operators. Concerned that training subsidies would hasten the industry's already rapid relocation to the South, the needle trades unions successfully blocked this effort on the grounds that "the ability to get a [sewing] job does not and did never depend on the possession of skill or on training."[43] Civil rights organizations, by contrast, had a different agenda, namely, increasing job opportunities for minority workers in the urban economies of northern cities. They were bitterly aware that the unions and their allies also admitted that, in New York, "there is a serious shortage of skilled sewing machine operators."[44] Ultimately, the legacy of wage restraint seemed to blur the lines between union leaders and employers, both of whom were mainly Jews. "Working for Goldberg, the cat who runs the garment center," as Claude Brown put it in his memoir, fanned the resentment bred on the shop floor and in other encounters between blacks and Jews in stores and schools: "I became aware of what I knew about the garment center and about Goldberg and his relationship to the Negro, the boy who worked for him . . . He never even tried to see us, and he tried to treat us the way he had treated [the older generation]. Most of the older folks were used to it. They didn't know Goldberg from Massa Charlie; to them, Goldberg was Massa Charlie."[45]

In the early 1960s, tensions came to a head with public accusations that the ILGWU discriminated against blacks. Ernest Holmes, a black cutter, lodged a complaint with the New York State Commission against Discrimination, charging unfair treatment by cutters' Local 10. The Holmes case resonated widely, not just because it crystallized the festering sense of black grievance, but also because it identified the barriers blacks encountered. Hired as a general helper, Holmes insisted that he soon found himself doing the job of a cutter's assistant, all the while continuing as a helper and receiving his original salary. To move into the higher classification, Holmes needed the nod from the cutters' local, approval he claimed never to have received, despite several petitions for recognition.

The state commission issued a preliminary finding of discrimination upon Holmes's complaint in 1962; a congressional hearing was then convened at the instigation of Congressman Adam Clayton Powell, focusing on the charges of unfair treatment but also spotlighting corrupt practices of which the ILGWU leaders were aware and not particularly proud. The conflict pitted the Union against its erstwhile ally, the National Association for the Advancement of Colored People (NAACP), whose labor director, Herbert Hill, led the charge against the garment workers. The complaint was eventually dropped; Holmes was admitted into the cutters' ranks;[46] and the top leaders of the ILGWU and the NAACP later made up.[47] Nonetheless, the conflict left deep scars.[48] It also lingered in the charges of discrimination that persisted, with one civil rights organization, the Congress of Racial Equality, announcing efforts to organize a new garment workers' union as late as 1967.[49]

In retrospect, the Holmes case was the siren song for African-Americans in New York's needle trades; shortly thereafter, the political and economic shifts of the late 1960s pulled them out of the industry's labor supply. Analysis of data from the 1970 Census of Population shows that black female sewers who had been working in the industry five years before were significantly more likely to have shifted to non-operative jobs than women sewers of most other ethnic groups (Table 5.2). That black women were more mobile than others reflected, in part, their educational advantages: having significantly more schooling than others, blacks were best positioned to exploit the opportunities that opened in the late 1960s when the labor market tightened and discriminatory barriers fell. But even after controlling for education, we see that black women were more likely than others to shift out of sewing jobs. The apparel pattern holds for other opera-

Table 5.2 Job changes, 1965 to 1970: Odds of native black women changing jobs compared to odds for other women

	Sewers to non-operative jobs		All operatives to non-operative jobs	
	Raw	Controlled	Raw	Controlled
Native-born whites	3.86	1.10	1.08	1.45
Foreign-born whites	5.67	3.66	2.81	1.67
Native-born hispanics	10.57	11.72	3.40	2.63
Foreign-born hispanics	2.69	3.04	1.14	1.03

Source: Census of Population, 1970.

tive jobs as well, but by no means as strongly, pointing to the rag trade's increasingly tenuous hold on its black labor supply.

Apparel's problems reflected its sinking wage position, which took it out of competition with other sources of lower-skilled black employment. While the superheated economic environment of the late 1960s gave New York's apparel producers a last reprieve, it also widened the gap between demand and supply. In 1967, employers launched their first recruitment drive ever, with advertisements in black and immigrant newspapers; though the effort received union endorsement, it had little effect.[50] Two years later, the local offices of the New York State employment service reported that they could fill only half as many requests for apparel operators as were needed.[51] Employers needed bodies but had less flexibility on wages and conditions than those in health care or government, which continued to expand while also generating constant improvements in wages and benefits. Claude Brown's generation of younger blacks born or brought up in New York was also increasingly unwilling to take on the jobs that their parents accepted. As one young Harlemite told Kenneth Clark and his Harlem Youth Opportunities researchers in the early 1960s: "You want me to go down to the garment district and push one of those trucks through the streets and at the end of the week take home $40 or $50 if I'm lucky. Come off it. They don't have animals doing what you want me to do. There would be some society to protect animals if anybody had them pushing those damn trucks around."[52]

Nor could the industry rely on compulsion to secure its low-wage labor force, since local government had relaxed eligibility rules for public assistance and brought benefits to a level close to ever-dwindling apparel earnings. "Field work conducted" in New York City in the late 1960s by the Wharton School's Racial Practices in American Industry Project "repeatedly elicited from employers the problem of scarcity of job applicants during periods when welfare rolls were climbing."[53] The militancy of the times swept over garment shops as well, inflaming earlier racial antagonisms. Employers surveyed by the Wharton School study reported growing discontent and intractability among their black workers.[54]

By 1980, when American-born blacks accounted for one out of every eight employed New Yorkers, they made up fewer than one out of every sixteen garment workers. The Jewish and Italian employers whom I interviewed in the early 1980s reported that few blacks were to be found in either the shops or the applicant pool. One of the younger employers—then in his late thirties, but with ten years of experience in the business—told me, "I've never seen a black sewing machine operator." The old-timers thought differently. "We used to have more," an Italian woman told me. "You don't see them around." A Jewish belt maker saw it the same way, noting that "blacks don't come around anymore." I did detect an occasional hint that blacks' withdrawal from the industry could be linked to the immigrants' in-flux. One employer, for example, related: "I never had many blacks, I've just had a couple. They seem to clash with Hispanics. I find that the Hispanics are more racist than the whites. It seems that the blacks sense it and leave." But most employers, like the Jewish dress con-tractor who told me that "it's not a turnover business—the children don't go in," ascribed the diminishing black presence to generational shifts and changing aspirations. "Blacks want better jobs," noted a South Bronx sportswear contractor in a comment echoed by numerous respondents. "They don't want to be operators. They're very tempo-rary at best." Said another, "The blacks were never numerous, and now we don't have any at all. They seem to disappear. The blacks are looking to better themselves and I don't blame them. They go to the banks where it's a steadier job. Ours is a seasonal line, so even if you can't get a better job you get a steadier one."

ENTER THE IMMIGRANTS

As it happened, the black exodus was but a sideshow, as the industry's work force underwent a much deeper change at the same time. For much of the postwar period, the ranks of skilled labor had been replenished by a small but continuing wave of immigrants from Europe. Employers and union leaders guaranteed jobs to Holocaust survivors, and though some of those who found their initial beachhead in apparel stayed with the industry, most appear to have moved on.[55] More important was an ongoing influx of skilled Italian tailors, many of whom were brought over at employers' behest.[56] In 1965, just before enactment of the Hart-Celler Act, more than fifteen hundred tailors immigrated to the United States under the occupational preferences of the time. As one large employer noted approvingly, "you not only get these workers, but they can also bring their families with them and many of the wives and children can sew".[57]

By the late 1960s, however, the story of the Jewish and Italian proletariat in New York's needle trades had at last come to its end. Emigration from Europe dropped off sharply in the late 1960s and the new immigration law cut down the number of occupational slots available to skilled tailors. But the problem was not just "that European tailors are not arriving like twenty to twenty-five years ago," as one union official contended. Rather, the social structure of the industry's traditional work groups had been completely transformed. "When I went into the business," noted one Jewish factory owner, himself an immigrant, "we had a lot of experienced people who wanted to work; they got older, retired, and their children don't want to go near a factory." With "85 percent of the union workers hav[ing] five years to retirement or less," as one Italian employer complained, those white ethnics who remained had an ebbing commitment to work. "At one point," explained an old-line contractor, "Italian workers were the best, but they are no longer as hungry or hard-working." Once the "skilled people [began] aging and retiring right and left," employers dependent on the industry's traditional sources of skilled labor were left hanging. "When a worker retires," commented one factory owner, "I put a wreath on her machine."

In the end, a new wave of immigrants from China and from the circum-Caribbean moved into the industry through a process of self-recruitment in response to vacancies. As in the past, turnover naturally led to a high level of vacancies; in effect, employers were always hiring. Having already adapted itself to Puerto Rican workers, the industry easily worked out the organizational patterns needed to absorb new waves of Spanish-speaking workers. And the proliferation of immigrant-owned shops—which grew phenomenally among the Chinese—brought the immigrant communities right into the shops. Once in place, informal immigrant networks funneled newcomers into the factories at lowest cost and with greatest efficiency for employers and job seekers alike.

In the immigrants, New York's garment employers found a labor supply for positions that natives, white or black, now shunned. As I learned from the immigrant garment workers I interviewed in 1980, many of them came ready to take "whatever there was." Indeed, most recounted that they had arrived expecting to work in the needle trades: "I didn't know what I was going to do," explained one Ecuadorian arrival, "but my uncle always told me that there was a lot of work in garments." With workers "ready to do anything that presented itself, because one doesn't arrive prepared to do office work or teach," the advent of the immigrants stemmed the upward pressure on wages. Wages for New York's garment workers, which had grown increasingly out of line with the rest of the nation's, moved onto a slower growth curve as the New York differential diminished. The presence of immigrants also buoyed apparel's position in the competition for labor, enabling garment employers to retain their work force even as wages for apparel workers slipped below the average for New York's manufacturing sector—itself badly depressed. As one employer commented, "without the immigrants, the needle trades would be out of New York."

Not only did the immigrants succeed established white and black workers, they did so without provoking the wrath of incumbents. Although competition between blacks and immigrants has inflamed relations between the two groups in certain instances, a deafening silence emanates from the garment industry case. The union response, though motivated by a complex of factors, also suggests that earlier competitive relations no longer hold. Whereas the ILGWU had opposed training programs for minority workers, it now supports—and has indeed organized—training programs for immigrants. Rather than seeking to exclude immigrants from the trade, the ILGWU has adopted the most inclusive policy of all unions, with a focus on organizing and defending undocumented workers.

Hotels: Who Takes Care of the Guests?

The epic story of the garment workers—with its cycles of oppression, revolt, and exploitation—captured the attention of reporters and researchers ninety years ago and has held it ever since. But most of the inhabitants of the "other New York" work in the shadows, where few social scientists or journalists go. In this section, I turn my attention to one of these unheralded trades, where less-skilled newcomers to New York have always managed to get a leg up—hotels. While the hotel account lacks the historical dimension of garments, it presents a more complex configuration, one that is also closely linked to New York's postindustrial future. Because hotels are connected to the city's newer economic functions, the industry has been able to grow: in contrast to the badly eroding rag trade, hotels added employment over the period 1970–1990. Like the garment industry, the hotel business is a black niche of the past, but one in which the African-American presence persisted until recent years. As black New Yorkers are but one of a varied set of groups on which the industry draws to fill its jobs, a look at current employment patterns in hotels lets us observe the factors shaping the ethnic division of labor at play.

GROWTH AND RESTRUCTURING

Unlike New York's factory sector, which has steadily eroded over the past fifty years, the jobs of low-wage service have kept their place during the postindustrial transformation. Suburbanization and sagging urban economic fortunes spelled bad times for big-city hotels in the 1950s and the 1960s. With the upswing of urban service economies, starting in the mid-1970s, and the new forms of urban agglomeration that emerged during this period, the downtown hotel took a new lease on life. The corporate service firms, whose growth fueled a massive office-building boom, thrived on their linkages with an increasingly national and international clientele. Not surprisingly, then, "companies that settled into the new downtown offices soon wanted modern hotels nearby where they could put up out-of-town clients and business colleagues in comfort."[58] A huge expansion in tourism accompanied this growth in business travel, further swelling the market for downtown hotel facilities.

An extraordinary burst in hotel construction has occurred over the past several decades. During the 1960s, hotel construction added an average of 4,000 rooms a year to the downtowns of the thirty-eight largest metropolitan areas; between 1970 and 1982, the rate increased to more than 5,400 a year.[59] Hotel construction in New York took off in the 1980s, under the stimulus of the city's boom in tourism and business and financial services, yielding many new hotels and more than 8,500 new rooms.

Renewed investment in hotels turned the job picture around. Whereas employment languished in the postwar period, as business sagged and older properties were converted to other uses, payrolls expanded during the years after 1970. Total employment increased by one-third between 1970 and 1990, a quite respectable gain for an industry that remains a cluster of entry-level jobs.

STRUCTURE OF EMPLOYMENT

In comparison to other immigrant-reliant industries, hotels stand out in several key respects. First, the hotel is a sizable establishment that often belongs to a much larger chain. New York's largest hotel has over 2,000 rooms and employs approximately 1,400 people. Second, whether large or small, hotels maintain an elaborate division of labor. Jobs fall into either the "back" or the "front" of the house, with the latter involving activities requiring direct guest contact. Functions create further distinctions, of which housekeeping, kitchen work, stewarding, and banquet services are generally the most important in employment terms. Differentiation within these functions varies considerably, with an elaborate hierarchy among kitchen workers, for example, and virtually none within housekeeping. Alongside the major functions are a plethora of smaller departments, with a large hotel maintaining a carpentry shop, upholstery shop, machine shop, locksmith, and so on, each one of which employs a complement of specialized workers.

These various characteristics have contradictory influences on the structure of employment. On the one hand, size and organizational form lead to a formal and elaborate employment structure along the lines of an internal labor market. Many hotels have formal training programs, developed either by the owner or the chain; job-posting systems are common, as is a preference for hiring and promotion from within. On the other hand, the distinction between the front and the back of the house, as well as the functional divisions, have the opposite effect of separating job clusters and career paths within the hotel. Although workers can move from the back to the front of the house, jobs at the front usually get filled from the outside. And outsiders rarely come from the same groups as workers in housekeeping. Hotels want workers with good communication skills and middle-class self-presentation at the front of the house, which gives the edge to whites with at least some college education. In the back of the house, kitchen workers come from differing sources: professional associations or culinary schools refer chefs and sous-chefs, while lower-level help gets recruited from other hotels, restaurants, or the open market. In either case, movement occurs via the external market.

Despite its complexity, the hotel is a large service factory from an occupational point of view. At a time when the shape of so many organizations is changing, the hotel remains the classic pyramid: in 1990, managers and professionals constituted barely 18 percent of the industry's employees in New York City. The great bulk of employment in hotels lies in one of a variety of service occupations, which engages almost 60 percent of the industry's labor force. The largest concentration of workers, approximately 25 percent, is involved in the heavy, menial work of housekeeping; approximately another 16 percent of employees work in one of a variety of food service occupations (of which waiting is the largest).

THE HOTEL WORK FORCE

With an occupational structure that emphasizes manual skills and ability to do heavy, menial work, hotels have always leaned heavily on minority and immigrant workers. Hotels had already evolved into a concentration of black and Puerto Rican employment on the eve of World War II. Employment shrunk over the next thirty years, as the industry consolidated, modernized, and phased out older properties and residential hotels, but the minority share of employment grew. By 1970, African-American and Puerto Rican workers each accounted for about a sixth of the work force.

Though a major component of the hotel rank and file, blacks historically found themselves confined to a narrow tier of positions. In the years immediately after World War II, hotels were often charged with discrimination, not just in lodging but in employment practices as well. A 1956 review of complaints filed with New York's State's Commission against Discrimination noted "an occasional breakthrough in the employment of Negroes as waiter, busboy, and bartender but the overall picture is not one of major or extensive advance."[60] As if the data from its files were not enough, the commission underlined the obstacles to black progress in a mid-1950s survey of the industry's employment practices that it undertook on its own. Blacks were trapped in low-skilled, low-paying, dead-end jobs in the back of the house, with few chances of moving into positions involving customer contact; two-thirds of the black labor force was crowded into housekeeping alone, a category that only employed a fifth of the total labor force.[61] All thirty-three of the hotels that the commission studied excluded blacks from bar service and front-service departments; the thousand and some waiters and waitresses at work in the higher-end hotels included only five blacks; and the top-paying banquet jobs remained virtually closed off to blacks. African-Americans rarely gained promotion from rear to front elevators, a shift that opened the door to still better-paying jobs in the front of the house.[62] Notwithstanding an agreement to use the state employment service for referrals, as part of an antidiscrimination plan, the range of job placements did not significantly expand: "Almost two out of every three nonwhites were referred and placed in housekeeping, laundry, and maintenance jobs, whereas white applicants were referred and placed in a greater diversification of jobs . . . A higher proportion of white than nonwhite referrals was accepted in each of the four major groups."[63]

Government regulators, joined by civil rights protesters, kept up the pressure in the 1960s. Picket lines mounted in front of some of the city's best-known hotels led the industry to put a training and upgrading program in place, but the job ceiling only gradually lifted. Results from a 1964 survey, which found that "a large number of Negroes [were] employed as maids, housemen, and elevator operators, but only a few or none in building maintenance positions, and as cashiers, clerks, auditors, typists, and telephone operators," showed that little had changed since the industry had been canvassed a decade before.[64] A 1967 survey discovered that, blacks made up one of every three workers in the back of the house but only one of every ten in the front of the house. Ironically, more progress was made in the clerical and managerial positions than in the skilled and waiting jobs, where the importance of networks and a buddy system among incumbents proved much harder to reform.[65]

After 1970, the industry's overall complexion changed abruptly, while the legacy of its racial hiring practices shifted much more slowly. European immigrants, previously a dominant presence, seeped out of the industry; as they did so, whites' share of hotel jobs dropped from just under a half in 1970 to a little over a quarter two decades later (Table 5.3). The seventies appear to be years of transition, with newcomers pouring into the industry, while the native minorities held on to their place. The industry's recovery in the 1980s added to the vacancies created by the old-timers' exodus, but the fruits of change went to the immigrants, who grabbed the positions vacated by

Table 5.3 Ethnic employment in the hotel industry, 1940–1990

		Whites		Hispanics		Blacks		Asians
	Total	Native	Foreign	Native	Foreign	Native	Foreign	Foreign
Employment								
1940	43,800	14,200	20,000	3,300	—	5,500	700	—
1950	41,486	15,094	15,773	3,595	545	5,771	652	NA
1970	19,750	5,600	3,700	3,500	2,250	3,400	1,100	200
1980	21,700	4,200	2,540	2,980	4,440	3,680	3,080	640
1990	27,176	4,840	2,375	3,153	6,076	2,625	4,613	2,987
Index of representation								
1940		0.60	1.21	8.16	—	2.33	1.54	—
1950		0.62	1.35	3.52	1.67	1.75	1.25	NA
1970		0.50	1.38	2.55	2.64	1.12	2.84	0.82
1980		0.41	1.11	1.53	2.62	1.08	2.45	0.71
1990		0.45	1.03	1.25	2.13	0.63	2.06	1.40

Source: Census of Population, 1940–1990.

Note: Index of representation = share of group in category ÷ share of group in total economy.

whites. By 1990, the transition to a new configuration had been completed. Almost 60 percent of the industry's work force was foreign-born, among the highest of all major industries in the city; Asian immigrants made the most sizable gains, making significant inroads for the first time, followed by immigrant Hispanics and immigrant blacks, in that order. Hotels also emerged as a niche for immigrant Dominicans and West Indians, as I noted in Chapter 4. The number of African-American workers eroded by over a thousand and their share of hotel jobs declined even more severely. Those black New Yorkers who remained in hotels found themselves repositioned: while waiting and kitchen jobs remained largely closed to them, employment in housekeeping plummeted, and front-of-the-house clerical and managerial jobs opened up. Despite progress on the last front, hotels underwent the changes of other black niches of the past, evolving into an industry in which African-Americans found themselves badly underrepresented.

LABOR SUPPLY CONDITIONS

The hotel industry exemplifies the problems afflicting America's service complex: rapidly growing employment, low productivity, and de-

clining available labor supplies. Nationwide, hotel employment increased from a little under 1.1 million workers in 1980 to almost 1.5
million in 1987. But in a report on labor productivity recently issued
by the Bureau of Labor Statistics, hotels ranked thirty-seventh of forty-
three selected industries in terms of the average annual percentage
change in output per employee for the years 1982 through 1987. Between 1983 and 1988, payroll and related expenses rose from 32 to
nearly 37 percent, "primarily reflecting high rates of hiring," according to a report by industry consultants.[66] Although current data
are not available, the industry's most recent growth followed a decade
in which local productivity declined: between 1972 and 1982, the ratio
of employees to rooms rose by 18 percent.

But while the industry's payrolls are growing and its productivity is
sagging, finding workers is becoming an increasingly difficult task.
The hotel is a relatively low-wage, service factory; hence, many industry observers contend that the industry faces "a human resources
crisis."[67] One consultant told the industry's weekly publication, *Hotel
and Motel Management*, that he considered "the labor shortage in the
market as the most difficult it's been in his 25 years of hotel experience and that it is 'just getting worse.' "[68]

In New York, however, "there are plenty of people in the industry,"
as one manager put it. "We just have to open the door." In part, the
density of hotel employment means that there exists a pool of circulating, experienced labor on which all employers can draw. Moreover,
the labor force lives close by, in the city, whereas many hotels near
new suburban office parks have no local pool of labor. But whatever
the precise explanation, labor supply conditions in New York differ
sharply from the national norm. "If I didn't have the hiring hall pre-
screen applicants," noted one manager, "I'd have a line wrapped
around the block." "We could get a hundred maids by tomorrow if we
needed," commented another. "We have a nonstop flow of people
coming in for jobs."

Whereas poor quality often aggravates the problems of insufficient
quantity, New York's hotels seem to do better on this count as well.
"The hard-core unemployed are a small percentage of the people who
apply for our jobs," one manager told me. And turnover rates, which
appear to be well below the industry average, suggest a more firmly
attached population as well. For example, the two New York hotels
operated by a large nonunion chain enjoy the lowest turnover rates
among two hundred properties. "I'm surprised," said one manager,

whose prior experiences had all been out of town, "that we don't have to go into the market and recruit . . . We can spend more time to find individuals who are a cut above. This further keeps turnover down."

THE ROLE OF IMMIGRANTS

Though New York's hotels had always drawn on an immigrant labor force—and which of the city's low-wage industries had not?—hotel managers have developed a new appreciation of the importance of immigrants since they entered the 1990s. "There's constant immigration," noted one veteran manager. "There isn't one department that doesn't have newly arrived immigrants." A large hotel found that its employees spoke forty-seven different languages, ranging from Creole to Twi, with Spanish, Vietnamese, Filipino, French, Polish, Russian, Italian, and Mandarin the largest language groupings. One personnel manager, a native Spanish speaker with twenty years of experience in one of New York's largest hotels, described the new immigrant influx at length: "The population in housekeeping and stewarding increasingly comes from Haiti, Jamaica, the Dominican Republic, and Central America. Asians are starting to come: we have a tremendous number of Asians applying for jobs. Lots of Dominicans: well represented, more so than Puerto Ricans. The Dominicans have come in over the last six or seven years, mostly replacing Puerto Ricans."

While the immigrants are important for "filling jobs from which other people have moved up the ladder," they also frequently import specific proficiencies that expand their role in the industry. "Many immigrants bring skills that we want," commented one experienced manager in a large hotel, who maintained that one-fifth of his immigrant contingent had arrived with home-country experience. Often, immigrant workers have backgrounds in related trades, acquired either at home or in the United States, that can easily be transferred to hotels. In general, "ethnic cooks—Italians, Chinese, Greek specialties—seem to be always needed," according to an employment service official. Certain cooking skills—for example, experience in the preparation of cold meats and hors d'oeuvres—favor the entry of Thai and Chinese workers into specialized kitchen occupations. "Filipinos with housekeeping experience in hospitals at home become housekeepers here," related one manager. "I get calls from lots of waiters in Indian restaurants," noted another.

However important the immigrant influx, there are no signs that it has occurred in response to deliberate employer efforts. On the contrary, the hotels seem to be the passive "bellwether[s] of what's coming into the population." "With more than enough workers," most employers are content to "satisfy needs from the applicant flow." Thus, as the city's population has diversified, new groups have spontaneously streamed into the labor force. "The ethnic group to choose from is Indians," reported one new manager in a comment echoed in other interviews. "They are the number one group of applicants." But the Indians are only one of a batch of newcomers, as I learned from the interviews, where one informant told of "all of a sudden getting lots of Irish," and another of "an influx of literate Russians and Poles, some mid-easterners." Thus, "with different groups now entering, looking for any kind of employment," natural turnover combined with ethnic differences in predispositions for hotel work have expanded the immigrant employment base. "Blacks and Puerto Ricans are being replaced by immigrants," noted the manager of a downtown tourist-oriented hotel. "This is strictly what the market has born."

WEAKLY ATTACHED WORKERS

The advantage of immigrants, as one personnel director pointed out, is that their "need to work is as great as our need to fill the position." But the supply of immigrants is not unlimited and, more important, their skill levels often preclude them from jobs that require communication with guests. Even housekeepers have contact with guests; as one informant noted, "95 percent of what a housekeeper does will not require English; the problem is what they do when they're stopped in the hotel by a guest." In contrast to the manufacturing sector, where sign language is sufficient for instruction and any continuing interaction with employers or workers, some English-language ability seems to be a prerequisite for employment in the hotels. One job developer for a refugee-placement program observed: "Service demands for English are much greater than in manufacturing. When I get someone an interview with a hotel personnel department, the expectation of the hotel personnel people is that the person will speak for himself, although I will accompany him. In a factory, the expectation is that I will do everything—fill out the interview, translate at the interview, explain what the job involves." Moreover, immigrants are looking for stable, steady employment, but hotels also want a labor force that can adjust to changing hours and uncertain, flexible staffing requirements.

For these needs hotels turn to actors and students, a veritable "blessing to me," exclaimed an interviewee who ran a Broadway hotel. In actors and students, the hotels secure "overqualified workers at bargain rates." "What are the advantages of employing these people?" asked one manager rhetorically. "Above-average people skills and communication skills." Another informant added that "their good educational background makes them easy to train." Where immigrants tend "not to work in guest contact areas," actors and students ideally suit these roles. They have an additional virtue as "people who want less than the traditional workday. Actors want to be available in the day, and are therefore willing to work nights." Since hotels operate as seven-day-a-week, twenty-four-hour enterprises, they have staffing requirements that many workers, especially those with families, find undesirable. If students or actors can be hired for part-time, weekend positions, it relieves the strain of having to find full-time adult employees to work during these undesirable shifts. Furthermore, hotel occupancy rates are notoriously volatile, but weakly attached workers like students and actors move out of the industry without friction. Rather than laying career workers off, hotels are able to adjust to slow seasons, such as summer, by waiting for the students and actors they employ to simply quit.

Clearly differentiated from the hotel rank and file, actors and students make attractive recruits. According to the white officials in the New York State employment service whom I interviewed, hotels prefer to fill their positions with a "younger, yuppie, white crowd. They'd like to present that image right down to the maid: a blue-eyed, blond kid." Moreover, these same recruits are unlikely to feel much sense of kinship with less-educated, more heavily minority back-of-the-house workers—a not unimportant consideration in the industry's changing industrial relations environment. Tastes in compensation and benefits also vary among these two groups in ways that work to the advantage of management. "At the Marriott," noted a former employee, now a manager with a unionized hotel, "actors don't want to join the union, with its $200 initiation fee and $25 monthly dues." And one large nonunion hotel with a sizable labor force of actors and students emphasizes that its employees do not have to use union clinics but can consult their own doctors—a feature more likely to appeal to workers of middle-class background than to the hotel rank and file.

NATIVE BLACK WORKERS

Although the hotel industry has long found a sizable share of its workers among African-Americans and continues to do so today, immigrants appear to provide a preferable labor force.

The entry and recruitment of immigrants seems to have little to do with wages or the immigrants' supposed susceptibility to exploitation. Those in immigrant-dominated occupations like housekeeping receive higher pay than those in front-desk occupations, where the immigrant penetration is much lower. Still higher wages are to be found in the kitchen, where the disparity between immigrant and African-American employment levels is the greatest. Nor can a strong case be made for employers' preference for immigrants on the grounds of the latter's greater vulnerability. Pay rates in the nonunion hotels equal, when not surpassing, the union rates, and the benefit packages are often better. Moreover, obtaining actors and students is a more effective union-avoidance strategy than hiring immigrants and one that large nonunion hotels have employed.

Despite their restrained labor market role, hotel employers still appear to prefer hiring immigrants. To some extent, employers evince "the philosophy that you get an immigrant who hasn't been spoiled by the welfare system, they're a lot harder working." More important, managers perceive a congruence between the hotels' competitive strategy—which increasingly emphasizes the quality and quantity of service—and workers' assumed traits. Hotels want workers known for their "friendliness," "service-orientation," and "smiling faces"—in short, "people-oriented intangibles that make people come back." Personnel officials think that these attributes, and an orientation more accepting of menial work, are likelier to be found among immigrants than among native minority workers. "Lots of new immigrants have more acceptable work ethics," noted one manager. "Asians have a culture for dealing with people in a courteous and respectful manner. They are here to work." An official in the state employment service advanced the same view, putting employers' motivation in a less flattering light: "The industry is elitist. They look for characteristics that are intangible, gratuitously hiring Orientals because they think they're hard working."

Ultimately, African-American participation in the hotel industry reflects a broad complex of factors—of which the entry of immigrants is just one part. Most important, the structure of incentives works less favorably for blacks than for immigrants.

Differences in preferences play a part. Interviews and statistical data both suggest that African-American workers are slowly moving out of the industry's effective labor supply. "For native black Americans in the past twenty years," reflected an official in the industry's joint labor-management training program, "the idea of service as a mechanism to make a living is simply not attractive." Similarly, many of the managers I interviewed agreed that the industry's legacy as a repository of the traditional jobs to which blacks had long been confined deterred younger African-Americans from taking hotel jobs: "American-born blacks see hotel work as servitude. They don't want to be a bellperson or a waiter. They don't want to do it. They say so. They're willing to take a lower paying job if it gives them a higher level of self-esteem."   (manager of a New York business hotel)

But if African-Americans judge the benefits of hotel work more harshly than do immigrants, they also confront problems in their search for upward mobility that further diminish the attractiveness of hotel work. To begin with, the natural starting point for movement into hotel management is the front of the house, an area in which blacks have historically been underemployed. The blatant discriminatory practices that previously kept blacks out operate with much less force than before, but the basic pattern remains in place. Until recently, African-Americans had been confined to the back of the house, which offers relatively few options for upward mobility. Currently, there are few takers for the available management positions— like executive housekeeper or executive steward—that open up: "the pay is not great for these jobs and the positions aren't great either. Managers have to fill in for workers if the latter don't show up for work: in other words, the managers have to make rooms or serve." These back-of-the-house managerial positions are also detached from the main lines of upward mobility, which are to be found in the front.

The case of food service occupations provides further insight to the barriers to black employment, especially since it highlights the difference between African-Americans and immigrants. Kitchen and catering jobs contain a range of opportunities for upward mobility, yet African-American employment in these categories remains well below parity. The kitchen, "where the average temperature is 120 degrees," is not an inherently attractive place in which to work. For those kitchen workers who start at the bottom without any skills, the appeal is diminished because "hotel kitchens don't have opportunities to train hands-on." Getting ahead in the kitchen requires entering with training, which gives other groups a leg up over African-Americans. As already mentioned, immigrants often arrive in the United States with cooking skills or else learn them in the burgeoning sector of immigrant restaurants. "Culinary schools are exploding with graduates," who, as it turns out, are mainly middle-class whites. Thus, African-Americans are the most likely to get stuck at the bottom of the kitchen hierarchy, which discourages them from starting there in the first place.

If lack of skills and exclusion from the skill-acquisition process impede access to high-paying cooking jobs, the case of banquet waiting illustrates other obstacles. Banquet waiting requires strength, quickness, and care but no skill that involves years of training. Still, it is "considered a high-prestige job," one of the industry's most desirable. Banquet waiters receive a salary supplemented by a tip, based on a predetermined percentage addition to a banquet's total costs. A worker attached to a hotel with a good volume of business can earn from $40,000 a year in a run-of-the-mill establishment in New York to over $100,000 a year in a top-of-the-line deluxe hotel, though these earnings will vary, depending on the ups and downs of a hotel's catering business.

The problem is that there is no fast road to banquet waiting in union hotels. One must have five years of prior service as a hotel waiter to apply to be sent out as a "roll-call" waiter when additional banquet staff is required; with enough seniority, one moves to a hotel's list of permanent "B" waiters, from which one eventually steps to the "A" list and serves on a more regular basis. Thus, to become a banquet waiter, one first needs to be employed in the front of the house. To maintain the long effort to gain a permanent banquet job, one also needs information about opportunities in the many different hotels, and contacts with waiters who are on the permanent A or B list. Those contacts are not equally available to all. "Banquet waiters have been cliquish," admitted one union official, himself a former banquet waiter. "Blacks and women have had a hard time breaking in. It used to be Italian; it's now more Greek and Latino." Today's cliquishness has long-standing roots: in the past, as we have seen, blacks seeking employment in a high-paying, low-skilled job like banquet waiter found few doors open, with informal practices that generally restricted access to whites. There is little evidence to suggest that things have since turned around.

Thus, the case of banquet waiting illustrates the vicious circle that keeps mobility opportunities closed. Discrimination, past and present, reduces access to this particular ladder; discrimination also lowers the probability of movement up that ladder, thereby reducing the incentive to obtain initial front-of-the-house jobs. Whereas African-Americans lack a network that might connect experienced and aspiring black banquet waiters, other groups are well-connected, possessing the contacts and ties to other waiters and banquet managers that blacks, given their history and smaller numbers, cannot possibly possess.

Other factors—limited skill backgrounds, problems in communicating, and lack of facility with computers—impede access to those front-of-the-house positions directly linked to managerial tracks. As the director of a union training program pointed out, minority workers who want to move up to front-desk jobs "must be trained explicitly for middle-class norms." Though rank-and-file hotel workers find the "front office very attractive, there's lots of competition, especially from middle-class whites." Large hotels maintain active college recruitment programs, which funnel an ample supply of new trainees from college and university hotel management programs. The Council on Restaurant and Institutional Education includes almost two hundred college hotel management programs among its affiliates and reports that the number of such programs has grown considerably in recent years. Yet, hotel schools appear to enroll a very small minority population. For example, New York City Technical College, a community college unit of the City University of New York where the student body is 87 percent nonwhite, maintains a hotel and restaurant management program in which at least half of the students are white and a high proportion of the remainder are foreign-born. Similarly, New York University runs a hotel program in its extension division, which enrolls a principally immigrant student body, while the students in the hotel program at the university's main campus are predominantly white.

PERIPHERALIZATION?

Perhaps the African-American exodus from hotel work is a response to the declining wages and work standards that sometimes accompany immigration. Although that hypothesis frequently appears in the literature, the hotel case offers little support. New York is an old union town, with a powerful branch of the Hotel and Restaurant Employees Union, which established firm control over its respective markets during the heyday of labor-movement activity over half a century ago.[69] Though union-management relations in the hotel industry changed during the 1980s—with nonunion chains experiencing growth and the industry's productivity squeeze motivating cost-cutting measures—these shifts had little impact on New York. Only two of the hotels that opened in New York during the 1980s remained nonunion, a status that has entailed substantial costs in wages and benefits, which compare favorably with union standards. Consequently, even in the market of the early 1990s—when demand was weak and unemployment rising—the very newest hotels signed neutrality agreements with the hotel workers.

The recent collective-bargaining experience attests to the stability of these arrangements. Negotiations over the 1985 contract broke down, leading to a thirty-five-day strike, the industry's first in over forty years. In the settlement, the union assented to only two of the more than thirty give-backs with which management had originally come to the table. The most important concession involved a two-tier wage agreement, which in contrast to that implemented in many other industries, held for only first-year employees, who would then automatically move up to the standard rate for their classification. In return, hotel workers received sizable wage increases. In 1990, however, negotiations pivoted around health care costs. But union and management averted the conflicts that had earlier led to stoppages in private hospitals and the telephone industry, successfully restructuring their benefits plan without imposing deductions or coinsurance and signing an agreement ahead of its expiration date.

Alternatively, we might expect to see an immigrant effect on wages, which could suggest a tie-in to broader arguments about the relationships among service growth, immigration, and earnings inequality. Nationwide, real earnings for hotel and motel employees declined, falling from $181 a week in 1972 to $160 a week in 1990. But in New York, hotel workers' *real wages*, which stagnated during the 1970s, rose during the buoyant 1980s. Likewise, a look at wages for detailed occupations in unionized hotels confirms the picture of rising real wages during the 1980s, while providing no evidence of growing inequality. On the contrary, wage trends showed a slight shift toward compression between more- and less-skilled occupations. Hotel workers also moved upward relative to their counterparts in manufacturing while holding their own in the overall economy.[70]

As Figure 5.1 shows, however, the hotel industry did pay immi-

Wages (in 1990 dollars)

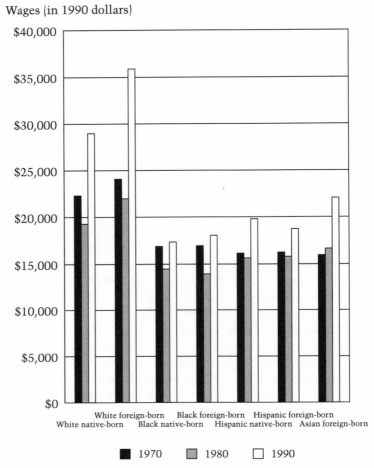

Figure 5.1   Wages of hotel workers in New York City, 1970–1990. (*Source:* Census of Population, 1970–1990.)

grants better than their native black counterparts. That advantage is hard to square with the usual claims of immigrant competition: after all, why should the hotel industry have substituted immigrants for African-Americans, if the result was a higher wage bill? But the disparity fits the argument I have made all along: that immigrants found a more supportive environment in hotels than did African-Americans, a difference that in turns helps explain the diverging supply curves between the two groups.

On Different Tracks

The portals to the bottom of New York's economy have run through the city's garment and hotel industries for the past hundred years. At midcentury, those characteristics led African-American New Yorkers to gravitate toward hotel and garment work. But now, when both industries remain concentrations of easy-entry jobs, their native black workers have largely gone. Instead, hotels and garments, like so much of New York's low-skilled sector, have reverted to the earlier pattern of immigrant domination.

The histories recounted in this chapter suggest that African-American trajectories have been shaped by a complex of interacting sociological and economic factors. The African-American experience in hotel and garment work coincides with the years of the great migration, as black workers converged on the lowest-level jobs, filling positions vacated by whites. In both cases, attempts to move up the hierarchy ran into the obstacle of competition with better-established white workers. Good jobs got rationed through informal ties among established workers and the younger members of their core networks. As long as white ethnics sought work as cutters, banquet waiters, cooks, or skilled seamstresses, opportunities for African-Americans remained largely foreclosed.

African-Americans subsequently moved out of both industries; the timing of those shifts casts light on the factors that triggered the outflow. The supply of native black labor began to fall short in the garment industry by the early 1950s, but not in hotels. The pace of wage change has much to do with this development, as wages in the garment industry fell behind in the city's wage hierarchy, while hotel wages pulled ahead.[71] Similarly, African-Americans' discontent with garment work conditions first showed up in the industry's recruitment problems; active protest emerged only later, toward the end of the 1950s, as the growing protest movement reflected shifting black aspirations. By the late 1960s, when the city's economy reached its postwar boom and apparel employers were searching for workers as never before, African-Americans dropped out of the industry's effective labor supply for good. Similarly drastic change did not occur in the hotel industry until the 1980s, a period of considerable improvement in the industry's real wages. As the interviews suggest, the attenuation of African-American ties was linked to the emergence of a new generation that rejected stigmatized service jobs to which blacks had long been confined.

In both industries, differences in economic aspirations put African-Americans and immigrants on different tracks. But the hotel case further suggests that the structure of opportunity systematically varied between African-Americans and immigrants, in turn yielding divergent motivations and incentives to develop the relevant skills. In hotels, African-American movement beyond the entry level is hindered by a variety of factors that do not hold for immigrants. The skills needed to enter at higher levels of the blue-collar hierarchy are *more* difficult to acquire for African-Americans than for immigrants; at the lower levels of the white-collar hierarchy, African-Americans encounter substantial and effective competition from whites; and African-Americans seem more victimized by discrimination than immigrants, as indicated by black underrepresentation in food service occupations.

What about the alternative hypothesis, that cheap immigrant labor pushed African-Americans out? Timing seems to rule that possibility out. African-American employment erosion began *before* the new immigrant influx; as noted above, the most severe African-American losses seem to have occurred in the 1960s, just when employers were most desperately seeking bodies. In hotels, the decline in African-American employment occurred in the 1980s, when real wages grew. The fact that relative wages for the most immigrant-dominated hotel occupations rose fastest makes the immigrant-displacement hypothesis still more implausible. In any case, African-Americans' chief competitive threat in hotels comes from actors and students, who provide the preferred sources of flexible labor, *not* immigrants.

But the seepage of African-American employment from industries like hotels and garments, and its replacement with immigrant labor, does seem to produce an irrevocable and irreplaceable loss. Once in place, immigrant networks have an inherently exclusionary bias, an effect that only grows when newcomers concentrate in an ethnic economy, as in the case of Chinese in the garment industry, or in an ethnic occupational niche, as in the case of hotel kitchens. Although the arrival of the new immigrants seems to be an instance of self-recruitment, not manipulation by employers, the evidence from the hotel industry indicates that employers prefer immigrants to African-Americans, when they have the choice. To some extent, employers also respond to the preferences of their immigrant workers, whose involvement in the struggle for place may yield an antipathy for African-Americans.

In the end, the immigrants may have hastened the African-American exodus from New York's low-skilled sectors, but if so, they only pushed along a development that was well under way before they arrived. African-Americans stopped doing New York's dirty work more than a generation ago, a change that has now run its course. Today's areas of African-American concentration are to be found in activities that require more schooling and provide much greater rewards. But this particular path of adaptation leaves behind the low-skilled. For these black New Yorkers there are no alternatives to work in the city's traditional, easy-entry industries. Unfortunately, that option is largely foreclosed: African-American recruitment networks into low-skilled industries like garments or hotels have dried up; and the advent of immigrants means that the newcomers have a lock on those jobs.

6 | Who Gets the Good Jobs?

This chapter is concerned with a single question, one that is simple and straightforward and yet almost always ignored: Why don't African-Americans get their fair share of good jobs when educational barriers don't stand in their way?

The infrequency with which this question is asked reflects the conventional wisdom about urban change and its underlying assumptions. The skills mismatch hypothesis assumes that the city of production—whose passing it so loudly laments—offered a hospitable welcome to blacks. It is not just the historical record that offers scant support for this view, but the contemporary situation as well. What remains of the urban manufacturing base is not a concentration of jobs for blacks, but rather the immigrant enclave par excellence.

Of course, one might still argue that the absence of factory jobs for African-Americans is not really so bad. After all, manufacturing has receded; and higher levels of black employment would just be further indicators of concentration in a mobility trap.

But goods production jobs are still to be had in the postindustrial city. They can be found in construction, the one urban blue-collar sector that has thrived during the years of manufacturing decline. The urban revitalization of the 1980s changed the landscape of downtown. In New York City alone, the value of construction contracts doubled in real terms between 1976 and 1987, which in turn doubled the size of the local construction labor force.[1] The workers who put up these buildings, though using more sophisticated equipment than in the past, brought little more than secondary-level schooling to crafts that they essentially learned on the job. As of 1990, New York's construction sector was a prime employer of less-educated workers, with four out of ten construction workers reporting completion of high school or less—a proportion matched only by manufacturing and exceeded only by personal services.[2]

Good times and abundant work for those with manual skills notwithstanding, the building boom of the 1980s left black workers out in the cold: construction remains an industry in which the force of long-established exclusionary practices has not yet been spent. Moreover, the persistence of discrimination in construction is not simply an unpleasant exception to the general case. By attracting such intense scrutiny, the flagrant discriminatory practices in the construction union have obscured the severe barriers to employment gains that confront blacks throughout the skilled trades. African-Americans have made no more progress in entering skilled manufacturing occupations—or for that matter, skilled blue-collar nonmanufacturing occupations—than they have in the building trades.

Empirically, construction is thus the most visible example of a widespread problem. It is also significant in another and deeper sense. Much of the debate has been focused on whether or not discrimination has in fact diminished. But demonstrating the continued virulence of discrimination in the construction case makes us ask why and under what conditions discrimination would persist or decline.

The proponents of the skills mismatch perspective, as I noted in Chapter 1, have an explanation for why discrimination continues. Whites' fear of low-wage competition from minorities, they contend, led to discriminatory actions in the past. But in recent decades, as the American state's expanded role in regulating industrial and race relations diminished wage competition between blacks and whites, white workers' motivation to discriminate against blacks lost much of its force. With these shifts in place, class—or to put it somewhat closer to the terms of the empirical debate, educational attainment—replaced race as the principal influence on blacks' labor market experience. Blacks' deepening employment problems reflect their educational and skill deficiencies relative to the demands of the new, service-based economy—not their vulnerability to discriminators.

But this theoretical perspective runs against the stark reality of the construction case. Neither tenet of the skills mismatch story applies. Low African-American employment in construction persists even though skills and education are not at issue. And while black-white *wage* competition has declined, the low levels of black penetration into construction's skilled trades are prima facie evidence of continuing discrimination—with many supporting details to be shown in the pages that follow. Thus, the persistence of employment barriers that bear little relationship to *school*-acquired skills raises theoretical questions about accepted explanations of discrimination's decline.

How can we understand the continued exclusion of African-Americans from an industry to which they have struggled for access over many decades? In this chapter, I argue that the answer lies in the shifting balance of power between black and white workers and in changes in their relative ability to affect state policy-making.

Construction has been the locus of ongoing racial conflicts that date back to the early days of civil rights protest in the northern cities. Those conflicts have yielded modest and disappointing job gains for blacks. For the past thirty years, white workers and unions have continued to oppose black employment in construction. Two factors— the importance of informal hiring and training practices, and the political power of construction unions—have prevented African Americans from achieving parity within the industry despite strenuous efforts to reach that goal.

The industry's reliance on informal social networks for both recruitment and training makes it difficult for newcomer groups to break into construction. Even in the unionized sector, which seems dominated by formal labor regulations and institutions, employment is largely based on informal relationships and mechanisms.

Informality not only creates natural barriers to outsider groups, it also thwarts public policies designed to counter discrimination. Since antidiscrimination policy proceeds through formal regulations, enforcement is more difficult and less effective in industries dominated by small firms that hire and promote through informal mechanisms.[3] Thus, the greatest gains in black employment and mobility have occurred in industries that have been within the reach of public policy influence. The most conspicuous example of this success, as we shall see in the next chapter, can be found in the public sector, where African-Americans are significantly overrepresented above parity and the level of black employment in managerial or professional occupations is far higher than in the private sector.[4]

The contemporary state's role in expanding employment for blacks represents a historic reversal: for many decades after the Civil War the state instead blocked black progress.[5] In the 1960s and 1970s, the

growing political power of blacks and their allies brought about a proliferation of government antidiscrimination policies aimed at the construction industry. As in other sectors of the economy, organizational
characteristics of the industry affected the scope of government's involvement. With its array of formal institutions and regulations, the
union (rather than the nonunion) construction sector provided the
more appropriate vehicle for equal employment efforts. Consequently,
the battle to open the industry to African-Americans has taken place
almost entirely on union terrain.

In this situation, black workers and civil rights organizations found
themselves pitted against labor unions that possessed considerable
political muscle. The unions successfully used that power in the conflicts that ensued, with the result that policy responses on all fronts
reflected the unions' underlying interests. Continuing black exclusion
from skilled construction jobs, therefore, is not so much the consequence of skill deficiencies as of power differences. My analysis brings
issues of power and conflict back to the study of the employment
problems of African-Americans.

African-American Employment Trends in Construction

Civil rights groups made opening up skilled construction jobs for minorities a top priority throughout the 1960s and early 1970s. Although
the fires of civil rights protest have died down, the embers linger: in
virtually every city, expanding minority employment in construction
remains a hotly contested, politicized issue.

The persistence of contention is a sign that protest has reaped limited rewards. Thirty years after the Civil Rights Act, blacks have not
yet gotten their fair share of construction industry jobs. Black males
were substantially underrepresented among construction workers in
the United States in 1980 and remained so a decade later. In New York
City, African-Americans made up a substantially larger proportion of
the industry's work force but were still employed at below parity.
New York's boom times in the 1980s did not help. Though construction grew by 63 percent between 1980 and 1990, outpacing every other
industry, African-American men gained a meager share of construction's newly created jobs. By the end of the eighties, black New
Yorkers had even less of a share in the industry than they had had
when the decade began.[6]

Black protest in the construction industry has been about more than

just jobs. The "trowel" trades of hod carrier and laborer have historically employed blacks, often in relatively well paying jobs. But the
problem has been how to move into the more skilled, and still better
paying, crafts. And here there is scant progress to report. In the United
States as a whole, blacks are still grossly overrepresented among construction laborers; for all skilled construction occupations they do not
even average 60 percent of parity, with lower levels of representation
in the most highly paid crafts like electrician and plumber. Given its
history of protest over discrimination in construction, New York not
surprisingly presents a more favorable picture. Yet the same pattern
prevails: overrepresentation in the lowest-level construction occupations, underrepresentation in the top-level crafts.

Ownership is common in an industry like construction, where firm
size is small, and one can do well working on one's own or with a
helper or two. Moreover, movement from craftworker to owner and
back again is common in construction, making the level of self-
employment a good indicator of the acquisition of higher-level construction skills and contacts. But the data on African-American self-
employment in the industry just add to the dismal record. Despite
two decades of efforts to spur black business by providing set-asides
on government contracts and other forms of business assistance, ownership remains much less common among blacks than among whites.
In 1990, African-Americans were even more underrepresented among
the ranks of self-employed persons in construction than they were in
the traditionally discriminatory skilled crafts.

Formal and Informal Organization in the Construction Industry

The outsider views the construction industry as a world of unchanging
work rules, jurisdictional regulations, formal licensing and training
requirements, and Byzantine provisions for contract bidding. But the
insider knows otherwise. Beneath the complicated regulations and
proliferation of collective-bargaining contracts lies a different reality,
one dominated mainly by personal contacts and informal networks.

The industry's employment system results mainly from the small
size of construction firms and the nature of construction markets.[7] In
1982, when the industry nationally did about $300 billion in business,
1 million construction contractors employed approximately 5 million

workers.[8] Seasonality, the unique and short-term nature of construction projects, as well as the industry's extreme sensitivity to the business cycle, make fragmentation and decentralization the industry's salient traits.

These characteristics create special problems for recruiting and training workers. Many construction jobs require extensive training and experience, but the industry's uncertainty and volatility complicate the acquisition of skills. Only the very largest firms can make stable commitments to a substantial number of employees. Usually, a contractor will have a small core of supervisors and skilled workers, but even these workers are periodically laid off. For most workers, the employer's commitment lasts only the length of a specific task.

These conditions impede institutionalized skill acquisition. Although the industry needs skilled workers, individual employers can benefit if they let others do the training. Free-riding employers can anticipate gaining access to workers who previously acquired skills, since those craftworkers are unlikely to be permanently attached to the employer who first provided the training. But if every contractor follows this same strategy, no one will be trained.

Traditionally, family and kinship relationships have been used to counteract the disincentives caused by the uncertainty and volatility of the construction markets. The family relationship alters the investment calculus. In place of an employer worried about losing an investment when a worker moves on to another job, the investor is now a parent interested in assuring a child's livelihood, of which both the level and stability of remuneration are key. The employer's interest lies in the production and maintenance of the minimally skilled labor force capable of executing required tasks. By contrast, the parent's interest tends toward the creation of a polyvalent worker capable of working on many jobs and able to ride out cyclical swings in the industry by moving from one specialization to another. These same considerations make the employer desire a larger, and the parent a smaller, work force.

While young workers acquire training and experience with the help of relatives and acquaintances, contractors draw on the same relationships to staff their projects. Given the short-term nature of the employment relationship, the contractors try to minimize screening and recruitment costs, and the quickest way of gaining reliable additions to a crew is to find recruits among the relatives and friends of incumbent workers.[9]

This informal system works effectively when the projects are small. When jobs are too large to be handled by the individual journeyperson and helpers, a vital worker can add to a crew by recruiting among friends and acquaintances. Thus, close ties from contractors to key workers, and from key workers to other skilled craftspeople, provide the channels by which members of a particular community gain entry into the industry. Because the skills required for success in any one of these positions come from prior employment, the training system creates strong barriers to outsiders. On the one hand, the industry's fragmented structure encourages contractors to rely on kin or kin-type networks to efficiently mobilize reliable, productive workers. On the other hand, the nepotistic nature of recruitment, which yields the incentive for training, provides an equally strong motive to exclude workers not associated with the core network.

But there are limits to the completely informal training system. Serious strains develop when jobs become larger. Individual connections are not likely to be adequate to mobilize the large numbers of specialized workers necessary to complete big jobs according to complicated schedules.[10] A variety of institutions have emerged to train and mobilize the work force; of these various institutions, the construction trade unions have historically been the most important.

The unions' training and mobilizing function has two essential components. The first, a "joint" (labor-management) training program, is financed by contributions from all union contractors, which means no contractor runs the risk of paying the costs of training for competitors. The second component, a referral system, can mobilize labor for short-term jobs when informal methods would be inadequate under conditions of constantly shifting demand.[11]

Despite rules and formal procedures, informal relationships still dominate the union sector's employment processes. Thus, training may go on within the union sector without any formal training arrangements. For example, the operating engineers have historically done without an apprenticeship program: experienced operators have passed on their knowledge about the various pieces of equipment to younger workers known as "oilers." Whether training is formalized or not, family connections are still important for passing on skills, particularly since much of the training must go on informally on the job. A high proportion of skilled workers report having fathers or relatives in the trade.[12] Though apprenticeship is the most important entry route for the industry's key workers and future supervisors, only a minority of union members have previously served as apprentices.[13] Many workers become sponsored for journeyperson status without ever having learned their skills or graduated from a formal apprenticeship training program; social connections to journeyworkers is even more important for workers who attempt to enter the industry through this route.[14] Construction training in the armed forces has provided a frequently used launching pad for civilian careers in the union sector;[15] work in the suburban residential housing market has been an alternative route of access, though one that is even more discriminatory against blacks than the central-city union sectors.[16]

The union's recruitment institutions operate in a similarly flexible fashion, emerging from and then collapsing back into the underlying informal networks as conditions change. Even at a formal level, the requirement that workers be recruited from among union members is by no means universal.[17] Whether mandatory or not, the hiring hall is often "a source of workers only at the margin," to be used when employers cannot "recruit sufficient help on their own."[18]

The workings of the apprenticeship system demonstrate how firmly embedded are institutional arrangements in underlying social networks. By creating a structure that channels the flow of entrants into the industry and regulates the characteristics of new workers accepted into the training system, apprenticeship fulfills the basic needs of the core, skilled work force. While the apprentice system is at once more restrictive with respect to numbers admitted and more intensive with respect to training required than most employers might desire, employers accept it because it works and appears to do so better than the alternatives. First, the financing of apprenticeship programs socializes the costs throughout the industry: every contractor is equally at risk of paying the costs of training a competitor's crew. Second, formalization counteracts the effect of fragmentation on the incentive structure facing workers acquiring skills. Uncertain and unstable employment prospects make workers reluctant to partially absorb the costs of skill acquisition. Apprenticeship keeps down competition for vacancies and reduces recruitment during down periods. These conditions improve the chances that young workers will find employment for their new skills, thereby increasing their incentives to devote the time and expense needed to become a skilled craftworker. Third, union control of apprenticeship keeps journeyworkers involved in the training process. Even apprenticeship programs depend on the journeyworkers to provide on-the-job training, especially since the most important skills are acquired on small jobs where apprentices work on a one-to-one basis with journey-level mechanics. Consequently, as long as the apprentice stream converges with nepotistic networks and never threatens to supplant journeyworkers with cheaper, less-trained workers, the apprenticeship system reproduces the familial system in providing incentives for journeyworkers to train new entrants.

Thus, formal regulations and processes play a less prominent role in the union sector than appears at first glance. Because groups not already integrated into networks within the industry find it difficult to firmly establish themselves in construction work, the industry's continuing informality has affected African-Americans with particular force.

But in the union sector, these informal barriers are also embedded in institutions. The institutionalization of the union sector has paradoxical consequences for government's responsiveness to black protest. On the one hand, a tight nexus links the state, at all levels of government, to the union sector. Government is a big spender of construction dollars and plays an important role in regulating construction industrial relations. The potential for altering existing institutional arrangements politicizes the industry's employment process. Moreover, government's levers can indeed be wielded with some effect. By contrast, the organizational characteristics of the nonunion sector—its greater fragmentation and its disconnection from the state—make it a less attractive policy target. And where the nonunion sector has developed training institutions, its employment practices compare unfavorably with the union sector.[19]

On the other hand, the very fact of skilled-worker organization and mobilization has given the crafts powerful levers in the political conflicts over training system control. When confronted with heightened black protest and governments mobilized to provide some response to blacks' demands, the craft unions have made strategic retreats. But the unions have been unrelenting in their efforts to maintain control over the training system; in the end, the weight of informal barriers, and the unions' ability to influence policy-making, sharply contained the African-American drive for equal employment in construction.

Racial Conflict and Antidiscrimination Efforts in New York City

Until the 1960s, New York's building trades were virtually impenetrable to African-Americans. Blacks had made some gains in construction jobs after World War I, but the impact of the Great Depression soon undid them, as craft union policies became more rigid. Powerful Local 3 of the electrical workers simply refused to admit blacks. Plumbers' Local 2, George Meany's home union, resorted to a different tack, enforcing racial exclusiveness through control of the licensing program—which barred black plumbers who might have gained experience or completed programs in other states. The carpenters, a less-skilled group in which African-Americans could make good use of proficiencies acquired on the farm, segregated its membership by race. The District Council assigned all black members to Local 1888, a mixed local based in Harlem; the white members gradually transferred membership to other locals; and as a final stroke, the District Council made Harlem the sole jurisdiction for which Local 1888 members could work. Not surprisingly, black membership in the carpenters' local plummeted from 440 members in 1926 to 65 in 1935.[20]

Although World War II helped redress the damage suffered during the depression, African-American workers remained on the margin of the industry. Most black construction workers continued to labor in the trowel trades; and even in these lower-level occupations, they enjoyed few opportunities to do more than low, unskilled "rough work." The black members of carpenters' Local 1888 found themselves confined to the hardest, low-paying jobs; until the 1960s, each New York City carpenters' local had its quota of two blacks who were allowed to do "finish work." Plumbers' Local 2 had three black members holding journeyworkers' cards who were rarely allowed to work with other journeyworkers. Sheetmetal workers' Local 28, where resistance to integration proved to be the most entrenched, was strictly a father-son local, with no black members at all.[21]

Contrary to William Wilson's claim that racial conflict in the post–New Deal era shifted out of the labor market, these job barriers became a lightning rod for black protest in the 1960s. The initial steps were relatively quiet: in the late 1950s, the New York State Commission against Discrimination published a scathing report that drew attention to the industry's discriminatory practices. Around the same time, the National Urban League began efforts to work with employers and unions. But once protest engulfed New York's African-American community, as it increasingly did in the early 1960s, it was inevitable that the construction industry would explode.

It was not just a legacy of blatant discrimination or the prospect of obtaining good jobs that made construction such a tinderbox. In those days of urban renewal, when the black ghettos of New York and other cities contained numerous construction sites, everyone could see the persistence of a lily-white work force. And so in May 1963, the Joint Committee for Equal Employment Opportunity announced plans to picket a construction site at Harlem Hospital. Picketing at the site led to violent clashes and suspension of work; pickets, demonstrations, and violence then spread to other construction sites throughout the city. The spring's protest activity led to daily sit-ins at the mayor's office (lasting ultimately for forty-four days), sit-ins at the governor's offices in the city, clashes with police, and more than 650 arrests.[22]

The following year another bitter fight ensued, though this time with the protagonists cast in opposite roles. In April 1964, Astrove Plumbing, which had just received a large city contract for work on the new public fruit and produce market being constructed in the Hunts Point section of the Bronx, succumbed to pressure from the City Human Rights Commission and agreed to hire four minority plumbers. Although these four did not belong to plumbers' Local 2, Astrove's contract with Local 2 allowed him to hire qualified workers in the geographic area of the union, regardless of membership status. This fact notwithstanding, Local 2 decided to call a strike as soon as the four minority workers appeared for work. The plumbers walked off the job on April 30; within the week, the strike spread to other crafts. On May 15, Mayor Robert Wagner announced a settlement: the plumbers would return to work if the four minority employees would agree to take a test; if they passed the test, they would be hired and admitted into the local. All four failed the examination, however. And though National Labor Relations Board and court decisions found the union's strike illegal and discriminatory, the four minority plumbers never made it into Local 2.[23]

These conflicts, sparked in the heyday of civil rights protest in New York, and which have remained an enduring part of the construction scene, produced policy responses. Those responses fall into four categories: (1) changes in formal, state regulation of apprenticeship programs; (2) equal employment strategies, which in turn can be distinguished into separate supply-side efforts; (3) demand-side efforts; and (4) court-imposed remedies. Examination of each case reveals the combined ability of the informal and formal power nexuses in the union system to avert effective integration.

STATE REGULATION OF APPRENTICESHIP PROGRAMS
The apprenticeship system in the United States derives from a broader set of legal relations that binds the construction industry to the state.

Modern apprenticeship was born under the New Deal, a product of the little-known National Apprenticeship Act of 1937—referred to as the Fitzgerald Act—which established standards for apprenticeship programs and set up an agency of government, the Bureau of Apprenticeship Training in the Department of Labor, to make sure that these standards were met. The law also gave states the option of establishing their own State Apprenticeship Councils, which, if approved by the bureau, could take over the regulatory responsibility. New York is one of the approximately thirty states with such a council, making the New York State Labor Department the designated agency for regulating apprenticeship programs.

Another New Deal progeny, the Davis-Bacon Act, has additional influence over apprenticeship programs. The act was yet another New Deal effort to keep a floor under wages and prevent the rounds of wage slashing that many considered a prime cause of the depression. Under the act, all workers on jobs funded by the U.S. government must be paid the prevailing wage—which in practice has meant the union rate. Little Davis-Bacon acts are a common feature at the state and local level. In New York State, section 220 of the labor law stipulates that any projects funded by the state or any of its subdivisions, which include municipalities, must pay labor at the prevailing rate. One class of worker is exempted from the prevailing wage requirement for journeyworkers: apprentices enrolled in government-approved, registered programs. Keeping a program registered is the only way that unions can provide contractors doing government work with a source of cheap union labor. Thus, the linkage between Davis-Bacon–type provisions and apprenticeship regulation is a potential hook that government can use to pry open apprenticeship doors.

In fact, however, government regulators have never employed this strategy. Ever since the inception of protest over discrimination, regulators in the federal and New York State Departments of Labor have resisted every effort to influence the programs they were mandated to oversee. Prior to passage of state and federal civil rights statutes, the regulators did their best to oppose extending antidiscrimination protections to apprenticeship programs. Thus, in the late 1940s, the New York State Apprenticeship Council and its director opposed amendments to the standards for apprenticeships that would have prohibited discrimination. In the mid-1950s, the council, in response to pressure for action from the New York State Commission against Discrimination, claimed that it knew of no discrimination in registered apprenticeship programs. And in the late 1950s, when the commission undertook a study of the industry, the council explicitly disassociated itself from the study and its procedures, findings, and recommendations and withdrew any cooperation.[24]

In the 1960s, the regulators finally bowed to pressure from protesters, legislators, and the courts. In 1964, closed apprenticeship programs were prohibited; programs had to undertake open and publicized recruitment drives, using a variety of objective and subjective criteria by which to admit candidates. The introduction of tests made it somewhat more difficult for relatives to be guaranteed an apprentice slot, but provided no direct payoff for blacks. Instead, the main beneficiaries were those white applicants whom nepotistic barriers had previously excluded.[25]

In the post–civil rights era, regulators are specifically charged with increasing minority participation in apprenticeships, and they have tools with which to do so; nonetheless, their basic approach remains unchanged. Federal regulations require that apprenticeship sponsors develop affirmative action plans to end the underutilization of minorities and women in their programs.[26] Furthermore, federal agencies can require the apprenticeship programs to develop a plan to achieve that goal. If the agencies decide that the program is not making a good-faith effort to achieve the plan, then they can deregister the program.

Under these circumstances regulators have opted to proceed publicly with antidiscriminatory procedures, while privately maintaining business as usual. In 1978, for example, the New York State Department of Labor set the minority population percentage as the target for the minority share of apprenticeships. But these goals could be blithely ignored since the department has never mandated action or pursued enforcement remedies. While the department is mandated to conduct regular compliance reviews, these consist of semiannual reports which demonstrate that almost every program fails to comply year after year.[27] To pick a typical example, the status reports for electrical workers' Local 3 show a decline in the minority apprentice share from 27.7 percent in 1982 to 15.3 percent as of May 1989, but the department's only reaction is to note "AA [affirmative action] discussed." Hence, the years of booming enrollment for apprentices during the 1980s proved to be bad years for minority workers. Between 1980 and 1987, the percentage of new apprenticeship registrants who were black or Hispanic declined—at a time when the minority population base expanded.[28] Apprenticeship opportunities disproportionately redounded to the benefit of whites; moreover, only small numbers of minority apprentices ever completed their training. In 1986, only 140 minorities completed apprenticeship programs, in comparison to 130 who dropped out prior to completion.

But this dismal record elicited a resounding silence from the State Department of Labor. As the department's deputy commissioner admitted in public testimony before the New York City Human Rights Commission in 1991, "There have been a number of [programs] that we have called before us for corrective action, but I think fewer than two or three."[29] In fact, the department has never moved to deregister an apprenticeship program on grounds of discrimination. The only program to suffer deregistration has been a small electricians' union, affiliated with the teamsters, that engages in bitter competition with the powerful and politically well-connected electrical workers' Local 3.[30] The department also has not referred any apprenticeship program to the division of human rights or the state attorney general for legal action.[31] As for training barriers that may be discriminatory in effect, if not in intent, the department has explicitly deferred to the unions' predilections: "We do not second-guess industry representatives on what or how much is needed to fully train for the occupation. Clearly, the industry is in the best position to know what it takes to succeed in their trade."[32]

There are several explanations of why the "watchdogs" haven't watched. First, the regulators are burdened with a contradictory mandate. The charge under the Fitzgerald Act gives them the job of expanding apprenticeships, yet their responsibilities under civil rights legislation turn them from promoters into police officers. Second, the policing mandate gets in the way of bureaucratic imperatives. Expanding apprenticeships yields the by-product of great bureaucratic visibility, importance, and personnel. The number of registered programs and the closeness of apprenticeship officials to program operators are the indicators of bureaucratic success. But it is precisely these goals that may vanish if officials push for greater minority employment. The fear that industry and labor might "withdraw from, or not join in, registered apprenticeship programs" has long provided an excuse for regulators to shy away from the issue of minority apprenticeship.[33] Third, and most important, industry and labor are the regulators' constituents; and the regulators represent their constituents' views and interests. The fact that teamsters' Local 363, of all the possible choices, should have been the only program to be deregistered, testifies to just who the regulators' constituency is and how responsive they are to those constituents' views.

SUPPLY-SIDE INTERVENTIONS: THE APPRENTICESHIP OUTREACH PROGRAMS

By the late 1970s, a supply-side strategy to increase the number and improve the quality of minority applicants for apprenticeship openings had become the principal weapon in the federal attempt to open up skilled construction jobs to African-Americans. By fiscal year 1980, the last year of full government support before the Reagan administration eventually closed the program down, the Labor Department was spending over $22 million for the Targeted Outreach Program, which in turn subcontracted to local recruiting and training agencies throughout the nation.[34]

The outreach approach grew out of the protests that erupted in New York City in the early 1960s. Among the various organizations participating in the wave of job-site protests and demonstrations in 1963 was the Workers Defense League (WDL), an offshoot of the Socialist Party with strong ties to organized labor.[35] WDL officials concluded that even if apprentice openings were to be made available, finding qualified and interested black applicants would be a major difficulty; they considered recruitment and training the key. Organizationally, WDL was part of that small cadre of civil rights leaders around Bayard Rustin that called on the civil rights movement to shift "from protest to politics."[36] WDL's apprenticeship outreach program embodied the strategic implications of that new thrust. Tactically and programmatically WDL broke with strategies of confrontation. It eschewed protest; it also accepted, as one veteran of the first WDL programs noted, "not only the apprenticeship system, but all of the requirements (based within the apprenticeship law) for entrance into apprenticeship."[37] As the program's early codirectors explained to a Ford Foundation evaluator, "We simply decided that we had to live with the tests and go on from there. Confrontations have not produced any basic changes in the structures of these unions. It was not WDL's job to challenge requirements."[38]

Financial support for the WDL's outreach approach first came through a small grant from the Taconic Foundation, which provided funds to establish a modest New York City operation. But the program soon gained the eye of the broader policy community. F. Ray Marshall and Vernon Briggs, in their mid-1960s survey *The Negro and Appren-*

ticeship, conducted under a grant from the U.S. Department of Labor, recommended the outreach approach as a template for efforts in other cities. In 1967, the Labor Department and the Ford Foundation took up the suggestion, providing $287,000 and $44,000, respectively, to expand the Workers Defense League program from New York to several other cities. Over the next thirteen years, the Labor Department's spending on outreach activities grew almost twentyfold, indicating that the outreach "strategy had been selected by federal officials as the primary method through which they would encourage integration of the skilled construction trades."[39]

This capsule history of the early WDL experience suggests how to read the broader context in which government policy developed. In construction, the Democratic Party policymakers at all levels were presented with their basic dilemma in particularly raw form. On the one hand, the industry was an especially egregious and unrepentant violator of equitable hiring practices that Democratic politicians had to endorse. Construction activity was visible, public, and clearly linked to the state. The logic of African-American demands for construction jobs—that these represented one of the few sources of good-paying positions for manual laborers—was hard to resist. And much construction work took place in black ghettos—increasing the local salience of discrimination and facilitating the protest mobilization.

On the other hand, the workers and the unions were a core element of the party's constituency and one whose political muscle and level of mobilization made them difficult to ignore. George Meany's original political base came from New York plumbers' Local 2, and Meany had previously served as New York State American Federation of Labor president.[40] The president of the New York State AFL-CIO during the period was also the business agent of the New York City ironworkers' local. Harry Van Arsdale, business agent of electrical workers' Local 3, also served as president of the New York City Central Labor Council.[41] Because the construction unions were so tightly linked to the state, racial conflict on the local job site quickly spread to the national level. Thus, the controversy over the Hunts Point market engulfed not just Meany but also President Johnson, who instructed Secretary of Labor Willard Wirtz to "see what could be done."[42] The connection between the building trades and the state became even more explicit when the head of the local building-trades council moved to Washington as secretary of labor under President Nixon.

Focusing on the supply side offered a convenient, and politically acceptable, escape from the Democrats' conundrum. By seeking to modify recruitment patterns, and no more than that, government policy left the institutionalized interests of unions and management unthreatened. Whereas whites often enter unions through direct admission into journeyperson status, blacks do so only through apprenticeships. But apprenticeship serves as the training ground for the industry's key workers and supervisors, with the result that its skill demands are far more rigorous than the typical journeyperson needs. Consequently, admission standards often bear little relationship to the job requirements of the typical skilled worker.

The outreach programs also served organized labor's interests in both material and organizational respects. The program became an instrument for cementing ties to emerging black labor and community leaders. Even unions received outreach funds to initiate their own targeted strategy; in 1980, more than $2 million in government funds went to the AFL-CIO's Human Resource Development Institute to run twenty-one different local programs.[43] Federal money also provided the glue for formalizing the previously informal connections between the WDL program and the AFL-CIO. In 1967, the WDL Apprenticeship Program became the Joint Apprenticeship Program of the Workers Defense League and the A. Philip Randolph Educational Fund, an entity directed by Bayard Rustin and appropriately characterized as an AFL-CIO "front."[44]

Participation brought political dividends, as noted even in a report written by proponents of the outreach approach prepared for the Department of Labor itself: "In resisting the affirmative action policies of the federal government, the unions pointed to the [Targeted Outreach] programs as evidence of their commitment to equal employment opportunity."[45] Involvement in outreach programs helped deflect potentially far-reaching and more damaging policies, observed the black organizers and administrators of what eventually became the Targeted Outreach Program.

In a sense, the fundamental strategic vision behind the apprenticeship outreach approach caused its ultimate demise. By not seeking to effect institutional change, the outreach strategy made itself dependent on its links to external allies and *their* strength in the political arena. But with the accession of the Reagan administration, support for even as mild an affirmative action strategy as apprenticeship outreach collapsed. When the flow of federal dollars dried up, the many outreach programs closed their doors.

DEMAND-SIDE INTERVENTIONS: HIRING "PLANS," IMPOSED AND VOLUNTARY

While policymakers at the various levels of government moved ahead on the supply-side front, they were also pushed into a demand-side initiative. The outreach programs somewhat boosted the proportion of apprenticeships provided to minorities, but the *number* of apprentice slots was severely limited. Decisions about how many new apprentices are to be admitted lie entirely in the hands of construction management and labor. And vigorously expanding apprenticeship programs is one course of action that these parties are reluctant to pursue, even in the best of times. Thus, programs designed to increase total minority employment in the industry became the focus of a parallel policy track.

This track took the form of hiring plans for work done under government contract. In September 1969, the Nixon administration launched the so-called Philadelphia Plan, requiring government construction contractors to commit themselves to goals in six trades (ironworker, plumber, steamfitter, electrician, sheetmetal worker, and stationary engineer [elevator construction worker]), in which minority participation was less than 1.6 percent. This tactic preceded federally imposed plans in five other cities—Atlanta, San Francisco, Washington, D.C., St. Louis, and Camden, New Jersey. To avert a similar fate, and moved by federal persuasion and dollars, unions and contractors in seventy other localities developed "hometown" plans or negotiated hiring plans. Like the imposed plans, the hometown plans specified minority hiring goals. But these goals were agreed upon after negotiations among unions, contractors, minority groups, and local political officials. Negotiated plans met the satisfaction of officials in the Office of Federal Contract and Compliance, who saw money-saving potentials and the possibilities of greater commitment from unions and contractors as well as more administrative flexibility.

Both imposed and voluntary plans sought to directly increase minority jobs, with any gain in minority union membership coming as an added benefit. Minority workers were to be brought into the plans under a special "trainee" category. This designation qualified them for apprentice, rather than journey-level, wages, making it more attractive for employers to hire the relatively unskilled trainees. Though trainees were to work alongside union journeyworkers and apprentices, the union had no obligation to extend union status.

New York was one of the cities where a negotiated plan was hammered out, the vestiges of which still survive. The tortuous history of the New York Plan, which I shall recount in summary form, provides a lesson in the shortcomings and sources of failure that afflicted this demand-side strategy.[46]

The original New York Plan, unveiled with great fanfare in March 1970, looked like many of the other hometown plans, with one major exception—no community participation. This first plan sought to enroll 800 minority trainees to work on government-sponsored or subsidized projects.[47] Although the plan had the backing of such usually antagonistic players as New York City Mayor John Lindsay and New York State Governor Nelson Rockefeller, as well as the Building Trades Council and the U.S. Department of Labor, it soon ran into trouble.[48] It took another seven months for Rockefeller and Lindsay to agree on funding.[49] In March 1971, four unions—including the powerful electrical workers', sheetmetal workers', and plumbers' unions—announced that they would refuse to accept trainees;[50] in response, the city froze all construction work for seven months, until all but the recalcitrant sheetmetal workers relented.[51] Despite the unions' eventual compliance, relatively few trainees moved through the pipeline. Bitter opposition from civil rights and community groups yielded protests, sometimes violent, at job sites; in other instances, union workers walked off the job in disputes over minority employment. In early 1973, the plan lost Mayor Lindsay's support;[52] later that year, the mayor issued an executive order to up minority membership in construction unions to 25 percent by 1976 by insisting on a one-to-four minority ratio on all projects undertaken by contractors working on city contracts, including those funded with federal dollars. Under the new program, all contractors bidding on city work had to submit plans detailing goals and timetables for employing minority workers.[53] But this plan stumbled into powerful opposition in the form of Peter Brennan, formerly head of the local Building Trades Council, now promoted to secretary of labor by President Nixon.[54] Brennan froze all federal funds for building projects in New York City until the city returned to the New York Plan. He received support from the New York State Labor Department, whose head had been elevated from a previous job working for Harry Van Arsdale.

An incredibly complex succession of lawsuits followed. After a federal court ruled in favor of the city's new program, Brennan withdrew his opposition and, with it, federal recognition of the New York Plan.[55] The next round of the waltz pitted city against state, with the latter promulgating less stringent hiring plans for its own projects, many of them built in New York City.[56] Meanwhile, the employers' association pursued legal action against the city in state courts, on the grounds that the mayor lacked legal authority to impose goals and targets. Finally, the whole affair came to a crashing denouement: in 1976, just when the collapse of the local construction industry had made the whole matter moot, the New York State Court of Appeals ruled in favor of the employers' association, finding that the mayor had exceeded his authority in setting goals and targets in the absence of legislative consent.[57]

The training controversy then briefly lay dormant, reviving with the turnaround in the city's economy, which occurred shortly after Edward I. Koch arrived at city hall. While Koch had been the recipient of considerable African-American support in the 1977 Democratic runoff primary and in the general election as well, he was personally opposed to racially based quotas, which were prohibited under the earlier ruling of the State Court of Appeals. Koch resolved the conflict by issuing an executive order that reinstated the one-to-four ratio proposed by Lindsay, but he did not stipulate any minority membership requirement. Trainees were to be supplied by the old New York Plan for Training, which had survived by performing a similar function for New York State agencies.

But New York State's support was not to be long-lived. Prodded by the powerful electrical workers' union, which had always opposed the New York Plan,[58] the State Labor Department decided in the mid-1980s that State Labor Law 220 recognizes only two classifications of workers—apprentices and journey-level employees, *not* trainees.[59] This determination reversed the state's policy on trainees: under the new ruling, government contractors who paid trainees the apprentice-level wage were now in violation of the law and at risk of debarment from state (or municipal) work. In 1984, the State Labor Department fined five electrical contractors, *all* under contract with teamsters' electrical union Local 363, for employing trainees at the apprentice-level wage. Upon appeal, the New York State Court of Appeals ruled in 1987 that trainee programs served a "compelling policy of eradicating discrimination from our construction industry," but that the wording of State Law 220 indeed provided no legal basis for the trainee program.[60] This decision left New York State (and its municipalities) without an affirmative action program in construction—a matter that appeared not to discomfit state officials at all. As the 1990s began, the

New York Plan limped along through a loophole, providing trainees to contractors working on projects enjoying a New York City tax abatement, and therefore not directly subject to State Law 220.

Two decades of conflict have yielded few journey-level jobs for minority workers. The rationale for the training program was provision of a parallel track, yielding jobs in the here and now and union status in the future. But the number of jobs provided in the here and now has always fallen far short of the promise—no surprise, since compliance efforts have been entirely toothless.[61] Nor has the New York Plan provided any support to the generally poor, generally unskilled workers it sends out to construction sites. Some undoubtedly do pick up a trade, but many are assigned "go-fer" jobs by contractors who are mainly interested in "checkerboarding"—moving the same black workers from job to job in order to meet government hiring goals. Consequently, the New York Plan has added few craftworkers to the union rolls: of the 5,000 trainees it placed on jobs between 1971 and 1988, only 800 were ever accepted into the unions.[62] Even that number is probably too high, since some of these trainees were already apprentices who were registered as trainees so that they could be counted toward the trainee goal on city and state jobs.

The history of the New York Plan is the story of an opportunity squandered. In the conflict over directly swelling minority jobs, protest groups and civil rights organizations never had a real chance. From the start, the unions and contractors froze them out, pushing them to the sidelines where they could picket, demonstrate, and slowly melt away.

By contrast, the unions exercised persistent influence through the allies they controlled at higher levels. At an early stage in the conflict, Peter Brennan (head of the New York Building Trades Council, then secretary of labor) played a crucial role in delaying the start of the New York Plan. Brennan signaled to building-trades unions throughout the country to dig in their heels further. In the 1980s the New York State Department of Labor, in response to pressure from the electrical workers, successfully moved in court against the New York Plan, leaving New York State without any training or affirmative action program in construction at all. Unlike the political leaders, the union leaders had the staying power and commitment to see their goals through. Long after Rockefeller and Lindsay were gone from the political scene, the union officials remained in place.

As of the early 1990s, Tommy Van Arsdale, Harry's son, was business agent of Local 3 and head of the New York City Central Labor Council; Edward Cleary, Van Arsdale's former right-hand man, headed the state AFL-CIO; and Peter Brennan remained entrenched in the Building Trades Council. With time, the underlying interest of public officials and building bureaucrats also came to the fore: find enough nonwhite bodies for the work sites to get the projects built. As I was told by a high state official, "Why pick on the construction industry to solve society's problems?" Why indeed?

COURT-IMPOSED REMEDIES

The building-trades unions have played a prominent role in employment discrimination litigation, to which New York's construction unions have made a particularly distinguished contribution. Numerous actions were brought against New York locals in federal courts, including steamfitters' Local 638, sheetmetal workers' Local 28, wire lathers' Local 46, ironworkers' Locals 40 and 580, operating engineers' Locals 14 and 15, elevator constructors' Local 1, and Local 3, International Brotherhood of Electrical Workers.[63] Of all these cases, the sheetmetal workers' is perhaps the most notorious; it highlights not only the crafts' tenacious resistance to integration but also the nexus between formal and informal training systems in impeding minority access to construction jobs.

In 1948 the New York State Commission against Discrimination ordered Local 28 to desist from "executing and/or maintaining constitutional or by-law provisions which exclude Negroes."[64] The "Caucasian only" clause was removed from the union's constitution, but fifteen years later no progress had been made: not a single African-American worker had been admitted into membership. In 1963, a black U.S. Air Force veteran initiated a complaint against Local 28 with the state civil rights agency. On March 4, 1964, the commission ruled that Local 28 had "automatically excluded" blacks during the entire seventy-eight years of the union's existence, in violation of the State Law against Discrimination. When Local 28 refused to comply with this order, the commission took the local to court. Later that year, the State Supreme Court upheld the commission's action and ordered the adoption of a new set of admission standards. Two years later, the New York State Supreme Court issued a restraining order against Local 28 when it rejected the results of a test for admission into the union-controlled apprenticeship program, because, according to the union, blacks received "phenomenally" high scores.

In 1971, the federal government began action in district court, with New York City and New York State joining as plaintiffs. Following a trial in 1975, the court found against the union on several counts: (1) the union had adopted discriminatory selection procedures, including the use of union funds to subsidize special training sessions for friends and relatives of union members taking the apprenticeship examination; (2) it had restricted the size of its members, refusing to administer journeyworkers' examinations despite demands from the Contractors' Association;[65] (3) it had instead called in pensioners and permit holders from other locals all over the country but never admitted workers from a heavily nonwhite local in New York City; (4) and it had selectively organized nonunion sheetmetal shops with few, if any, minority workers and only extended union status to white employees. The district court then established a membership goal for the local of 29 percent, to be met by 1981, and empowered an administrator to devise and implement a recruitment and admissions program. Noting that the 29 percent goal had not been met, the city and the state sued the local for contempt in 1982; the district court imposed a $150,000 fine on the local. In 1983, the city brought a second contempt proceeding, which led to a 1983 district court ruling affirming the administrator's proposed "Employment, Training, and Recruitment Fund." This fund, designed to pay for special services for minority apprentices, was to be financed by the $150,000 fine imposed by the court as well as by an additional payment of 2 cents for each hour worked by a journeyperson or apprentice. In approving the administrator's plan, the district court also extended the deadline for the 29 percent minority membership goal to August 1987; imposed a quota of three minority apprentices for every one apprentice; and required that the Joint Apprenticeship Committee assign one apprentice to every four journeyworkers. When the union appealed this ruling to the Supreme Court, the court upheld the lower court's ruling and finally put an end to this tortuous history.[66]

The importance of this case extends beyond its obvious legal significance. In searching for remedies to discrimination, the courts and their officials provided confirmation for my basic argument: to undo discrimination, it was not sufficient to make changes in the formal training system. Despite a court-appointed administrator empowered to increase the number of minority apprentices, minority enrollment in the program was difficult to sustain because the minority apprentices lacked access to the informal support system.

> The [minority] kids don't know tool recognition. They're thrown out on the job site and can't get a tool if asked for. That sets up conflict and confrontations right from the start. There's a racist aspect on the job site when non-tool recognition occurs. If a white kid doesn't know, the foreman will explain. If the guy is black, the foreman sees a dummy, impairing the job. We're still finding in the regular apprenticeship group a high number of whites with relatives in the trade. They're already going in there knowing the tools and the names of people on the job sites. They've got a leg up from day one.[67]

The particulars of the sheetmetal case magnified the importance of these connections: the trade is highly decentralized, with the largest shop employing only 180 people and the smallest employing only 1 mechanic; the typical minority apprentice was likely to work with few other minorities and in considerable isolation from counterparts in other shops; and workers had to find jobs on their own, without assistance from a hiring hall. To remedy these problems, the court-appointed administrator established a surrogate skills-training and support system, organized around a tutorial and counseling program financed by federal job-training monies as well as the court-imposed fines.[68]

There is a further lesson to be drawn from the sheetmetal case. When faced with the most egregious forms of employment discrimination, state-supported efforts at integration may eventually overcome the informal and formal power nexus in the union system. The key words are "eventually" and "may." It took almost forty years for white workers in the sheetmetal workers' union to desist. The record of other litigations provides scant encouragement: where the unions choose not to be as provocative as the sheetmetal workers, draconian measures can usually be averted. Even severe penalties and the imposition of administrative oversight, such as placing control over a hiring hall in the hands of a court-appointed administrator, may not be sufficient to override the workings of the informal system. And those unions that prolonged their resistance into the 1980s found that time was not an enemy but a friend. With the advent of the Reagan administration, monitoring the behavior of construction unions under consent decrees no longer took high priority.

The Continuing Significance of Race

If the employment problems of African-Americans result from a mismatch of their skills with the job requirements of urban employers, then construction should be one industry with plenty of black workers. As this chapter shows, the construction industry has many jobs requiring little schooling but few African-American workers. That the mismatch prediction should be so wrong on this count leads naturally to the question of why. The answer, I suggest, lies in a theoretical error in the skills-mismatch framework.

The essential work is undoubtedly Wilson's controversial *Declining Significance of Race* (1978). Most of the debate has focused on the status of Wilson's empirical claims, and not on the theoretical synthesis he forged. This is an important omission, since the synthesis provides Wilson's explanation of why class, rather than race, mainly influences the life chances of African-Americans. Wilson follows Edna Bonacich's theory of a split labor market in ascribing racial conflict to a competitive struggle between two groups with different wage norms.[69] As "low-priced" labor willing to work at rates well below the rates acceptable to whites, blacks lend themselves to employers' efforts to "undercut the white labor force by hiring cheaper black labor." Thus, fear of wage competition fuels white workers' antagonism toward blacks.

According to Wilson's argument, the expansion of the state into labor market regulation altered these racial dynamics. By protecting unions, the New Deal sharply diminished the competitive threat posed by cheaper African-American labor. Because employers had previously recruited blacks into the mass production industries, unions also had to include blacks in their organizing drives. Passage of equal employment legislation forced employers to equalize pay for black and white workers in similar jobs, further reducing the incentive to use African-Americans as cheap labor. Therefore, in the present period, "the structural relations between blacks and whites in the labor market have significantly reduced racial confrontations over jobs . . . virtually eliminating the tendency of employers to create a split labor market, in which black labor is deemed cheaper than white labor regardless of the work performed, the market that provided so much of the antagonism during the earlier years of the period of industrial race relations."[70]

Wilson's argument implies that racial conflict over construction jobs should have significantly declined. Institutional arrangements such as collective bargaining or prevailing wage requirements insulate the industry's labor market from straightforward wage competition. The continuing centrality of skills that are acquired on the job means that the skilled elite of electricians, plumbers, sheetmetal workers, and others have no worry that unskilled workers might displace them.

Even where collective bargaining might not protect white workers from the threat of wage competition, there is no evidence to suggest that construction employers could find blacks who would be willing to work for less than whites. The theory of a split labor market attributes a "low-priced" orientation to a group's status as migrants, recently recruited from less-developed societies. As Bonacich notes, compared to current immigrants, African-Americans now belong to the class of "high-priced" labor, having "rejected the sweatshop as had white workers before them." One therefore rarely hears the complaint that blacks are potential strikebreakers who are pushing wages down; the view more commonly expressed is that blacks, like whites before them, "are unwilling to work under rough conditions for low wages."[71]

Thus, "structural conditions" in construction contain the conditions for discrimination's demise. And yet the case study shows that conflict between whites and African-Americans cannot be collapsed to wage competition, as Wilson contends. In this industry, where outsiders pose little threat to the wages of established groups, racial conflicts revolve around the allocation of scarce jobs. Established groups have an enduring interest in restricting hiring to the members of incumbents' core networks, even if outsider groups share the prevailing wage norms.

Construction's position in the job hierarchy maintains that interest, with construction wages in New York ranking among the highest in the country, first for ironworkers, second for carpenters, and third for electricians and laborers. In good times and bad, the building trades enjoy a plentiful supply of new recruits. In 1978, when the industry had badly slumped, 1,000 people camped out for five days in front of the electricians' union hall in order to receive apprenticeship applications.[72] A decade later, when employment boomed, the electricians' union received an annual average of over 4,000 applications for approximately 500 apprenticeship slots a year between 1986 and 1989. Whites dominated the electricians' applicant pool, with 4 whites to every 1 nonwhite applicant.[73]

With little slackening in whites' attachment to construction's high-paying manual jobs, the advent of African-American protest in the 1960s sparked a competitive conflict over job allocation that has continued to this day. Historically, exclusion resulted from the formal and informal arrangements which connect craftworkers to one another and their employers and through which construction workers and their unions control access to the trade. But those practices came under intense scrutiny in the 1960s, as blacks began agitating for access to skilled, unionized trades. Although white dominance was rooted in informal processes, government was a potentially important player, owing to its role as a consumer of construction services and the prevailing wage policies it used when awarding contracts. Racial conflict at construction sites activated this latent influence: by the mid-1960s, shifts in the power of African-American protesters relative to white-dominated construction unions led governments at various levels to open up apprenticeship programs and impose minority hiring goals on public jobs.

Though thirty years of protest over discrimination in construction have produced progress, the gains are disappointing and severe barriers remain in place. To the extent that African-Americans made inroads into the union sector, they did so under conditions of intense community mobilization and alliances to other white interest groups and actors.

The conditions that produced black influence over public policies did not last long. A 1969 survey of New Yorkers' racial attitudes convinced one major pollster that "a potential explosion could take place in the building trades area."[74] Not surprisingly, local government remained acutely sensitive to African-American demands for construction jobs: after seventeen demonstrators had been arrested in a melee at a plumbers' work site in 1974, the *New York Times* wrote that "the dispute over hiring of more members of minority groups has grown into a major crisis for the (new) Beame administration."[75] By 1976, however, building in New York City had virtually come to a halt; when construction resumed on a large scale in the early 1980s, controversy never really reignited. Mayor Koch did revive the New York Plan, though it now applied a hiring ratio for low-income residents of any ethnic background and was used for government-subsidized projects only. For a brief while, Koch felt impelled to maintain a special Mayor's Office on Construction Industry Relations, but concern about continuing political support from the building-trades unions soon led him to shut that office's doors. Occasional violent clashes engulfed construction sites, but contractors usually worked out hiring arrangements with community groups to ensure peace. The 1987 report of the Mayor's Commission on Black New Yorkers called on the city to open community hiring halls—thus resurrecting a long-held demand of African-American protest groups—but the election of New York's first African-American mayor in 1989 left city policy unchanged. In 1991, when African-American protest groups and minority contractors organized a coalition, they could do little more than appeal to state and city officials to enforce the laws already on the books.

Even those policies that originally emerged in response to black protest involved instruments that were far blunter and less powerful than what the protesters had sought. As I have argued, the nexus between the unions and the state shaped the policy matrix in construction. On the one hand, the unions' and the industry's dependence on the state made civil rights policy in construction an intensely political affair: in this context, as the only component of the industry in which hiring and training were institutionalized, the union sector was the only actor on which policy instruments could be brought to bear. On the other hand, the unions were themselves highly political entities, embedded in the political parties, and with long-established strategies for controlling those state policies that affected the industry. The history of affirmative action policies in construction bears witness to the unions' ability to control those policies to meet their ultimate ends.

Discrimination and the Ethnic Niche

To contend, as I have, that African-American exclusion from construction jobs reflects black-white power differences, begs the question of why blacks had as little power as they did. The example of other outsider groups that have successfully circumvented discriminatory barriers helps answer that query.

In construction, the apposite comparison involves Jews in the first few decades of the twentieth century. Although many Jews had been in building in Eastern Europe, the Irish-dominated construction unions kept them out of road-building and large-scale construction projects in New York. Consequently, Jewish builders and craftworkers, as the Committee on Economic Adjustment noted in 1937, were "typically active in smaller developments rather than in construction of large apartments and office buildings."[76] Conflict suffused Jewish-gentile relations in the lower-paying alteration trades: when Jewish painters held a citywide strike just before World War I, rival non-Jewish construction unions "sent scabs to undermine the struggle of the alteration workers."[77] While the gentile and the Jewish unions in the alteration trades learned to live with one another, confinement to smaller projects and alteration jobs had another, perhaps more important effect: it taught Jewish painters, glaziers, and carpenters how to run and manage older buildings.[78] These skills, in turn, allowed Jewish craftworkers to buy and run their own buildings; the growth and dispersion of the Jewish population spurred these new landlords to develop new real estate. Jewish builders put up large sections of Brooklyn and the Bronx, as well as the garment center constructed in the mid-1920s in midtown Manhattan, providing work to a cadre of Jewish craftworkers.[79] Thus, the Jewish ethnic economy furnished a protected market for Jewish contractors, who in turn hired Jewish employees, notwithstanding Irish dominance over most of the building-trades unions. Confronted with a growing population of Jewish workers who had found a way into the trades, the unions swallowed their ethnic dislikes and relaxed the criteria they used to control entry.

Business provided Jews with a strategic platform for niche expansion: as Jewish employers hired co-ethnic workers, the power differential shifted in ways that weakened exclusionary pressures. By contrast, the dismal state of black construction businesses has meant heightened black vulnerability to discrimination.

Over the long term, discrimination has eroded the base of potentially skilled African-American workers. Marshall and Briggs contended in the early 1960s that black workers "have often not applied for apprenticeship openings . . . Civil rights and union leaders have been surprised at the apathy shown by Negro youngsters toward apprenticeship programs even when they had a chance to get in."[80] But this characterization probably underestimated the elan and drive created by the protests of the day. At the time, the Workers Defense League accepted the entry criteria required by the construction trades, a decision that inevitably led to a "creaming" strategy oriented toward minority applicants who were best qualified and most likely to pass written and practical exams. Creaming was a viable approach as long as the protest organizations could mobilize a population of highly selective, potential recruits, as in the case of one of the first African-American entrants into the sheetmetal workers' union: "In the early sixties, I was involved in the civil rights movement, starting in high school. At one point Bayard [Rustin] said we'll need some people to take these [construction] jobs. I was in Community College at the time. I took a pre-test in 1963; I then took the Local 28 test. I didn't need any tutoring: I was always good in math and did very well in the test." Even if the rank-and-file black applicants did not make up quite as selective a group, the "dropouts of the period were different," as a former official in the WDL program recalls: "The dropouts in the sixties were functioning at ninth-grade level and could read. The kids didn't know math because they had had four to five teachers a year and never got to algebra. But they had basic arithmetic skills. Dropouts is really a misnomer. We ran a program in which we said, we'll give you nothing for free. You've got to work your ass off. Got to commit for six days a week. The kids came for long hours, for two months."

The few training programs still in business as of the late 1980s had a very different experience to report. Minority youth expressing serious interest in going into construction were difficult to find. Having few connections to the industry, they lacked the familiarity with the trade that would breed interest; and knowledgeable about the prospect of discrimination, they were deterred by the prospects of receiving relatively low apprentice wages for the first two, if not three, years of a four-year program.[81] Although vocational programs in construction can be found in over thirty of New York City's high schools, most programs were severely underenrolled when I surveyed them in 1988. As school officials saw it, there was little interest in preparing for a career in the building trades. One source told me that "the parents of today's youth and youngsters themselves don't look for careers in construction: everybody's charging head on into computers"; and most of the officials I contacted felt that the building-trades programs did poorly in the competition with more technologically advanced programs. Not surprisingly, a Brooklyn-based social service program, oriented toward low-income young adults, registered better success in attracting a sizable applicant pool for its heavily subsidized construction jobs. But if these low-skilled recruits found construction jobs appealing, they began the process with several strikes against them, as one counselor explained:

> We try to *convert* them by supplying them with the proper skills for being economically independent. We're dealing with high school dropouts. We try not to get rid of them. We try to take someone hanging

out on the corner and make him a taxpayer, not a dependent. The kids are economically disadvantaged. Many are fathers, some with a history of drug abuse; others are ex-offenders. We take a counseling approach. You're dealing with people off on the wrong foot already, so you can't expect to have the cream of the crop; they wouldn't be eligible. These kids' success in construction is dependent on luck and their ability to give a good impression, because it is an extremely competitive industry in which these minority dropouts are at the bottom of the barrel.[82]

Even in the sheetmetal program, where the administrator had the power to install three minorities for every one white applicant and had substantial training resources at his disposal, he found that "we're not drawing the same pool as twenty years ago." On the one hand, the type of highly selective applicant available during the civil rights era now enjoyed better alternatives: "We had an experience three years ago where the union recruited three of the top twenty minority guys from the city's best vocational school. We accepted five or six, but only one came in. The top three guys were given scholarships to the . . . Institute of Technology." On the other hand, "if the goal is to find an economically disadvantaged native New Yorker who can do the ninth-grade math needed to get into the trade, it's awfully hard": "In 1991, we tested 250 people for our training program test. Less than one-quarter have been able to pass the math test. This has been consistent over the past couple of years." The training programs were by no means unique in their reports of problems on the recruitment front; as we shall see in Chapter 8, African-American building contractors recorded the identical complaint.

If black New Yorkers registered little progress in finding construction jobs during the years of the city's building boom, immigrants did considerably better. The newcomers with the best prospects, naturally enough, were Irish immigrants (part of the new wave of emigration that began in the 1980s), who were able to mobilize contacts with the industry's core work force. True, even these workers found the going tough. Those with "hard-to-find skills and with good union contacts" gained access to high-paid jobs in the unionized sector, as ethnographer Mary Corcoran found; their less fortunate counterparts moved into the nonunion, informal sector. However they made their route into the trades, by the late 1980s, no one could mistake the enhanced Irish profile in construction; the reports from my own contacts were entirely consistent with Corcoran's claim that the majority of Irish illegals had found work in the construction sector.[83] But the Irish made up only one—at that, relatively small—component of the new foreign-born presence. Black, Hispanic, and even Asian immigrants streamed into construction; whereas African-American representation levels in the building trades sank after 1970, the newcomers saw representation levels grow. Caribbean immigrants became particularly important players, as I shall discuss in Chapter 8.[84] For now, suffice it to say that a combination of factors—relevant skills, exposure, contacts, and a predisposition toward a type of work that was not so different from what many of the newcomers had done before—facilitated the immigrant influx. As my contacts in the sheetmetal program told me, "We're now seeing more recent immigrants," and those new arrivals were far better equipped to succeed than the minority youth whom the program sought to attract. "We're now seeing Eastern Europeans with master's degrees applying. NYANA [the agency working with Russian Jewish refugees] always has half a dozen guys with air conditioning background. We hired two Pakistanis as apprentices for the sheetmetal program last month. The group that is passing our test has quite a few immigrants; of the twenty people we accepted in our last cycle, about ten were foreign-born."

By contrast, the supply of African-American workers seeking skilled construction jobs falls short, even while native-born, white ethnics remain attached to the trades, a development that can be interpreted in light of my earlier argument about the ethnic niche. Construction became an ethnic niche for successive waves of white immigrants and their descendants, who, once entrenched in the industry, succeeded in using both informal and formal means to exclude blacks. Discrimination impelled African-Americans to look elsewhere for jobs; once the public sector emerged as the principal locus of black employment, black concentration in the public sector undermined the skills base, motivation, and connections needed to move into alternative specializations. Thus, while civil rights organizations succeeded in mobilizing protesters for demonstrations at job sites, they have yet to produce an African-American labor supply that seriously threatens the source of white craftworkers' job control. As in the other components of New York's economy, the newest immigrants have begun to exploit the opportunities associated with ethnic succession—a development unlikely to help African-Americans in their quest for good jobs.

7 | The Ethnic Politics of Municipal Jobs

Government employment offers the one bright light in the generally dim jobs scene for blacks: the public sector now stands as the largest, highest-quality employer of African-Americans. In 1990, one out of every four employed blacks held a government job; close to half of the country's African-American civil servants worked on municipal payrolls.[1] Blacks hold a much higher share of upper level jobs in the public than in the private sector; discrimination exerts a less powerful influence on public sector employees than on their private sector counterparts; and the public sector seems to act as a ladder of mobility into the middle class for blacks more than for whites.[2]

The contrasting trajectory of private and public urban employers puts questions about the politics of jobs back into the broader debate about minority employment. Simple skill-based sorting processes cannot explain why African-American overrepresentation in municipal employment almost everywhere exceeds parity, with more than 30 percent of employed blacks in the largest cities working in the public sector. Moreover, the educational requirements of government work preclude the possibility that government has become a black niche because its jobs demand low skills. In 1990, for example, New York's typical black municipal worker was far better schooled than his or her private sector counterpart, and the African-American concentration in the public sector professions was particularly strong.

The circumstances of African-American entry into city jobs also stand at variance with the skills-mismatch point of view. Black penetration of municipal government came at the cost of intense and persistent conflict, often through the imposition of quotas and hiring targets. Conflict suggests that interests, not just neutral job requirements, limit the potential for black employment gains. Since the occurrence of conflict over black employment in city jobs varies across functions, its intensity and incidence tell us when and under what conditions racial shifts in employment occur.

But the story of black employment in the public sector is not simply a story about blacks alone. Moving into public employment has been an ethnic mobility strategy since the mid-nineteenth century. Although the changing ethnic profile of city workers suggests a game of musical chairs, transitions have been abrupt, not gradual, and marked by alternating tendencies toward inclusion and exclusion. Successful machine building in the late nineteenth century led the Irish to dominance over city jobs, though WASP efforts at civil service reform contested Irish control.[3] By the 1920s, Irish dominance was threatened by immigrants from southern and Eastern Europe and their children, who swept into the public sector on the heels of the New Deal.[4] With the onset of the civil rights movement, blacks and other minority groups began clamoring for their share of city jobs. Passage of the Equal Employment Opportunity Act of 1972, which extended Title VII of the 1964 Civil Rights Act to public employers, gave hope that local government might once again be a direct lever of ethnic mobility, as it was in days gone by.[5] But for which ethnic group? African-Americans entered the 1990s as the dominant player in the public sector job game; their conflicts with Hispanics point to continuity in the cycle of ethnic competitive jockeying that dates back over a century.

This chapter provides a case study of the ethnic politics of municipal jobs in the New York City government, from the 1890s to the 1990s. As we shall see, interethnic conflict has focused on the rules of access and promotion, with each phase yielding a change in the structure of employment protecting incumbents and impinging on the prospects of the newest entrants. As with other ethnic groups, the African-American concentration in government fits into a complex organizational matrix, molded over time and evolving in tandem with the changing interests of diverse parties.

Making the Patronage System

By the end of the nineteenth century, government employment had become one of a series of arenas over which traditional WASP elites and immigrant competitors struggled for control. New York's growing economic and ethnic heterogeneity undermined the traditional pattern of elite control, and provided "contenders for office with an incentive to mobilize new voters into the electorate."[6] Through patronage the Tammany Society mobilized votes and consolidated support, allowing it to structure the city's employment system in ways that maximized benefits for the political machine. As Wibur Rich argues, "the Tammany-controlled departments were labor-incentive organizations, which had the flexibility to respond to an unstable marketplace."[7] In the pre–civil service city, transactions between various city departments and the public were conducted without records, files, or transcripts; workers were assigned according to experience and could rely on receiving job preferences as long as the needs of the machine were met. Sponsorship was crucial for entry and mobility, with workers given no promise of security. The use of temporary day laborers was an essential and deliberate employment strategy, enabling the machine to keep its visibility high in immigrant communities. By the 1870s, one out of every eight New York voters was on a local payroll.[8]

The machine's hold on local government met opposition from WASP reformers, whose antagonism toward immigrants old and new was fed by cultural conflict as well as economic interests that were threatened by the machine's depredatory ways. Reformers sought to break the machine's power by severing the link between political activity and government employment. The institution of civil service ranked high on the reformers' list of priorities, not just for ideological reasons but also because it provided a means for undermining Tammany Hall's base of support and institutionalizing a new class of employees and positions. By imposing entrance standards, by testing applicants for fitness, and by reorganizing government procedures, reformers sought to achieve two goals at once: attract native-born middle-class recruits for a professionalized government service; and reduce the machine's ability to influence who got into government and, once inside, got ahead.

Despite eventuating in an 1883 statewide civil service law, which established a municipal civil service commission, reform efforts were of little avail. On the one hand, control over the mechanisms of entry and promotion never really eluded Tammany Hall's grasp. The city continued hiring workers to many positions that did not require exams, leaving a substantial number of jobs embedded in the patronage system. For those jobs technically accessible through formal exams only, the politically connected enjoyed a decisive edge. Only insiders had good access to opportunities, as the Civil Service Commission rarely posted notices of job openings.[9] Tammany-linked cram schools, which prepped job seekers for essay exams graded by Irish examiners, held a virtual stranglehold on the flow of applicants to the Irish fiefdoms in police and fire, "training" most of the applicants and almost all of the successful candidates.[10] Such bureaucratic pressure groups as the Civil Service Forum, which served as an adjunct of the Democratic Party, provided privileged access to the decisions of the Civil Service Commission.[11] And the commission maintained a loose classification system, giving politicians considerable discretion over employee salaries.[12]

On the other hand, the Irish encountered few effective competitors for city jobs. As Robert Fogelson's analysis of that classic Irish niche—the police—shows, WASPs never seriously threatened to dislodge the Irish.[13] Notwithstanding the episodic efforts of reformers like Theodore Roosevelt, the number of native applicants was small; few of them were interested in public service; and even fewer were attracted to police work. The increasingly numerous Poles, Jews, Italians, and others who were just off the boat had little chance of doing well in essay-type exams against the Irish, who were, after all, native English speakers. Consequently, the introduction of a civil service system had the opposite of its intended effect—increasing the opportunities for the Irish.

The Irish made the most of those opportunities and by the turn of the century had already established dominance in public employment, as can be seen from data in the census of 1900. On an index of representation, in which a score of 1 for an occupation equals a group's share of employment in the total economy, Irish men scored 1.74 among government officials and 2.36 among policemen and firemen, higher than British men, who shared the same linguistic advantage (1.12 and 0.91, respectively), and towering above the newly arrived Russian Jews and Italians (each with identical scores of .01 and .15, among police- and firemen, respectively).[14]

As long as city government stayed small, Irish dominance yielded relatively few jobs. The years following the turn of the century saw a major expansion in New York's role as employer—eclipsing the employment potential attained even in the Tammany system's earlier period of unhindered patronage. The consolidation of the five boroughs in 1897 brought Tammany Hall a windfall of 20,000 new patronage jobs. Thereafter local government grew substantially, especially at the lower, blue-collar levels, thanks to investment in large-scale public works. "Thousands of unskilled and semi-skilled Irish," notes Stephen Erie, "took jobs in [New York City's] municipally owned subways, street railways, waterworks, and port facilities."[15] Erie estimates that municipally owned utilities accounted for over one-half of Irish public sector jobs in New York City between 1900 and 1930, with employment in the city's expanding police and fire departments accounting for another 21 percent. Irish employment in New York City government almost quadrupled during these years, increasing from just under 20,000 to 77,000, while the total number of city workers climbed from 54,000 to 148,000, less than a factor of three.[16]

The liabilities of the new immigrants lasted hardly a generation; with the Jews' rapid educational and occupational advancement, another competitor entered the scene. By 1912, as one contemporary journalist wrote in *McClure's*, the Jews were "rapidly driving out the Irish, the Germans, and the native Americans. . . The Jews study hard and long, and their examination papers are so immeasurably superior to the average offered by representatives of other races that they invariably secure preferred places."[17] But as long as the Irish, through Tammany Hall's grip over city government, could control municipal hiring, interethnic competition posed little threat. To begin with, competition was structured in such a way as to minimize the value of Jews' educational advantages. Improved qualifications for government employment had ranked high on the agenda of the efficiency experts, social scientists, and social workers who made up an important component of the city's "reform vanguard." But the reform program made little headway. The Civil Service Commission increasingly emphasized experience over education. It imposed few absolute educational qualifications, issued exams at irregular intervals, and ensured that tests included only material directly relevant to the duties to be performed. These changes gave the cram schools a continuing, strategic role and postponed appointments until two or three years after an exam had been held.[18]

Moreover, the patronage system functioned unencumbered, throughout the period of Tammany control, between 1917 and 1933. In 1920 city hall had almost 23,400 positions to which it could hire its preferred candidates without exams; by the end of the decade, the city had added another 10,000 noncompetitive positions, falling under Tammany Hall's sway.[19] As late as 1933, barely half of the city's work force was chosen by competitive exams; the magistrate and municipal courts appointed clerks without relying on civil service lists; 6,000 jobs on the locally owned Independent subway lines, almost 30,000 laboring jobs, and 11,000 positions for orderlies, untrained nurses, and scrubwomen were filled at the mayor's discretion—or more appropriately, at the whims of his political mentors.[20] Some portion of this patronage could be handed out to the newcomers, without endangering core Irish support, thanks to the overall growth of government. Conditions in the rapidly expanding schools, which hired an additional 9,000 teachers between 1903 and 1925, made it easy to ladle out relatively attractive jobs to Jews, who were also helped by changes in certification procedures as well as stepped-up educational requirements. But Tammany Hall did not abandon its gatekeeping role: as one historian noted, "the Board of Examiners regularly penalized Jewish applicants for certification if their speech was Yiddish-accented."[21] The Irish made sure to retain the very best positions: in a city where Jewish students made up almost half the school population, only one of the thirty high school principals was Jewish.[22] Still, the Jews enjoyed benefits as junior partners in the Tammany system, as Erie argues; the Italians did less well, confined to jobs as garbage collectors, street cleaners, and laborers on the politically sensitive docks.

Making the Civil Service System

The depression brought these harmonious arrangements to an end. Fiscal stringency forced Tammany-led city hall to prune city employment—with the bulk of the cuts borne by teachers and social workers, whose ranks were disproportionately filled by Jews. LaGuardia's election in 1933 delivered the coup de grace.

LaGuardia's own political imperatives pushed him to restructure the competition for government jobs in ways that favored the Jews. Keeping control of city hall required that he undermine the material base of Tammany Hall's power and consolidate his support among groups not firmly under the machine's tow—the most important of which, the Jews, had split between LaGuardia and his Tammany opponent in 1933.[23] Both goals could be accomplished in the same way, namely, by giving the green light to the administrative changes long championed by the reform vanguard, which played a crucial part in LaGuardia's coalition.

As Wallace Sayre and Herbert Kaufman observed, the reformers used "the Civil Service Commission to exclude the party organizations from any influence upon the appointment, promotion, and tenure of city employees."[24] In detaching public employment from the influence of political actors, the reformers transformed the entire structure of competition for government jobs. Their strategy proceeded along several fronts. First, they took over old Tammany preserves. They transferred labor positions from the noncompetitive to the competitive class, with 12,000 in the Department of Sanitation alone, another 10,000 in the municipal hospitals, and an entirely new, competitive classification created for skilled workers. They whittled down the ranks of provisional workers from 13,530 in 1938 to just over 3,000 in 1940 by transferring the home relief division of the city's welfare office, which had been set up on an emergency, appointive basis. By obliging incumbents to take the appropriate exams, the commission overhauled their ranks, as the exams winnowed out as many as 90 percent of the workers in some occupational categories, with one-third of those in the professional social service category failing. By the end of 1939, 90,000 workers had been brought into competitive positions, accounting for three-quarters of the city's payroll and up from 58 percent in 1933.[25]

Second, the reformers limited entry portals to the bottom and established career lines for promotion through the ranks. They restructured access to the vast array of basic clerical functions, establishing the high school graduation or its equivalent as a prerequisite for entry-level jobs, closed the next grade to open competition, and raised the third grade to college graduates only. The commission made "filling higher positions by promotion examination . . . a prime objective," creating an administrative service for jobs paying more than $3,000.[26] Increasingly, the commission sought to fill the highest jobs through exams, attempting at one point to bring the entire staff of the Department of Water Supply, Gas, and Electricity into the competitive civil service up to and including the post of commissioner.[27]

Third, the reformers established new criteria for hiring and promotion. Long critical of the traditional techniques that "ignore[d] or even indirectly penalize[d], the training embodied in public education," they raised the entrance requirements for examinations, changed the relative weights given to the evaluation of experience and education, and increased the educational content of tests.[28]

The depression provided the labor market conditions under which this strategy could be successfully pursued. In contrast to conditions at the turn of the century, when reformers could entice few highly qualified applicants to the government jobs they wished to transform, mass joblessness made public employment attractive. And the reformers avidly grasped this opportunity. As the civil service commissioner noted at the end of the war: "In the years of depression . . . the Commissioner's general policy was to take advantage of the existing labor market and to encourage many well-trained citizens seeking employment to enter City service."[29] Moreover, the city's work force had been upgraded during the 1920s, as a result of longer school attendance.[30] With the ranks of the unemployed filled with high school graduates, as well as a large number of persons who had spent at least some time in the city's burgeoning public college sector, circumstances were ripe for restricting employment to persons who met the reformers' desired criteria.

The transition to the new civil service regime took the route of replacing experience by educational qualifications. The commission's 1937 report enunciated its basic policy:

> There is no way in which the Commission can test in 4 or 5 hours what a college or high school faculty can test in 4 or more years, no matter how expert the Commission may become. Not only is the area of civil service testing definitely limited but certain factors cannot be summarily tested. Diligence and application, patience and perseverance are vital elements of character for all public servants which can hardly be measured in a limited test. But if a candidate has done well over a 4 hour test in school, it means that he has these qualifications. To secure them, this Commission must rely heavily on education.[31]

The commission lowered the maximum age for nearly all positions, especially in the labor class, so that the "city can have the benefit of the longest possible period of useful service from trained employees."[32] In 1934 and 1935, the commission raised requirements in favor of additional training for 34 of the 110 position titles and grades for which examinations were given.[33] The 1936 exam for social investigator in the home relief bureau required a college degree, where previously no college education had been required, and it set the experience equivalent at a maximum of four years. The commission provided further incentives to highly educated job seekers, by adding educational credits to scores in examinations for positions like chemist, lawyer, and even police officer, a decision that proved highly controversial.[34] And it allowed education to be accepted in partial ful-fillment of experience requirements.

In sum, the reformers revamped the structure of competition—which they also encouraged by embarking on a vigorous recruitment campaign, with special efforts focused on the high schools and col-leges. Made hungry for jobs by the depression, competitors arrived in droves. In 1933, under Tammany dominance, 6,327 individuals ap-plied for government jobs; six years later, 250,000 job seekers knocked at the municipal service's door. Openings in just one city agency, the newly competitive Welfare Department, attracted 100,000 test takers in 1939. The search for upward mobility through civil service also accelerated, as applications for promotional exams climbed from 6,270 in 1935 to 26,847 in 1939.[35]

Whether or not the depression allowed the city to "command the best personnel available for public service," as the reformers con-tended, it clearly furnished government with its most highly educated work force ever. One night in 1938 5,000 men waited in line till day-break to apply for a porter's job: among the first 500, nearly 40 percent had attended high school and 10 percent were high school graduates.[36] The commission pointed to the results of the 1938 patrol officers' exam, which attracted 30,000 test takers, as evidence that its "positive recruiting program has shown impressive results":[37] the top 200 men who headed the new police list had an average of three years college education, with 12 percent possessing professional training. The next year, more than 85,000 men applied for the sanitation labor jobs that had been transferred to the competitive service, among whom were "an unusual number [of] college graduates and a few [with] post grad-uate degrees."[38]

The new structure of competition displaced those who had previ-ously enjoyed privileged access to city jobs—namely, the Irish—while increasing access to Jews. In 1935, Paul O'Dwyer, of the United Irish Counties Association, argued that the commission's new emphasis on education worked to the detriment of applicants with relevant experience—such as those that he represented.[39] Later in his life, O'Dwyer contended that educational requirements eliminated many Irish, particularly of the first and second generations, who did not have the necessary schooling but nonetheless desired civil service jobs.[40]

The depression, and the new structure of competition, triggered Irish-Jewish conflict throughout the city's bureaucracy. In the schools, where Irish administrators held sway, union activity attracted the allegiance of Jewish teachers and the ire of their Irish counterparts. One historian reports that evidence of anti-Semitism—in the form of hate mail and anonymous letters addressed to Jewish union officers—abounds in the files of the teachers' unions of the time.[41] Tensions flared in the Welfare Department as well, where the replacement of appointees by the finalists on exams led to heavy Jewish incursions. Far more explosive was the police situation, where 300 men were selected to join the department in 1940, out of 29,000 who took an exam in 1939. This class of 1940 contained the first significant numbers of Jews to enter the police, as indicated by a survey of the surviving members of the class, which found that 38 percent were Catholic and 36 percent Jewish, with Russia and Ireland the leading countries of origin of the respondents' grandparents.[42]

Success on exams took the Jews through the Police Department's door, but it left them exposed to incumbents' hostility.[43] As one Jewish veteran of the class of 1940 recalled: "The police was an Irish enclave: how do you think they felt about it? There was overwhelming prejudice. A lot of our people were sent to punishment districts. It took a long time for Jews to be accepted in the Police Department. Took a lot of good physical efforts—some times fights—to show that we could be cops."[44]

The Jewish incursion into the police fanned the flames of resentment, which had already been kindled by the depression, the daily encounter with Jewish shopkeepers, the competition over geographical space. When LaGuardia's civil service commissioner sought further control over corrupt police, Father Coughlin, the Irish, anti-Semitic radio priest, waded in to protect "the boys from Cork and Galway and Yorkshire and Bavaria . . . 90 percent of them good Christians" against their opponents, "who could not tell a nightstick from a streak of salami"—code words for Jews. As reported in *Social Justice*, the Coughlinite paper read by many Irish, LaGuardia's preference for "college boys" meant that "a man must be up on his Greek, mathematics, zoology, astronomy, and Hebrew before he can be a good cop"—a development that boded ill for the heretofore "vastly Christian" force.[45]

Consolidating the Civil Service System

Up to the end of World War II, the politics of municipal jobs were driven by a sequence of competitive conflicts, in which political elites contended with one another over votes and control over personnel systems, with competition among workers for government jobs conditioning efforts to close off or open up avenues for municipal employment. In the aftermath of the war, however, all of these competitive processes subsided.

As Martin Shefter has argued, the post–1945 political regime halted the cycle of electoral competition.[46] When the Democrats returned to power in 1945, they accepted the status quo in the civil service, rewarded Jews and Italians with a greater share of influence and appointments, and made administrative and budgetary concessions to the reformers. Accommodation yielded two results: the machine eliminated earlier sources of conflict while maintaining the exclusion of less powerful groups—blacks and Puerto Ricans.

The attenuation of political competition had an equally potent effect on the city's personnel system. Reformers and the machine had previously battled for control; each group had sought to bolster its position by developing satellite relationships with employee groups. But acceding to civil service reforms was the price the machine paid for regaining power; and the reformers, having achieved victory, "fell away, their mission seemingly accomplished."[47] Thus control slipped away to the bureaucrats themselves, who benefited handsomely from the structures and ideologies that the reformers had developed. The bureaucrats gained further influence from the new political arrangements, as the postwar Democratic machines gradually eased the road to unionization and full-fledged collective bargaining emerged in the early 1960s.

Finally, the advent of postwar prosperity diminished competition in the labor market, with consequences for municipal employment. As the labor market tightened, government's former advantages in recruitment receded, weakening its bargaining position relative to its employees. The 1952 report of the Mayor's Committee on Management Survey found that "the City does not seriously compete, from a salary point of view, with other employers in the New York area,"[48] a conclusion seconded by other assessments appearing over the next ten years. In contrast to the 1930s, the surplus of highly skilled labor could no longer be used to refurbish the ranks of the civil service; instead the city attracted less qualified, security-oriented workers who met its hiring requirements. But these workers were beginning to flex their muscles: maintaining the prewar system became one of the goals that the fledgling public employee unions sought to achieve.

Contention among white ethnics for public jobs subsided, replaced by a stable ethnic division of labor. Jews took over professional and technical jobs, most notably the school system, where the 35,000 or so Jewish public educators "set the tone much as the Irish [did] in Boston."[49] Irish and Italians shared the uniformed services and skilled or laboring jobs. Earlier flash points, like the police, no longer provoked conflict: on the one hand, the civil service structure allowed for upward mobility for those Jews who had entered the department; on the other hand, Jewish recruitment into police work dwindled, as well-educated Jews now found better opportunities elsewhere.[50]

Under these circumstances, the structures established in the 1930s hardened, sheltering incumbents while heightening barriers to newcomer groups. The mantle of reform ideology proved to be remarkably well suited to the interests of civil servants and their organizations. The doctrine of the "impartial" or "neutral" career civil servant provided a well-tuned instrument for increasing status and influence. The creed of "promotion from within," advanced by reformers to limit the intervention of party leaders, was transformed by civil service interests into a method of limiting the discretion of all outsiders.

More important, the force of inertia pushed the system of personnel control in a direction that satisfied the bureaucrats' ends. Although the city increasingly lost out in the competition for the most qualified workers, the inflated eligibility requirements developed during the 1930s remained in place. The written test similarly remained the principal selection mechanism, as test-mindedness proved "a policy that [was] easy both for management and for some employee groups to accept."[51] Not until the late 1960s, when city officials realized that "many of our examinations tested for education and training achievement levels higher than those required for satisfactory performance on the job,"[52] were entry requirements relaxed. Indeed, the elaborate mechanisms devised to "protect" civil servants and "preserve" the merit system lived on long after the political machine had lost the ability to influence personnel matters, with distinctive and unintended consequences. As one former director of the Personnel Department wrote, "procedures . . . emphasize pre-audit and double checks, and policies . . . discourage line agency initiative and authority."[53] Chronic underfunding and understaffing reinforced this tendency, as personnel policy came to mean selecting and promoting by the rules, with few if any attempts at either oversight or support functions. Bureaucratic debility made the personnel system still less responsive to either agency or staff needs, since budget officials, concerned with curbing expenditures, exercised control over lines and positions.[54] Thus, hiring policies, while complying with the "merit system," rarely produced meritorious results. The laborious application procedures and the long waiting times required to make appointments discouraged the most attractive candidates; too often, the city was left with those applicants who passed civil service tests but had less than brilliant prospects elsewhere.[55]

Whereas the reformers had pursued internalization to develop a career civil service, that strategy now served a different purpose, namely, reducing competition and maintaining the bureaucracy's stranglehold over the allocation of jobs. Jobs at the very bottom tier—low-skilled positions in "noncompetitive" titles—were detached from the job ladders established for moving ahead. Promotional routes were in turn narrowly circumscribed, with experience at the next lowest title usually the most important qualification for movement to the next step up.[56] By ensuring that mobility would proceed from the ranks—one study from the late 1960s found that 72 percent of the city's top managers had never changed agencies[57]—internalization wedded bureaucratic managers to their subordinates, while distancing both from their nominal, appointed leaders, as one veteran tartly pointed out. "The stability of the work force is paramount, since the heads change every four years. If we were to change people all the time, it would be chaos. We run the department out of people's heads. They know what has to be done, what are the rules . . . nobody knows how to get things done except for the old-timers."

As with so much else in the civil service system, promoting insiders and reducing opportunities for lateral movement meshed neatly with the interests of the newly ascendant unions. Narrowing the scope for competition came to rank high on the unions' agenda. They compiled an enviable scorecard: successful opposition to open, competitive exams; agreements to give priority to departmental, rather than city-wide, promotional lists; and strong pressure on managers to accept the "rule of one" instead of the "rule of three" in making appointments from examination lists.[58]

Under these circumstances, the civil service, notwithstanding its size and importance, became a hermetic, self-enclosed entity. Because the weak, understaffed Personnel Department was preoccupied with administering exams, doing little to either encourage new workers to seek out city employment or encourage incumbent workers to upgrade their skills, recruitment had become a peripheral function as early as 1952, as noted by the Mayor's Committee on Management Survey. A report prepared for the city by the Brookings Institution in 1963 was even more scathing, deriding the "budget and staff for the central recruiting and public relations work" as "pathetic."[59] Ten years later there had been scant improvement; the Personnel Department rarely departed from its legal mandate to advertise openings in "certain, specified, obscure places, and in formidable terminology: the formal descriptions, in 'bureaucratese,' of . . . narrow kinds of specialties."[60]

With little in the way of an active recruitment effort, potential applicants with no prior connections had few signposts to an appropriate source of vacancies. Indeed, a 1963 survey of more than 7,000 civil servants in professional occupations found that almost half learned about their initial job through friends or family, with an additional 18 percent obtaining information in a civil service paper.[61]

Thus, whereas the events of the 1930s overturned the preexisting ethnic division of labor, the developments of the postwar era consolidated the ethnic division of labor that had emerged out of the depression. The transformation of the 1930s increased Jewish and Italian access to municipal jobs; as these networks were embedded in the municipal system, they became self-reproducing. But power shifts gave the change in the composition of the city's recruitment networks added impact. With the city's retreat from an active personnel policy, the population of people with ties to municipal workers virtually became the applicant pool. Prosperity diminished the city's appeal to the type of high-skilled competitors who had displaced the previous era's incumbents, while the eligibility requirements inherited from the 1930s kept less-skilled competitors at bay. The altered balance of political power gave further influence to employee views; once in place, the new groups of white ethnic workers became engaged in bargaining games that sheltered them from competition. In the end, the civil service became reconstituted as a protected enclave for white ethnics.

Consolidation occurred just as a new set of outsiders were becoming a sizable presence. At the beginning of the twentieth century, local government, like most other New York employers, closed its door to blacks: in 1911, Mary White Ovington counted 511 black city employees, almost all of whom were employed as laborers.[62] In the early 1920s, Tammany Hall installed the leader of its black client organization, the United Colored Democracy, as a member of the three-person Civil Service Commission, but black access to public jobs changed only marginally. By the late 1920s, the city's payroll listed 2,275 black workers, including 900 in laboring jobs and an additional 700 in other noncompetitive or per-diem positions.[63] Few opportunities opened up for the higher skilled: in 1930, for example, W. E. B. Du Bois wrote to the highest-ranking black city government official, complaining that library branches, even in black districts, had rarely hired black librarians and refused to promote the few they employed.[64] Only one black educator made it to the ranks of school principal before the 1930s.[65] The Fire Department stayed lily-white until 1919, and its first black firefighter remained its only officer until the 1940s.[66]

Historians have concluded that the reform regime did more for blacks, and there is certainly evidence to support that point of view.[67] The 1938 "Report of the New York State Temporary Commission on the Condition of the Urban Colored Population" noted "an unmistakable apprehension among Negro applicants" about the discriminatory potential inherent in civil service codes that allowed appointing officers to select any one out of the top three finalists for promotion or employment; but the commission also found that "in no case during the period covered by our inquiry [1936 and 1937] was a Negro eligible passed over in favor of a lower white eligible."[68] In some segments of the bureaucracy, the effects of the new regime—combined with pressure from civil rights organizations and militant unions sensitive to the concerns of their black members—gradually helped to expand hiring opportunities. When the new, municipally owned subway line opened in 1932, blacks found themselves confined to menial jobs, with access barred to the system's skilled and better-paying positions.[69] Two years later, the Board of Aldermen placed black employees under seniority rules, and in the following year it instituted civil service procedures. But making the best of the new system proved hard. Of the roughly 260 black workers employed in the city's municipal line in 1936, 200 were still working as porters, for poor pay and under miserable conditions, and another 40 were engaged as ticket agents in stations in Harlem; civil service coverage did little for the porters, since they were placed in a classification system that lacked promotional lines.[70] Not until the late 1930s did a small but still significant number of blacks succeed in finding work as conductors and motormen.[71] As blacks had fared even worse in the two, older private subway lines, they stood to benefit when municipalization occurred in 1940. Nonetheless, they first had to overcome the considerable resistance of the largely Irish rank and file, whom, as Roy Wilkins noted in an internal NAACP memo, "still think of union brotherhood as applying to whites only."[72] Only when wartime pressures made for labor shortages did conditions substantially improve.[73]

A close look at the overall record suggests a still more somber view. True, black employment in municipal government moved above parity by 1940, but only because of the many African-Americans enrolled in emergency, public works.[74] Within the civil service proper, only a few agencies made substantial additions to the ranks of black employees: mainly the preexisting, black niches like hospitals, sanitation, and public works, where more than 80 percent of the city's black jobholders worked in 1935.[75] Moreover, blacks remained vulnerable to discriminatory practices, as in the city hospitals where 979 of the system's 982 black nurses were employed in just four of twenty-six municipal hospitals as of 1937.[76] Provisional appointments proved hard to obtain, with the consequence that "very few Negroes have had the opportunity for the kind of experience which they need for preparation for different kinds of Civil Service positions," as the Citizens' Coordinating Commission complained in 1938.[77] Under pressure from civil rights organizations, the newly formed Welfare Department added 150 black employees to its provisional roster,[78] but these new workers were soon displaced by regular civil service appointees.[79] Black firefighters, always a small number, struggled in vain against discriminatory practices that kept them employed as a group, prevented transfers to those firehouses without black employees, restricted them from the more elite formations, and effectively barred promotion through the 1940s.[80] Most important, the employment system that emerged during the depression put blacks at a structural disadvantage in competition with whites. Lacking the educational skills and credentials needed to qualify for most city jobs, blacks and, later, Puerto Ricans found themselves channeled into noncompetitive positions, concentrated in the municipal hospital system. From here there were few routes upward, as these bottom-level positions were disconnected from the competitive system, which promoted from within. Thus, the initial placements of outsiders of the post–World War II period, which strongly affected their later employment trajectory, took place within an organizational matrix that reflected the interests of an earlier group of outsiders; reordering that matrix became the issue that dominated the ethnic politics of municipal jobs from the 1960s on.

Contesting the Civil Service System

Though leaders like Adam Clayton Powell had been pressuring New York's mayors to increase black employment in government ever since the LaGuardia years,[81] race only gradually transformed the politics of municipal jobs. For the first two decades of the postwar era, personnel policy revolved around unsuccessful attempts to regain administrative control over a system that had been captured by the bureaucracy. By the early 1950s, the personnel system had come under attack, as some of the disillusioned reformers of the 1930s realized that they had created a cumbersome system more oriented toward protecting civil servants than responding to governmental needs.[82] Reflecting the machine's sensitivity to reform complaints, reorganization followed in 1954, though with little effect. While personnel officials realized that "the system of the 1930s and 1940s couldn't continue," as a former personnel director recalled, the city's difficulties in recruiting professional workers dominated personnel concerns. These priorities led the city to commission the Brookings Institution study, a report that contained no mention of issues involving race.[83] Efforts at reform focused on ways of "broadening the market" when the city could no longer "get the best of the market": in 1963, the city finally repealed the depression-era Lyons Act, which required employees to be residents of New York City. Rather than widening the pool of potential applicants and improving work force quality, repeal facilitated white migration out to the suburbs, yielding the unintended effect of making civil service jobs more attractive to incumbents and the members of their core networks. As a symbol of how fast and completely the tables would turn, reviving the residency requirement became a clarion call of the new generation of reformers preoccupied with equity rather than efficiency concerns.

Race jumped to the top of the agenda in 1965 when John Lindsay arrived in office, the first reformer elected mayor since LaGuardia. Elected with the votes of liberals and minorities, Lindsay lacked his predecessor's commitments to the interests of civil service workers and pledged to increase black and Puerto Rican employment in city agencies. But the new mayor quickly discovered that the civil service structure was not amenable to change. The requirement that low-paid clerks and typists be high school graduates—a product of the depression—remained in force until 1968.[84] And after revoking this rule, the city continued to rely on tests to screen its clerical applicants—which provoked protest from minority workers on provisional lines who were being pushed into the competitive service.[85] Reducing eligibility requirements went on in dozens of other low-ranking titles, but resistance proved severe when officials attempted incursions in the better-paid ranks. Firefighters, for example, successfully opposed a city proposal to drop the minimum height requirement of five feet, six inches, so that more Puerto Ricans could be employed.[86] Recreation leaders blocked efforts at hiring minority high school graduates as playground assistants. Street workers in the city's youth services agency successfully disputed an attempt to reduce the requirement of a college degree for that position.[87]

But Lindsay's main focus, in contrast to that of earlier reform administrations, was to evade the civil service system and its unionized defenders. The Lindsay administration embraced the "new-careers" movement;[88] the city created new, less-skilled positions—for example, nurse's aide or case trainee—in which minority residents could be more easily hired. But the new-careers movement never involved large numbers. More important, it left existing eligibility requirements unchallenged, shunting minority recruits into dead-end jobs. Trainees in the Police Department, for instance, could move up one step beyond the entry-level spot but could never reach the ranks of police officer.[89] Even where promotional ladders were developed, trainees often lacked the requisite skills: despite considerable coaching, many of the case trainees never succeeded in meeting the qualifications for the next title.[90] Agency officials often proved unenthusiastic about the new-careers project. And union officials were prone to foot-dragging, seeing efforts at creating promotional opportunities for trainees as unfair "to current employees, many of whom are poor at city salaries and stuck in dead end jobs." In the end, as one analyst concluded, the city was unwilling or unable to "pay the price" to implement new careers on a widespread basis.[91]

Far more resistance arose when the administration sought to use the Model Cities programs to create positions that would direct minority residents into the uniformed services, always vigilantly defended by their incumbents. No sooner did the Brooklyn Model Cities program create a new title in firefighting for a "model cities fireman's aide," calling for a separate exam and job classification, than the fire-fighters' union successfully challenged the action in court. A later attempt to a create a salvage corporation that would clean up the debris left after a fire had been extinguished—which would have put Model Cities residents in competition with the members of *private* salvage companies—was squashed after firefighters threatened to act in concert with their brethren in the private sector.[92] The uniformed services received judicial relief again when courts struck down a third initiative designed to require applicants for uniformed jobs in Model Cities areas to live and work in those areas.[93]

The pattern of ethnic specialization within municipal functions guaranteed that conflict over jobs would escalate beyond the confines of labor-management relations, leading to heightened ethnic mobilization when challenges to the civil service system threatened core ethnic interests. The school system proved the best, and most explosive, case in point.

Although the Jewish presence among teachers had been noticeable by the 1920s, the school systems had only recently become a Jewish stronghold. The depression had effectively stopped the hiring of new teachers; only after the war, with the influx of thousands of new teachers, did Jews replace the Irish as the dominant players, not only among the educational rank and file but also in the upper echelons of the bureaucracy. The student population was rapidly moving in a different direction, however; thanks to the influx of African-American and Puerto Rican migrants, and the white outflow to the suburbs, minorities climbed to over 50 percent of the student body by 1966. These new minority students encountered few minority teachers and virtually none in administrative positions. Until 1964, only three black educators had ever been appointed to a principal's position; another three black principals were appointed between 1964 and 1965;[94] it took until 1969 for the system to name its first, regularly licensed, black high school principal.[95]

To some degree, these disparities were inevitable: simple differences in age structure created a majority minority student body two decades before the rest of the city's population followed suit; the same factor, combined with the historically lower levels of education among African-Americans and Puerto Ricans kept the supply of minority educators low. Nonetheless, civil rights leaders and their allies among the white reformers argued that the civil service system, with its cumbersome licensing requirements and its impermeability to outsiders, made matters worse. In this criticism, they were probably right, but their pressure, combined with Lindsay's antagonism toward the civil service structure, made for a head-on attack. With the 1968 teachers' strike—which erupted after a community school board removed a number of teachers and pitted the largely Jewish teachers' union against the black- and Puerto Rican–supported community boards—friction heightened into conflict of a cataclysmic sort. Civil rights groups accused the teachers' union of racism; the teachers and their white allies replied in kind, depicting their opponents as anti-Semites.[96] As Louis Harris noted, in a survey conducted just after the strike had wound down, "the whole episode divided New York City as it has rarely been divided before."[97] The badly bloodied teachers' union emerged victorious, but a war of attrition continued in the immediate years that followed. In 1970, the NAACP Legal Defense Fund convinced a court to stop tests for supervisors, on the grounds that they discriminated against qualified blacks and Puerto Ricans, and install a quota system to protect the jobs of recently appointed minority supervisors, much to the distress of Jewish defense organizations.[98] By 1974, the B'nai Brith was complaining of anti-Jewish bias in the selection of principals; two years later, a higher court prohibited the use of quotas, returning matters to the status quo ante.[99] The same type of conflict flared throughout the city's bureaucracy, especially in the uniformed services, where civil rights organizations sought to open up jobs to affirmative action procedures, and ethnic defense organizations and fraternal societies representing groups of white ethnic civil servants lined up behind the unions and the Personnel Department to defend the "merit system."

Lindsay backed off from his confrontations with the civil service system and its defenders in the aftermath of the disastrous 1968 teachers' strike. Where the mayor could both accommodate the unions and pursue his earlier goals of increasing minority employment, he did—mainly, by tripling the number of exempt workers and shifting them from agency to agency to avoid the requirement of taking an examination.[100] But in other instances, pressure from civil service interests proved overwhelming. Thus, when the city received funding from the 1971 Federal Emergency Employment Act, designed to provide transitional public service jobs for the un- and under-employed, it defined the new jobs in terms of regular civil service requirements and filled them with white, college-educated employees.[101]

Abe Beame's election as mayor in 1973 seemed to presage the return to the status quo ante of the 1950s—combining ardent defense of civil service structures with adroit manipulation of the remaining patronage opportunities. But the city's worsening fiscal condition soon put an end to patronage games, as the ranks of exempt and provisional employees plummeted precipitously in his first two years. And when bankruptcy loomed, in 1975, even civil servants were let go. Layoffs initially threatened minority workers under the principle of last in, first out, but the city and the unions instead opted to reduce the work force through attrition. While this policy entailed a more onerous workload for remaining workers and left the city with an aged work force, it accelerated ethnic transition. As the most senior employees, whites left city service at a higher rate than African-Americans or Hispanics. Consequently, the city's work force became more representative of its population, with minorities composing almost 37 percent of employees in mayoral agencies by 1979.[102]

Pluralizing the Civil Service

With the election of Edward Koch as mayor in 1977, the prospects for expanding the minority base in city employment seemed to dim. Koch's election coincided with a precipitous drop in African-American political influence. Blacks lost representation in the city's highest governing body, the Board of Estimate, for the first time in twenty-five years. Moreover, Koch's electoral base allowed him unprecedented independence from minority leaders, leading to the political isolation of the city's African-Americans, a condition that endured until the late 1980s.[103]

The city's official employment and hiring policies quickly revealed the change in priorities. Entering office as an avowed opponent of racial quotas of any kind, Koch immediately shelved an affirmative action plan, complete with goals and timetables, that had been developed in the waning days of the Beame administration. He then sought to shift equal employment monitoring functions from the City Human Rights Commission to the Personnel Department, in effect proposing to let the Personnel Department monitor its own activities. After first backing away from the idea in the face of protest from minority leaders, he later pushed the proposal through.[104] Growing pressure to increase minority hires led him to appoint an Equal Employment Opportunity Committee (EEOC) in 1981, but the committee had little power and seemed to yield results only when its chair—a deputy mayor close to Koch—personally intervened.[105] To further allay criticism, the mayor also established a Talent Bank, ostensibly to "ensure that the City service attracts the widest possible array of candidates, particularly in the protected groups—women, minorities, handicapped individuals, and Vietnam veterans."[106] But the Talent Bank was later exposed as a patronage device that mainly provided high-paying but low-skilled jobs to whites as a favor to the machine politicians with whom Koch had allied himself. By 1989, New York remained the only major city without a public sector affirmative action plan. In the end, as one high personnel official told me: "There was no EEO policy under Koch. On paper [there was]. But the EEO bureau was a backstore operation. It wasn't computerized; it was a lip service to everything. When Koch lost the governor's election [in 1982], he just threw EEO straight into the trash. Unless commissioners felt personally responsible, they didn't care. It was just business as usual. The corrupt talent bank had no impact. There was really no EEO policy."

Notwithstanding Koch's opposition to affirmative action, and the disfavor with which minority leaders greeted his hiring policies, the Koch years of 1977 to 1989 saw the ethnic composition of the municipal work force completely transformed. By 1990, whites made up 48 percent of the 375,000 people working for the city and just slightly more—50 percent—of the 150,000 people working in the agencies the mayor directly controlled.[107] The declining white presence in municipal employment chiefly benefited blacks. Constituting 25 percent of the city's population, and a still smaller proportion of residents who were older than eighteen and thus potentially employable, blacks made up 36 percent of the city's total work force and 38 percent of those who worked in the mayoral agencies. Though blacks were still underrepresented in some of the city's most desirable jobs, they had overcome the earlier pattern of concentration at the bottom. The municipal hospital system, which employed two-thirds of the city's black employees in the early 1960s, now employed less than a fifth, reflecting the dispersion of blacks throughout the municipal sector. Higher-level jobs were clusters of considerable black overrepresentation as well, with blacks accounting for 40 percent of the administrators and 36 percent of the professionals employed in the direct mayoral agencies.

In both the magnitude and pattern of change, the Koch years represented a sharp contrast with the record of the earlier Wagner and

Table 7.1 Change in black employment, 1963–1990

Agency	Total employment			Black employment			Percent Black			Components of change			
										1963–1971		1971–1990	
	1963	1971	1990	1963	1971	1990	1963	1971	1990	Size	Share	Size	Share
All agencies	196,870	271,249	314,474	41,162	67,219	111,172	20.9	24.8	35.4	15,551	10,505	10,712	33,242
All non-mayoral	98,861	140,599	171,053	27,836	42,583	58,513	28.2	30.3	34.2	7,906	6,841	8,134	7,796
Board of education	55,840	88,641	111,923	6,108	16,303	28,810	10.9	18.4	25.7	3,588	6,607	4,282	8,225
Hospitals	34,511	40,646	47,604	18,720	22,032	23,246	54.2	54.2	48.8	3,323	−16	3,772	−2,558
Housing authority	8,510	11,312	11,526	3,008	4,248	6,457	35.3	37.6	56.0	990	250	80	2,129
All mayoral	98,009	130,650	143,421	13,326	24,636	52,659	13.6	18.9	36.7	7,248	3,553	6,411	21,635
Police	25,000	35,310	32,572	1,407	2,650	6,807	5.6	7.5	20.9	580	663	−205	4,362
Social services	10,485	23,237	31,069	4,218	10,304	19,738	40.2	44.3	63.5	5,130	956	3,473	5,961
Correction	2,910	3,681	12,849	1,036	1,600	7,291	35.6	43.5	56.7	274	290	3,985	1,706
Fire	13,320	14,873	12,727	554	614	751	4.2	4.1	5.9	65	−5	−89	226
Sanitation	13,890	15,304	12,545	1,088	1,909	2,770	7.8	12.5	22.1	111	710	−344	1,205
Transportation	4,151	4,097	7,757	251	548	3,281	4.5	11.0	42.3	−2	299	401	2,332
Environmental protection	1,433	4,107	5,428	58	165	1,123	4.0	4.0	20.7	107	0	53	905
Housing	872	4,863	4,456	185	509	2,141	21.2	10.5	48.0	847	−523	−43	1,675
Health	3,988	5,962	4,455	1,487	2,165	2,498	37.3	36.3	56.1	736	−58	−547	880
Parks	5,963	4,895	4,426	774	939	1,342	13.0	19.2	30.3	−139	304	−90	493

Sources: 1963: City of New York Commission on Human Rights, *The Ethnic Survey* (New York: Commission on Human Rights, 1963); 1971: City of New York Commission on Human Rights, *The Employment of Minorities, Women, and the Handicapped in City Government: A Report of a 1971 Survey* (New York: Commission on Human Rights, 1973); 1990: City of New York Department of Personnel, *Equal Employment Opportunity Statistics—Agency Full Report, 1990*, and unpublished reports to the Equal Employment Opportunity Commission: Health and Hospitals Corporation, Board of Education, and New York Housing Authority.

Note: Employment in specific mayoral agencies shown for top ten as of 1990 only. 1963 data for police estimated.

Lindsay administrations. Data from two earlier city-sponsored ethnic surveys of its work force, one conducted in 1963 and the other in 1971, provide a comparative view; as the city did little hiring from 1975 until the early 1980s, the 1971 survey provides the best benchmark for assessing shifts over the Koch years. In 1963, as Table 7.1 shows, blacks made up 20.9 percent of the municipal work force; by 1971, after eight years of intensive efforts to expand minority employment, the city had added another 26,000 black workers. By contrast, blacks gained 44,000 jobs between 1971 and 1990, more than their total in 1963, with the sharpest proportional growth occurring among the direct mayoral agencies

Moreover, the dynamics of change varied sharply between the two periods. During the Lindsay years growth provided the driving force behind change in black employment, as the city's payrolls expanded and hospitals and social service agencies in which blacks had originally concentrated grew correspondingly. Black gains in share, resulting from increases in the proportion of blacks employed in specific agencies, were far more meager, reflecting the resistance of entrenched whites. Consequently, blacks piled up in their original clusters—many of them concentrations of dead-end jobs. By contrast, when government expansion stalled, as it did during the Koch years, growth generated far fewer new municipal jobs for blacks. Instead, the black employment base expanded owing to gains in the black share of specific agencies. The direct mayoral agencies felt this shift with particular force: whereas gains in share were less than half the gains from growth during the Lindsay years, they exceeded three times the gains from growth during the Koch years.

Thus, unlike Jews and Italians, whose convergence on New York's public sector occurred during a period of growing ethnic influence, African-Americans concentrated in municipal government just when their political influence in city politics had sunk to its postwar nadir. Notwithstanding this divergence, the underlying processes of employment change were similar in both cases, as African-Americans, like their predecessors, benefited from simultaneous shifts in the structure of employment and in the relative availability of competing groups.

Changes in the structure of employment came from a variety of sources. The Equal Employment Opportunity Act of 1972 prohibited discrimination in local government. By requiring local governments to maintain records on all employees by race and gender and to submit them to the EEOC, with the clear expectation that governments would show improvement over time, the act also led to institutional changes. As EEO functions were established in each city agency, recruitment and personnel practices changed in ways that benefited previously excluded groups. Recruitment became focused on minority and immigrant communities, as the EEO director of the Sanitation Department explained:

> I control recruitment for the sanworkers title. In 1984, I hired an ad company and they created a campaign. And we got 87,000 people, of which better than 55 percent were protected candidates. We did this by targeting candidates. We spent close to $300,000 on that campaign. We know from census tracts where minorities are highly concentrated. We had people go into buildings with leaflets, recruiting people. They sold the job. With my first list, I affected the department for four years; [as a result of the second exam] we now will have an effect for ten to twelve years total. If you take all the fraternal organizations, the unions, etc., they won't put half a million [dollars] into a campaign. From the perspective of who can put out resources and affect process, this has enduring impact. That's what you do. Create policies that are going to survive. You institutionalize . . . it's hard to go back to the old ways.

Notwithstanding contrary signals from city hall, commissioners tended to endorse an affirmative action approach. "If you consider yourself a professional manager in the 1980s and 1990s," noted one informant who had occupied two important commissionerships during the Koch administration, "one of the issues you have to deal with is managing diversity." Thus, control over recruitment and promotion tended to slip away from previously incumbent groups. As one long-time Jewish union official representing workers in a heavily black agency complained: "The agency goes to black organizations, the black press for recruiting. There's no real effort to recruit white workers, other than ads in the *New York Times* and the *Chief.* When the agency was soliciting [job applicants], it tried to reach out to minorities. There was no honest effort to try to recruit whites."

Moreover, the 1972 Equal Employment Opportunity Act provided minority employees with new levers on more recalcitrant agencies, which they used with greatest effectiveness in the uniformed services. In 1973, the Vulcan Society (the organization of black firefighters) successfully challenged the results of a 1971 exam, leading to an imposition of a one-to-three quota for the duration of that list (1973–1979).

In 1977, the Guardians Association (the organization of black police officers) along with their Hispanic counterpart sued, with partial success, to prevent the Police Department from firing or recalling any police offers until seniority lists were reordered to account for past discrimination. The Guardians and the Hispanic Society again challenged the 1979 police officers' exam; court findings of disparate impact led to the imposition of a 33.3 percent minority quota for the duration of the list. This decision was applied to settle a Guardian-initiated challenge to the 1978 sergeants' exam, resulting in a quota that reflected the ethnic and gender composition of the test takers. A challenge to the 1981 police officers' exam, also brought by the Guardians, led to a change in the passing score and the selection of officers from broad bands of scores rather than strict rank order. The last challenge involved the 1983 sergeants' exam; when the city concluded that it would be impossible to defend the 1983 exam as sufficiently job-related, it established a quota system that would reflect the racial composition of the police officers who took the test.[108]

While African-Americans endured weakened political influence during the Koch years, so too did civil service interests. In the years after the fiscal crisis, the push for efficiency rearranged job ladders and requirements; the twin gospels of "civilianization" and "specialization" altered mobility structures to the detriment of incumbent workers while creating new portals of entry for previously excluded groups. The saga of caseworkers and eligibility specialists in the Welfare Department highlights the ethnic dimensions of these organizational shifts.

Historically, a caseworker had two functions—determining welfare eligibility and working with clients to resolve financial and other problems at home. To cut costs, the Welfare Department chopped the caseworker's job in half in the mid-1970s, separating out intake functions and assigning them to a new title, "eligibility specialist," while confining the college-educated, professional caseworkers to field activities alone. With half the job gone, the agency suddenly found itself with a surplus of caseworkers. "The bottom line," as a union official explained, "was no new hiring for ten years after reorganization." And for those who remained, many "couldn't even get a promotion from caseworker to sup1 [the next highest title]. Many of us waited ten years for a promotion."

The other side of the coin was the expansion of job opportunities—and the development of a new promotional ladder—for the largely black labor force that had previously been confined to clerical tasks. For most of the 1970s and much of the early 1980s, "all of the hiring was done in eligibility specialist" jobs. "The clerks who were there" took these new jobs: "At first, it was primarily civil service, entrance-level people already employed in civil service who took the promotional exams. In the explosion of the early 1970s, it became an open competitive position, with people coming in from the street. In the beginning as it is now, [the eligibility specialists] were primarily female, primarily minority, who had been taken in in the 1960s and who had taken entrance level jobs."

With the new title came a new ladder of mobility, allowing specialists to move up to a unit supervisor position and from there up a few steps more into managerial ranks. As it happened, "an awful lot of those people did get promoted. And that group of people historically had been from an area where the agency, on EEO, was very, very good." Thus, organizational restructuring yielded ethnically divergent effects, closing down promotional paths where whites clustered, but opening them up in functions that mainly employed blacks. As one official in the caseworkers' union put it, rather bitterly, "what had been a white caseworker function became a mainly black female function." But the representative of the eligibility specialists saw the change in different terms: "I know several black females who are office managers or directors who have nine to thirteen years on the job. They came in as entrance level clericals and worked their way up. They had talent and went to school."

Higher-paid, mainly white career workers were not pushed aside by specialists in every corner of the bureaucracy. Thus, while minority women filled the ranks of "911 operators" (a new specialty title), the dispatchers who performed an essentially identical job for the Fire Department remained a group of largely white males—with salaries several thousand dollars higher than their counterparts working for the police.

More important than organizational changes was the attack on the civil service itself from the mayor and a new generation of reformers. The reformers saw the civil service as a major impediment to badly needed administrative changes. Koch also considered it a brake on the executive's power and a source of strength for the public employee unions, with which he was locked in conflict. Whereas the leaders of the bureaucracy, and later the public employee unions, had always sought to control personnel systems, the Koch administration tried to shift influence to city hall. At first, Koch tried to convince the state legislature that municipal managers were lacking in number and authority and that the city needed relief from restrictive civil service laws. But the municipal unions prevented the mayor's proposal from reaching the floor of either the State Assembly or the Senate; from then on, as one well-informed observer noted, "municipal officials . . . tried to beat the system rather than change it."[109] Beating the system meant subverting the civil service process, as a 1989 report of the New York State Commission on Government Integrity discovered: "The New York City civil service system is in a state of crisis. Anecdotal evidence related by experts and confirmed by a number of commission staff interviews, suggest that Civil Service Law is now widely regarded as something it is desirable to bypass or avoid, when possible. Adherence to the law is viewed as hampering the effective recruitment, deployment, and retention of employees."[110]

Though the crucial factor, according to a personnel official, was city hall, other factors further weakened the traditional civil service approach. Equal employment laws and guidelines made for a much more complex process in civil service examination preparation. As one high-level personnel official explained, "Where we used to be able to grind out one of our standard multiple choice tests—which used to take us a few months—we now have to do research to show that the test is job related." Consequently, "it could now take two to three years from when we start [preparing a test] to actually establishing an eligible [hiring] list. So you have a proliferation of provisionals because we didn't get lists out."

For these reasons, "people hired whom they wanted," in the words of a high-level Department of Personnel official. The city relaxed its hiring requirements, bringing the great bulk of new hires into the bureaucracy as "provisional" employees. Between 1979 and 1990, when permanent employment in the direct mayoral agencies grew by only 7,500, the number of provisional employees soared from 6,583 to 40,340.[111] With the exception of the uniformed services, where law prohibited the hiring of provisional employees and needs for specific training made provisional hiring undesirable, virtually every agency saw its roster of provisional employees increase. Unlike civil servants, "provisionals" were hired directly, without recourse to exams and bypassing lists.

If, as a labor relations manager in a large agency argued, the preference for provisional hiring was designed to "keep people in line, keep them controlled," the policy had the unintended effect of opening up a hermetic system, whose slowly grinding, complex procedures had excluded outsiders. These circumstances put a premium on incumbents' knowledge of vacancies and on their referrals. "Our biggest recruitment is by word of mouth," explained a labor relations director. "People who are in the department are sharing with their respective communities openings that they became aware of." A leader of the heavily black, clerical workers' union, with over 30,000 members, made a similar point: "My people have an excellent communications system: they know that jobs are available; they refer cousins, sons, daughters. People walk into personnel and drop off résumés like there's no tomorrow. You'll find that many people are relatives." An executive in an engineering agency explained how this "communications system" affected his recruitment efforts: "There seems to be a tremendous network of friends and family; real contacts socially. Even in the past when we were first conducting our own provisional hiring pools, with no lists, we would post or gather résumés, send out call letters, and then have them come to hiring pools. We would invite fifty people and eighty would show up, oh my brother's friend's cousins called and said there would be a position."

While provisional hiring opened the city's door to the external labor market, the municipal services had always relied on network recruitment, as noted earlier. But whereas incumbents' contact networks had previously furnished a flow of white ethnic workers, they no longer functioned with the same effect. The city's attraction to its traditional white ethnic labor force had begun to diminish even before the fiscal crisis. Professional occupations were the first to suffer: by the early 1960s, vacancies in selected professional, technical, and managerial occupations were in the neighborhood of 20–25 percent. The staffing problem had diverse origins. In some instances, the city suffered from an absolute shortage of trained personnel; more commonly, it could not compete on salary and compounded this problem with bureaucratic delays that chased qualified people away. Finally, new hires proved unstable, with one out of every five newly recruited workers with college degrees having to be replaced each year.[112]

"I'm a dinosaur, I'm a relic," reflected one Jewish union leader on the diminishing attraction of city work for white ethnics. The veterans and bureaucrats I spoke with felt that the fiscal crisis and its aftermath had exacerbated and extended the city's recruitment difficulties among its traditional work force. The layoffs and hiring freeze of the mid- to late-1970s disrupted networks between white incumbents and their contacts who had been accustomed to seeking city jobs. By the time large-scale hiring resumed in the early 1980s, public employment had become a less attractive option than it had been before. As one veteran executive reflected: "Civil service has become tarnished, because of the layoffs. Before the last round of layoffs people looked at civil service, the only time you got fired was when you stole something. Now layoffs are publicly discussed. People think it's just another job."

Moreover, municipal salaries and benefits took a severe beating during the fiscal crisis;[113] though compensation edged back upward during the 1980s, real gains often failed to recapture the losses endured during the 1970s. By 1990, for example, the salaries of teachers, police officers, and the lowest-paid civilian workers had finally returned to mid-1970 levels. But mid- and upper-level civilian ranks—the jobs that had long attracted white ethnic workers—fared worse: by 1990, real wages were down more than 10 percent from 1975 levels.[114]

Under these conditions, the strength enjoyed by New York's private sector during the 1980s pulled native white workers up the hiring queue and out of the effective labor supply for many city agencies. Many civilian agencies reported annual turnover of more than 20 percent.[115] The city's diminished attraction for its traditional white ethnic workers particularly stung agencies with technical and professional responsibilities. "The fundamental reality," explained a Hispanic human resources manager for an agency in the engineering area, "is that the city has not been able to get people to come and get these jobs, except for . . . immigrants." Even though starting salaries improved during the eighties, and the city continued to offer superb opportunities for hands-on training, it could not compete with private employers. "In the private sector," noted one manager as he looked over his workers, "a data base expert making 55,000 [dollars] could get 20,000 more; a girl who is a crackerjack programmer could get another 10,000." Under these circumstances, the city could occasionally succeed in recruiting but "could not keep up over time," and all too often its best people "jump[ed] ship for the dollars."

In a situation where "the city was hiring a great deal and not turning away anyone who was qualified," as one deputy commissioner explained in an interview, the disparity in the availability of minority and white workers led to rapid recruitment of minority workers. Minorities had constituted only 40 percent of the new workers hired in 1977, making up the majority in only two, low-paid occupational categories. By 1987, minorities made up 56 percent of all hires, dominating the ranks of new recruits in five out of eight occupational categories.[116]

One final factor contributed to the ethnic transition of the Koch years: the accelerated departure of its older, white ethnic cadre thanks to a wave of early retirement plans. In 1991, for example, the school system lost one of every four principals;[117] a group of largely minority principals moved through the revolving door, substantially diluting the once formidable Jewish presence, as the *Jewish Forward* mourned.[118] As the attachment of white ethnic groups to municipal work ebbed, so too did their organizational presence and influence wane. The Council of Jewish Civil Servants, for example, reported a membership loss of 60 percent over the 1980s, with entire chapters disappearing in agencies like transportation, environmental protection, and buildings.

Thus, in most city agencies, diminished competition with whites and a shift in control over personnel systems—with the bureaucracy losing influence relative to city hall—produced the dramatic growth of minority employment that we have already seen. Where neither condition held, traditional barriers to minority employment remained in place. Three brief profiles outline the different patterns of change.

The Uniformed Services

Because resistance to change has been fiercest in the Fire Department, analysis of this deviant case underscores the dynamics that either promote or impede the ethnic transformation of the municipal work force. The Fire Department—where whites made up about 93 percent of the work force in 1990, down from 96 percent in 1963—presents a glimpse of municipal service as it functioned in days gone by. Inter-ethnic conflict runs deep in the uniformed services, in part because of the peculiar character of fire (and police) jobs—which isolate their occupants from the civilian world and heighten their dependence on one another—and in part because of the historic connections between the Fire and Police Departments, on the one hand, and the political machines, on the other. But the entry of blacks has been particularly charged. Historically, whites sought not only to control access to police and fire jobs but also to segregate those blacks who surmounted the entry barriers. In the Police Department, the factors that led to the hiring of blacks—namely, their utility for policing black neighborhoods—also confined them to those precincts and to lower-level patrolling jobs. Black-white conflict in the Fire Department also focused on issues of assignment and promotion, though, owing to the special living arrangements in the firehouse, it revolved around regulating accommodations. Black firefighters were typically assigned to "opposite," that is, sequential, shifts in the same firehouse, which meant that beds would never be shared by blacks and whites. While allowing whites to maintain social distance from the black colleagues with whom they literally lived in the same house, the assignment patterns had another, more important function: that of confining blacks to firehouses where they had already established a presence and keeping the rest of the houses white.

Although these blatant discriminatory practices have abated under the impact of civil rights and affirmative action laws and programs, professionalization, and the waning influence of political patronage, racial conflict persists. Antagonism continues to flare at the interpersonal level, but now mainly over the allocation of jobs—both at the entry and promotional level. Minority organizations have mounted repeated challenges to hiring and promotional decisions; the content of the legal challenges shows that the conflict focuses on the rules of the game.

The Fire Department exemplifies the relationship between job competition and racial employment change. None of the city's jobs beckons like firefighting, all of its dangers notwithstanding. Monetary compensation makes the job attractive, but its informal fringe benefits, in particular, its flexibility, provide the most desirable rewards.[119] Although scheduling requirements bring firefighters to work fourteen days a month, informal arrangements, or "mutuals," typically cut this level to seven, twenty-four-hour days. "Mutuals are an inherent part of this department," noted one firefighter. "I do twenty-four hours on Monday, you do twenty-four hours Tuesdays. It's the best of all worlds." As personnel officials see it, flexible hours make the job "very attractive: the hours permit you to have another business, get another degree, get an education." Finally, the firefighter's job generates unique social rewards: "There's something peculiar to firefighting. People live together; they fight fires together, inspect together, eat meals together, socialize together. This solidifies the group and engenders a close knit, family orientation. It makes for a family-type occupation. There's a fraternity in the Fire Department that's impossible to duplicate."

Consequently, the department attracts a large, qualified, and motivated applicant pool, retaining a high proportion of the workers it accepts. Firefighting enjoys a well-deserved reputation for intergenerational succession, with as many as one-third to one-half of firefighters having kin in the city's Fire Department or in firefighting in other communities.[120] Key informants with whom I spoke agreed that sons continue to follow fathers into the department. "Usually, it's father-son," noted one captain. "I know as many as four or five people with five or six sons in the department." As an assistant commissioner told me: "I see a lot of people who have that motivation passed on through their families. Lots of people have families—they view it as the ultimate profession. A good deal of people want the fire job because they see it as a lifetime profession, because they're familiar with it, and they apply for it."

"People who get in never leave," a personnel officer observed; instead, they "stay until they're 65." As of the late 1980s, almost 30 percent of the department's active firefighters boasted more than twenty years of seniority, and the department's overall attrition rate—3.5 percent—made it the most stable of all the city's uniformed services.[121] Although "few firemen transfer out," there are "lots of cops who transfer in," attesting to the attraction of the firefighter's job. Indeed, transfers to the Fire Department account for the single most important source of attrition during the first five years on the force.[122]

Thus, the Fire Department, unlike the rest of the civil service apparatus, still ranks high in the job queue, which means that it attracts an extraordinarily large, highly qualified applicant pool. The 1987 exam, for example, which included both a physical and a written component, attracted almost 40,000 applicants, of whom 33,000 actually sat for the exam. With so many test takers, the department rarely opens up to the general labor market, unlike the rest of city government: the city's Personnel Department administered only five firefighter exams between 1978 and 1992 and, as of this writing, the last group of new hires came from the 1987 exam. Even the Police Department, with its high attrition and turnover rates, "exhausts the list quickly," which means that newcomers continuously flow into the department. By contrast, the Fire Department "list lasts for years." The department's personnel director remarked, "I've worked in four city agencies and in no place have I experienced anything like this.

People at the top of the list are highly motivated and they jump at the chance to go into the department. You tell people 'you have to be there tomorrow' and they say 'ok.' They know that 'this is it, I'll be here for at least twenty years.' It's very different."

Consequently, whites continue to dominate the ranks of test takers and, most important, of those who score well. In 1987, whites made up almost 72 percent of the test takers but 95 percent of the 8,000 applicants who passed high enough to be hired over the life of the list.[123] The complexion of the applicants has an enduring effect: in 1993, when the department selected its last class from the 1987 list, 96 of the 100 new rookies were white.[124]

The disparity between white and nonwhite scores reflects, in part, the social and geographic differences between the two groups of recruits. Since the uniformed services are exempt from residency requirements, they draw from and employ a heavily suburban population. In 1987, nonresidents constituted 36 percent of all the test takers who passed the test and 46 percent of those who ranked in the top third.[125] Just over half of the firefighters that joined the department in 1993 lived outside city boundaries.

While white incumbents maintain networks that keep whites in line for jobs, "black firefighters are not being replaced," noted an assistant chief. Despite the success of the Vulcan Society's challenge of the 1971 exam, the suit produced a "one-time shot in the arm," since minority hiring flagged once the quota expired. "That's been the last sizable chunk." The department and the black and Hispanic fraternal societies have tried massive recruitment drives several times without success in moving blacks onto the hiring line.

Even concerted efforts by the administration of Mayor David Dinkins, the city's first black mayor, did little to turn things around. The 1992 exam sought to decrease test anxiety among minority applicants through a corrective testing method that asked test takers to pick three answers on multiple-choice questions and gave them partial credit if they picked the right answer as their second or third choice.[126] Not surprisingly, the white fraternal organizations vociferously opposed this departure from traditional exam procedures.[127] But they need not have been so alarmed—whites were overwhelmingly preponderant among the ranks of applicants and sufficiently so to prevent any recoloring of the department.[128]

Thus, not only do whites continue to vie for jobs in the uniformed services; given their higher social and cultural capital, they dominate the formal recruitment mechanisms. As with construction, the jobs' high standing ensures an ample supply of new white recruits; the distinctive characteristics of the jobs, as well as the long traditions of ethnic network recruiting, reinforce a keen sense of corporate identity and attention to group boundaries. Consequently, the Fire Department continues to reflect an old New York, as the power of white incumbent groups keeps ethnic change at bay.

Social Services

The Department of Social Services can be considered the quintessential black niche, with blacks making up more than 63 percent of the department's 31,000 workers in 1990 and 58 percent of its professionals, far higher percentages than in any other agency. The sources of black concentration in social services can be traced relatively far back: the agency had been a hotbed of radicalism in the 1930s, and a dissenting tradition lived on through the 1950s, notwithstanding the witch-hunts of the McCarthy years. More significant, as an agency with a disproportionately large black clientele, the Welfare Department was a focal point for civil rights organizations that sought both to increase job opportunities for black public servants and to add a cadre of workers who would be more sensitive to their clients' plight. By 1950, the commissioner could claim that his department had "no peer" in hiring blacks, with the "largest Negro employment in high places of any government department."[129] At the time, black welfare workers were less impressed with the department's record, complaining that they were passed over for promotions, segregated into units with a mainly black clientele, and subjected to supervisors known for discriminatory practices.[130] Nonetheless, one union official, a long-time veteran, was probably right when he told me that "social services was the place where minorities felt least unwelcome. Generally speaking, whites in the agency were liberal." By the late 1950s, blacks had begun to move up the hierarchy: James Dumpson, a black social worker, became director of the department's Bureau of Child Welfare in 1955 and was named commissioner before the decade's end. The 1963 Ethnic Survey found a high level of black employment in place, with blacks well-represented at all levels of the bureaucracy.

As in the rest of the public sector, however, the crucial influence on the department's ethnic composition involved the mechanisms of control over entry and promotion. The tight embedding of recruitment within ethnic networks that characterized the uniformed services never applied to social services. Far from hermetic, the agency was a haven for college-educated newcomers from out of town, seeking an easy start in the big city. "I haven't heard of anyone who came to this agency for a career," acknowledged an executive, unknowingly highlighting the contrast to the uniformed services. Moreover, entry criteria posed few obstacles. As the department's labor relations manager explained, "Whenever there's been recruiting by Personnel, it's a straightforward process, the test is for a fourth-grade education, and all you need is a B.A. in any topic." Unlike the uniformed services, where all newcomers enter at the bottom and have to move up in lockstep fashion, the agency maintained numerous portals to the external market, keeping down the thresholds to less-skilled arrivals, as illustrated in this black veteran's account:

> At the time [1961] this was a walk-in, noncompetitive job. I had just graduated [from] a black college in the South. In order to file for the job, you had to have at least two years of college. They would take you right away. The program really needed staff. My being black, we take the jobs that we're offered. It was a city job, with all the benefits of all the other city workers [and] pay that was not much less than a caseworker. And you had options: this was a stepping stone, work with kids, and move ahead to caseworker. Most of the workers at that agency were predominately black, had two Hispanics, and 2–3 percent white. Ninety-five percent were black American. Most of the kids were minority: about 5 percent white, 20 percent Hispanic.

Although blacks were well ensconced in social services, the turbulence of the 1960s had the ironic effect of maintaining a strong white presence. The temper of the times played a part as well, luring plenty of "pretty naive, bright-eyed caseworkers coming out of school." The advent of unionization had the same effect, with a 1965 strike forcing the city to cut the caseload in half, which in turn produced large-scale hiring and rapid promotions for incumbent workers.

But by the mid-1970s, organizational changes altered the shape of the caseworkers' careers, in effect putting a halt to hiring and keeping careers on hold for almost a decade. The wheel turned again in the 1980s, when the social crises of the era—homelessness, crack, and particularly child abuse—sent the agency scurrying for caseworkers. "Thousands and thousands were hired," yielding "tremendous promotional opportunities." But if the agency was "no longer as closed as it was," with openings for people who "walk in the door," the new recruits who sought out careers in social services no longer resembled the caseworkers of the 1960s. By choking off the flow of new hires, separation had detached the agency from its traditional, white labor supply. Moreover, conditions offered few incentives for higher-skilled workers with reasonable alternatives. "People have always said," a shelter manager with a twenty-year career in the department told me, "you work for welfare, you get treated like you're on it. The personnel practices in this department are barbarian: you get treated like shit." Nor did physical surroundings help: "We don't put welfare centers on Wall Street," complained one union official. "If you look where welfare centers are put, they're in areas where people are serviced." The increasingly desperate, heart-rending situations that caseworkers encountered did little to make the job more attractive. "Since it gets so difficult and so hairy out there, white workers are afraid. Hell, black workers are afraid." Within the agency itself, racked as it was by a series of interminable crises, the sense of mission and purpose was lost: "If a person wants to do good, that can't happen here. We're an assembly-line agency."

Under these circumstances, the supply of new white labor faded away. As one union leader noted, speaking of the agency's training classes that he had addressed: "For the longest time, the vast majority, 95 percent [of the hires in the training classes] were minority, predominantly black. White faces were very rare. It was much more than demography." Beyond demography lay the divergent supply curves of blacks and whites and the embedding of the department's recruitment mechanisms in ethnic networks. "There are lots of families," remarked one veteran, repeating a theme heard elsewhere in the city's bureaucracy, but one that would not have been heard in social services a generation ago. "Virtually everyone here is related to someone else."

Unlike the veterans of the 1960s, whose mobility had been arrested by the organizational changes of the 1970s, the workers who entered the agency in the 1980s found opportunities aplenty. As in so many other parts of the city's bureaucracy, the agency brought most new hires on as provisional employees. But nowhere else did provisional employees account for such a large portion of personnel—almost 40 percent in 1990;[131] hence, their impact on the makeup of social services' staff was disproportionately great. "In entry titles, the provisionals helped EEO," noted the department's labor relations manager. "Had they had a more formal test-taking thing, more people directly out of college would have taken it, somewhat lesser minority, than word of mouth."

By 1992, the department was so desperate to fill caseworker ranks that it gave a no-fail exam that virtually guaranteed provisional employees passage from temporary to permanent civil service status.[132] When it came to promotion to the agency's highest-level, civil service positions, however, the specter of interethnic competition flared up again. The caseworkers' union charged that agency leaders scrapped a promotion list because the candidates were "too white, and too male."[133] Notwithstanding official denials, the Dinkins administration eventually gave raises and promotions to seventy-five supervisors who contended that they had been passed over for advancement because they were white.[134]

Thus, the pattern of ethnic change in social services provides a miniature of the processes of ethnic transition that I earlier, and more abstractly, described. A variety of factors—detachment from white ethnic networks; a deviant, more liberal cultural stance among white caseworkers; and the nontechnical nature of the department's jobs— made social services an easy point of black penetration at a very early stage. For a brief period, in the middle and late 1960s, when social services moved up in the job queue, it retained a sizable white applicant flow. Thereafter, the situation changed. First, organizational changes opened up opportunities for less-skilled, heavily African-American, mainly female labor. Later, when turnover and expansion created higher-level vacancies, whites had largely dropped out of the supply curve, allowing African-Americans to move into and rapidly move up within the agency, without interference from the competitors that closed the doors to the Fire Department. But at the very top, competition for the best jobs kept the embers of interethnic conflict alive.

The Professional Services

Whereas native minority employees abound in those professional categories that are entirely or largely monopolized by government (like welfare caseworkers and teachers), a different pattern holds where government employs professionals in technical jobs for which there are competitive equivalents in the private sector. Here native minorities are underrepresented; immigrants have instead emerged as the successors to the white ethnics who long dominated these functions.

The case of the professional services, though relatively small in the total public job picture, offers new insight on the processes that sort native minorities and immigrants into different labor market segments.

Like the Police and Fire Departments, the professional services were a classic ethnic enclave. To a large extent the public had little contact with these functions. Consequently, the ranks of such specialists as the engineers in the Bureau of Sewer Maintenance or the accountants in the Department of Finance had come to resemble a "secret society," as one black manager described the assessor's bureau when he entered it in the late 1970s: "Looked at institutionally, there was no recruitment or effort made to encourage people. You almost didn't know that these guys existed. I just kind of stumbled across the [exam] notice." In fact, the doors to the professional services had begun to open in the 1960s, as city managers became concerned about the impending retirement of the "depression virtuosos" upon whom they had so long depended. With the city's position in the market for educated replacements eroding badly throughout the 1960s, personnel policies strove to widen the recruitment pool, dropping the residency requirement, as noted, and persuading the State Civil Service Commission to wave the requirement of U.S. citizenship for appointees to forty-three hard-to-fill titles, including engineers, chemists, and architects. Thus, in the mid- to late-1960s, a small number of seedbed immigrants slowly began to trickle into the civil service:

> I'm from Egypt. I didn't know anyone in the U.S.; I came in 1968. I applied just before the 1967 war; I came in under the accountants' quota. The first job—you know immigrants—I came in and worked at all different kinds of jobs for the first two weeks. Then I got a job with a Jewish company: it was in the Empire State Building. They gave me a job as a figure clerk. I worked for them for two to three months and I said, "hey, I'm an accountant." They said "we'll give you a thirty-dollar increase." So I decided to join a government agency which doesn't discriminate and where everyone gets equal treatment. What happened is that when I decided to leave private industry, I went to the New York State employment office and said I want a government job. And the person called up and sent me over and I had an interview with a Jewish person who said, "———, that's a Hungarian name," and they hired me right away as a provisional. . . I was the first Egyptian hired [into the Finance Department]. It was mainly Jewish and Italian. Because they

were discriminated against during the depression, so they all came in then. They were not Anglo-Saxons, WASPs. Then when I came, there were two black accountants. And then it started from that time, other ethnic groups joining in.

Once a small immigrant cluster was implanted, networks among newcomers and settlers quickly directed new arrivals into the appropriate places in the bureaucracy. Although the city's deteriorating fiscal situation put an end to the immigrant buildup by the mid-1970s, it left a nucleus in place, which kept the portals open when the city resumed hiring in the 1980s.

Growth led to disproportionate gains in those titles and agencies where the earlier immigrant employment base had been established. In the Finance Department, which benefited from the city's stepped-up and increasingly sophisticated tax collection operations, expanding payrolls led to greater immigrant penetration. "During my six years in the agency there's been a dramatic increase in foreign-born employees," recounted the department's first deputy commissioner. "They comprise a high proportion of the professional staff." Greater staffing needs in agencies with engineering responsibilities brought similar results. In the Transit Authority, the chief engineer, himself an Indian immigrant, estimated that Asian immigrants alone constituted 25 percent of the organization's 1,500-person engineering staff. An assistant commissioner in the Department of Highways said, "60 to 70 percent of my staff is immigrant and that includes people in supervisory positions."

Whereas white ethnic professionals could no longer be drawn to municipal work, the city was a magnet for immigrants, who appeared impelled by a different set of motivations. To the immigrants, the city offered a more readily permeable environment, one more likely to provide employment commensurate with their skills and prior training. "In the audit area, we have many people who are extremely well educated, with advanced degrees," explained a high-level official in the Department of Finance. "The pattern is that government is the first employer: these are not people who could get jobs at the big eight [accounting firms]." Moreover, immigrants found attractions in the civil service environment that native whites no longer saw. "Immigrants view government as a stable and secure environment," one manager pointed out. In this respect the newcomers seemed to "be the same as the older generation," noted the Jewish president of the assessors' local, a forty-year veteran of the civil service. "People who are not immigrants, their motivation is different." In addition to security, the city bureaucracy provided the immigrants with a more hospitable environment. "We don't discourage people from speaking their own language among themselves, we allow for religious observances," noted an EEO officer. "We tend to make reasonable accommodations of their requests." Immigrants also valued the city's highly structured environment, which seems to offer a more predictable and less arbitrary pathway to mobility. One of the city's most senior Indian engineers contended that, "Foreign trained engineers, when they come in, they feel from the security point of view that they're better off in the government. I know quite a few foreign trained engineers who came back from the private sector. Their motivations were the extent of responsibility and their inability to advance. There's comparatively greater discrimination [in the private sector]."

As immigrants and native whites fell out along different supply curves, the disparity in the availability of immigrant and native white professionals created a steep rise in immigrant employment. As in other parts of the city's bureaucracy, once the door to the external labor market opened up during the 1980s, connections among newcomers and veterans played a crucial role in expanding the immigrant employment base. Having a richer array of contacts to workers seeking government employment than natives, immigrants were well suited to funnel new recruits.

Immigrant insiders gained an initial advantage because they could immediately learn of vacancies, all of which were posted. More important, network recruitment provided management with a means of quality control, as the head of an information service department told me: "When I came in 1983 the people I got through the [civil service] lists were natives. They were marginal. The tests were not conducive to eliciting the best technical knowledge. A lot of the people I got in the beginning for analysts, data base managers, couldn't cut it. So I found a way around the civil service list. I found a way to circumvent it. I hired mainly provisionals. I got them through people I knew."

The promise of greater reliability led managers to encourage insiders to refer applicants and made them eager to tap into the recruitment stream that incumbents could generate. One union official, previously a manager in the Finance Department, offered the following case in point:

> The extension out to the Third World came through the . . . division. When they set up the . . . division, no exam was needed to get hired. It

allowed a lot of people to come in. It was an open bridge into the rest
of the agency. Finance didn't have a pool of provisionals lying around.
People were retiring and there was no list; so they hired provisionals.
Management engaged in active recruitment among the people already
there. Supervisors would say "give me your résumé." The theory was
these hires are per diems. In the interviews we would say, this is a data
collection unit. The job will last from September to June. No guarantee.
But we think that it will last for two years or more. The people [inside]
knew the kind of work we were doing. It was an established practice
that people wouldn't turn you on to knuckleheads. Generally those that
we contacted were those that were recommended from the inside. For
example, Z . . . came to me and said my wife is coming over, can you
hire her. Then his brother came over and I hired him. The agency would
love the foreign-borns. They came in prepared. They had engineering,
accounting backgrounds. They were easy to train and used to the engineering, math environment. Management recognized that [the im-
migrants] had a hard work ethic. Not tainted by the American work
ethic of stretching out three hours into eight hours of work. They recognized that immigrants work much harder. They'd bring their lunch
to work. The immigrants' work habits were different.

"Once you get in, you work your way up," said one assessor who
came into the Finance Department "from a temporary agency, quite
by happenstance," and then acquired civil service status and several
promotions. "My story is not that unique." With a foothold in the
bureaucracy, immigrants had ample opportunities for gradual conver-
sion from temporary to permanent status. One immigrant assessor
noticed a posting for a per-diem position in the Finance Department
shortly after his wife, the holder of an M.B.A., arrived from South Asia:
"She was initially hired [in that position]. Per diems have no rights at
all. At the time, they were expanding, she was given another eight
months. Based on her evaluation, she was given a provisional test.
From there, she took the test. She is now an assessor." Just as insiders
are the first to know about vacancies for provisional workers, so these
workers "have a six-month lead time in terms of knowing when the
exam [for a civil service title] would be given." Moreover, both management and the union have interests in encouraging provisional employees to convert to civil service status—management, to gain a return on its investment in training, and the union, to reduce the
potential for conflict between permanent and temporary workers. As
one EEO director explained:

Provisionals will be encouraged to take the exam when it comes out. Working with the union, we will let them know about prep courses for exams and will work with the union to make sure that all eligible employees can take the courses. The union generally holds prep courses. Everyone is eligible to go. The union has a setup where they have an educational fund—this subsidizes prepping. The department encourages people to do this, to make sure that the union has a Saturday class. And we follow up to see you are getting into the prep course, might try to work out different hours for studying, try to see if they can be reasonably accommodated, maybe coworkers will bring home study materials. I spend a lot of my time on this, because I want to attract minorities and keep them.

The immigrant propensity for security has played a role as well. As one manager put it, "the immigrants take every test available," since "they want to be protected [and] don't want to be exposed to the possibility of layoffs. They're great test takers."

Thus, immigrants made a niche for themselves in the city's professional services once the supply of native competitors dwindled and bureaucratic barriers to the entry of outsider groups declined. Ethnic networks channeled immigrants into government, allowing for rapid transmission of information about openings *outside* the bureaucracy, while also providing better information *within* the bureaucracy, thus reducing the risks associated with initial hiring. Since the immigrants tended to be "more conservative about leaving government service," the immigrant base built up at a particularly rapid rate. Opportunities for growth and promotion provided further stimulus to the self-perpetuating recruitment processes of the immigrant networks. As immigrants converted their status from provisional employee to civil servant, they became integrated into the established channels of mobility and promotion. "In the last two to three years, the [civil service] list's gotten better," noted a manager who complained about the quality of the civil service referrals he received in the early 1980s. "The most intelligent Russian, Chinese, and Indian immigrants have taken the test." Since eligibility for many upper-level positions is restricted to civil servants in lower titles, the structure of the bureaucracy itself reduced competition from the outside and encouraged efforts at internal mobility. Because "immigrants have people from their countries working as supervisors and see opportunities to advance," they have special incentives to seek out public employment.

Conflict in the Pluralized Civil Service

By 1990, when Dinkins became mayor, the phase of black for white succession in municipal employment was nearly complete. Blacks held just over 35 percent of all city jobs; though unevenly represented among the city's many agencies, they were often a dominant presence, accounting for more than 40 percent of employment in six of the ten largest agencies, and more than 50 percent of employment in three of the largest ten. As in the past, the city's strong tendency to rely on incumbents' networks to furnish recruits led to a process of cumulative causation, as African-Americans moved into government at a quicker rate than others.

The comparison with Hispanics underlines blacks' advantage in the new ethnic division of labor that has emerged in city government. Whereas the city's Hispanic and black populations are equal in number, Hispanics hold one-third as many municipal jobs as do blacks. The discrepancies are even greater as one moves up the occupational hierarchy into the ranks of managers and professionals. Blacks have been far more successful than Hispanics in gaining new permanent civil service jobs, rather than the provisional appointments on which Hispanics have mainly relied. The disparity has not gone unnoticed, as the Mayor's Commission on Hispanic Concerns pointed out in a 1986 report:

> Hispanics are significantly underrepresented in City government and, further, even in an era of increased awareness of the need for minority recruitment. Hispanics have not been as successful as Blacks in obtaining city jobs . . . What accounts for the fact that Blacks have continued to enjoy a percentage of the new hires in excess of their representation in the population, while Hispanics remain at lower levels? The Commission believes that one answer to th[is] question is that "minority" is too often taken to mean "Black."[135]

Of course, other answers might be invoked to explain Hispanics' municipal jobs deficit relative to blacks. As in the past, human capital factors—most notably higher rates of high school and college graduation and of English-language facility among blacks than among Hispanics—helped in the competition for public jobs. So too did resource bearing capacity in the political arena—with blacks far less fragmented and more politically active than the heavily immigrant Hispanic population.

Whatever the precise explanation of the African-American advantage, conflict with Hispanics has emerged as a continuing undercurrent. The Police Department, headed by black commissioners between 1984 and 1992, provides a perfect case in point. What had been a working alliance between black and Hispanic fraternal organizations began to break down under the leadership of African-American commissioner Benjamin Ward.[136] "As Latinos, we have no voice in the hierarchy," complained the leader of the Hispanic officers' association. "We don't get our piece of the pie. Blacks are in the top management team."

New York's first African-American mayor confronted similar concerns. Hispanic leaders put Dinkins on notice from the onset: "We're going to be monitoring . . . the Dinkins administration to make sure our community gets its fair share. And one of the things that we point out on the question of appointments, that as much as people may be hitting on Mayor Koch, he appointed a fair number of Latino commissioners. . . So what we say at the Institute [for Puerto Rican Policy] is that we hope David Dinkins will not simply match the Koch record in terms of appointments, but will surpass it."[137] In the end, black-Hispanic tensions over jobs plagued Dinkins throughout his tenure. With the advent of a Republican mayor determined to shrink municipal payrolls, internecine battles pitting African-Americans against Hispanics over public jobs can only grow.[138]

The case profiled in this chapter shows that the development of ethnic specializations in New York City's government can best be understood as part of a continuing, interethnic conflict over access to jobs. Irish immigrants and their descendants were the first to move into public employment in large numbers, and they gained dominance over entry portals and promotional ladders through a web of interlocking formal and informal mechanisms that effectively barred outsiders. Irish dominance persisted well after their population crested, not only because recruitment networks into government were self-perpetuating, but also because the political environment kept employment controls within Irish hands. When the balance of power shifted to the city's newer ethnic groups during the depression, control mechanisms shifted as well. Reformers restructured the civil service, encouraging competition and the influx of new, better-educated workers; in the straitened circumstances of the depression, job conflict took on heavily ethnic overtones. With the advent of the postwar recovery, the depression-era conflicts among white ethnic groups subsided, yielding a stable ethnic division of labor within city government and a sharp decline of competition in the electoral arena. Under these circumstances, control over personnel systems shifted again, this time to organized civil servant interests themselves. As these interests consolidated their gains, the structures put in place during the depression hardened, sheltering incumbents, while heightening barriers to the latest arrivals—blacks and Puerto Ricans. In the mid-1960s, the revival of electoral competition, accompanied by a rising level of ethnic mobilization, encouraged these groups to expand their employment base; these attempts involved direct attacks on the depression-era structures, reigniting the types of ethnic job conflicts characteristic of the 1930s. Although these first confrontations at best succeeded only partially, later changes in the power and social structure of white incumbent groups yielded a new ethnic division of labor in the 1980s. Blacks replaced white ethnics who moved up the labor queue and fell out of the city's labor supply, a process facilitated by political changes that opened up civil service structures. By 1990, African-Americans had emerged as the successors to the Irish, while other outsider groups, most notably Hispanics, enjoyed much scantier access to the public's jobs.

But there is an ironic twist to government's emergence as the African-American niche par excellence: public sector concentration yields increased intra- and interethnic divisions. Black civil servants have inherited the structure bequeathed to them by the earlier interethnic conflicts, and that structure continues to influence the characteristics of those recruits who make it through government's door. The depression's legacy of inflated job requirements has not been erased: as described in Chapter 4, average African-American educational attainment exceeded the high school level in *all* of the black public sector niches. Lowering educational requirements would expand access to African-Americans with lower skills and experience levels. But as in the rest of the economy, entry thresholds legitimate the perks and privileges that civil servants enjoy; and it is precisely those perks and privileges that increase the competition for municipal jobs. As one ranking personnel official noted, in speaking of the city's highly paid garbage collectors: "102,000 people took the sanworkers' test in 1990. New York is the only major city in the country that administers a test in Sanitation. The staff at Department of Personnel is always at a loss to design a test for Sanitation. What do you put on the test to assess whether a person can be a good sanman? We're thinking of getting rid of the test. But if we did this, and made hiring open, we'd weaken the San union's claims to parity with Police and Fire."[139] Today's civil service unions, highly responsive to the interests of their African-American members if not actually led by African-Americans, are no less opposed to flattening the civil service hierarchy than they were a generation ago.

While the black middle class largely works in government, the black poor are its dependents. The interests of civil servants, regardless of ethnic stripe, leads them to push for higher wages and ever greater public jobs. The record shows that government has been extraordinarily responsive to these demands. Civil servants found that the 1980s were good times indeed, reaping more than half of the considerable increases in municipal expenditures that occurred during the 1983–1989 period. By contrast, the poor did a good deal less well, with public assistance payments actually declining and much of the increase in redistributive spending going to organizations designed to serve the poor.[140]

Fiscal stringency returned to New York City at the very end of the 1980s; as of this writing, there is no indication that the city's coffers have returned to good health. Municipal payrolls, however, remained unscathed, until the advent of Republican Mayor Rudolph Giuliani in January 1994. The city employed more workers in 1993 than it had in 1989, and just 8,000 fewer than it had when the work force peaked in 1975.[141] And in this fiscal crisis as in those of the past, the city has been less solicitous of its residents' needs, not to speak of the concerns of the indigent.

Public sector concentration thus pits the interests of the city's black middle class against the interests of its black poor. But as the poor have few resources, and rarely venture into the street, intrablack conflict remains latent. African-Americans' relations with the newer New Yorkers follow a different pattern. Competition for public jobs is only one component of the rivalries that pit blacks against Hispanics, and increasingly Asians, over the goodies that government has to give out. "La gran estafa"—the great fraud—was the headline that New York's Spanish newspaper chose to characterize the reapportionment plan endorsed by the Dinkins administration.[142] The same resentment filters into Hispanic views of the divvying up of government jobs, as can be detected from one Puerto Rican leader's disappointment in "the traditional black politician's notion of simply seeing black/Latino relations as a question of group competition. Simply one group against the other, fighting for finite resources."[143] Whether indeed the accusations are justified is not the point. More compelling is the message they send about the reversion to an earlier interethnic pattern from the fundamental opposition of blacks to various groups of ethnic whites during most of the postwar years. African-American New Yorkers now occupy an ordinary ethnic role in New York's segmented system, as just another, albeit important, self-interested player in the same old game of splitting up the pie.

8 | Small Business: The Interplay of Economy and Ethnicity

Twentieth-century New York may be one of the capitals of capitalism, but it is also home to an extraordinary array of small firms. New York's small-business sector has long acted as a seedbed of ethnic mobility, and the terrain it provides today's ethnic entrepreneurs seems no less fertile than it was when European immigrants came ashore at the turn of the twentieth century. Indeed, newer arrivals busily replicate the older immigrant experience of converging on small business. By now, the phenomenal business success of the Koreans is old news, one familiar to the residents of virtually any big American city. And the Koreans are only one among a legion of newcomer groups that have made their way into New York's economy as petty entrepreneurs. Greeks, Chinese, Arabs, Israelis, Dominicans, recent Russian immigrants and others have all registered considerable success playing the entrepreneurial game.

But not African-Americans. Business never provided black New Yorkers with fertile terrain for growth. To be sure, black-owned businesses did sprout up as the city's African-American population grew. As with other groups, the densest areas of black settlement often boasted a concentration of black-owned firms. If not empty, the scorecard of African-American business success has never been high: relatively few black New Yorkers have gone to work on their own. More controversial, outsiders—Jews, Italians, and more recently, the new immigrants—have captured the great bulk of black patronage.

Accounting for the underdevelopment of African-American business has been a persistent scholarly concern. There is no shortage of explanations, starting with that of E. Franklin Frazier, who speculated that slavery deprived blacks of a tradition of buying and selling. Nathan Glazer and Daniel P. Moynihan later contended that black entrepreneurs, unlike their immigrant counterparts, never enjoyed a captive market, since blacks had few distinctive ethnic consumer needs.[1] Ivan Light, whose landmark book *Ethnic Enterprise in America* showed that ethnic solidarity was the engine that propelled business growth, maintained that individualism, competition, and status differences fractured African-American communities far more than the communities of other visible minorities, such as the Japanese, Chinese, or even black immigrants from the Caribbean, who all did significantly better in business.[2]

All of these accounts are plausible, indeed insightful, and by no means mutually exclusive. The authors, however, all sought to illuminate earlier entrepreneurial differences between African-Americans and the immigrant groups of the first half of the twentieth century. But the current question is no longer a matter of simple historical concern. The burgeoning of immigrant business has involved a transformation in the composition of New York's small-business class: the newcomers have taken over from the Italians, Jews, and other white ethnics who dominated the ranks of the city's petty entrepreneurs up until a generation ago. But if succession provided an opening to the very latest arrivals, why didn't better-established black New Yorkers take up the same opportunity?

The latest scholarly research suggests a different tack, moving away from the cultural explanations favored by the earlier research. Instead, analysts now look to ethnic social structures as the source of actions propelling business growth. Thus, Ivan Light, in his recent book on Los Angeles's Korean entrepreneurs, coauthored with Edna Bonacich, developed the concept of "ethnic facilitation," referring to the way in which the clustering of earlier immigrants in business lines sends signals to newcomers as to the most appropriate economic pursuits.[3] Thomas Bailey and I developed the concept of "training systems" to show how ethnic networks increase the quality and quantity of information exchanged between co-ethnic employers and employees, reducing the risks associated with investment in skills on both sides.[4] Alejandro Portes and a variety of collaborators coined the concepts of "bounded solidarity" and "enforceable trust" to show how the characteristics of immigrant communities promote altruism and create mechanisms that reduce the likelihood of opportunism. In sum, the new approaches emphasize the embeddedness of immigrant economic behavior in the communities from which the businesses spring. In this view, the social structures that connect ethnic entrepreneurs and communities form a source of "social capital" that facilitates entrepreneurial growth.[5]

This perspective links ethnic entrepreneurial disparities to differences in ethnic social structures. The networks and institutions created by the process of migration itself provide the structural seedbed out of which business activity emerges. But the migration experience is now history for most black city dwellers, among whom black New Yorkers, more than half of whom were already northern-born as early as 1970, are a prime case in point. In effect, black New Yorkers have moved further down the road toward assimilation than the new immigrants, in due course losing the ingredients that make for business success.

If ethnic business is embedded in ethnic social structures, then the types of structures a group establishes have a fateful effect. As I have discussed, blacks' search for opportunity led them into the public sector. Once African-American networks became implanted in government jobs, those networks transmitted signals that led other black New Yorkers to converge on public employment. By contrast, burgeoning business activity among groups like Koreans or Chinese sends out a different type of signal, suggesting to newcomers that they set up shop on their own.

In my mind, these arguments explain much of the difference in new immigrant and black entrepreneurial success, and the material to follow will provide additional support for that view. Yet, I find troubling a perspective that accents endogenous ethnic characteristics to the neglect of ethnic competition and its effects. Newcomers jostle with one another for jobs. Newcomers also flow into areas where earlier immigrants moved up through economic specialization, establishing ethnic niches to which they or their descendants often remain strongly attached. Consequently, immigrants and ethnics participate in a segmented system, in which one group's ability to mobilize resources through social structures serves as a strategy for limiting another group's chances for advancement. Under these conditions, the embeddedness of economic life may yield a particularly negative effect for business, generating both pressures and motivation to exclude outsiders, as the previous chapters attest.

This chapter examines the changing profile of New York's ethnic entrepreneurs and inquires into the source and consequences of business growth and success through case studies of three quintessentially ethnic, quintessentially small, business sectors—retail, garments, and construction. The first two cases, through which I pass quickly, illuminate the sources of immigrant business success; the third case, to which I devote the bulk of the chapter, sheds light on the obstacles facing African-Americans in business and on the factors that give immigrants an edge, though one that is less impressive than often thought. In all three cases I quote from my field notes as well as from interviews.

Retail: A Case of Ethnic Musical Chairs

The ethnic neighborhood looms large in the popular iconography of the American ethnic experience as well as in its scholarly interpretation. The mass migrations of the turn of the century created ethnic enclaves—Germantowns, Little Italys, Chinatowns, and the like—where the immigrant masses huddled together for sustenance and support. Over time, the immigrants and their descendants moved on to newer, better neighborhoods, but the original areas of settlement often remained a concentration of ethnic stores and services, and thereby a symbol of common ethnic identity.

Although New York's European immigrants and later generations dispersed from older settlements like the Lower East Side to newer neighborhoods in the Bronx, Brooklyn, or Queens, they continued to live in considerable isolation from others. The "urban village" of the mid-twentieth century, as Herbert Gans showed in his classic portrait of Boston's Italian-Americans, was a world circumscribed by the converging contours of class and ethnicity, in which everyone knew everyone else.[6] The centrifugal forces of the American city have since emptied many of these older urban villages, but the post-1965 immigrants have placed their own stamp on the urban landscape, even as attachment to the old neighborhood has waned. With the growth and emergence of Chinatowns, Koreatowns, and others like Brooklyn's "Little Odessa on the Sea," the post-1965 arrivals seem to have replicated the experience of their turn-of-the-century predecessors.

The advent of new immigrant neighborhoods has also transformed the face of local commerce. Manhattan's Chinatown, the largest, densest, and most vibrant of all the ethnic business districts, has all but swallowed the older Jewish and Italian ethnic shopping districts

that used to abut it. In Brooklyn's Brighton Beach, the world's largest
Soviet émigré community, stores with signs written in Cyrillic line
the main shopping streets, as newcomers install fancy pastry shops,
"international-style" groceries, bookstores, and a dozen new night-
clubs and restaurants.[7] In central Brooklyn, West Indian groceries,
barber shops, restaurants, and record shops dot the landscape; here,
businesses often show "a Caribbean referent: a flag, a country's name,
a few words in dialect or perhaps just a painted palm tree."[8] As
northern Manhattan has evolved into a miniature Santo Domingo, its
business sector has come to resemble "a giant Caribbean bazaar."
Broadway, the area's major thoroughfare, "abounds with *bodegas, far-
macias,* unisex beauty salons, bargain clothing outlets, restaurants
serving *pollo* and *platanos,* and travel agencies offering bargain
[flights] to the Dominican Republic."[9] On the other side of the East
River in Queens, Jackson Heights has become an international emporium: with one cluster of blocks serving as "Little India," the area
also contains the city's largest concentration of Colombian merchants, who do business cheek by jowl with Argentines, Uruguayans,
Koreans, and Filipinos. On any given street, the shopper might find a
Colombian bakery, a Korean fish store, a Chinese supermarket, a Pak-
istani-owned drugstore, and an Irish bar, the first four reflecting the
neighborhood's new diversity, and the last the preferences of its old-
time residents.

One could continue with this Cook's tour of New York's ethnic
neighborhoods, but these examples suffice to make the point: the
growth of immigrant populations, with their distinctive ethnic tastes
and wants, has fueled a vast market for the goods and services that
their fellow ethnics are best positioned to sell. Immigrants not only
want special consumer goods they also have special problems caused
by the strains of settlement and assimilation—difficulties usually aggravated by their unfamiliarity with, or fear of, the institutionalized
mechanisms of service delivery. The business of immigrant adjustment provides yet another track for ethnic commercial development,
as evidenced by the ethnic travel agencies, law firms, realtors, and
accountants that proliferate in immigrant communities.[10]

But a second factor promotes the growth of a local ethnic market,
and it has to do with the effects of local demographic shifts on the
supply of potential entrepreneurs. When a neighborhood changes from
Jewish, Italian, or Irish to Dominican, Jamaican, or Chinese, the store-
owning population among the older groups begins to decline. The de-

cline is due to a few factors: in part, to the tastes that the newer groups bring; in part, to self-segregating processes in personal service businesses; and in part, if the newcomers are poor, to income effects, which means that specialty shops and stores carrying high-quality goods also lose their market. Most important, however, is the high turnover rate of small businesses, whatever the ethnicity of their owners. And when Jewish, Italian, or Irish businesses go under in neighborhoods experiencing ethnic transitions, new Jewish, Italian, or Irish owners rarely appear.[11]

I observed just how this process worked in 1986 and 1987, when I surveyed white, Korean, and Hispanic business owners in two quintessentially ethnic neighborhoods—Jackson Heights, in Queens, and Sunset Park, in Brooklyn. At the time, whites were already substantially underrepresented among the business population. The white store owners were significantly older than either their Korean or Hispanic counterparts. Their businesses also tended to be older establishments: at the time, the average white-owned establishment had been in existence for just over thirteen years; by contrast, the Korean- and Hispanic-owned businesses were newly founded, averaging six and four years, respectively. The composition of the white store owners provided further testimony to the shrinking pool of white ethnic petty entrepreneurs, as almost half of the white owners were themselves foreign-born.[12] Four years later, when my colleague Greta Gilbertson and I conducted a follow-up survey, we found that the state of neighborhood business was thriving, with virtually no vacancies among the stores I had originally surveyed. Nonetheless, the struggle for survival had exacted a considerable toll among the owners I had originally interviewed, with just over a third of the businesses either going under or changing hands. The existing white businesses fared reasonably well, turning over at rates slightly lower than those experienced by the Hispanics or the Koreans. But whites appeared infrequently among the group of replacements: whereas whites had made up a third of the original sample, they were now only a sixth of the new owners.

Still, there is more to the transformation of New York's small-business class than neighborhood succession. In New York, as in other cities, Jews, Italians, and Greeks have played disproportionately prominent roles in retail, selling goods and providing services, not only to co-ethnics but to customers from virtually every ethnic group as well. As in so many of the other trades and occupations that I've examined in this book, the white ethnic role in New York's small-scale commercial activities has now come to end, as the present-day descendants of turn-of-the-century immigrants have moved on to choicer positions. Their exit from commerce has provided opportunities for a new, diverse group of entrepreneurs—Arabs, Israelis, Persians, Indians, Bangladeshis, Chinese, and, above all, Koreans—as Illsoo Kim remarked in his pioneering book on Korean immigrants:

> The majority of Korean retail shops . . . cater to blacks and other minorities located in "transitional areas" where old Jewish, Irish, and Italian shopkeepers are moving or dying out and being replaced by an increasing number of the new minorities . . . Korean immigrants are able to buy shops from white minority shopkeepers, especially Jews, because the second- or third-generation children of these older immigrants have already entered the mainstream of the American occupational structure . . . In fact, established Korean shopkeepers have advised less experienced Korean businessmen that "the prospect is very good if you buy a store in a good location from old Jewish people."[13]

Koreans, as Illsoo Kim and Pyong Gap Min have explained, began by securing a few, narrowly circumscribed business lines, such as wig stores, which could succeed because of Korean ties to cheap manufacturing sources back home, and the low-margin, labor-intensive, fruit and vegetable businesses. From these beginnings, the Koreans branched out considerably. Korean entrepreneurs spilled over into other retail businesses like groceries, the liquor business, and fish stores. They pioneered new, personal service businesses, like the nail salons that became ubiquitous during the 1980s. They exploited their homeland connections to set up wholesaling businesses that imported low-priced novelty items from Korea, which in turn distributed merchandise to Korean retailers.[14] And as with other groups, the growth of the Korean population created a market for Korean accountants, doctors, brokers, hair stylists, and restaurant owners. By 1990, 28 percent of New York Korean males were self-employed. The 1991 Korean Business Directory illustrates the range of Koreans' commercial ventures, with over 120 business specialities in which Korean firms are to be found.

Koreans moved into the openings created by the commercial exodus of New York's older, white ethnic groups; so did other immigrants, but not as successfully as the Koreans, a disparity that can be ascribed only to the characteristics of Korean immigrants and to the social structure of the community they have established. As middle-aged newcomers, with high levels of education and poor English-language skills, relatively few Koreans have managed to steer a route into the middle-class, professional fields for which they trained. The social structure of the Korean community itself generates resources that assist business success. Many Koreans emigrate with capital and those who are cash-poor can raise money through rotating credit associations, known as *gae*; because Koreans migrate in complete family units, family members provide a supply of cheap and trusted labor; the prevalence of self-employment means that many Koreans have close ties to other business owners, who in turn are a source of information and support; and the high organizational density of the Korean community—characterized by an incredible proliferation of alumni clubs, business associations, and churches—provides additional conduits for the flow of business information and the making of needed contacts. As I found in my survey of Korean, Hispanic, and white business owners, these community resources distinguish the Koreans from their competitors, who are less likely to have ethnic or family ties that can be drawn on for assistance with business information, capital assistance, or staffing problems.

Thus, petty commerce in New York City has undergone a game of musical chairs. Immigration and the greater diversity it has engendered have wrought much of the change. But changes in the shape of the ethnic queue, conforming to the model sketched out in Chapter 1, moved the process along, producing additional opportunities for middleman-type groups with a specialization in business and trade. The retail story is hardly unique, as the following thumbnail portrait from the rag trade will show. Returning to the garment case provides another perspective for thinking about the ethnic business phenomenon, since it also tells us something about the broader consequences of an ethnic niche in business.

Garments: The Employment Consequences of an Ethnic Niche

Like the retail case, the garment industry story shows what happened to New York's petty entrepreneurs when small business lost its allure for the later generations of white ethnics. For the first half of the twentieth century, the industry had no shortage of Italian or Jewish sewing-machine operators, cutters, salespeople, and pattern makers eager to step up and start up a contracting factory on their own. But things began to change by midcentury, when better opportunities emerged; by the time I interviewed white ethnic and immigrant garment contractors in 1985, white ethnics were clearly on their way out. Those Jews and Italians still active in the running and managing of clothing factories were an aging group, in charge of long-established factories and reaching the end of their productive lives. Many of the contractors I spoke to were second-generation owners; yet, virtually none wished to pass their factories on to their heirs. "Going into the garment industry?" asked one Jewish contractor rhetorically, "I wouldn't wish it on a dog." Few of the younger Jewish or Italian owners showed any entrepreneurial flair: all of those under age forty had succeeded their parents in business and not one had established his or her own firm.

If old-timers predominated among the white ethnic owners—with the average firm dating back more than three decades before my survey—young entrepreneurs with new businesses were the common currency among the immigrants, where the average firm was five years old. In certain crucial respects, the newcomers were not unlike the old-timers: both groups had begun from modest origins, with employment in garments or some other low-level occupation the most common stepping stone to starting out on one's own. And neither immigrant nor white ethnic firm was immune to the rag trade's vicissitudes: the records of the unionized firms affiliated with the garment workers' union attest to appallingly high business mortality. But the immigrant populations produced a steady stream of neophytes willing to try their hand despite the odds—if for no other reason than that "for the immigrants, it's either the restaurant or the garment business." Thus, with few white ethnics stepping forward to fill in for failing entrepreneurs, differences in the rate at which new firms were founded led newcomers to replace old-timers among the ranks of New York's petty garment capitalists.

As an example of occupational succession, the garment industry's changeover from white ethnic to new immigrant entrepreneur recapitulates the retail case, furnishing yet another illustration of changes in the shape of the queue and the effect that those shifts can yield. But as the industry still provides plenty of jobs, in addition to the opportunities it supplies the self-employed, it points to the broader rewards generated by a small-business niche.

As in the past, garment jobs attract entrepreneurs of various ethnic stripes. Dominicans and Latin Americans have established small shops in northern Manhattan, parts of Queens, and in the garment center itself. Koreans have set up over 300 shops, mainly located in Manhattan, where they draw on a polyglot labor force among the newest, most easily exploitable of New York's immigrants. But the chief inheritors to New York's rag trade, tattered and torn as it may be, appear to be the Chinese.

Clothing production had long been a feature of San Francisco's Chinatown, but not New York's, which did not develop an ethnic garment shop until 1948.[15] By 1952, there were apparently 3 Chinese garment shops, with the largest employing forty workers and the smallest fewer than ten.[16] As the flow of female immigrants slowly increased, so too did the number of garment shops, reaching 18 in 1960, according to S. W. Kung's count.[17] But as soon as immigration began to burgeon, the number of garment shops also began to grow: by 1970, there were just over 100 small factories; five years later, the number had more than doubled; by 1980, there were 430 Chinese shops; since the mid-1980s, the count has stood somewhere between 450 and 500.[18]

A variety of factors spurred the growth of Chinatown's garment industry. The movement of family units in the new immigration, and the rapidly increasing numbers of women, furnished a ready supply of labor for this traditionally female-dominated trade. Clothing also had the advantage of being a field in which getting started in a business of one's own required only a little capital and access to family and kin labor, and the Chinese community's social organization facilitated such resource mobilization.

Field notes: S.C. came to New York in 1972 from Hong Kong, where he had graduated high school and worked as a salesman. But in New York, he went into his uncle's garment factory; working as a helper, he "learned everything." Two years later, S.C. and his wife opened up their own factory, with an investment of $10,000. "I had no choice. As a new immigrant, it's not easy to get into American society. And if you work for someone else, you can't make a living. I thought if I put in the time, I would get something back." By 1982, S.C. was employing forty-five workers, all Chinese, but of diverse origins, some from Hong Kong, others from the People's Republic of China, others from Southeast Asia.

Once in place, the immigrant garment industry quickly acquired a dynamic of its own. The demand for labor to staff the local garment factories affected the stream of newcomers to New York; compared to other cities, New York received a disproportionate number of lower-skilled newcomers arriving from China, Hong Kong, and

Taiwan.[19] Moreover, while many of the newcomers to New York moved to quasi-suburban areas within the city's boundaries, those immigrants who gravitated into the garment industry were far more likely to settle in Chinatown. In 1980, for example, just under half of the roughly 20,000 Chinese workers who belonged to the garment workers' union lived in Chinatown, compared to a quarter for the city's Chinese population as a whole. For the immigrants, residence in Chinatown provided the convenience of being able to walk to work. Living close to the concentration of jobs was also a sort of unemployment insurance, since if any employer went under or laid off workers, there was likely to be another job in one of the score of factories close at hand. Employers also gained from this arrangement: a nearby source of labor provided a constant supply of workers looking for jobs. Proximity kept teenagers, mothers of young children, and older workers, who might not have commuted long distances to work, readily available for work in a local factory.

> *Field notes:* Along with her brother and her mother, P. ran one of China-town's larger, better organized shops. Though P. kept strict rules by local standards, insisting that "workers maintain regular hours," she nonetheless allowed flexibility for mothers who had to pick up or de-liver students at school. "We have about twenty part-time workers, mainly college students who might work afternoons," she told me; the factory also employed six older workers, for part-time, finishing jobs.

In a sense, the emergence of a Chinese garment sector harked back to turn-of-the-century developments; it also altered the role of ethnicity in organizing the industry's economic life. By the 1980s, the exodus of the old-timers and their replacement by immigrants left nonimmigrant employers uncoupled from the networks that previously structured their labor market. "These days family recruitment is fairly infrequent," lamented one old-timer, a Sephardic Jew who had inherited his factory from his father. To find and recruit workers, the remaining white ethnic employers have fallen back on formal inter-mediaries, like the New York State employment service and the union hiring halls. But the hiring halls only circulate the existing labor force from one factory to another, and while the employment service does infuse new labor, there is another catch: the information employers can acquire about an applicant is of much lower quality than the in-formation they might receive when a recruit is referred by someone already in the plant. Because employers lack knowledge about the stability and reliability of the workers referred to them by the employment service, they are unwilling to make a commitment to training and upgrading. As one official in the employment service noted: "Employers in this industry are unwilling to train. They don't like to hire a worker even if she's an operator who has to be broken into a different line. Employers have to be on the edge of desperation to do any training, even if it's a matter of training for a related skill."

The other side of the coin is that few employers consider the employment service to be a source of reliable skilled labor. "The employment service hasn't sent me a decent worker in more than thirty years," more than one employer told me. Of course, employers do make wide use of the service, which belies their insistence that it is often useless. But their negative views reflect the problems in hiring and holding on to workers who lack any attachment to a firm and its stable network of employees.

Substantial wage increases would certainly help attract new workers to the industry, but intense international competition and widespread seasonality make it difficult for employers to compete on pay. The menial character and low status of many jobs compound the problems that low earnings cause. The owner of one large factory admitted, "Even if we were willing to pay 3, 4, 5 dollars more, you can't find people: nobody wants to work as a lay-up girl or stand with scissors and cut threads." Similar considerations also make workers reluctant to undertake the long training required for the industry's most skilled positions. The problem is exacerbated, as employers insisted time and again, because workers seem to "prefer the fast food industry where one needs no skills to get a job." Finally, low earnings mean that apparel firms are vulnerable to competition with industries that can do better on wages; the standard complaint among men's clothing makers is that the alteration rooms of department stores "soak up our skilled labor and pay them better."

Thus, in the nonimmigrant sector one finds the paradox of a "tremendous void in skilled labor" and a "labor situation [that] is good for bad operators," despite the continued loss of jobs. But in the expanding immigrant sector, "we work with our own ethnic group," and that linkage has rekindled the industry's dormant training system, giving immigrant firms a leg up on their white ethnic competitors. Although help-wanted ads for garment workers have apparently appeared in Chinese newspapers since the mid-1950s,[20] ties between new arrivals and immigrant owners play the crucial role in steering newcomers into the ethnic economy. "When new immigrants come in, they need a job," explained one well-established contractor in Chinatown. "We know they are hard workers." As in the past, immigrant owners provide newcomers with some instruction, material, and a place to work. According to one Chinese contractor:

> Most of my workers, they've been with me for a long time. Lots of them have been trained here. When they first started I gave them a little basic training on a machine and some pattern stitching. They start with simple operations like sewing straight seams. I hire unskilled workers and train, mostly through recommendations of other workers. They seem to have more confidence in the shop. They must hear something good about the shop. Of course, I have had problems; I expect that some workers will go. The only thing is I have to let people know that if you're looking for a temporary job, this is not the right place. I want someone to work here for a while. This is not a shop that goes out of business one day and opens up the next under a new name. It happens often that people are coming from China: I have no problem, I will train them, but I want someone that stays after the training. If they're looking for training alone, this is not the place. People are responsive to that.

Ties between owners and newcomers provide the information that both sides need for decisions about hiring and training: "We mainly recruit through word of mouth," noted the owner of a fifty-person shop. "Workers know what it's like beforehand." Those connections also foster a social structure in which skill acquisition can readily take place: "We prefer to train referrals; we know them; they also have friends or relatives in the shop. At least if they have anything difficult, they can help each other out; they will show them how to do this [particular operation]."

An invisible wall keeps immigrant workers tied to the ethnic economy, giving immigrant employers an advantage over their white ethnic competitors. The same informal connections that lubricate entry into the immigrant sector make workers reluctant to leave immigrant firms where they are more comfortable, work in a familiar environment, and enjoy ties to other workers who share their culture and language. According to one recent book on New York's Chinatown economy, "many garment workers who had once worked for *lofan* ['whites,' in Cantonese] eventually turn back . . . because they are frustrated at not being understood."[21] Many old-line employers echoed this observation when they told me of their eagerness to recruit Chinese workers and the frustrating experiences they encountered: "I hear about the Chinese and would love to have some [in the factory]. But until I get a few [Chinese workers] I will never have a lot. They need to have people in the shop to relate to; I don't have anyone in the shop who can communicate in Chinese; and the area where I'm located is not conducive to the travel patterns of the Chinese."

Thus, ethnic connections help to organize an otherwise unstructured industry; the ties that connect immigrant owners to the broader ethnic community generate the resources that have kept Chinatown's garment industry growing, even while the city's rag trade has continued to decline. Although growth has come at the price of low wages, the employment effect has offset the wage effect. As I noted in Chapter 4, the Chinese ethnic economy has been a kind of job machine for the low skilled, generating employment at sufficient rates so that men, in the restaurant industry, and women, in garments, can cobble together a living that moves them out of poverty and into the ranks of the working and lower middle classes.

The garment and retail cases can both be read as stories of ethnic disadvantage turned to good account, in which new immigrants have been able to compensate for the background deficits of their groups and the discrimination they encounter. In both instances, succession processes allowed newcomers to replace old-timers with little of the conflict widespread in the public sector and in construction. By converging on New York's small-business sector, the new immigrants have succeeded in building an employment base that creates opportunities for workers and entrepreneurs alike.

Construction: The "Other Side" of Embeddedness

The immigrant push into business makes the persistently low rate of African-American entrepreneurship all the more puzzling. After all, the white ethnic exodus from petty commerce and manufacturing created a window of opportunity not open when African-Americans first came to the metropolis: why didn't they seize the chance, when opportunities for succession arose in the 1970s and 1980s?

To answer that question, I turn to yet another industry, construction, and a case study of African-American, Caribbean, Korean, and white ethnic entrepreneurs. Construction is an ideal setting, since its competitive structure and low capital-to-labor ratios has made it a time-honored ethnic pathway into business. Construction has the further virtue of being an industry in which black entrepreneurs have a significant presence, in part, due to public policies that have sought to leverage government resources to increase opportunities for black entrepreneurs. As with most minority business development policies in the United States, these efforts have produced disappointing results, but the record of black business growth in construction still reads better than it does in the economy overall.[22]

Construction also provides a vehicle for returning to the theoretical discussion with which I began this chapter. Few other industries could provide a better example of embeddedness, as construction businesses live and die on their ongoing relationships to clients, key workers, sub- or general contractors, suppliers, and a host of other actors. The comparative framework of the third case study will allow us to see how social structures affect economic behavior in *inter-* and *intra*ethnic settings.

Though construction has received little consideration in the expanding literature on ethnic and minority business, it deserves a good deal more attention. In the past, the industry served as a seedbed of immigrant business; the characteristics that attracted newcomers to construction and allowed them to succeed—the industry's plethora of actors and its low requirements for capital and formal schooling—remain in place. Construction still stands out as an area where immigrants concentrate: in 1990, 46 percent of all New York's construction personnel were foreign-born; the same proportion held among those working in construction on their own account. While Caribbean immigrants were overrepresented in construction, employment levels among African-Americans and Koreans, as with other Asians, fell below parity. For African-Americans, underrepresentation reflects past and continuing tendencies toward discrimination, matters to be discussed in the pages that follow. Discrimination plays a part in the Korean story too, but the recent establishment of the community is probably the most important factor behind its limited penetration into the industry. While the Korean, and general Asian, presence in the industry and among its self-employed grew substantially between 1980 and 1990, neither Koreans nor any other Asian group have matched the success they have achieved in other business lines—which makes the comparison to African-Americans all the more interesting.[23]

As in other sectors where immigrant and ethnic businesses thrive, the segmented nature of the construction industry provides ample scope for neophytes to begin.[24] Construction's cyclical pattern repeatedly dislodges workers who then turn to contracting as a survival strategy. A number of the contractors I interviewed owed their start to the recession of the mid-1970s. A West Indian was working as a "permit man" in the jurisdiction of a union to which he didn't belong, when work slowed down in 1972. "So I bought a welding machine, rented a truck, bought some gauges, and went to a pawn shop to get tools. I started out doing small jobs, window guards, odds and ends." Similarly, an African-American electrician found himself laid off in 1976 and discovered that "the union encouraged fellows to get licenses and then hire other members as helpers." He "bought a truck and just started in" without any capital: "I shared floor space with a contractor on 86th Street on the east side of Manhattan. I would pay $25 a month to share an office. The desk was a door on two saw-horses. The shop was the desk and everything I had was on the truck or at home."

But the vagaries of construction's business cycles transform workers into contractors only because the persistently small size of construction firms and the industry's segmentation provide fertile terrain for fledgling entrepreneurs. One old-timer, a European immigrant, "got started by taking small jobs, neighborhood jobs, wherever I could get work. You have to start with nothing, there's nobody to back you. Everybody has to start small, go step by step." Entry thresholds were undoubtedly lower earlier in the century, but the most successful of the African-American contractors surveyed offered an almost identical account of his experience starting out in the mid-1950s: "I bought an auto for $10 and went into business by myself, doing jobbing, plumbing, minor repairs. I worked by myself. Finally got big enough to get a helper. Next thing, I started doing larger plumbing jobs. Putting in bathrooms, kitchens, repiping smaller houses. And then I started working for real estate brokers."

The interviews with owners of the newest businesses indicate that capital barriers to entry remain low. "I went into business on a shoestring," recounted an African-American electrician. "If you wait until you get sufficient money, you won't ever do it." A recently established Korean contractor found himself "mainly doing repair work and service work, sometimes new construction, alteration. When somebody opens a store, I put up lights, the outlets, power for the machines and the refrigerator." A young black New Yorker, struggling under the brunt of the recession, explained, "I grew from being a small, jobbing contractor. Doing at first $800 to $900 a job; then $1,500 to $2,500 a job. Jobs grew slowly. When I made a buck, I put a percentage back in." A Korean contractor, who had gone into business while still an illegal immigrant, started his own business with basic tools and a car in the garage of the house where he rented a room. Two Greek brothers went out on their own in 1985, doing lots of $25 and $50 jobs. As one of them put it, "We did anything."

Fledgling contractors often choose neighborhood work because these jobs are too small to attract larger operators and information flows by word of mouth, but construction contains a myriad of specializations that provide a somewhat protected market. A sheetmetal contractor who ran "the oldest shop in the city" represented a classic example of how the differences in small and large firm efficiencies *within* construction specialties created opportunities for small-time operators like himself. "I work for people who are doing giant projects. They have small jobs that the big houses don't want to do. They would put in a nonunion firm and then have a problem with the [union] delegate. So they'd turn to me. I'll do a job for two men's pay plus overhead." Cost and capital disparities among the various trades work with similar effect, as one of the city's few African-American sprinkler contractors explained to me:

> In my previous job, I worked for an architectural firm as a project engineer doing plumbing and fire protection. This gave me exposure to all types of sprinkler systems and plumbing/piping systems. It was a matter of choosing what type of plumbing to go into: mechanical, plumbing, or sprinklers. I picked sprinklers: of all the mechanical systems, the contracts were much smaller. And the sprinkler business doesn't need a lot of capital. Just tools. Occasionally I need a lift and I rent it.

As these examples suggest, patterns of entry into the industry reflect two processes at work. Segmentation lowers threshold barriers and multiplies product markets. Neophytes in turn adapt with strategies that reduce their exposure, either to more efficient producers or discriminating competitors. "I would look for jobs where I wouldn't find prejudice," explained one African-American electrical contractor. "Small public jobs where low bids win. Companies that want good service and don't give a shit about who gave it."

But if contractors can get started with little or possibly no physical capital, they still need social or human capital. Not only are the latter two forms of capital more decisive for the neophytes, they also play a crucial role in gaining access to physical capital, which becomes imperative for those entrepreneurs who hang on long enough to expand their operations. The interviews underscore the contrast between the abundance of human and social capital that the industry requires of its entrepreneurs, and the paucity of physical capital with which they can get by.

Let me begin with the oldest contractor I spoke to, whose deviation from the white ethnic norm helps highlight the distinctive social matrix out of which the traditional contracting businesses typically begin.

Field notes: Of Russian Jewish background, B. was born in England and came to New York when he was three years old. He went to the old Baron DeHirsch trade school, then located on East 64th Street in Manhattan, where he took electricians' classes, with some math and English. "I had had no previous experience in construction: I had been working in an office. In 1923, when I got out of school, it was very bad, I experienced a lot of discrimination. I wanted to go to certain places, big companies. Everything was alright, but when they asked about religion, they said, 'we'll let you know.' " So he began working for Jewish electrical contractors as a nonunion apprentice. "Working for them I got experience and learning. The mechanics that I was with were willing to let me work, because I was willing to break my back."

Thus, B. began as an outsider, not eligible for employment in gentile-owned firms and lacking kin-based contacts who could have provided him with practical exposure. But access to the ethnic economy allowed him to gain the skills and contacts needed to effectively go out on his own. B.'s case illustrates a key principle: first, one negotiates the barriers that keep outsiders excluded from an economic milieu where skills and contacts are naturally generated; then, one learns how to be an entrepreneur. This principle applies throughout the small business world, but general considerations about the importance of prior experience, contacts, and know-how apply with special force in construction. Construction skills are socially generated: neophytes learn the proficiencies they need on the job through interaction with experienced workers: "I fell in with a group of guys," noted an African-American sheetmetal contractor, looking back on his entry into the trade. "They took me for what I was. I helped them, they were thankful for it. When they needed help [to finish the job] I couldn't help them if I didn't know. So I had to learn. Working together they found out I wasn't an animal—just another guy with a wife and a baby."

Getting customers is akin to eliciting the cooperation of skilled workers, in that both depend on trust. Any one job is likely to differ significantly from the next, making price no more, and possibly less, important than getting the work done right and on time. Since construction is "a very small world," developing a good reputation is essential.[25] "It's very important to know these people," a general contractor explained. "You have to be somebody who knows the market . . . The most important thing in this business is experience and background. If you don't know the manufacturers and the subs, it would be impossible. If nobody knows you, it's difficult to get credit. If you don't have credit, you're dead."

Thus, established players operate in a framework where prior dealings reduce risk. Just as developers or general contractors seek subcontractors with a track record, contractors are concerned about the reputations of the people who engage their services. "If you're working private for people you know, you get paid," explained one contractor. "If you're working for people you don't know, you're going to get killed." Developers may insist that contractors be bonded, which provides insurance in the event of nonperformance or nonpayment to companies that have furnished suppliers. But "once owners and contractors are familiar with you they don't want a bond," as one black contractor noted, making an observation that earlier research supports.[26] "The question is: are you qualified to finish the job? Once they think your head is stabilized and you know what you're doing, they waive the bond." Suppliers operate on similar principles, allowing ample leeway for customers "with a twenty-five-year record of paying their bills." While suppliers would "cut some room to breathe . . . because of the name," a second-generation Italian-American contractor explained, newcomers receive different treatment.

Field notes: When his business was new, a West Indian contractor used to pay his chief supplier in cash. "At the time, I would go in person: I got helped quicker. After about three years, the owner says, 'Give the guy some credit. His check never bounced.' The accountant says, we'll send you two loads, pay for one and take the other on account. When the truck came, the deliverer said, I'll unload it and I'll say you weren't here. Ever since then we've been on credit."

In the end, actors in as fragmented an industry as construction have no choice but to be interdependent. That interdependency provides a framework for establishing confidence and assessing reliability, making "New York a small town [where] good and bad news travel fast." But it also yields a systematic bias for known players, making it difficult for outsiders to gain access to the crucial social relations of trust.

Social Capital in the Transmission of Human Capital

Rephrased in terms of the concepts used to illuminate the sources of ethnic entrepreneurial success, a construction business grows through the development of social capital. But insertion into the industry and the networks that hold it together is itself a mechanism for the accumulation of social capital.

WHITE CONTRACTORS

Because the relevant social capital is most likely to be a property of those already in the industry or with connections to it, kinship figured prominently in the accounts that white contractors gave of the origins and operations of their firms.

Field notes: After H. got a license, he got work through friends, putting in oil burners. "But I had no administrative ability; I was a great mechanic but I had no experience running a business. I hadn't been in enough different positions to learn the business angles of electricians' work." Even worse, the city started leaning on him because he did not know the rules and was getting a lot of violations. In short, "I was dying." Then, his uncle, who had a large business doing electrical work on schools, housing projects, and subways, hired him. "I was as good as out of business anyway . . . so I joined him." He made a good salary and was learning the business: an apprenticeship of sorts. When H. went out on his own, he benefited from a gift from his uncle. By this time his uncle was very big, but he still had a lot of service contracts from the early years when his business was new. These were subcontracting jobs that his uncle was no longer interested in because he was now a prime contractor, but he could not drop them since they had given him a break when he had nothing. So H.'s uncle asked him if he would take these jobs off his hands for him and H. did.

Fathers and sons were active in most of the white-owned firms I studied, including two that had been handed down across three generations. Some father-son pairs were classic cases of encapsulation in the ethnic networks that bind the industry, as in the case of an Italian plumber who had inherited the business from his father, who had gone into plumbing under his uncle's sponsorship. Those with an engineering background were somewhat more likely to start without any direct tie to the industry, though not in every instance, and were also likely to later bring their sons into the firm.

Of course, not every white contractor could lay claim to a relative, or even a contact, in the industry; notwithstanding the importance of inside connections the structural characteristics of the industry ensure that it remains permeable to outsiders, especially those sharing other, relevant characteristics with the industry's dominant groups. But the interviews show that however my respondents entered construction, prior employment provides an ideal platform for starting out on one's own.

BLACK CONTRACTORS: IMMIGRANT AND NATIVE-BORN

The typical white contractor began from a milieu connected to, if not ensconced in, the industry, which generated know-how and contacts. African-American builders, by contrast, were outsiders who had to pick up skills and knowledge without the social capital whites enjoyed. Only one of the African-American contractors I interviewed had followed his father into the trade, and none of the others had close relatives in construction. Whereas white neophytes entered familiar terrain, surrounded by friendly, or at least familiar faces, the black contractors found that going into construction meant learning an entirely new world: "When I got in I saw white people as a mass. No Jews, Catholics, Germans, etc. One monolithic mass. When I came in I discovered different. I heard You Wop, Jew-bastard, etc. All kinds of stuff happening. It was crazy. I had no idea." Moreover, the same social capital that facilitated the transmission of human capital among whites hindered skill acquisition among African-Americans. "You had to fight for things," explained one contractor, a graduate of the civil rights era. "If you wanted to learn, you had to make them know you wanted to learn." "People were extremely prejudiced," commented a New York–born electrician recalling the conditions under which he entered the trade. "What the hell was a black guy doing in a father-son union like Local 3? . . . Those guys . . . I had one job where the guys walked off the job. I walked into the shanty and the guys said if I would work with them they'd walk off." "I worked with a guy for three weeks and we never talked during that period," a sheetmetal contractor told me. "The first day I said good morning, he turned his head. That was it."

Field notes: C. told me about an incident that occurred when he was an apprentice. He used to go to the job and the guys would talk with him on the job but then ignore him when they met him on the subway or anywhere else, before or after the job. So one day, he got them their coffees and said, "Look, if you're not going to talk to me, don't talk to me. Just write down your instructions and I'll do what you want. But don't talk to me." So then the white workers started talking to him all the time.

These traditionally discriminatory practices had the greatest effect on those who moved up in the time-honored way, through the trades. Others, possessing more education, began from technical or managerial jobs, but even so, almost all my interviewees complained of discrimination.

Although I began this study looking for African-Americans, I stumbled across a large concentration of black immigrant contractors from the Caribbean. In contrast to African-Americans, whose employment in New York's construction industry has been receding since 1970, immigrant blacks have done significantly better. In 1990, black immigrant construction employment stood at 1.35 on an index of representation where a score of 1 was equal to the group's share of the total economy; by contrast, African-Americans scored only .61.[27] The situation among contractors resembled the pattern for the industry overall. Fourteen of the twenty-five black contractors interviewed for this study had been born in the Caribbean, a distribution that squared with the perception of those respondents who were long familiar with the industry and its ways. "All of the big black mechanical contractors are Caribbean," reported a seasoned official with a public authority. "Over there they're trained in trades." In fact, almost half of the black-owned firms registered with his agency as minority business enterprises (MBEs) were run by Caribbean immigrants. The director of a minority business association told me, "Caribbean blacks are present to a much greater extent than natives. I deal with a lot of Caribbean people."

The Caribbean advantage stemmed from the ways in which the social and economic structures of the islands expanded the opportunities for relevant skill acquisition. To some extent, these immigrants benefited from exposure to a rural environment in which many of the skills needed for construction work were "naturally" acquired in the course of growing up:

> *Field notes:* "Though my father was a railroad worker," recounted J., a Trinidadian, "he had his own farm. We cut our own sugar cane and sold it to the factory. We were brought up to be independent; to provide for your own self. You have to find the way to survive for yourself." J. started out in house wiring for a contractor who didn't pay him for a year. "I did my own shoe making. Bought my leather, got a last from the shoemaker. This was the only way I could learn—to work for free."

Other contractors learned the traditional way, through apprenticeship, even though they had only received the rudiments of formal education. "You learn it in school as an apprentice . . . house building, cabinets and kitchens, roofing," reported a barely literate contractor from a rural district in Jamaica in a discussion of his five-year apprenticeship. "I put up buildings . . . doors, floors, joists." Opportunities for employment in construction, or construction-related jobs, also encouraged the Caribbean immigrants to invest in skills; those whom I spoke with had had experience in local building, oil fields, shipyards, and bauxite. The history of a successful Jamaican contractor gives an idea of the career range and learning opportunities to which these immigrants had access:

> *Field notes:* O. had gone to a trade school, to work with the Bauxite Company, and after that to a construction company doing iron work. After working in the field, he then went into the shop. "There the shop is more crafted," he said. "I learned technical aspects, layout, proper techniques." Next he worked in a refinery. His last job before coming to the United States was in the Bahamas in 1964, where he worked with a large, international construction company.

KOREAN CONTRACTORS

For the Koreans, the milieu in which they originated also provided access to the contacts and interactional settings where construction skills could be learned. But they differed from the West Indians in terms of class characteristics. As I noted earlier, Koreans arrived in the United States with high levels of skill, but many found that there were few appropriate outlets for their prior training and that the small business industries in which so many Koreans have concentrated make no use of their premigration skills. Construction was an exception, since skills and experience acquired prior to immigration could be transferred to the United States. Indeed, many of the Koreans active in the industry not only arrived with high levels of technical proficiency but brought ample technical training as well, often acquired through years of work abroad.

> *Field notes:* In Korea, J. used to work as a civil engineer for the government, doing estimating, field inspection. "I used to handle big projects, oil refineries, cement projects, things like that. We learned how to handle a project, how to bargain, how to negotiate. It was a big help in this country."

J. was no exception. The great majority of the Korean contractors interviewed held a bachelor's degree, usually in engineering or architecture; some had also received advanced schooling in the United States. All but one had had construction experience, usually at high levels. Several had owned their own companies; some had worked for giants like DaeWoo or Hyundai or Bechtel; others had worked in the Middle East. One contractor boasted of six years of experience at DaeWoo and Hyundai, managing and administering hundreds of construction workers.

Koreans nevertheless encountered problems in transferring their human capital to a U.S. setting, some of which their Caribbean counterparts could more easily circumvent. Language was a big problem, to which the many engineers running dry cleaning or grocery stores could certainly testify, but not an insuperable difficulty: "When I started my English was very poor. I was scared to pick up the phone. I couldn't speak a word of English. In Korea, you learn English for ten years, but not for conversation, rather grammar, writing, comprehension. I got over my problems within three months. Based on my vocabulary and comprehension, my English-speaking ability improved quickly. Within six months I could communicate with people." Similarly, contractors in the mechanical trades needed to be licensed, but as one Korean banker pointed out, "electricians may have a Korean license but can't get [one] here." This banker maintained that "Korean electricians or plumbers in New York are working for [American] licensed people" rather than on their own. Architects and engineers had similar problems, although those who had received some U.S.

schooling or had worked for U.S. firms were likely to have obtained the necessary credentials. All these obstacles notwithstanding, the Koreans came with skills that prepared them for business ownership. Moreover, favorable market conditions, the next topic, helped them make a rapid transition into entrepreneurship.

Social Capital and the Market

The problem of weaning clients away from older competitors stands out among the liabilities of new organizations. "One of the main resources of old organizations," noted Arthur Stinchcombe in a classic piece, "is a set of stable ties to those who use organizational services. Old customers know how to use the services of the organizations and are familiar with the channels of ordering, with performance, qualities of the product, with how the price compares and know the people they have to deal with."[28]

Access to information ranks among the advantages of established construction firms. As in other economic arenas, information moves through both formal and informal channels. The *Dodge Reports* provide a weekly source of information about upcoming projects; government bid lists and procurement conferences let contractors know about opportunities in the public sector. But as one West Indian contractor admitted, "At the beginning I didn't know about these established ways of finding about business." Lack of familiarity or failure to use these formal sources of information appears to be a common trait among minority construction entrepreneurs.[29]

While access to formal sources is undoubtedly helpful, contractors rely on their reputation and their customers' preference for maintaining ongoing relationships, which means that information may not always leak out of private channels. Neophytes are constantly struggling to get business; by contrast, the more established firms live off the reputations and contacts developed over the years. "We get customers almost exclusively through referrals or from recalls from old customers," reported the owner of the oldest firm visited. "All the business comes to us—we never send out salesmen trying to drum up business, or solicit any business." A roofer similarly noted, "We have such an extensive list of references through the old jobs we have done that we always have business coming in." A black mechanical contractor elaborated on this same point, drawing out the implications for race: "In the private sector, you get business by word of mouth, recognition, people look for you . . . [so that] the color thing is not a problem at that point . . . they know I can deliver a product."

Reputation reduces the need to seek out work or bid for jobs; more important, according to my respondents, is the "owner-builder network," the ongoing relationships to those actors responsible for initiating work. "We have developed several key relationships with larger entities," explained one contractor, "which provide us with steady work which we do not have to seek out"; as an illustration he described a sizable contract with one of the city's largest builders.[30] While obtaining contacts at this level eludes even established firms— one Jewish veteran complained that he was frozen out of bigger jobs because he "never had a lot of contact with the owner-builder network,"—other contractors assiduously seek to insert themselves in these networks:

> *Field notes:* F., who relies mostly on personal contacts and networking to get business, stressed over and over again the importance of networks and the conscious development and maintenance of them for the success of a business. While I was there he had at least six phone calls where he was thanking people for this or that favor and talking to people about whom he met at which foundation benefit. He was quite explicit about this kind of networking being a strategy of his. He works for the Juvenile Diabetes Foundation, the Building Mangers Association, and various other groups, all of which "give me access to a network of big building managers and real estate people in Manhattan . . . And even though things are slow now, you still must be seen at these functions . . . 'Out of sight out of mind.' "

The widespread preference for transactions with contractors that boast track records and enjoy steady relationships makes entry problematic for untested entities. The liabilities of newness weigh heaviest on neophytes who are also outsiders and lack the ethnic traits that established parties might look for as proxies of trust, reliability, or simple membership in the occupational community. "Had I been a white electrical contractor," recounted one African-American entrepreneur, "I would have walked into the supply house and they would have said, there's this association. Now if *I* walk into a supply house they assume that I'm a homeowner or a small guy. They don't know me. People don't know who you are. It's hard to help someone you don't know."

Market factors make it particularly hard for black builders, whether native- or foreign-born, to develop the relevant occupational identity. Whereas the demand for contractors' services comes from property owners, disproportionately few blacks own property of any kind, let alone engage in the development activities that generate the bread and butter of most contractors' work. Consequently, both African-American and Caribbean construction entrepreneurs must go outside their communities to find a customer base; practically speaking, this entails confronting a white clientele that may be distrustful, when not actively hostile. Since black contractors cannot change their visible characteristics, they might attempt to circumvent the suspicions of white clients by altering social identities, as one entrepreneur explained: "I put together $6,500 in 1968 and rented an office in the Castle Hill section of the Bronx, at the time a very Italian neighborhood. I called my firm Woodman Associates; the card said Joe Woodman, 'Representative.' The idea was to obscure the fact that I owned my own business. People in the area knew me, but they didn't know I was the owner." Similarly, a Trinidadian began at a neighborhood business in Brooklyn, working for "Jewish real estate owners— they weren't that bad. When I started out I would go and say, 'I'm from John's Electric,' and do service calls on big apartments. People always think you're working for someone else being black and I don't mind that."

Of course, those African-American and Caribbean contractors who go into business with a history in the industry can trade on their track records or contacts, just as whites do. "I diversified through word of mouth," recounted an African-American electrician. "I was known in the industry for being one of the few black supervisors. Lots of people knew me from that." A West Indian who had moved up to management from a skilled crafts position carved out a business from the jobs he had been running while still employed:

Field notes: S. had gone from Supervisor to Service Manager to Field Operations Manager and Junior Partner. In 1974 one partner retired and he was going to try and buy him out, but he and the other partner could not come to a mutually acceptable dollar figure. As S. put it, "I was technically running the company myself" at the time, so he decided to go out on his own. He took several significantly sized clients with him when he left. "Not huge accounts, $25,000, $50,000, maybe $60,000, but big enough to keep you going."

But even the most experienced black contractors find that the problems of effecting relationships to white general contractors and developers, combined with the greater opportunity in the public sector, leads them to shy away from private work. Whites enjoy "the golf course advantage," as one southern-born bricklayer put it; without this asset, many of the Caribbean and African-American contractors instead pursue public jobs. "I think that the reason I haven't taken the next step—to having steady big contracts with X—is because I'm not in the social circles where those kinds of deals are made," noted one of the larger Caribbean builders interviewed. "I can't go play golf or go on boats with people . . . I don't have this kind of entertainment to offer." A mechanical contractor made a similar point, commenting, "I'm not good at politics, or being a social butterfly, networking, lunches, etc. . . . I never found time for this, so I gravitated towards the public sector."

Not only do black contractors, native- and foreign-born feel constrained from pursuing the personal relationships with the owner-builder network that their white counterparts cultivate, they also find that transactions with larger, white entities are unlikely to evolve into stable, mutually beneficial relationships. Both African-American and Caribbean contractors rarely receive recognition as regular players, except in those fields where larger white firms need to engage them to fulfill affirmative action guidelines. A West Indian contractor who began working with one of the country's largest construction firms in the mid-1970s told me, "We built a good name with ABC and since then have been doing a lot of ABC's work. We get a particular job from ABC in an area where they need a minority contractor and where someone in that area knows us. If there is not a job that does not bind ABC to a minority contractor to some degree, I won't get it." Private work also entails greater exposure to opportunistic or predatory actions by the larger, richer firms that provided the work. "We're in a safe zone," exclaimed one African-American contractor in accounting for his reluctance to take on larger jobs. "Ain't nothing fuckin' whitey can do to us. If we get big, they can kill us." Though white contractors express similar concerns—"it only takes one SOB to put you out of business," remarked an Italian-American contractor—blacks feel more exposed. "This industry is tough for white people," complained an African-American electrician with more than twenty years of experience in running his own business. "I can't begin to describe what it's like for blacks." With private sector jobs come collection problems of the sort described by a Haitian electrician who complained that "GCs [general contractors] were failing to pay me and I didn't have the money, time, or energy to chase them in court."

> *Field notes:* G., an experienced black contractor, had been forced into Chapter 11 in 1983, mainly because a general contractor refused to pay him on a $300,000 job which G. had finished. The job had been one where the GC needed a minority subcontractor to apply, got G., and then never paid him. G. ended up losing $250,000 in real estate collateral. He spent over $30,000 in legal fees but has not gotten any results. He said the GC lives in Florida and flies into New York City, and told him to forget about the money because: "Kid, I'll keep you in court for years," wearing you down financially.

Concerned about "private people [who] declare bankruptcy and just don't pay you," most African-American and Caribbean contractors choose the path opted by a Trinidadian contractor who decided "to do public work. If you have patience and the funds to keep you going, you eventually get paid." Minority contracting goals—and, in some instances, continued set-asides—provide white construction managers and general contractors with strong incentives to use minority firms. Still, public work has its own pitfalls, above and beyond greater exposure to unionization, a matter to which I will turn below. The interviews resounded with complaints that public jobs were notoriously slow to pay, though the bottom line was generally that "most of the agency jobs are sound because there are monies there." Contractors also fretted over the consequences of disputes with the managers and bureaucrats who supervised their work. "Working for the public sector can be great—when they pay—but terrible, when they don't pay," noted an experienced African-American plumber. "The X Authority will use any excuse not to pay you. There comes a time when your retainages put you out of business." A mechanical contractor linked public sector problems to the "lower-echelon people" within the agency with which he was dealing. "These people often bear hostility: they feel you're being patted along . . . because you are black."

Although the public sector helps level the playing field for some minority contractors (and their smaller white counterparts as well), its push to increase minority participation often yields a perversely negative effect, enticing minority neophytes who lack the resources and experience to succeed on the job. As one project manager for a public agency explained:

> The problem is: should we let them do a job that's too big for them to do? What are the realistic expectations? A prime [contractor] goes to them and says, "you're on the list." They say, "sure I'll do it." Then the guy doesn't have enough money to do the job. The agency is not very hard on MBEs in terms of saying, "this is too big for you." We end up giving them contracts that you wouldn't give to a non-MBE.
>
> These guys tend to be tradesmen who are trying to have businesses. I think a lot of other guys would wait longer to go in. They'd get more backing, get more jobs on the line. No subs on this job are as small as the minority contractors. They're making very low profits. They need to get in [a project]; think they have to bid low; then they get killed by change orders [when the agency wants to change the project]. A contractor can either make an estimate and reach an agreement with the agency—good estimators can make money on this. Or they can say, as do minority contractors, "watch us and count it." That's when you lose money. Some guys are change-order artists: that's where you make money. You need to be secure enough and knowledgeable enough to make money on changes. The minority guys haven't been exposed enough to the business part—negotiating, estimating. They're so surprised when the negotiations don't work out.

Thus, the difficulties in effecting stable ties to larger, white entities, coupled with the liabilities of newness and skill deficiencies, have moved both African-American and Caribbean contractors to a dependent niche in government work. While affirmative action provisions encourage firms doing public sector work to use minority contractors, they also inflate demand beyond the carrying capacity of many smaller African-American and Caribbean firms. Korean firms, by contrast, do no public work. "I won't touch jobs for the city," declared the most sophisticated Korean contractor contacted. "If they don't trust me," he argued, referring to city requirements for bonding, "I won't do it." These considerations touch on the reasons for Koreans' exclusion from government work, but a Korean official with an American bank in Flushing, New York's de facto Koreatown, offered a fuller explanation: "Koreans feel that they can't qualify for public bids. They don't have the experience and hesitate to compete for these jobs. And they're not open to getting more information about public work because of the language barrier. They're not familiar with the process of fulfilling the documentation required to qualify and are less likely to become an MBE. They're also trying to avoid union problems."

Moreover, Korean contractors have less need for public work. Unlike their African-American or Caribbean counterparts, Koreans have an ethnic market to which they can turn; the burgeoning of New York's middle-class Asian populations has meant work for Korean builders. One electrician told me that he "mainly gets business through ads, Korean newspapers, and also the Korean Business Directory." About two-thirds of his business consisted of store renovations, of which over half involved work for other Koreans. A general contractor developed a specialty remodeling Korean-owned small businesses, especially stores, as well as co-op apartments and houses. His business reflected his clients' growing prosperity: with lots of orders for building marble-tiled bathrooms, this contractor had recently moved from Queens to New Jersey to be near his increasingly suburbanized clientele. Another general contractor, who reported that the Korean market picked up in the late 1980s, had completed building a $3.5 million house for a fellow Korean in one of the fanciest New Jersey suburbs just before the interview.

But I found few contractors who did without non-Korean clients altogether. The broader Asian community represented an important source of demand. Capital flows from Taiwan and Hong Kong generated new construction in the Flushing area of Queens, and the benefits from these investment patterns spilled over to the emerging group of Korean contractors. One contractor had developed a business specializing in the needs of Indian entrepreneurs, branching out from building newsstands—the most visible Indian business niche—to store and home repair jobs that he got through recommendations from his old customers. Most contractors also did work for white customers, but only two depended on a mainly white clientele. All the usual factors—deficiencies with respect to language, reputation, and familiarity with clients' preferences—made it hard to build up a business among whites. Like their black counterparts, the Korean contractors found that business dealings with white customers and white-owned entities led to perilous situations:

> White clients sue Korean contractors intentionally. They take advantage of the situation. Let's say 20 percent of the balance is left behind. Whites sue over a defective problem. Contractors who don't know are scared. They say, "what am I supposed to do?" They see a lawyer, whom

they have to pay. They get further scared. They try to forget about it. Or they negotiate and give back 10 percent. You keep on giving back 10 percent and you go right out of business. In my case I don't let customers push me around. Fight to the end. If I give up, I have to give up everything.

Thus, the growth of New York's middle-class Asian community spurred the development of a Korean construction sector in two different ways. First, the prevalence of Asian property ownership created the ethnic demand for construction services, lacking in black communities. Second, ties to the ethnic clientele made this a protected market. On the one hand, Korean clients were less likely to engage in the type of opportunistic or predatory actions described in the quotation above. On the other hand, the social organization of the Korean community helped connect contractors to their clientele. Information flowed through ethnic channels, both formal, like Korean TV and newspapers, as well as informal. "Korean customers prefer to call Korean firms rather than go through the Yellow Pages," noted the bank officer cited above. An electrician pointed out that "American customers are very sensitive to the price. It's easier to deal with somebody who [has been] recommend[ed]." Moreover, the contractors were highly integrated into the networks and organizations that spanned their communities, increasing their visibility to potential customers and their exposure to relevant information. Contractors belonged to Korean alumni associations, the marine corps association, social clubs, and rotating credit associations; these affiliations did not necessarily generate business, but nonetheless provided a framework for establishing and identifying reputations. Community standing made a difference; one contractor argued that the prestige associated with the university he attended in Korea was a source of considerable status among his fellow Koreans in the United States. For most of the contractors, though, a Korean church was the most likely focal point of their organizational activities. While the religious life was pursued for its own motivations, its fringe benefits could often be measured in dollars and cents. One contractor who refused to conduct business at church gatherings nonetheless reported that fellow church members became aware of his business after seeing his ads on Korean TV. In another case, church affiliations gave a general contractor his start:

Field notes: J. began his construction career in the United States on a project involving the first new Korean church building in Queens. The church was the general contractor on this project and J. was the field/ site engineer. His job was to control the subs and handle the building department.

Capitalizing on Relations with Labor

The pace of construction waxes and wanes with the business cycle, and the industry's volatility weakens workers' attachment to the firm. Having little control over the broader forces of supply and demand, contractors maintain a floating work crew. But they strive to retain a core of key journeyworkers, who know the types of jobs in which the firm specializes and have the proficiencies that those specializations require. The importance of these workers also reflects the high level of skill and autonomy inherent in construction work. Each job is different from the next and has to be done to specifications. The ability to get the job done, in time and at the agreed-upon price, determines the degree of the contractor's success.

For these reasons, the social structures that attach contractors to skilled workers and send reliable signals about characteristics of workers and firms constitute an important source of social capital. Explaining how he secured his labor, one white contractor stressed that he hires new employees through the workers whom he already knows "because when someone works for you for awhile you get to trust these guys." The search for trust and for risk reduction leads contractors to recruit through ethnic networks: ethnicity provides a rough and ready proxy of the characteristics an employer is likely to be seeking; and ties among co-ethnic workers powerfully influence a worker's behavior on the job. Consequently, network recruitment reproduces the characteristics of the existing work force; the example of a long-established, white-owned roofing company is a perfect case in point:

> *Field notes:* When A. came to the XYZ company, most of the workers were Irish. A lot of them still are, including Patty the foreman, whom I saw in the office and who had a stiff brogue, as did Jimmy, one of the workers. They usually hire through their present workers, and so it is sons, uncles, and nephews who get hired.

Although network hiring has historically excluded minorities from construction jobs, immigrant and minority business development depends on minority-owned firms' hiring and training minority workers. Certainly, the interviews provide ample evidence that African-American and Caribbean construction contractors, like their counterparts, rely on ethnic contacts to recruit their key workers. A Haitian general contractor reported that he gets new workers through his existing hires, a practice that maintains a "tight group." At the time I interviewed him, a Trinidadian had fifty-four workers on the payroll, of whom only three were white. The key workers in a West Indian firm consisted of the owner's two brothers, his foreman, a southern-born African-American, and two black bricklayers, one born in the Caribbean and one born in the South. An African-American plumbing contractor said that he employs "ten to twelve guys who've been with me for the last twenty years, and I have another twenty-five to thirty who fluctuate. All black. A core of guys whom I've trained. Some of them have fathers who worked for me." A Caribbean-born mechanical contractor, more explicit about the imperatives that led him to hire minority workers, noted, "I tried and always used black or Puerto Rican fitters in the beginning. The first workers I hired were minority workers and I hired them for two reasons: I'm very sensitive to my own people and want to look after my own. And also because of affirmative action: when you get these jobs, construction managers expect you to have minority workers." Though white workers have come to play a more prominent role as this firm has expanded, the core group remains black and Puerto Rican, as do the supervisors.

THE LIMITS OF ETHNIC RESOURCES

While African-American and Caribbean contractors have strong motivation to use networks as a preferred source for their key workers, they are not always free to do so. The constraints, in part, have to do with the broader social structures of the groups to which they are attached and the institutional patterns that dominate the industry. The ideological claims of black business notwithstanding, the ties between black contractors and black workers have often seemed too tenuous to furnish a sufficiently large and consistently reliable labor force. Part of the problem relates to the ethnic divisions within New York's increasingly heterogeneous black population, in particular, the divide between African-American and Caribbean immigrants. Despite differences of opinion on the extent of the Caribbean presence ("bullshit!" was how one African-American electrician responded when asked whether Caribbean immigrants are more likely to do well in the industry than native-born blacks), the interviews suggested that the immigrants are supplanting their native-born counterparts. "Most of my black workers are Caribbeans," reported a Trinidadian masonry contractor. "Most of the black Americans are employed as laborers, not as tradesmen, unless they're guys who came from the South." Similarly, a West Indian welder with a large plant in the Crown Heights section of Brooklyn and a sizable field operation told me, "I hire a lot of people at the door. They're all foreign-born except for the secretary and a few of the office help." The welder couldn't explain this situation, but other respondents could. "Island boys are hard workers," remarked one of the city's largest, most reputable black builders, himself Brooklyn-born. "They're aggressive. That's what it takes. And lots of islands have oil and sugar refineries. They work in plants and get experience."

That opinion was widely held. "The stronger contractors come from the islands," observed a white project manager for one of the public agencies, himself a former skilled tradesman: "When I was with the fitters, the best workers came from the islands. I think these guys have much better training. And a longer tradition of skilled labor." Others, like a contractor from one of the smaller Caribbean islands, who thought that "the average black New Yorker doesn't want to do this type of job," put the accent on motivation. "If you pick up a guy from Bed[ford]-Stuy[vesant]—they don't show up on Monday, want time off, and want you to loan them money." "My explanation of why so few native blacks?" asked one Bronx-born electrician with an office in the neighborhood where he grew up. "Crack. I've had several experiences of employing people who were strung out on dope." A Haitian electrician argued that Caribbean immigrants "come from a smaller community and are all interrelated; the discipline of the family underlines the difference—you don't find this in black Americans." A southern-born bricklayer considered the "island-born . . . more successful":

> Not because of education or training, but their zeal. I don't think it's skill but zeal. They have a certain desire: house, business, family, personal needs. I'm not saying that American blacks are lazy, but that the zeal of the Caribbeans is much greater. There's a certain taint for American blacks; why get involved in construction because of past problems. The West Indians are first generation: they don't know of these problems. They only came from the Caribbean because things weren't that great there.

Even beyond immigration's segmenting, perhaps divisive impact on New York's black population, other factors seem to circumscribe the degree to which African-American and Caribbean entrepreneurs follow the Korean strategy of looking to their communities as resources. The ties linking contractors and workers are often too weak to engender loyalty among both immigrant and native-born communities. The literature on black business abounds with observations of this kind, most notably black business owners' oft-recorded complaint about the failure of black customers to support them. Of course, the contractors are less concerned about the absence or presence of a black clientele than about the availability, and dispositions, of a skilled black labor force. As one southern-born bricklayer noted, "There's no guarantee that blacks will work better for you than anybody else. You're looking for qualified workers—not asking for race, creed, or color." A masonry contractor contended, "I get more production out of some whites than out of black workers. I have some white workers who show me a lot more interest than my own black workers." An electrician reported that he was "20 percent minority. That's all I want. I don't want all minority: it's not a good business. And black workers wouldn't want to work for a black shop." "I'm looking for guys who can produce," remarked a Trinidadian in a comment that seemed to sum up the views of most of the black contractors interviewed. "I'm not looking for black or white."

The ethnic preferences of black workers and contractors aside, constraints on the supply of black workers, especially in the more skilled trades, compel both African-American and Caribbean contractors to look to other groups for labor. Part of the problem is simply that exclusionary mechanisms persist in full force. Even a long-time mechanical contractor with an established reputation among the black business community conceded, "I don't think I could get twenty blacks and Puerto Ricans to maintain my crews. There are even some blacks who don't want to work for black companies." Similarly a steamfitter who said, "I would hate to have an all white crew," nonetheless admitted, "I have had the situation where most of the available workers are white." And when contractors work on unionized jobs, control over the flow of labor slips out of the minority owner's hands. "When I get a big job, most of the workers become white," noted one respondent. "I can't tell the union whom to send me." The fact that "white guys who come out of Long Island are scared [of working in black areas]," as one Caribbean contractor claimed, may keep some slots reserved for blacks. According to one African-American electrician, however, the union was likely to have the last say: "As an MBE, you're expected to get minority workers, but the union doesn't always send them. You go to the union and say you need to have 25 percent minority. But the union tells you that they have to send by the list."

"The bottom line," an older contractor from the Caribbean concluded, "is that it is very difficult to get black electricians in New York." But if black contractors often find themselves hiring whites as skilled labor, they are even more likely to recruit outsiders to fill their technical and supervisory positions. According to the director of a minority business association, black contractors attract Asian technical personnel, who encounter difficulty moving into white-owned firms: "You show me a black company anywhere in the Northeast and I'll show you an Asian engineer, architect, and often an Asian controller. Many black companies have Asians working for them. The largest black excavating company, X, has an all-Asian technical staff. Its owner can barely read or write, but he can excavate. He has surrounded himself with the people who have the technical know-how." While I did not encounter Asian technical workers among the firms visited (the excavator referred to above refused to talk to me), I did find numerous examples of both African-American and Caribbean contractors employing whites in their highest-level jobs. A successful African-American contractor with a large facility in Queens told me, "I've had a mixture of foremen. These are guys I know from the business. It's guys who can do the job whom I know. I know a lot of people." A long-established Brooklyn-based contractor with a mainly black office staff had a white superintendent and other whites at key positions in his organization. An electrician reported, "I've had whites and blacks as supers. Lost a lot of money with all of them. All no f'n good." A West Indian who worked with his brother and his son had a Jewish purchasing agent and an Italian foreman. Somewhat of an exception was a large black contractor whose "office consists of my brother, who has managerial experience in the grocery store industry; my controller, a minority; my secretary, a minority; and my engineer, a black." But in this case, the key field people were white, with the following consequences:

Field notes: "Times are tough now," C. told me. "I had as many as 110 employees, but I'm now down to 10." He traced the problem to his white construction manager [CM], who "didn't trust my judgment. I'm dealing with college grads and they've been taught the technical aspects. I have to hire someone in the organization to do it." He implied that his clients felt that his organization was weak, and that this was what led him to hire a CM and a superintendent. "These guys screwed me." He then told me about a conversation he had with his white super, after hearing about conflicts between black and white workers, in which the blacks seemed to feel they were "getting shafted": " 'Here I call this the League of Nations. There's grumbling that you're treating the black and Hispanic guys differently. I'm telling you it's no good. Something must be done about it.' More and more of the black guys were getting laid off of jobs. I should have laid off the super early. He just betrayed me."

THE IMPACT OF UNIONS

The classic studies of ethnic business have focused on highly competitive industries where connections between a business and members of the ethnic community (either as customers or workers) provide an underlying structure to an otherwise unregulated arena. But in construction, unions play an important structuring role. Given the complexity and volatility of construction work, the unions serve to organize and structure the labor force, providing access to a supply of skilled labor beyond the reach of the employers' kin, ethnic, or community networks.

Black contractors experience the advent of unionization with disproportionate force, because reliance on public work makes unionization a near inevitability for most black contractors. "Once a job gets big, there are teamsters at the gate," observed an affirmative action officer for one of the public agencies, with years of experience in the industry. "They'll turn you out and won't let you bring in supplies or men if you're nonunion." The interviews provided numerous examples to support this view. For example, one electrician who got his start in the late 1960s reported:

> At that time I worked in mainly black neighborhoods. Then I worked on a supermarket on the same block as the Bed[ford]-Stuy[vesant] Restoration Corporation. Then Local 3 came down. The Business Agent said: "I don't want your men, I want your shop." I told him, "I can't join, you know, with the price I have on this job, I can't employ Local 3 help." He said, "I'll let you finish this job, but then you better come see me." I finished the job and then started working in Brooklyn on a

rehab job on Atlantic Avenue and got a call from Local 3, saying, "we saw your truck." So then I signed up.

Given the prevalence of unionization, "a minority contractor must learn to deal with union labor, if he wants to grow in the New York area," explained a black mechanical contractor. Labor's vigilance means that black-owned firms, usually undercapitalized to begin with, "must work on a smaller profit margin." Unionization also forecloses certain options, since "as a union contractor, you can't do any neighborhood work. You're priced out of the market." Most important, black contractors "go union" before they are ready to handle the increased costs and administrative problems that accompany unionization. As one of the larger black contractors put it: "It would be better if you could grow in an environment where you could have a little leeway. A lot of minority businesses have not had the chance to develop their skills before they end up having to pay union wages and compete with others with experience." In the end, as one Caribbean electrician complained, "You can't afford to put union workers on a job 'cause you can't control them. But you can't get a job if you're not union."

Beyond its bottom-line impact, unionization also constrains the contractors' ability to directly shape and control the work force—a matter of particular consequence for black contractors for reason of both firm size and race. Since construction work is so volatile, with periods of famine following years of feast, unions typically want a contractor's shop and its jobs, not its workers. "A good contractor ought to be able to bargain his guys into the union," asserted one official with a public agency. But not all contractors can. Whereas one black contractor brought thirteen of his twenty-three men into the union when his shop was organized, one of his contemporaries, who had employed a mainly minority work force prior to unionization, brought only one of his key workers into the union with him. The example of the black electrician cited above is another case in point: the electricians' local accepted his men but moved them into a lower-paid division that did maintenance work only.

The advent of unionization also curtails the contractor's ability to manage the selection process. Although union problems in this regard are generic, established contractors are more likely to gain control over their labor supply: not only do they enjoy a reputation but their track record provides reassurance that, once engaged, a craftworker is likely to find a steady stream of work. "I get workers because people call me when they are out of work," reported a white contractor in a highly specialized sheetmetal and roofing line. "I have a name in the business so I get a lot of calls." Smaller, newer firms—a category into which the minority contractors often fall—cannot count on steady work, which means that they resort to the union's hiring hall as a source of labor. But recourse to referrals brings vulnerability. "The best thing to do is to avoid the hiring hall," noted a Caribbean mechanical contractor. "Most of the labor going to the hiring hall is bad. The worst thing you can do is to go through the union." Though the problem is hardly confined to blacks—a long-established white roofer emphasized his unhappiness with the union practice of sending "anyone who is available"—minority contractors, who are smaller, less well-known, and not as rich in connections to skilled workers, are still most likely to suffer the baneful effects of hiring through union referrals. "If I just call the hall and ask for four men," complained a successful West Indian, "they send people whom you can't get any productivity out of."

In addition to the general control problem afflicting unionized contractors, minority contractors face another set of issues. Few black contractors of any size and none of the union operators can avoid recourse to white workers, and they often do so without hardship, notwithstanding the interethnic tensions that permeate the trade. "You will always find a white worker who will work with you," explained an experienced African-American contractor, "because you'll always find a guy who'll put making a living above that kind of shit." Nonetheless, the combination of third-party involvement in screening and racism among white craftworkers makes control over the work force a particularly salient issue for blacks, native- and foreign-born alike. A successful Haitian contractor reported severe difficulties in dealing with the union, whose workers "are white lower middle class, blue collar, with limited education: resentment is very high when they work *for* a black man who is clearly doing better than they are." "As a black contractor," said one with an architectural background, "I have to be ready to factor in bad help from the union into my work more than a white contractor would."

KOREANS: ETHNIC RESOURCES AS A STRATEGIC OPTION

As with their white and African-American or Caribbean counterparts, ethnic ties among Korean contractors and the communities to which they are linked provide access to a reservoir of skilled labor. But the Koreans differ in two crucial respects. First, the structural characteristics of the Korean community increase the resources to which Korean ethnic networks can connect. Second, the Koreans seem to use the networks in a more strategic way, preferring Koreans for key technical jobs, while mobilizing immigrant outsiders for lower-skilled positions.

Korean workers, as well as Korean contractors, arrive with highly developed construction skills that facilitate their entry into the industry. "There are so many people with experience in Saudi Arabia," noted one contractor. Likewise, a general contractor contended that "Koreans have excellent skills due to their prior experience in the Middle East." "My helper has a lot of experience in the field," recounted a small electrical contractor. "He graduated from vocational high school in Korea, worked there as an electrician, and also worked in the Middle East for three to four years. He has experience of maybe three years here."

One contractor, with extensive Korean and U.S. experience, contended that Korean construction workers enjoy significant technical advantages over other ethnic groups. Whether this claim is true or not, the interviews do suggest that Koreans have access to a cadre of highly trained technicians and mechanics, an asset that permits contractors to pursue an employment strategy that differs significantly from that of their black, or even white, counterparts. A successful general contractor with a Korean supervisor who had worked for Hyundai in Korea and Iraq told me, "I don't have any white employees, I don't have to hire whites." He went on to explain his employment practices in these terms:

> My staff is all Korean. I'm trying to make the best experience for them, giving them a chance. But even though they have Korean experience and outside experience in the Middle East, they don't speak English well. After I hire them, within one year they start to speak English. This is a professional field. They know the professional terminology. They can pick up English words for technical terms quickly. I tell them: "I'll give you a good chance. You'll find out that you can speak good English in one year." I also employ Koreans because they're cheaper. I can pay less in salary and benefits. In my firm, I bid a job with a low price. That's why I have a good chance. I can't pay a nice salary and only provide limited health insurance.

At the same time, this contractor drew on a more diversified labor force—"Koreans, Turks, lots of Spanish"—to fill the ranks of his manual labor force, who mainly did carpentry and demolition work. In the course of my survey, some variant of this strategy often appeared. One contractor said that he hired Koreans as skilled workers, but that the "helpers are usually Spanish." A second contractor, with a similarly mixed labor force, explained that his Korean workers, who usually had five to six years' experience, earned about $600 a week, whereas his lower-level black and Spanish-speaking workers made just over half that sum. A third relied on a street-corner labor market in northern Queens to recruit casual laborers from a heavily immigrant, Hispanic population. In yet another instance, a contractor used a mixed Korean and Hispanic crew on regular construction jobs but had developed connections to Polish workers with a specialty in interior carpentry.

With the growth of New York's new immigrant economies, the always intriguing question of why a significant African-American business sector never emerged has gained new salience. The scholarly literature leads us in various directions, suggesting alternatively cultural or social-structural factors that have weakened the black push into business. To the extent that the debate focuses on first causes and seeks to explain a counterfactual—namely, why black business did not follow the entrepreneurial trajectories of other ethnic groups—one is hard-pressed to produce a definitive conclusion about the source of the current entrepreneurial disparities between immigrants and blacks. As I have argued throughout this book, history has a long-lasting effect: blacks' adaptation, both to the weakness of their business sector and to their overall economic situation, has set in motion a vicious circle that impedes the further development of black business. Given the paucity of *earlier* entrepreneurial opportunities, on the one hand, and widespread discrimination in the private sector, on the other, blacks' search for advancement led them into the public sector. Once in place, government employment established an ongoing, selfperpetuating alternative to business as a mechanism of social mobility.

That being said, the construction case study deepens our understanding of the obstacles to black business growth and of the factors that keep African-American and immigrant entrepreneurial development on two different paths. Construction, like other industries in which immigrants and minorities cluster, draws on an ethnically diverse population of workers and entrepreneurs who compete for jobs and customers. Under these circumstances, one group's successful mobilization of social capital has profound consequences for another group's access to desired resources. In construction, the embeddedness of economic behavior in social relations among a myriad of actors impedes access to outsiders. Embeddedness contributes to the liabilities of newness that all neophytes encounter, breeding a preference for established players with track records. But the convergence of economic and ethnic ties has a further baneful effect, since outsiders also fall outside those networks that define the industrial community.

While African-American, Caribbean, and Korean outsiders all experience these barriers in similar ways, they differ in the adaptive strategies they have pursued. African-Americans appear to be most disadvantaged, in part because they have been the most exposed to the social closure that results from the mobilization of white ethnics' social capital. By contrast, Caribbean and Korean immigrants entered the labor market in societies where racial domination played little or no role in labor market outcomes—a considerable asset since construction skills are transferable from one society to another. As the earlier research would suggest, the effect of intergroup differences in social structure can also be detected among the construction contractors I studied. The Koreans appear to be the most embedded in ethnic networks, through which they secure jobs and skilled labor, though class factors play a role here as well, and even the Koreans must reach out beyond the ethnic community for a clientele. Ethnic solidarity operates less powerfully among the black contractors, who are tied to a community where intraethnic diversity and internal competition have grown as a result of immigration.

But ethnic differences among African-American and Caribbean contractors make for only partly diverging fates. Foreign origin may help the immigrants get a start and secure a more skilled labor force, but it doesn't seem to provide much shelter from the force of discrimination; Caribbean immigrants were no less vocal than their U.S.-born counterparts when complaining of the opportunism of white developers and general contractors, and the racial animus that lay behind such behavior. Though black immigrants seem to be slowly progressing, the community is far from affluent, and thus does not provide the type of "protected market" that works to the advantage of

Koreans. In the end, both Caribbean and African-American contractors turn to the state.

Despite qualities that make it a case of particular theoretical relevance, construction differs from the bread and butter ethnic business lines, like garments and retail, on one crucial count: white ethnic workers and entrepreneurs remain far more attached to construction than to many of New York's other entry-level trades. Consequently, ethnic succession has not moved far in construction, unlike in the garment industry or the retail sector, where one can observe a game of ethnic musical chairs.

Other characteristics, however, push construction closer to the prototypical ethnic business lines. As in construction, business development brings ethnic entrepreneurs into conflictual, sometimes competitive, relationships with other economic actors. The black boycotts of Korean retail stores—of which the first began in Jamaica, Queens, in 1981, and the most explosive occurred in Brooklyn's Flatbush area in 1990—provide the most notorious examples.[31] But conflict has suffused Koreans' relationships with the largely white ethnic wholesalers from whom they buy produce, fish, and other goods; interestingly enough, Koreans have sought to use tactics like boycotts to remedy their grievances against white wholesalers.[32] Though overt interethnic conflict has not yet been activated among the city's petty garment capitalists, its sources are certainly present in competitive processes bound up with the structure of the industry. The Dominican contractors whom I interviewed in the mid-1980s, for example, viewed the Chinese competitive threat with considerable concern. "In Chinatown they make clothing more cheaply," commented a sportswear maker, who himself admitted to employing numerous workers off the books. "They work twenty-four hours a day, exploiting their employees." Another entrepreneur said, "About four years ago, the Chinese and the Koreans began to grow more numerous. They work day and night and most of them don't report [what they pay]. When I go to look for work, the [manufacturers] tell me, 'No, the Chinese are doing it cheaper.' " But if the Chinese's success has curbed Dominicans' growth prospects in the garment industry, Chinese factory owners have their own competitive worries, with the burgeoning Korean garment sector—a concentration of lower-wage factories relying on recent immigrants from Mexico and Central America—posing a particular threat.

As in construction, the job opportunities generated by small ethnic businesses, if not quite restricted to members of the club, do not extend equally to all. By definition, an ethnic business niche, like New York's Chinatown garment industry, excludes outsiders; the Chinese factories I surveyed in the 1980s employed a work force that was uniformly Chinese. The Hispanic garment capitalists open the hiring door a little more widely, mainly relying on hometown and home-country connections, while also drawing on workers from a variety of Latin American countries. Korean garment owners also employ their own but apparently with less frequency, since the high rate of Korean self-employment forces them to find a labor force outside the bounds of their community, a quest they fulfill by recruiting the newest, most easily exploitable of New York's immigrants.

Likewise, ethnic shopkeepers tend to recruit among their own kind, as I found in my survey of white, Hispanic, and Korean businesses in Jackson Heights and Sunset Park. Compared to whites, Korean and Hispanic shopkeepers were a good deal more likely to employ relatives and co-ethnics. As the garment and construction cases show, considerations of trust and risk-aversion lead ethnic owners to hire their own kind. But however rational network recruitment may be, it is inherently exclusionary, as black leaders and protestors have charged. Moreover, immigrant entrepreneurs appear to practice exclusion with a twist. When they first emerged, Korean store owners avoided hiring natives, for reasons outlined by the president of the Korean Produce Retailers Association: "We should be especially cautious in employing Americans, because union officials may encourage them to become union members. Once they belong to the union, extra expenses such as overtime payments, the hourly minimum wage, and social security taxes follow. Small Korean fruit and vegetable stores cannot afford to pay all these extra costs."[33] Employment practices have since changed as the Korean ethnic economy has grown and Korean workers increasingly "insist on the highest pay." Like their counterparts in garments and construction, Korean shopkeepers have connected with the newest New Yorkers. By 1991, almost a third of the Korean-owned stores in Brooklyn and Queens that I had surveyed four years earlier were employing Mexican helpers. Mexicans invariably worked alongside Koreans, and Koreans were seen as better workers. Still, these newest arrivals did have their virtues when it came to filling dead-end jobs—namely, their acceptance of low wages, the store owners' universal explanation for their shift to this new source of outside labor. The owners were also impressed with the Mexicans' capacity for "diligence," "hard work," and "obedience," qualities they did not always perceive in Dominican or Puerto Rican workers whom they previously employed. As one owner put it, "Mexicans are milder and more obedient than other Spanish workers."

In the end, many of New York's new immigrants do appear to be getting ahead by going out on their own. But a proper appreciation of ethnics as entrepreneurs requires critical distance from the ideologically loaded image of immigrants pulling themselves up by their bootstraps through business. The ethnic business phenomenon does not epitomize rugged individualism: ties to kin, co-ethnics, and community are the key to immigrant business success. True, the burgeoning of immigrant business can be read as story of turning disadvantage to good account by mobilizing informal resources; however, it also provides a second, less pleasant side. By shoring up New York's small business sector, ever-expanding immigrant businesses reinforce a structure inimical to outsiders, one more difficult to monitor, whose *modus operandi* cuts against the grain of policies that equalize opportunities for all.

Outsiders fare poorly when immigrant entrepreneurs rely on their own kind; the variations among ethnic business communities aside, job opportunities tend to be withdrawn from the open market, a change that hurts low-skilled, native minorities who lack the networks needed to connect with an ethnic business niche. By yielding an economy and labor market where particularistic ties play a more important role, the ethnic business phenomenon makes ethnic affiliations more significant and ethnic boundaries more salient. Thus, New York's new ethnic economies accentuate the city's segmented system, providing new incentives and mechanisms for contention over the ethnic division of labor and its fruits.

9 | Beyond Black and White

American cities today differ sharply from the models and theories with which social scientists have sought to study urban life. The old urban reality was captured by the twin transformations in cities' economic and population base: manufacturing, the historic engine of urban growth and mobility, began a phase of continued decline just when a massive wave of nonwhite, largely black newcomers moved cityward. As home to new cohorts of migrants, the big cities seemed to relive their role as magnets for the earlier wave of immigrants from abroad; this time, however, the magnet was no longer golden, and the urban promise tarnished quickly with time. Just why cities failed to work for African-Americans as they had for other groups has framed social science debates from the 1950s on.

Amid the plethora of answers, we can distill two basic views into which most explanations fall. One emphasizes the beliefs and actions of whites; from this perspective, the problem is that whites prefer not to employ or work with blacks; or else they believe that blacks work less well than comparable whites and therefore assign them to dead-end jobs. The second, more influential view links the source of black economic distress to neither actions nor beliefs; the culprit, instead, becomes the service city and the global economy, which together have wiped out the mechanisms whereby low-skilled city residents had earlier gotten ahead.

But now that immigration has returned America's biggest cities to the diverse, multiethnic worlds they once were, analysis in black and white will no longer do. There are still grounds for ascribing blame to the actions and beliefs of whites, as the reader has already seen. In the city of the turn of the twenty-first century, however, employers pick among a variety of visibly identifiable and often stigmatized groups— not just between blacks and whites. If prejudice motivates employers, why they should give first crack to Jamaicans or Dominicans, and not African-Americans, is simply not clear. The burgeoning of immigrant employment suggests that the city's role as reception point and staging ground for newcomers remains strong—structural transformations notwithstanding. At the very least one can conclude that the scope of urban economic changes has been overdrawn: there are plenty of "lousy jobs"—and relatively fewer competitors angling to grab them than before. Since the immigrant job base has expanded as the service city has grown, why have African-Americans experienced an utterly different fate?

In this book, I have sought to explain the ethnic differences that stamp the economic reality of late-twentieth-century New York—a rather different venture than the enterprise that engaged the earlier wave of urban research. Accounting for exclusion no longer suffices in an economy where the majority of jobs are held by an increasingly scrambled population of "minority" groups. Those jobs are not simply divided up by random or by the conventional mechanisms of skill or longevity. Instead, ethnic New Yorkers, new and old, have converged on narrow branches of economic activity. Establishing, maintaining, and sometimes reconfiguring specialized roles that distinguish their position in the city's economic life, ethnic New Yorkers have carved out niches that serve as employment shelters for members of the group but prove inhospitable to outsiders.

The reordering of New York's ethnic division of labor highlights the question of who got which jobs and why, and puts it at the top of the intellectual agenda. On that issue I depart from conventional frameworks with their emphasis on impersonal economic forces inexorably shaping urban life. Instead, this book moves to a new perspective that places the people and groups that have made, maintained, and changed the structures of today's postindustrial urban economy at the very center of the discussion. As those structures reflect the legacy of earlier ethnic contentions over the spoils of urban economic life, my analysis emphasizes longer-term, historical experiences, and thus joins past and present.

Networks and Niches

This book tells us that getting a job remains very much a matter of whom you know. Hiring through social networks conveys significant advantages for workers and managers alike. The prevalence of network hiring and the benefits it engenders lead ethnic groups to converge on specific economic activities; as they do so, they establish a conc.ntration or ethnic niche. New arrivals are particularly likely to cluster in a niche, lacking information about the broader labor market and reliant on the support of their own kind. Size plays a role in niching as well: numbers are usually small at the early phase of a group's settlement, and so many (if not most) of the newcomers can be accommodated in just a handful of industries or occupations.

But in the conventional view, it is all downhill from here. Niches should decline in relative importance as ethnic numbers increase and established members of the group learn how to penetrate beyond the sectors to which they were initially confined. However important the niche may remain for the first generation, ethnics of the second or later generations should disperse into the broader economy, perhaps leaving behind a residual concentration or two.

As detailed in the preceding chapters, the tendency to cluster in a limited set of economic activities turns out to be far more persistent, even if the precise mix of activities undergoes significant change. Although every group does not retain a sizable economic concentration, the longevity of ethnic clustering remains impressive. The economic base of New York's Italians, for example, bore the imprint of the original immigrant concentrations up to the 1970s; only then did the traditional ethnic niches undergo severe erosion. For other groups, new and old, ethnic niching continues to flourish. While New York's Jews have left the garment industry far behind, they have moved up the ladder collectively, following a trajectory that has taken them from an industrial to a postindustrial niche. African-Americans have followed a somewhat similar path, abandoning their earlier concentrations, while maintaining a sizeable niche capable of absorbing a good portion of this large group. The newest New Yorkers are no less niched than their predecessors. Generally, the degree of ethnic concentration tends to slowly subside—with an accent placed on the slowness of the decline. In 1990, for example, more than half of Chinese and Dominican New Yorkers worked in industries that could be classified as an ethnic niche. Even once it has begun, the downward curve can often flatten out, as in the cases of Jewish and African-American New Yorkers.

Niching is pervasive and persistent because it is self-reproducing. Outsiders get excluded when employers rely on ethnic networks: insiders' contacts are the first to find out about job opportunities; and employers know more about the associates referred by their own employees than they do about newcomers with no prior connections to the workplace. In this respect, networks and niches are a source of social capital, providing enduring social structures that promote and direct economic action.

But as the case studies have shown, a purely social structural explanation of niches engenders an underpoliticized account of who gets which jobs and why. Moving into a niche first requires getting past the owners, managers, and established workers who act as gatekeepers; and these groups of gatekeepers are rarely indifferent as to who gets into a niche and, once in, gets ahead.

Ethnic owners often have a preference for their own kind, not out of sympathy for their co-ethnics but as a result of the tangible benefits that co-ethnic hiring confers. Alternatively, ethnic owners may be on the lookout for the most malleable groups of ethnic labor available. Or they may combine the two strategies, as do Koreans who hire co-ethnics and kin for more skilled jobs and newly arrived Mexicans and Central Americans for the most menial, low-paid positions. Ethnic and other social criteria appear to be no less important to hiring outside the ethnic economies. Hotel and restaurant managers pursue a policy of recruiting white middle-class workers for jobs that require customer contact, while relying on immigrants to fill invisible positions in the back of the house.

But managers hardly have a free hand: incumbents often influence the hiring process, reflecting their ability to wield power relative to management and competing labor market groups. Since newcomers to a workplace usually learn their skills from incumbents, established workers can make it hard for outsiders to get started simply by withholding assistance: the strategy that Jewish and Italian sewing-machine operators followed when African-Americans began to move into the needle trades in the 1930s and 1940s, and that white workers in the skilled construction trades copied when faced with black apprentices and trainees in the 1960s and 1970s. Incumbents can also engage in concerted activity to discourage or harass outsiders. The history of interethnic conflict in the uniformed services or in the construction industry, where workers' ability to fulfill tasks rests on their ability to work as a team, demonstrates how effective this technique can be. Ethnic dominance also conveys signals to outsiders, who draw their own conclusions about the likelihood of entering niches controlled by established groups. As a black firefighter on detail in recruitment explained, "The problem is that it's not enough to say that the career is great. The problem is that the candidate doesn't see the fire truck, he sees white boys."

No less important are the terms of exchange between labor and management. Unionization robs black construction contractors of the ability to control hiring portals; as a result, they hire white ethnic workers, who may be unsympathetic, if not actively hostile, to their black bosses. By contrast, Korean owners, who face no such hiring constraints, can access highly vulnerable workers. Not only do the terms of exchange vary among industries or groups; they change over time. When war-induced prosperity depleted the supply of skilled garment workers in the 1940s, Italian-American contractors were at last able to override the objections of their co-ethnics and bring in black workers. In the 1930s, New York's Civil Service Commission actively sought to improve the number and quality of workers applying for city jobs, thereby infusing new groups into the ranks of civil servants; when the city lacked active personnel policies—as in the prereform and post–World War II eras—the ties linking incumbents to members of their core networks effectively detached vacancies from the open market. In the 1980s, managers in the public sector oriented toward affirmative action successfully used their muscle to reopen hiring doors.

Managers' and incumbents' repeated tendency to control hiring and promotional practices shows how a purely social structural approach overlooks another politicized aspect. Niche formation results from activities of which employers and workers are only partly aware. Once the niche is in place, however, frequent interaction in a highly concentrated niche promotes a sense of group identity. Participation in the niche, one of the salient traits that group members share, helps define who they are. Thus, greater attention is paid to the boundaries that define the niche, and the characteristics of those who can and cannot cross those boundaries. The niche, in other words, identifies an "us" and a "them."

That niche formation helps identify ethnic boundaries and interests can be seen from the proliferation of ethnic associations within New York's economic life and the prominent role they have played in defending ethnic turf or opening the niches controlled by others. In the building trades, many of New York's union locals are nominally open but fundamentally ethnic: in Manhattan, for example, the Irish control the west side carpenters' locals, the Italians the east side locals. Even small business owners turn to concerted, ethnic action to protect their interest: the 1991 Korean Business Directory lists over twenty-five Korean business associations, ranging from the Korean American Chamber of Commerce to the Washington Heights Korean Merchants Association. The Koreans may appear to be more organizationally inclined than others, but they are not alone. The Chinese garment contractors formed their own organizations, until they grew large and powerful enough to take over the association that bargains with the garment workers' union.

Once again, the civil service case provides a particularly nice illustration of concerted ethnic action. In the 1930s, Paul O'Dwyer, representing the United Irish Counties Association, argued that the commission's emphasis on education worked to the detriment of applicants with relevant experience—such as those whom he represented. In the 1960s and after, the Association of Jewish Civil Servants emerged as a vigilant defender of the "merit system," that is, hiring and promotion on the basis of test scores, a principle that happened to serve the interests of better-educated Jews. Similarly, the associations of black and Hispanic police officers have criticized psychological tests used in screening for their supposed racial biases; while an adverse selection effect is clearly visible, the deficiency in the test mechanism is more difficult to discern.

The linkage between niche development and the specification of ethnic identities and interests explains why groups have engaged in concerted action; the job-competition model of the labor market specifies the nature of that concerted action, showing why established groups have been motivated to exclude outsiders and why that strategy has generally proven successful. In structured labor markets, like government or construction, entry into employment occurs at the bottom of the hierarchy and wages are detached from movements in the external market. Thus, applicants compete for vacancies, and employers allocate openings to the applicants most likely to work out on the job, not to those with the lowest wage bids. Under these circumstances, exclusion results from incumbents' pursuit of social closure strategies. The scarcity of good jobs is a major consideration: incumbents will seek to control or influence hiring procedures as long as the number of applicants from their core networks exceed the number of vacancies. One way to maintain leverage is to control hiring standards, and this is precisely the strategy that civil servants and construction workers pursued. Neither civil service managers nor construction contractors have much inclination to oppose their underlings. As long as they can get enough workers, they have little motivation to make it easier for less-skilled newcomers to get in—indeed, the opposite holds, since lower hiring thresholds would probably increase training costs. Thus, unionized apprenticeship programs in construction are deluged with qualified applicants, in good times as well as bad; by contrast, the New York City Social Services Department, the densest black concentration in the municipal sector, constantly seeks qualified employees. In any case, managers may share the views of their key workers. Civil service management was "captured" by the civil service rank and file; likewise, many construction contractors have moved up to management through the ranks of skilled workers.

Beyond narrow self-interest, normative considerations wed incumbents to rules and practices that may have an exclusionary effect. Stable occupation of a niche breeds not only common understandings among workers and managers but also beliefs in the fairness and legitimacy of established procedures. Consequently, ideological considerations lead incumbents to defend existing recruitment and promotional structures. Thus, in the earlier period of Irish-Jewish conflict in the civil service, defenders of the existing system spoke up for the virtues of experience as against the attractions of hiring "college men." At a later stage, civil servants and their organizations became wedded to the principle of the merit system, an ideology they took over from the "good government" reformers of yore and then passed on to today's generation of largely minority, public sector unionists and labor leaders. Currently, the African-American leader of the city's largest municipal union waves the banner of efficiency and quality control in his effort to keep the city from contracting out services—a policy that would shift employment from better-educated, largely African-American workers, to a lower-paid, less-skilled, more heavily immigrant work force, which has not made it into civil service.

Labor Market Factors

Ethnic groups frequently contend with one another over access to jobs and promotion up the job ladder, but they don't always do so. Groups often vacate a niche voluntarily, with the result that outsiders replace established groups through a process of succession. The case studies show that the extent and sequencing of shifts in the order and shape of the hiring queue and in the preferences of workers determine the likelihood of competition and succession.

Succession occurs when the *shape* of the queue tightens the supply of established groups; applications from the members of incumbents' core networks fall off; lower-ranked groups then get pulled up the totem pole, replacing a previously established group with little or no conflict. Black New Yorkers made their first giant step beyond the confines of domestic work when job shortages induced by World War II produced vacancies in garments and other light manufacturing industries that whites had previously controlled. After the war, prosperity widened the ambit for replacement, especially in sectors like health care, where whites poured out of bottom-level jobs even as demand for low-skilled workers increased. The same sequence of events recurred in many parts of the public sector, especially after 1975, when whites left municipal service for better opportunities elsewhere.

Succession also furnishes the backdrop for the new immigrant story that has progressively unfolded since 1965. At the population level, the disproportionately declining white presence had a ladder effect, creating empty spaces for newcomers up and down—though mainly down—the economic totem pole. Reflecting the influence of *prior* migration histories, the impact of white population decline rippled through New York's diversified economic complex in an uneven way. With the exception of construction and a few other skilled trades, New York's white ethnic proletariat disappeared after 1970. Consequently, immigrants could move in and replace departed white workers, without conflict or opposition from incumbents. Ethnic succession even generated opportunities in declining industries, where the rate of white outflows often outpaced the rate of job erosion. New York's small-business sector experienced the same changes: newcomers repeatedly moved in as white ethnics abandoned petty retailing, garment contracting, and other less remunerative business lines.

As the case studies show, generational shifts in opportunities and predisposition move groups out of occupations or industries to which they had earlier been attached. Italian and Jewish workers first left the needle trades proletariat, all the while remaining involved in skilled and entrepreneurial activities, from which they departed still another generation later. During the 1930s, civil service was the employer of last resort for highly educated labor. When opportunities improved after the war, the city ran into increasing trouble when recruiting younger college-educated workers, even though the "depression virtuosos" remained on city payrolls until their careers came to a natural end. Since changes in the standing of occupations *relative* to a group's opportunities or preferences determine shifts in or out of a niche, succession processes can occur at relatively high levels of the occupational structure—as can be seen by looking at municipal engineers or accountants, who were once uniformly Jewish, Italian, or Irish, but are now increasingly dominated by Asian, Middle Eastern, and Russian professionals from abroad.

Succession is most pervasive and noticeable at the bottom of the labor market. Because New York's employers have repeatedly found lowest-level workers among migrants, attachment to unskilled jobs has rarely survived beyond the first generation. Thus, African-Americans have gradually fallen out of the market for low-level labor, in a process outlined by the various case studies. First, the garment industry lost its black labor supply, as eroding wage conditions deterred young applicants and experienced workers found better prospects elsewhere. Then, the same fate befell the hotel industry in the 1970s and the 1980s, when it added large numbers of West Indians and Dominicans to its ranks. By the 1980s, even black construction contractors were complaining about the skills and commitments of the African-American workers whom they could attract. From the 1960s on, changing predispositions among African-Americans added to the replacement opportunities that immigrants exploited. We may already be seeing the same pattern among new immigrants—as indicated by the growth of Mexican and Central American laborers in industries or occupations in which Dominicans or Colombians had previously predominated.

Competition occurs when the job rankings of outsider groups change more quickly and more extensively than either the order or shape of the labor queue. In this case, the ambitions of outsiders extend to higher-level jobs to which established groups remain firmly attached. Competition tends to focus on jobs that rank relatively high in the relevant wage hierarchy. In the 1950s, as Chapter 5 showed, minority workers in the city's low-wage manufacturing complex began to get restive; in the following decade, black workers shifted out of garments and other low-wage industries in the factory sector, only to press with ever greater militancy for access to more stable, skilled jobs, like those in the high-paying construction trades. Civil rights groups seized the time to campaign against employment discrimination in hotels; civil rights pressure helped open up some front-of-the-house jobs, but African-Americans have never been able to circumvent the stranglehold that Italians, Greeks, and now new immigrants have enjoyed over the richly remunerated jobs in banquet waiting. The pattern in small business further pinpoints the sources of ethnic competition: Korean fish dealers or produce merchants have encountered no opposition from white ethnic retailers, but antagonism has suffused their relationship with food wholesalers, a higher-profit line in which white ethnics remain solidly entrenched.

Perhaps the dynamics of competition can best be observed in the civil service case, where ethnic conflict has alternated with periods of succession and segmentation. The most intense forms of Jewish-Irish conflict flared during the depression, when highly skilled Jewish outsiders, pushed down the queue by the depression, sought entry into protected Irish niches; conflict occurred in the police and the school system, not in the Irish-dominated transit system, where blacks were the outsiders seeking in. As the return of prosperity pulled white ethnics up the hiring queue, accommodation replaced competition, and a stable ethnic division of labor emerged. In the school system, Jewish-Irish conflict subsided as Jews moved up the hierarchy, but matters then reverted to the status quo ante after the 1960s, as a generation of black and Hispanic outsiders sought access to jobs to which various groups of white ethnics remained attached. As in the earlier period, the fiercest interethnic conflicts of recent times have pivoted around the school system and the uniformed services, where the best jobs are concentrated.

Resource-Bearing Capacity

Group characteristics and resources play an important role in accessing jobs within a given employment structure while also affecting the potential for changing the structure. Within a given structure, the human and social capital of contending groups affects their order on the hiring queue. In manual fields like hotels and construction, where occupationally specific skills make a difference, the training that immigrants received prior to migration give them a leg up over African-Americans. In the uniformed services, established white ethnics, often suburban residents, outperform minorities on entry-level and promotional exams; efforts at sensitizing test instruments to reduce "adverse effects" have so far produced disappointing results. The same pattern appears in construction apprenticeship programs, which shifted from nepotistic recruitment to an exam-based system, without prejudicing the chances of better-qualified white applicants. Even when special slots are set aside for black applicants, as in the case of the sheetmetal workers' training program profiled in Chapter 6, low skills keep African-Americans from effectively pursuing these jobs.

While the labor market gets its informal structure from the networks that criss-cross it, ethnic ties differ in strength and these differences matter. Immigrant economic activity appears to be particularly embedded in ethnic networks, as almost all of the case studies demonstrate. But the same type of connections work less well among African-Americans. The strength of immigrant networks counts for reasons beyond their role in lubricating the newcomers' movement into New York's low-skill sector and then up the job ladder. As the case study of construction contractors reveals, African-Americans not only have difficulty mobilizing their own but also find themselves depending on outsiders—public sector managers, who provide them with work, and white tradesmen who do their skilled jobs. By contrast, immigrants, with their greater success at social closure, often escape this fate.

Shifts in the relevant characteristics of a low-ranked group can reorder its place in the hiring queue: thus, rapid educational advances among Jews made them competitors for government jobs even during the heyday of the machine system. The diversity of today's new immigrants has a similar effect, allowing better-educated newcomers to enter the economy at middle and even higher levels of the occupational structure. Likewise, rising educational attainments among today's middle-class African-Americans give them a leg up when competing for public jobs against Hispanic New Yorkers—whether native- or foreign-born.

Since externally initiated policy changes can open up a defended and previously closed ethnic niche, a group's resource-bearing capacity in the political realm also comes into play. In construction, shifts in the power of black protesters relative to white-dominated building-trades unions transformed government from a latent to an active influence on employment and training policies. Governments at all levels pursued policies that opened up apprenticeship programs and imposed minority hiring goals on public jobs, changes that in turn led to substantial increases in the number of black apprentices and black building-trades union members by the late 1970s. In the public sector, connections to advocacy and legal rights organizations, embedded in a nationwide matrix of black political and civil rights organizations, enabled associations of black civil servants to pursue legal strategies that dismantled discriminatory practices. A similar concatenation of events changed hiring practices in hotels: government turned its spotlight on the industry's hiring practices as early as the mid-1950s, and the subsequent combination of protest and continuing public scrutiny impelled hotels to open front-of-the-house jobs to blacks by the late 1960s.

If the political pendulum can shift influence from insiders to outsiders, it does not always do so: established groups have also proven adept at protecting their own interests. When black influence over government policies in construction waned in the 1980s, white building-trades workers effectively reasserted control. Similarly, the well-organized and symbolically potent police and firefighters' unions have effectively killed any attempts to alter residency requirements, thus foreclosing efforts at increasing access for minority city residents. In other instances, outsiders' efforts to open up protected niches have been totally forestalled, as in the mid- to late 1960s, when the clothing workers' unions ended any public effort to set up training programs that would prepare minority workers for employment in the needle trades.

African-Americans

The framework outlined above provides a new twist to our understanding of African-Americans and their changing role in the economy of today's multiethnic city. With the allocation of jobs at the center of the story, one is hard-pressed to make the case for the skills-mismatch hypothesis and its scenario of a collapsing low-skilled base and an ensuing social disaster. New York's demographic changes over the past half-century created widespread opportunities to replace the whites who either moved out of the city's economy or moved up to the better jobs that its postindustrial transition created. Like other New Yorkers, African-Americans profited from ethnic succession and the jobs it opened up—but in a limited way, circumscribed by the experience of the past.

For much of the twentieth century, black New Yorkers have competed economically with whites. Until the recent past, African-Americans had little recourse against the weapons of white job control. Even at the bottom of the city's economy, white attachment to better jobs impeded black advancement. In the garment industry, Jews and Italians rarely provided blacks with the same informal assistance they extended to co-ethnics; in hotels, blacks struggled, with little success in moving to the front of the house; in construction, African-Americans could find laboring jobs, but not much else, as skilled craftworkers were unstinting in their efforts to keep doors closed.

Under these conditions, African-Americans searched for the best opportunities they could find; that quest took them to the public sector. Public sector employment offered numerous advantages—not least of which were easier access to jobs and an employer that provided better, more equitable treatment. Government did not automatically extend a welcome hand. Black New Yorkers entered municipal service at the bottom and there found a structure—bequeathed to them by interethnic conflicts among whites—that made it hard to get ahead. In the 1960s and the 1970s, the search for mobility led to open and intense conflict with white ethnic workers; though that conflict has largely subsided, contention persists wherever well-paying and attractive government jobs remain.

African-Americans' shift into the public sector can only be understood as a rational search for advancement in an environment where superior alternatives have been few. African-Americans do better in their largely public sector niche than they do outside it. Government offers them rewards comparable to those whites receive. As a particularly big employer in New York, government creates a sizable niche. The white outflow from government has also given the African-American employment base ample room to grow. Relative to other minority groups, whether foreign- or native-born, citizenship and English-language ability give African-Americans an edge in finding public work.

But convergence on government employment has had the corollary effect of heightening the skill thresholds of the chief African-American economic base. Public jobs were advantageous for those who could get them. As in other fields, contacts helped; black civil servants, and their associates who were seeking government jobs, knew how to put those contacts to good use. Civil service positions, however, held promise only to those members of the community with the skills, experience, and credentials that government required—qualities not shared by the many African-American New Yorkers who find themselves at economic risk.

Of course, work in the bowels of New York's economy could have been a possibility. Yet the data and the case studies depict a steady erosion of African-Americans' share of the large number of remaining, low-skilled jobs—even as the number of low-level jobs held by minorities, native and immigrant, steadily grew. On the one hand, the black concentrations of old, from the most menial occupations in domestic service to later clusters like garment or hotel work, largely faded away. On the other hand, African-Americans failed to make headway in sectors where they were previously underrepresented—and where immigrants found their main opportunities.

Historical experiences conditioned the role that African-Americans came to play in late-twentieth-century New York. Blacks moved to New York when whites were solidly entrenched in the city's working class; while white job control was widespread, it naturally varied in intensity and extent. Over time, blacks converged on the most supportive economic environments, while gradually departing from sectors where discrimination and other factors limited opportunities. Thus, when ethnic succession stirred up New York's ethnic division of labor, the ladder effect created by the declining white presence pulled blacks up—but mainly in the concentrations that they had earlier developed. Elsewhere, low-skilled African-Americans found that they increasingly lacked the connections to entry-level jobs.

But the story also involves New York and its own effect on economic expectations: earlier cohorts of black workers were willing to accept jobs in the city's traditional immigrant industries; their children and grandchildren wanted more. If high aspirations kept low-skilled blacks from seeking entry-level jobs that whites no longer filled, they also oriented better-skilled blacks toward the good jobs that whites still retained. That quest led to competition on unequal terrain, since past and present discrimination in housing and schooling make black workers less prepared than whites. In the end, the mismatch between the aspirations of the *partly* disadvantaged and the requirements of the jobs to which they aspire has provided the spark for persistent economic racial conflict between blacks and whites.

And yet . . . one can imagine a different telling of the story I've recounted, even if one agrees that the central question concerns who got which jobs. The most plausible alternative would lay the blame for African-Americans' deteriorating economic position at the immigrants' door. After all, the economic problems of black New Yorkers have gotten a good deal worse during the years that the immigrant presence has grown. The newcomers have also grabbed the lion's share of the city's diminishing, though still ample, storehouse of low-skilled jobs.

The case for displacement would have to rest on a finding that immigrants pushed African-Americans out of jobs that the latter once held; evidence of that sort, however, is hard to find. African-Americans have played a role in New York's economy quite different from that filled by the new immigrant groups. Industrially, black New Yorkers are far more segregated from Dominicans and Chinese than they are from Italians or even Jews. For the most part, the new immigrants have converged on industries, like retail or light manufacturing, that had never become large employers of blacks. Nor have African-American concentrations undergone a disproportionate immigrant influx. Just a handful of the niches that African-Americans had established by 1970—a mere five years after the new immigration had begun—have since become immigrant concentrations. Overall, U.S.-born blacks occupied a different mix of industries than the immigrants, and for good reason, since African-Americans had already made large incursions into government, whose characteristics as an employer create inherently large barriers to the employment of the foreign-born. Although immigrants subsequently made some progress toward overlapping with African-Americans, persistent separation from immigrants gave the 1990 African-American industrial distribution its distinctive feature.

The case for competition might be salvaged if one made its claims a little more modest: one might argue that although immigrants did not *directly* displace U.S.-born blacks, they still diminished African-Americans' job prospects. Without immigrants, employers might have made greater efforts to recruit African-Americans. The availability of a cheap, hard-working immigrant labor force reduced the incentive to improve wage and working conditions, which in turn might have attracted more native-born blacks.

Marshaling evidence for indirect displacement, at least when stated so starkly, still proves difficult. As the garment industry case shows, African-Americans moved out of low-level jobs well before the advent of the new immigrants. When the labor shortages of the late 1960s led garment employers to recruit African-Americans, going so far as to advertise in the city's weekly black newspaper, their efforts fell flat. Wage depression in the garment industry, certainly a deterrent to African-American job seekers, can hardly be attributed to immigrants: relative wages started dropping in the 1950s; today's immigrants notwithstanding, New York's garment workers still earn a good deal more than clothing workers anywhere else in the country. One cannot assess displacement without looking at the positive side of the balance sheet: immigration accounted for almost all of New York's net population gains in the 1980s, adding to the local demand for goods and services, and providing a fillip to employment growth. Since immigrants receive the same public services as everyone else, from street cleaning to schooling, their presence provided support for the African-American employment base in the public sector.

Yet, the material developed in this book does suggest that immigration has redefined the contours of New York's economy in ways that circumscribe job availability to native-born blacks. While changing aspirations and expectations weakened African-Americans' attachment to bottom-level jobs, the crucial fact about the current labor market is that low-skilled jobs essentially belong to the foreign-born. Since connections play an important role in getting a job, the newcomers enjoy privileged access to inside information, which tends not to leak out to black New Yorkers. African-American exclusion gets more pronounced when immigrants establish ethnic economies, converge on occupational niches, or cluster in specialized business lines; under these circumstances immigrants play a more active role in the hiring and recruitment process, and their preferences clearly do not extend to African-Americans. Furthermore, immigrant networks provide a mechanism for getting the skills one needs to move beyond entry-level slots; informal ethnic training systems effectively exclude outsiders from the processes that teach proficiencies to those workers with the right ethnic connections.

Whatever the immigrant impact so far, it is likely to deepen in the years to come. African-Americans have had the best of economic times when a vigorous economy swelled payrolls, encouraging employers to move down the hiring queue and pull in workers whom they previously excluded. While the hopes of the black policy community seem to lie in a return to full employment, the immigrant incursion into New York's economy makes it unlikely that African-Americans will reap the dividends of any future urban economic growth. Just as full wallets lead American consumers to buy goods made in Tokyo or Seoul rather than Detroit or North Carolina, tight labor markets in the United States mobilize potential immigrants in countries abroad. When New York's next economic boom depletes the supply of dishwashers and janitors, the existing immigrant lock on low-level jobs will lead employers to find replacements abroad—not in Harlem or Bedford-Stuyvesant. Indeed, tomorrow's low-skilled immigrants have already arrived—in the form of the Mexicans who work in Korean grocery and garment shops—and the connections needed to signal additional opportunities to impoverished kin and acquaintances left behind are already in place.

Prospects further up the job ladder also look poor: the African-American concentration in public jobs has sheltered them from immigrant competition, but that situation is unlikely to persist much longer. The long-standing conflict between African-Americans and Puerto Ricans only presages things to come; immigration simply means that there will be more claimants for a piece of the public sector pie. Comparisons of the 1980 and 1990 censuses show that immigrants have already begun to move into government employment, though not yet in numbers that threaten African-Americans' privileged place. Moreover, the new immigrants need not wait for greater political influence to gain a growing share of government work: the combination of high skills and private sector discrimination directs newcomers into public sector professional or managerial jobs, a trend that will surely accelerate in the future. The background to growing ethnic competition includes New York's continuing fiscal difficulties, which almost certainly guarantee a shrinking supply of public jobs.

Immigrants

What no one expected in the early 1960s, when the United States reformed its immigration laws, was that New York would again become an immigrant town. In a sense, the city has come full circle, reverting back to the polyglot mixture of days gone by. The view that the earlier immigrants were good for New York and that the city did well by them—or least by their descendants—has helped place the most recent newcomers in a favorable light. If the past predisposes New Yorkers to an optimistic reading of the new immigrant experience, a good deal of factual support for that point of view exists as well. In the three decades since the Hart-Celler Act, immigrants have become a pervasive element in New York's economic life. Their high employment rates, the bustling ethnic economies that they have established, and their gradual infiltration of higher-level activities confirm that New York retains its role, not just as an immigrant port of entry, but also as a staging ground of upward mobility for America's newest arrivals.

Although many aspects of the new immigrant experience suggest a replay of earlier history, at least one major difference stands out: whereas the newcomers who streamed into Ellis Island entered a rapidly growing economy with ample opportunities for workers who made their living off their muscles and brawn, in troubled, post-industrial New York, job seekers' prospects lie in the processing of information and the making of deals. In this respect, the mystery of the new immigration concerns New York's continuing attraction for the foreign-born. Although one well-known answer links immigration to the growth of the city's advanced services, this book gives plenty of evidence that the opportunities for new immigrant labor came from ethnic succession.

Popular wisdom celebrates the immigrants for their efforts to pull themselves up from the bottom on their own. Nothing in this book contradicts the view that immigrants, today and before, have worked long and hard. But immigrants' progress in New York is not simply due to individual effort, since newcomers are linked to settlers and their networks help them from the start. Ethnic connections within immigrant communities provide an informal structure to immigrant economic life; that structure, in turn, furnishes explicit and implicit signposts of economic information and mechanisms of support that help ethnics acquire skills.

Thus, the new immigrant phenomenon is largely the story of the ethnic niche. The past quarter-century has shown that the initial immigrant concentrations have found ample room for newer arrivals, claims of limited absorptive capacity notwithstanding. The niche provides a privileged place for new arrivals: established kin and co-ethnics steer the way into New York's economy, which helps explain why so many low-skilled newcomers have found a berth in postindustrial New York. Unlike the African-American niche, the immigrant concentrations do *not* appear to reward immigrants in particularly favorable ways. Nonetheless, they furnish jobs aplenty and in so doing help many of the newcomers take modest, gradual, but still significant steps up New York's economic ladder.

The social structures of migration account for much of the immigrants' progress. Until recently, the match between immigrants' aspirations and broader labor market dynamics produced another ingredient of success. On the one hand, the immigrants' social origins predisposed them to embrace jobs that native New Yorkers would no longer accept; meager as they appeared to New Yorkers, the paychecks in the city's garment, restaurant, or retail sectors looked good in comparison to the going rate in Santo Domingo, Hong Kong, or Kingston. On the other hand, the city's factory sector was suffering a hemorrhage of older native workers that outpaced the leakage of jobs.

But neither the supply nor the demand sides to this equation will forever remain the same. Immigrant expectations change with acclimation to the new style of life they adopt in New York; one cannot project immigrants' willingness to labor at the bottom in perpetuity. Time also affects the opportunities that result from ethnic succession. The newcomers of the 1970s took over from the city's white ethnic proletariat; but now that white ethnic workers have essentially left the scene, one can no longer count on the factory's revolving door to furnish jobs to the newest arrivals. Once replacement processes have worked themselves out, manufacturing's continuing decline will put a ceiling on immigrant job growth in this sector.

A related issue is how the arrivals of the future will affect those immigrants who have already settled down in New York. The econometric literature is inconclusive about the degree of immigrant-native competition in the labor market; it does tell us that immigrants compete with other foreign-born workers. Two factors give this finding particular relevance. First, unlike earlier waves, the new immigration appears not to respond to the ups and downs of the business cycle: immigrants kept coming to New York during the economic crisis of the 1970s; the same pattern emerged after the city's economy stumbled in 1987, and this time the numbers actually increased and by a sizable amount. That immigration no longer falls off when the economy slackens probably mattered less in the 1970s, when there were relatively few immigrants and relatively more opportunities to get ahead through ethnic succession, than it will in the 1990s, when there are many more immigrants and a less active game of ethnic musical chairs. Second, many of the immigrants have converged on declining sectors where the future employment of one group may come at the expense of another. That scenario seems well advanced in New York's rag trade: the Chinese ethnic economy has burgeoned while Dominicans and other immigrant Hispanics—a presence in the apparel industry since the early 1960s—have already begun to lose jobs.

Indeed, for some groups, the interaction of supply and demand factors already appears less favorable than it was in the phase of initial implantation, with consequences that raise concern over the immigrants' future. Consider New York's largest new immigrant group, the Dominicans. By 1990, the number of Dominicans in manufacturing had tumbled from its apex of a decade before. In a sense, Dominicans recouped these losses through gains in a wide swath of service and retail industries, while also building a vibrant ethnic economy. But the new niche that Dominicans carved out tends to be a concentration of jobs that pay poorly and compare unfavorably with opportunities elsewhere in the city's economy—even after background factors have been controlled. And the effects of bleak job prospects do seem to be detectable—in the diminishing proportion of employed Dominicans and, still more ominously, in the high proportion of Dominicans receiving public assistance.

Of course, the incredible diversity of New York's new immigrant population makes generalizing about the prospects for *all* immigrants a hazardous business: each group follows a somewhat distinctive path. Though danger signals can be found for both the Chinese and the West Indians, the groups seem to be doing quite well overall, with firm and expanding footholds in the city's economy. The same can be said for Russians, Colombians, Koreans, and others who have contributed significantly to the explosion of New York's new immigrant population base.

Even if most of New York's new immigrants move onward and upward, this book suggests that ethnic progress comes with a cost measured in the types of conflicts that I have repeatedly portrayed. While the underlying social structures of ethnic communities provide the basis for immigrant absorption, settlement, and economic incorporation, maintaining the boundaries that separate ethnic economies, niches, or even neighborhoods always proves problematic. Newcomers jostle with other, identifiably different, new arrivals for the resources they all value. In the scramble for jobs, the same ties that bring communities into the workplace also produce the motivation and the opportunity for excluding those New Yorkers who aren't members of the same ethnic club.

By converging on New York, the immigrants have also come to an area where earlier immigrants and domestic migrants moved up through economic specialization, establishing niches to which they often remain strongly attached. Until now, those specializations have largely gone unchallenged—since the newest arrivals have been content with the modest positions they have obtained to date. But the economic orientations of New York's newcomers will inevitably change, and when they do, immigrants will begin to compete for natives' jobs. Since the next New York is likely to resemble today's New York—an economic world where ethnic connections have much to do with who works where and with whom—New Yorkers' extraordinary propensity to come to blows over racial and ethnic differences should persist for the foreseeable future.

Appendixes
Notes
Index

Appendix 1

Shift-Share Analysis

In Chapter 3, I adapt shift-share analysis, a technique used most often in regional analysis, to break down the components of employment change. For purposes of readability, I mainly present pictorial results of the analysis; space precludes me from providing the many numbers that lie behind the pictures. Nonetheless, for the quantitatively inclined, I thought it would be useful to present a more detailed account of the calculations, as well as an example that begins to illustrate how the results were generated.

The "absolute change" refers to the differences between the total employment of the group (in the economy overall, or in a sector, or in an education-specific category) at the beginning and at the end of an intercensal period.

The "growth effect" is computed by multiplying employment (in the sector or in the category) in the base year by the growth rate of the economy as a whole for the intercensal period.

The "industry effect" (or the "category effect") is computed by multiplying the base-year employment of the group in the industry or the category by the difference between the growth rate for the industry or the category and the overall growth rate.

The "population effect" is computed by multiplying the base-year employment of the group in the industry or the category by the "adjusted population rate." This number is derived by first calculating the difference between the actual change in the group's population and the change that would have occurred had the group not grown or shrunk at the same rate as the total population. This difference is then divided by the actual group employment at the beginning of the period. Thus, if the group grew at the same rate as the overall population, the population effect would be zero.

The "shift" is a residual. It is calculated by summing the growth, industry (or category), and population effects, and then subtracting this sum from the absolute change. It represents the change in employment for the group that is not explained by any of the other effects.[1]

For example, consider the graph for the 1980–1990 period that appears in Figure 3.13. Here, I try to account for the different components of employment change among native whites in jobs requiring less than a high school education. In 1980, 155,040 native white New Yorkers worked in jobs requiring less than a high school education; since the same category employed only 70,013 native whites in 1990, the absolute change for the period was 85,027. During this same period, however, New York's economy grew by almost 16 percent. In calculating the growth effect, I multiply .16 times 155,040 (the number of native whites employed in these low-skilled jobs in 1980), to estimate how many such jobs native whites might have gained had employment in this category increased at the same rate as the total economy. Had the change in native white employment in jobs requiring less than a high school degree been directly proportional to the growth of the city's economy, native whites would have gained roughly 25,000 such jobs.

Total employment in jobs requiring less than a high school degree actually declined by 12.8 percent between 1980 and 1990. But the extent of the job change (loss or gain) directly attributable to shifts in this category is the difference between the change in the category's size (−.128) and the growth effect for the total economy (.159). To estimate the category effect, I then multiply the size of this difference (−.287) times total employment for the category in 1980 (155,040). This calculation shows us that native whites would have lost almost 45,000 jobs, had their decline in this low-skilled category been directly proportional to the category's decline.

In calculating the population effect, I assume that native whites would have lost jobs in this category (and in every other category as well) owing to a decline in their relative size: relative to 1980, there were fewer native whites available for work in New York City's labor market. (The same reasoning assumes that growing groups, like immigrants, would add jobs simply because numbers grew during the period.) In estimating the population effect, I first calculate how many additional native white residents the city would have gained had the native white population increased at the same rate as the total economy. Thus, I multiply the number of adult native whites living in New York in 1980 (1,528,700) times the growth rate for the total economy (.159). I then subtract this predicted change from the actual change in the white population and divide the difference by the 1980 native white population. This procedure tells us that native whites would have lost almost a quarter of their jobs in every category, had the native white job change been directly proportional to the change in their relative population size. Applying this estimate to jobs requiring less than a high school degree, I attribute a loss of 38,400 native white jobs due to the population effect.

Looking at each of the effects calculated so far, we see that the growth effect should have increased native white employment in low-skilled jobs, whereas the other two effects, each working independently of the other, should have decreased native white employment in low-skilled jobs. But employment in a category could also change because a group changed its *share* of such jobs. For example, had native whites held on to their earlier share of low-skilled jobs, after adjusting for the growth, category, and population effects, they would have lost 58,188 jobs between 1980 and 1990. In fact, during the 1980s, they lost 85,027 jobs requiring less than a high school education. This difference represents the shift.

Appendix 2

Field Research Methods

Chapters 5 through 8 are informed by a variety of field research projects that I undertook between 1980 and 1991. This brief appendix summarizes the various studies I conducted as part of the data collection efforts for this book.

Chapter 5: While in the chapter's first section, on the garment industry, I mainly focus on historical developments prior to 1980, I also quote from interviews I conducted with employers and workers in the industry. In 1980, I interviewed a randomly selected sample of 100 Hispanic members of a large garment workers' union local in New York City; these interviews, which I tape-recorded, typically lasted from one to two hours. During the interviews, I collected a complete work and migration history, in addition to obtaining information about respondents' attitudes toward work. In 1984, I interviewed 41 Jewish and Italian contractors; I describe the selection of the sample and provide a copy of the questionnaire in my book *Through the Eye of the Needle: Immigrants and Enterprise in New York's Garment Trades* (New York: New York University Press, 1986). Between 1987 and 1989, Thomas Bailey and I conducted additional interviews with 70 apparel employers, union officials, and directors of employers' associations in conjunction with an evaluation of training programs for the apparel industry, an evaluation of the impact of the Immigration Reform and Control Act, and a study of technological and organizational change. These interviews centered on matters related to recruitment, training, labor force characteristics, factory organization, and customer linkages. They also inform portions of Chapter 8.

The chapter's second section, on the hotel industry, draws on 26 interviews I conducted in 1990 in New York and Philadelphia, with hotel personnel managers, union officials, trainers, representatives of employers' and industry associations, government officials, and officials in immigrant service agencies. Although the majority of interviews (18) were conducted in New York, I incorporate material from the Philadelphia interviews where they illuminate aspects of the industry and the jobs that are common to both cities. The interviews lasted from one to four hours and covered a broad span of topics ranging from changes in the market for hotel services, to specific skill requirements, to patterns of recruitment and training. I spoke with informants connected with both the union and the nonunion segments in both cities, and I stratified the sample to include hotels catering to the various major submarkets.

Chapter 6: This chapter has its origin in work I did with Thomas Bailey to develop an affirmative action strategy in construction for a large regional transportation agency, which was then planning its long-term capital spending strategy. In the course of this work, done episodically between 1984 and 1989, we undertook more than 120 interviews with union leaders, directors of apprenticeship programs, trainers, government officials, and contractors. We supplemented this material with several additional, lengthy interviews with key informants involved in the policy developments recounted in the chapter. These interviews mainly provided background material for understanding the construction industry and its workings, though certain parts of the chapter draw directly from the interviews, as indicated.

Chapter 7: The historical and statistical material that figures prominently in this chapter is supplemented by 62 in-depth, open-ended interviews that I conducted with a broad range of government officials, past and present, occupying positions from top to lower levels, as well as officials of public sector unions. The interviews lasted from forty-five minutes to three hours; in a number of cases, I conducted repeat interviews, which allowed me to cross-check information and assess new hypotheses. The interviews were tailored to the individual's circumstances, varying in content depending on whether the informant was a rank-and-file bureaucrat or a manager. Interviews with the former were more likely to focus on the individual's own career trajectory, with an emphasis on factors impeding or promoting entry and mobility within government service; interviews with the latter tended to concentrate on hiring, recruitment, and promotion policies, though wherever possible I tried to collect a brief career history. Most of my respondents were connected to the cases profiled at the end of the chapter—the Fire Department, the Human Resources Administration, and a variety of agencies employing large numbers of accountants and engineers. I also interviewed a number of contacts in the Personnel, Sanitation, and Police Departments, as well as two past directors of personnel.

Chapter 8: The field material for the retail case comes from a study I first conducted in 1986 and 1987: I took a complete ethnic census of all retail and service businesses in the Jackson Heights section of Queens and the Sunset Park section of Brooklyn. From this census I generated a random sample of 240 stores, equally divided among white, Korean, and Hispanic owners (80 each). I interviewed 213 store owners from this list. Further details are given in my article "Structural Opportunity or Ethnic Advantage? Immigrant Business Development in New York," *International Migration Review*, 23, no. 1 (1989): 48–72. With some assistance from me, Greta Gilbertson, of Fordham University, returned in 1991 and 1992 to the original white- and Hispanic-owned stores I had surveyed several years earlier. A Korean graduate student undertook the follow-up interviews with the Korean owners; in addition to inquiring about ownership patterns, he also asked some labor force questions, which provide material discussed at the very end of the chapter.

The apparel section of this chapter draws on the interviews described for Chapter 5, as well as 10 interviews I undertook with Chinese contractors as part of the *Chinatown Garment Industry Study*, conducted by the consulting firm of Abeles, Schwartz, Haeckel, and Silverblatt, for Local 23-25 of the International Ladies' Garment Workers' Union.

The construction case study is principally based on interviews from late 1990 and early 1991 with 50 construction contractors, of which 25 were black, 13 were Korean, and 12 were white. The interviews with white and black contractors were generated from lists of "minority" and "small" business enterprises (MBEs and SBEs) maintained by two public construction agencies. Given the vast differences between white and black construction firms—with the former likely to be larger and distributed over a wider range of specializations—this procedure promised to generate white and black firms that would be more or less comparable. In selecting among firms doing at least some public work, I was concerned that I would generate a skewed sample of black firms, eliminating those with private sector specializations only. But interviews with key informants, attendance at a meeting of a "black workers/black contractors association," and discussions with respondents made it possible to outline the network of black contractors. By adding referrals to lists obtained from the agencies, I was able to ensure that our interviews sampled from the full range of black contractors and their specializations. Since no Korean contractors had been certified as MBEs, I instead drew my sample from the 1991 New York Korean Business Directory, which listed 138 Korean construction firms.

The interviews were open-ended, typically lasting from ninety minutes to three hours. In the interviews I sought to obtain information about the contractors' career histories; the business history; linkages with and the composition of customers, suppliers, related firms (general contractors or subcontractors, depending on the case); financing; and labor, including questions having to do with its composition, recruitment, and labor relations. I personally interviewed 12 black contractors, 3 white contractors, and 3 Korean contractors; a white graduate student conducted the remaining interviews with the white and black contractors; and a Korean graduate student conducted the remaining interviews with the Korean contractors. These interviews were supplemented by interviews with 3 officials in government agencies as well as with a Korean banker.

Notes

1. The New Urban Reality

1. William J. Wilson, *The Truly Disadvantaged: The Inner City, the Underclass, and Public Policy* (Chicago: University of Chicago Press, 1987); Christopher Jencks and Paul Peterson, eds., *The Urban Underclass* (Washington, D.C.: Brookings Institution, 1991).

2. Sharon Zukin, "Gentrification," *Annual Review of Sociology*, 13 (1987): 129–147; William Frey and Alden Speare, *Regional and Metropolitan Growth and Decline in the United States* (New York: Russell Sage Foundation, 1988).

3. George Sternlieb and James Hughes, "The Uncertain Future of the Central City," *Urban Affairs Quarterly*, 18, no. 4 (1983): 455–472; John Kasarda, "Jobs, Mismatches, and Emerging Urban Mismatches," in M. G. H. Geary and L. Lynn, eds., *Urban Change and Poverty* (Washington, D.C.: National Academy Press, 1988), pp. 148–198.

4. Saskia Sassen, *The Mobility of Capital and Labor* (New York: Cambridge University Press, 1988) and *The Global City: New York, London, Tokyo* (Princeton: Princeton University Press, 1992); Bennett Harrison and Barry Bluestone, *The Great U-Turn* (New York: Basic Books, 1988).

5. The two perspectives also contradict each other on the issue of the direction of job change: is the problem the disappearance or the proliferation of low-level jobs? The answer is that neither polarization nor mismatch proponents are sure. Thus William Wilson and his collaborators emphasize the decline of manufacturing but then point out the "explosion of low-pay, part-time work" (L. J. Wacquant and W. J. Wilson, "The Cost of Racial and Class Exclusion in the Inner City," *Annals*, 501 [January 1989]: 11), the growth of sweatshops, and the "peripheralization and recomposition of the core," code words for economic polarization (L. J. Wacquant, "The Ghetto, the State, and the New Capitalist Economy," *Dissent*, 36, no. 4 [1989]: 512).

6. Our society's problems in talking about race make a note about terminology necessary. This book centers on the contrasting experiences of African-Americans

and a variety of immigrant groups, most of whom came to New York after 1965. Where I am concerned with native/foreign contrasts, I use the term "African-Americans" to designate a U.S.-born population, with long-term origins in Africa and proximate origins in the U.S. South; I also use the terms "black New Yorkers" and "native-born blacks" or "U.S.-born blacks" to refer to the same population.

Of course, New York has experienced a large influx of blacks from abroad, mostly from the West Indies, though there is a small, rapidly growing population of persons from Africa. In this book, I distinguish these foreign-born New Yorkers from their U.S.-born counterparts by using the term "black immigrants" or "foreign-born blacks." At various points in the book, I am specifically concerned with black immigrants from the West Indies; I use the terms "West Indians" or "Caribbean immigrants" when referring to this group.

I use the term "black" when not concerned with native/foreign contrasts; in these cases, "black" refers to native- and foreign-born persons. In many instances, the population designated by the term "black" is in fact a mainly native-born population, as is true for my discussion of most events prior to 1970. There were undoubtedly immigrant blacks among the garment workers, construction workers, and government employees I discuss in the historical sections of Chapters 5, 6, and 7, but their numbers were small, in both relative and absolute terms. Moreover, the sources on which I rely for the historical cases almost always make it impossible to distinguish between native- and foreign-born blacks. This holds for some of the contemporary cases as well, for example, that of the public sector. Administrative data, such as those compiled for equal employment opportunity purposes, count persons by race, not by national origins, and hence groups native- and foreign-born blacks together. In other instances, as in Chapter 8, I use the term "black" to refer to both African-Americans and West Indians; though ethnic differences divide these groups, as the chapter's case study recounts, outsiders treat them as if they were one, making "black" the appropriate category.

7. Unfortunately, the public use sample from the 1960 Census of Population does not provide a code for specific areas below the state level, making it impossible to isolate New York City from the rest of the state. Hence, I have not been able to use the public use tapes for 1960. The printed census volumes do not provide much help either, as very little employment data at the city, as opposed to metropolitan, level is provided.

8. Frank Levy, *Dollars and Dreams: The Changing American Income Distribution* (New York: Russell Sage Foundation, 1987), p. 112.

9. John Kasarda, "Cities as Places Where People Live and Work: Urban Change and Neighborhood Distress," in Henry Cisneros, *Interwoven Destinies: Cities and the Nation* (New York: Norton, 1993), p. 82. The article I cite here provides a particularly succinct and clear expression of Kasarda's views, which he has elaborated in many publications over the past fifteen or so years. For other examples, see "Entry-Level Jobs, Mobility, and Urban Minority Employment," *Urban Affairs Quarterly* 19, no. 1 (1984): 21–40; "Jobs, Mismatches, and Emerging Urban Mismatches"; "Structural Factors Affecting the Location and Timing of Urban Underclass Growth," *Urban Geography*, 11, no. 3 (1990): 234–264. William J. Wilson, a still more prominent mismatch proponent, liberally cites Kasarda's findings and endorses Kasarda's views in his influential book *The Truly Disadvantaged.*

10. Kasarda, "Cities as Places Where People Live and Work," p. 83.

11. Ibid., p. 84.

12. Hudson Institute, *Workforce 2000: Work and Workers for the Twenty-first Century* (Indianapolis: Hudson Institute, 1987), p. 100.

13. Edward Fiske, "Impending Jobs 'Disaster': Work Force Unqualified to Work," *New York Times*, September 21, 1989, p. 1.

14. Hudson Institute, *Workforce 2000*, p. 91.

15. National Advisory Commission on Civil Disorders, *Report* (New York: Bantam, 1968), p. 278.

16. Joleen Kirschenman and Katherine Neckerman's well known essay, " 'We'd Love to Hire Them, But . . .': The Meaning of Race to Employers," in Christopher Jencks and Paul Peterson, eds., *The Urban Underclass* (Washington, D.C.: Brookings Institution, 1991), pp. 203–234, is a major exception to this general trend.

17. Stanley Lieberson, "A Reconsideration of Income Differences Found between Migrants and Northern-born Blacks," *American Journal of Sociology*, 83 (January 1978): 940–966; and Larry Long, "Poverty Status and Receipt of Welfare among Migrants and Nonmigrants in Large Cities," *American Sociological Review*, 39 (February 1974): 44–56.

18. George Peterson and Wayne Vroman, "Urban Labor Markets and Economic Opportunity," in Peterson and Vroman, eds., *Urban Labor Markets and Job Opportunity* (Washington, D.C.: Urban Institute, 1992), p. 12.

19. Unless otherwise specified, the data reported for the text are for employed adults aged 25–64.

20. David Howell and Edward N. Wolff, "Trends in the Growth and Distribution of Skills in the U.S. Workplace, 1960–1985," *Industrial and Labor Relations Review*, 44, no. 3 (1991).

21. A rereading of Kenneth Clark's 1964 classic *Dark Ghetto* (New York: Harper and Row) brings the point home. Noting that "Negroes in the ghetto have long been concerned with the quality of their children's education," he first mentions E. Franklin Frazier's report on Harlem conditions in the mid-1930s, which highlighted "the flagrant deficiencies of the ghetto schools." He then refers to a 1955 study produced by the Public Education Association and "the picture they discovered . . . of sub-standard staff, facilities and pupil performance." Clark concludes that *"the situation has deteriorated since then"* (pp. 118–119; italics added).

22. Data on enrollment from Census of Population for 1970 and 1990; as noted in the text, data apply to persons aged 18–24. Jencks's data apply to those aged 16–24 (Christopher Jencks, *Rethinking Social Policy: Race, Poverty, and the Underclass* [New York: Basic Books, 1992], p. 174).

23. See the discussion in Alejandro Portes and Ruben Rumbaut, *Immigrant America* (Berkeley: University of California Press, 1990), pp. 42–48.

24. Michael P. Smith, *City, State, and Market: The Political Economy of Urban Societies* (New York: Basil Blackwell, 1988), p. 200. For further arguments in this vein, see Alejandro Portes and Saskia Sassen-Koob, "Making It Underground," *American Journal of Sociology* 93, no. 1 (1987): 30–61, and Patricia Pessar, "Sweatshop Workers and Domestic Ideologies: Dominican Workers in New York's Apparel Industry," *International Journal of Urban and Regional Research*, 18, no. 1 (1994): 127–142.

25. Saskia Sassen-Koob, "Exporting Capital and Importing Labor: The Role of Caribbean Migration to New York City," Occasional Paper, Center for Latin American and Caribbean Studies, New York University, 1981, pp. 28–29.

26. Bennett Harrison and Barry Bluestone, *The Great U-Turn: Corporate Restructuring and the Polarizing of America* (New York: Basic Books, 1988), p. 70.

27. Joe Feagin and Michael P. Smith, "Cities and the New International Division of Labor: An Overview," in Feagin and Smith, eds., *The Capitalist City* (New York: Basil Blackwell, 1987), p. 15.

28. Sue E. Berryman and Thomas Bailey, *The Double Helix of Education and the Economy* (New York: Institute on Education and the Economy, Teachers College, Columbia University, 1992), pp. 30–35.

29. U.S. Department of Labor, *The Effects of Immigration on the Economy and Labor Market* (Washington, D.C.: Government Printing Office, 1989), p. 158.

30. The queue theory of the labor market was developed by Lester Thurow in his books *Income and Opportunity* (Washington, D.C.: Brookings Institution, 1968) and *Generating Inequality* (New York: Basic Books, 1975); while modifying his formulation, I have developed a model that derives from his work. In *A Piece of the Pie* (Berkeley: University of California Press, 1980), Stanley Lieberson applied queue theory to examine the effect of compositional differences in black and immigrant employment across a sample of U.S. cities in 1900. Here, I am less interested in cross-sectional differences than in the effect of compositional changes over time. Though the concepts of queue order and shape and of workers' rankings were implicit in these earlier writings, they were first made explicit in Barbara Reskin and Patricia Roos's chapters in their edited book *Job Queues, Gender Queues* (Philadelphia: Temple University Press, 1990).

31. Cf. Michael Piore, *Birds of Passage* (Cambridge: Cambridge University Press, 1979), chap. 3.

32. Though Lieberson uses the term "special niches" in *A Piece of the Pie,* he conceptualizes the process of niche formation in much the same way as do I, arguing that "most racial and ethnic groups tend to develop concentrations in certain jobs which either reflect some distinctive cultural characteristics, special skills initially held by some members, or the opportunity structures at the time of their arrival" (p. 379). He goes on to argue that "such specialties can only absorb a small part of a group's total work force when its population grows rapidly or is a substantial proportion of the total population"; however, the history of New York's ethnic niches, which I present in Chapter 4, paints a different picture. New York's ethnic and immigrant groups have maintained large and persistent concentrations of precisely the kind that Lieberson discusses; and though the niche tends to absorb a diminishing *proportion* of a group as the group increases in size, the niche still remains an impressive employment cluster in both relative and absolute terms. Suzanne Model's chapter "The Ethnic Niche and the Structure of Opportunity: Immigrants and Minorities in New York City," in Michael Katz, ed., *The "Underclass" Debate: Views from History* (Princeton, N.J.: Princeton University Press, 1993), conceptualizes the ethnic niche in ways that come close to mine. She defines a niche as a "job" in which the "percentage of workers who are group members is at least one and a half times greater than the group's percentage in the labor force" (p. 164); I use this definition, with modifications to be explained later, in the discussion that follows in Chapters 3 and 4.

33. John Bodnar, *The Transplanted: A History of Immigrants in Urban America* (Bloomington: University of Indiana Press, 1985).

34. Piore, *Birds of Passage,* chap. 3.

35. Note the contrast to Piore, whose work has strongly influenced my own views. He depicts the labor market for immigrant workers as fundamentally unstructured, with neither formal institutions nor informal mechanisms, like ethnic networks, playing much role. Chance clearly has a good deal to do with job-finding patterns at the early stage of a migration stream; and there is no doubt that long-distance migrants engage in a good deal of churning, whether from job to job or from the host to the home society. But there is ample evidence, in both the secondary literature and in the material to follow, that ethnic networks among settlers and newcomers get activated at an early stage in the migration process, providing a source of structure in otherwise unstructured environments. On the role of networks, more generally, in matching workers with jobs, Mark Granovetter's book *Getting a Job* (Cambridge, Mass.: Harvard University Press, 1974) is a basic source. The afterword to the second edition (Chicago: University of Chicago Press, 1995) brings the discussion up to date with new references. Other useful sources include Mark Granovetter and Charles Tilly, "Inequality and Labor Processes," in Neil Smelser, ed., *The Handbook of Sociology* (Newbury Park, Calif.: Sage Publications, 1988), pp. 175–231; David Stevens, "A Reexamination of What Is Known about Jobseeking Behavior in the United States," in *Labor Market Intermediaries* (Washington, D.C.: National Commission for Manpower Policy, report no. 22, 1978), pp. 55–104; and Margaret Grieco, *Keeping It in the Family: Social Networks and Employment Chance* (London and New York: Tavistock, 1987).

36. Thomas Bailey and I developed this argument in our article "Primary, Secondary, Enclave Labor Markets: A Training Systems Approach," *American Sociological Review,* 56, no. 4 (August 1991): 432–445; for additional empirical examples, see Bailey's book *Immigrant and Native Workers: Contrasts and Competition* (Boulder, Colo.: Westview Press, 1987) and my *Through the Eye of the Needle: Immigrants and Enterprise in New York's Garment Trades* (New York: New York University Press, 1986), chap. 6.

37. On the concept of social capital, see James Coleman, "Social Capital in the Creation of Human Capital," *American Journal of Sociology,* 94, supplement (1988): S95–120; Alejandro Portes and Julia Sensenbrenner, "Embeddedness and Immigration: Notes on the Social Determination of Embeddedness," *American Journal of Sociology,* 98, no. 6 (1993): 1320–1351; and Portes's edited volume *The Economic Sociology of Immigration: Essays in Networks, Ethnicity, and Entrepreneurship* (New York: Russell Sage Foundation, 1994). For a friendly critique of the Coleman and Portes formulations, as applied to ethnic contexts, see my article "The 'Other Side' of Embeddedness: A Case Study of the Interplay of Economy and Ethnicity," *Ethnic and Racial Studies,* 18, no. 3 (1995), and the material in Chapter 8.

38. On ethnic economies, their characteristics, and their consequences, see Roger Waldinger, Howard Aldrich, Robin Ward, and associates, *Ethnic Entrepreneurs* (Newbury Park, Calif.: Sage Publications, 1990), and Howard Aldrich and Roger Waldinger, "Ethnicity and Entrepreneurship," *Annual Review of Sociology,* 16 (1990): 111–135. The role of ethnic economies figures prominently in the work of Alejandro Portes, whose research on the Cuban "immigrant ethnic enclave" in

Miami has been enormously influential, though quite controversial. See his books, *Latin Journey* (Berkeley: University of California Press, 1985; coauthored with Robert Bach) and *City on the Edge: The Transformation of Miami* (Berkeley: University of California Press, 1993; coauthored with Alex Stepick). I discuss Portes's work, the reactions it has engendered, and the problems with the enclave concept in my article "The Ethnic Enclave Debate Revisited," *International Journal of Urban and Regional Research*, 17, no. 3 (1993): 428–436.

39. Model, "Ethnic Niche," p. 168.

40. This argument was anticipated by Nathan Glazer and Daniel Moynihan in *Beyond the Melting Pot* (Cambridge, Mass.: MIT Press, 1963), where they argued that "ethnic groups in New York are also *interest groups*," with the consequences that the " 'rational' economic interests and the 'irrational' or at any rate noneconomic interests and attitudes tied up with one's own group are inextricably mixed together" (pp. 17–18). For later, more explicit efforts to show how ethnic concentration in residential or economic niches structures interaction patterns in such a way as to promote ethnic identity and sensitivity to ethnic boundaries, see William Yancey, Eugene Erickson, and Richard Juliani, "Emergent Ethnicity: A Critique and Review," *American Sociological Review*, 41 (1976), and Michael Hechter, "Group Formation and the Cultural Division of Labor," *American Journal of Sociology*, 84 (1978): 293–318.

41. Peter Doeringer and Michael Piore, *Internal Labor Markets and Manpower Analysis* (Lexington: Heath, 1971); Howard Wial, "Getting a Good Job in a Segmented Labor Market," *Industrial Relations*, 30, no. 3 (1993).

42. This is precisely what has happened in Miami, where white building-trades workers blocked Cubans from getting union jobs, whereupon the Cubans took their revenge by building a flourishing nonunion sector that now threatens the viability of the remaining union firms. For the full story, see Alex Stepick and Guillermo Grenier, with Steve Morris and Debbie Drazin, "Brothers in Wood," in Louise Lamphere, Alex Stepick, and Guillermo Grenier, eds., *Newcomers in the Workplace: Immigrants and the Restructuring of the U.S. Economy* (Philadelphia: Temple University Press, 1994), pp. 145–163. The Jewish experience in New York's construction industry provides an analogous example, as I note briefly toward the end of Chapter 6.

43. The fundamental work remains Gary Becker's pioneering book *The Economics of Discrimination* (Chicago: University of Chicago Press, 1957); for a more recent review of the economic literature, see Glen Cain, "The Economic Analysis of Labor Market Discrimination: A Survey," in Orley Ashenfelter and Richard Layard, eds., *Handbook of Labor Economics*, vol. 1, (Amsterdam: North-Holland, 1986), chap. 13.

44. Ray Marshall, "The Economics of Discrimination: A Survey," *Journal of Economic Literature*, 12, no. 3 (1974): 849–871.

45. William J. Wilson, *The Declining Significance of Race* (Chicago: University of Chicago Press, 1978). Wilson's argument here draws on the "split labor market theory" developed by Edna Bonacich in her articles "A Theory of Ethnic Antagonism: The Split Labor Market," *American Sociological Review*, 37 (1972), and "Advanced Capitalism and Black/White Relations in the United States: A Split Labor Market Analysis," *American Sociological Review*, 41 (1976): 34–51. For a further critique of split labor market theory, see Chapter 6.

2. People and Jobs

1. Robert J. Lichtenberg, *One-tenth of a Nation* (Cambridge, Mass.: Harvard University Press, 1960); Edgar Hoover and Raymond Vernon, *Anatomy of a Metropolis* (Cambridge, Mass.: Harvard University Press, 1959).

2. Temporary Commission on City Finances, "Economic and Demographic trends in New York City: The Outlook for the Future," thirteenth interim report to the mayor, 1977; Matthew Drennan, "Economy," in Charles Brecher and Raymond Horton, eds., *Setting Municipal Priorities, 1982* (New York: Russell Sage Foundation, 1981), pp. 55–91; Drennan, "The Local Economy and Local Revenue," in Charles Brecher and Raymond Horton, eds., *Setting Municipal Priorities: American Cities and the New York Experience* (New York: New York University Press, 1984), pp. 43–70.

3. George Sternlieb and James Hughes, *Post-industrial America: Metropolitan Decline and Inter-Regional Job Shifts* (New Brunswick, N.J.: Center for Urban Policy Research, 1976).

4. Kirkpatrick Sale, *Power Shift: The Rise of the Southern Rim and Its Challenge to the Eastern Establishment* (New York: Random House, 1975).

5. Sternlieb and Hughes, *Post-industrial America*; Larry Sawers and William K. Tabb, *Sunbelt/Snowbelt: Urban Development and Regional Restructuring* (New York: Oxford University Press, 1983); D. Perry and A. Watkins, eds., *The Rise of the Sunbelt Cities*, Urban Affairs Annual Review (Beverly Hills, Calif.: Sage Publications, 1977).

6. Matthew Drennan, "The Decline and Rise of the New York City Economy," in John H. Mollenkopf and Manuel Castells, eds., *Dual City: Restructuring New York* (New York: Russell Sage Foundation, 1991).

7. Robert Cohen, "Multinational Corporations, International Finance, and the Sunbelt," in D. Perry and A. Watkins, eds., *The Rise of the Sunbelt Cities* (Beverly Hills, Calif.: Sage Publications, 1977), p. 212. See also Cohen's article "The New International Division of Labor, Multinational Corporations, and Urban Hierarchy," in Michael Dear and Allen Scott, eds., *Urbanization and Urban Planning in Capitalist Societies* (New York: Methuen, 1981), pp. 287–315.

8. Eli Ginzberg, Matthew Drennan, and Robert Cohen, *The Corporate Headquarters Complex in New York City* (New York: Columbia University, Conservation of Human Resources, 1977); Thierry Noyelle and Thomas M. Stanback, Jr., *The Economic Transformation of American Cities* (Totowa, N.J.: Rowman and Allenheld, 1984).

9. Thierry Noyelle and Penny Peace, "Information Services: New York's New Export Base," Conservation of Human Resources Working Paper, Columbia University, 1988, p. 31.

10. Hugh O'Neill and Mitchell Moss, *Reinventing New York: Competing in the Next Century's Global Economy* (New York: Urban Research Center, Robert F. Wagner Graduate School of Public Service, New York University, 1991).

11. Mitchell Moss, "Telecommunications, World Cities, and Urban Policy," *Urban Studies*, 24 (1987): 534–546.

12. David Vogel, "New York City as a National and Global Financial Center," in Martin Shefter, ed., *Capital of the American Century: The National and International Influence of New York City* (New York: Russell Sage Foundation, 1993), pp. 66–67.

13. Susan Fainstein, *The City Builders: Property, Politics, and Planning in London and New York* (Cambridge, Mass.: Blackwell, 1994), p. 35.

14. Andrew Herod, "From Rag Trade to Real Estate in New York's Garment Center: Remaking the Labor Landscape in a Global City," *Urban Geography*, 12, no. 4 (1991): 324–338.

15. Elizabeth Bogen, *Immigration in New York* (New York: Praeger, 1987); City of New York, Department of City Planning, *The Newest New Yorkers: An Analysis of Immigration into New York City during the 1980s* (New York: Department of City Planning, 1992); Ellen Percy Kraly, "U.S. Immigration Policy and the Immigration Populations of New York," in Nancy Foner, ed., *New Immigrants in New York* (New York: Columbia University Press, 1987), chap. 2.

16. Nathan Glazer and D. P. Moynihan, *Beyond the Melting Pot* (Cambridge, Mass.: MIT Press, 1969), p. 8.

17. Oscar Handlin, *The Newcomers: Negroes and Puerto Ricans in a Changing Metropolis* (Cambridge, Mass.: Harvard University Press, 1959), pp. 49–50; Ira Rosenwaike, *Population History of New York* (Syracuse, N.Y.: Syracuse University Press, 1972), pp. 117, 141.

18. Emanuel Tobier, "Population," in Charles Brecher and Raymond Horton, eds., *Setting Municipal Priorities, 1982*, (New York: Russell Sage Foundation, 1981), p. 36.

19. Data on place of birth and residence from *U.S. Census of the Population: Social and Economic Characteristics, New York, 1970*, section 2, table 91.

20. Lawrence Chenault, *The Puerto Rican Migrant in New York* (New York: Columbia University Press, 1938).

21. Handlin, *The Newcomers*, pp. 50–53; Tobier, "Population," p. 36; Rosenwaike, *Population History*, p. 138; *Census of the Population*, 1970, table 97.

22. Tobier, "Population," p. 36; Rosenwaike, *Population History*, p. 136.

23. Clara Rodriguez, *Puerto Ricans: Born in the USA* (Boston: Unwin Hyman, 1989).

24. David Reimers, *Still the Golden Door: The Third World Comes to America* (New York: Columbia University Press, 1985).

25. Calculated from *1991 Statistical Yearbook of the Immigration and Naturalization Service* (Washington, D.C.: Government Printing Office, 1992).

26. Calculated from the *Statistical Yearbook of the Immigration and Naturalization Service*, annual volumes published by Government Printing Office.

27. Eugenia Georges, *The Making of a Transnational Community: Migration, Development, and Cultural Change in the Dominican Republic* (New York: Columbia University Press, 1990), p. 81.

28. Robert Warren and Jeffrey Passel, "A Count of the Uncountable: Estimates of Undocumented Aliens Counted in the 1980 United States Census," *Demography*, 24, no. 3 (1987): 375–393.

29. Susan Gonzalez Baker, *The Cautious Welcome: The Legalization Programs of the Immigration Reform and Control Act* (Santa Monica, Calif.: Rand Corporation, 1990).

30. In point of fact, IRCA enabled two groups of illegal aliens to become temporary and then permanent residents of the United States: aliens who had been living illegally in the United States since January 1982, technically known as le-

galization applicants; and aliens who were employed in seasonal agricultural work for a minimum of ninety days in the year preceding May 1986 (Special Agricultural Worker [SAW] applicants). As of 1992, the Immigration and Naturalization Service had received 1,759,705 legalization applicants and an additional 1,272,143 SAW applicants.

31. Barry Edmonston and Jeffrey Passell, "The Future Immigrant Population of the United States," in Barry Edmonston and Jeffrey Passell, eds., *Immigration and Ethnicity: The Integration of America's Newest Arrivals* (Washington, D.C.: Urban Institute, 1994), chap. 11.

32. Robert Warren, "Estimates of the Unauthorized Immigrant Population Residing in the United States, by Country of Origin and State of Residence: October 1992," Immigration and Naturalization Statistics Division Report, 1994, p. 30.

33. The immigration data profiled in Figure 2.3 excludes persons admitted under the legalization program between 1988 and 1990. This procedure maintains the distinction between flows and stock, since persons legalized in, say, 1988 or 1989 were already present in the United States at an earlier period of time (as explained in the brief discussion of IRCA above). And though related, the legal and illegal flows represent two distinct migration flows, with the latter disproportionately oriented toward the southwest and overwhelmingly dominated by Mexicans. While New York is a relatively unpopular destination for undocumented immigrants, it has continued to capture a disproportionately large share of the legal immigrant flow—as shown in Figure 2.3.

34. Rosenwaike, *Population History*, p. 117.

35. For further discussion of West Indian migration, see Chapter 4 and the references cited therein.

36. *Annual Yearbook of the Immigration and Naturalization Service*, various years.

37. A more extensive discussion of Dominican migration to New York, with references to the appropriate literature, appears in Chapter 4.

38. Calculated from *U.S. Census of the Population: Social and Economic Characteristics, New York*, 1990, section 2, table 167. This calculation includes persons from Guyana and Belize within the Caribbean category.

39. Steven Lowenstein, *Frankfurt on the Hudson: The German-Jewish Community of Washington Heights, 1933–1983* (Detroit: Wayne State University Press, 1989); William Helmreich, *Against All Odds: Holocaust Survivors and the Successful Lives They Made in America* (New York: Simon and Schuster, 1992).

40. Annelise Orleck, "The Soviet Jews: Life in Brighton Beach, Brooklyn," in Nancy Foner, ed., *New Immigrants in New York* (New York: Columbia University Press, 1987), p. 275.

41. Fran Markowitz, *Community in Spite of Itself: Soviet Jewish Emigres in New York* (Washington, D.C.: Smithsonian Institution, 1993).

42. Between 1982 and 1989, 10,778 refugees from the Soviet Union moved to New York, along with 7,880 Poles, 5,440 Romanians, 3,086 Yugoslavs, and 2,045 persons from other Eastern European countries; City of New York, Department of City Planning, *The Newest New Yorkers*, p. 51.

43. Mary Corcoran, *Irish Illegals: Transients between Two Societies* (Westport, Conn.: Greenwood Press, 1993).

44. Roger Waldinger, "Immigration and Urban Change," *Annual Review of Sociology*, 15 (1989): 215.

45. Warren, "Estimates," p. 30.

46. See Stanley Friedlander and Charles Brecher, "A Comparative View," in Eli Ginzberg, ed., *New York Is Very Much Alive* (New York: McGraw Hill, 1973), pp. 20–41.

47. Tobier, "Population," p. 37.

3. The Ethnic Division of Labor Transformed

1. Unless otherwise specified, all numbers in this chapter refer to employed, prime-age adults and are derived from the Public Use Microdata Samples of the Censuses of Population.

2. The data for Asians that are reported in this chapter, whether in text, tables, or figures, apply to immigrants only. As of 1990, there were barely 16,000 adult, native-born Asians employed in New York City, and the numbers for earlier years are considerably smaller.

3. The index of representation equals group A's share of employment in industry X divided by group A's share of total employment.

4. I am using the definition proposed by Suzanne Model in "The Ethnic Niche." Model writes, "It is difficult to generalize about just how overrepresented in a job a group must be before niche conditions obtain. . . In this chapter, a job is considered a niche if the percentage of workers who are group members is at least one-and-a-half times greater than the group's percentage in the workforce" (p. 164). Model's formulation leaves some ambiguity as to what constitutes a "job," as she writes that "in this essay, a 'job' may mean an occupation, an industry, even a set of related industries." For my purposes, industries best define the contours of a niche. As I argued in Chapter 1, exchanges and mutual assistance among co-ethnics who have concentrated in some specialized economic activity create the basis for movement to related, higher-level jobs. Whereas an occupation involves a single set of jobs that may span many different and unrelated industries, an industry contains a multiplicity of related jobs arrayed in some hierarchical order; hence, the best way to think of an ethnic niche is in terms of an industrial concentration or specialization. Because government employment has played such an important role for various groups of ethnic New Yorkers, in particular the Irish and African-Americans, I further distinguish between private and public sector industries. Consequently, public and private sector hospitals or public and private rail systems get defined as two distinctive industries. The import and appropriateness of this distinction will become fully clear in Chapter 4.

5. Michael Katz, "Reframing the 'Underclass' Debate," in Michael Katz, ed., *The "Underclass" Debate: Views from History* (Princeton, N.J.: Princeton University Press, 1993), p. 447.

6. John Kasarda, "Cities as Places Where People Live and Work," p. 84.

7. Katz, "Reframing," p. 447.

8. L. J. Wacquant, "The Ghetto, the State, and the New Capitalist Economy," *Dissent*, 36, no. 4 (1989): 510.

9. Ibid.

10. William J. Wilson, Robert Aponte, Joleen Kirschenman, and Loïc Wacquant, "The Ghetto Underclass and the Structure of Urban Poverty," in Fred R. Harris and Roger Wilkins, eds., *Quiet Riots* (New York: Pantheon, 1988), p. 142.

11. Ibid.

12. By 1990, according to census data, 38,750 African-Americans were employed in the FIRE sector, one-third again as many as worked in manufacturing.

13. Isabel Sawhill, "An Overview," *Public Interest*, 96 (Summer 1989): 9.

14. Unlike the rest of the chapter, this paragraph and the next focus on the entire prime-age adult population, both employed and not employed.

15. John Kasarda, "Urban Industrial Transition and the Underclass," *Annals of the American Academy of Political and Social Science*, 501 (1989): 35.

16. Sawhill, "An Overview," p. 10.

17. Recall that the odds ratio tells us the odds that the members of a group will be in category X relative to everyone else. In 1970, the odds were .74, or three-quarters for African-Americans with some college education. By 1990, the odds had changed to 1.29, which is roughly equivalent to four-thirds (1.33).

4. The Making and Remaking of the Ethnic Niche

1. A few notes are in order concerning the definition and classification of these various groups. The main difficulties involve the identification of the native-born, white ethnic groups. The first problem concerns the identification of Jews. Since the census does not ask questions about religion, researchers have used the convention of classifying persons who give Russian birth, parentage, or ancestry as Jews, on the grounds that most Russian immigrants to the United States were in fact Jewish. Of course, a substantial number of Jews did not emigrate from Russia; and we have no way of knowing how the boundary changes that have occurred in Eastern Europe since the great migration of 1880–1920 affect ancestry responses (what was then Russia often no longer is so today). Still, as Stanley Lieberson and Mary Waters note in *From Many Strands* (New York: Russell Sage Foundation, 1988), the Russian category captures a predominantly Jewish population. While the Russian category imperfectly identifies Jews, it does so at the cost of under-estimating their exceptional socioeconomic performance. Hence, I follow the conventional procedure in identifying native-born Russians as Jews.

The second issue involves changes in census procedure that affect the classification of the foreign-origin population. The data reported for Jews and Italians in 1940, 1950, and 1970 concern the native-born children of foreign-born parents; the data reported for Jews and Italians in 1980 and 1990 concern native-born persons with parents born at home or abroad. This shift reflects a basic change in census data collection procedures. Starting in 1880 and continuing till 1970, the census asked not only about respondents' place of birth but also about the place of birth of their parents. This procedure worked well as long as a substantial portion of the white population had direct European roots; but with the passage of time, increasing numbers of whites were native-born children of native-born parents whose ethnic origins ineluctably slipped into statistical obscurity. In 1980, the census changed procedure; rather than asking about parentage, it instead inquired into respondents' ancestry, permitting open-ended responses, including multiple ancestries, and excluding only responses that implied religious affiliation. In one fell swoop, the census thus brought the increasingly hidden ancestral roots of white Americans back into light.

Given the inconsistencies introduced by the ancestry question, the change in census procedures is clearly troublesome for the type of venture in which I am engaged. Nonetheless, there are grounds for arguing that in New York, at least, the populations defined by the older parentage and the newer ancestry questions may be reasonably alike. Recall that my populations consist of adults aged 25–64 and that the Jewish and Italian immigrations were compressed between the years 1880 and 1920; hence, between 1940 and 1970, most native-born Jewish and Italian adults were likely to have been the children of the foreign-born. By 1980, and certainly by 1990, a much larger proportion of adult Italian and Jewish New Yorkers were now the grandchildren, or even great-grandchildren, of the earlier immigrant generation. Thus, the ancestry question allows me to identify ethnics of the third generation and beyond *just when they became quantitatively significant;* their invisibility in 1940, 1950, and 1970 is likely to be of less importance.

Finally, a note on the definition of the West Indian population. For purposes of comparability to African-Americans, I define West Indians as immigrants from the anglophone Caribbean, eliminating immigrants from the Dominican Republic, Haiti, other francophone countries, and the Dutch West Indies. This definition allows me to compare two black groups that differ only with respect to immigrant status. Unfortunately, only a limited number of Caribbean countries are identified in the place of birth variable in the 1940 public use sample; hence, data presented for 1940 refer to all black immigrants.

2. While the abbreviated description of the statistical comparisons provided in the text seems appropriate, given the needs of narrative symmetry, I expect that some readers will be interested in the more elaborate explanation that follows. Tables 4.2 and 4.5 show the comparisons of earnings inside and outside niches; Table 4.2 presents the data for all groups, men and women separately, for 1990 only; Table 4.5 presents data for African-Americans only, from 1940 through 1990. The contrasts are both internal, comparing the earnings of a single group inside and outside its niches, and external, comparing a group's earnings inside and outside its niches with those of a common reference group inside and outside the same set of industries. The reference group consists of non-Italian, non-Jewish, native-born whites; all of the problems of comparability and consistency of census definitions, discussed in note 1, apply to this reference group as well.

Each cell in Tables 4.2 and 4.5 represents a ratio constructed from at least two of the following eight numbers:

1. raw mean earnings, ethnic group in its own niche industries;
2. raw mean earnings, ethnic group in its own non-niche industries;
3. raw mean earnings, reference group in ethnic group niche industries;
4. raw mean earnings, reference group in ethnic group non-niche industries;
5. adjusted earnings, ethnic group in its own niche industries;
6. adjusted earnings, ethnic group in its own non-niche industries;
7. adjusted earnings, reference group in ethnic group niche industries;
8. adjusted earnings, reference group in ethnic group non-niche industries.

Numbers 1–4 were calculated by first flagging the industries that met the criteria as niches for a given group and then calculating mean earnings for that group and for the reference group for all niche industries and for all non-niche industries.

Numbers 5–8 were calculated by first regressing individual earnings on a set of human capital variables (YRSED, EXPER, EXPERSQ), work-related variables (HOURSN, WEEKSL), an immigration-related variable (YRSUS) used for the three foreign-born groups only, and a dummy indicating NICHE status and an interaction between NICHE and YRSED: NIED.

$$\text{EARN} = B0 + B1 \times \text{NICHE} + B2 \times \text{NIED} + B3 \times \text{YRSED} + B4 \times \text{EXPER} + B5 \times \text{EXPERSQ} + B6 \times \text{HOURSN} + B7 \times \text{WEEKSL} + B8 \times \text{YRSUS}.$$

Regressions were done separately for each ethnic group studied and for the reference group. The last term was present only for immigrants. Regressions were calculated separately for group members and for the reference group, still using group niches. The equation above, evaluated at group means for all independent variables, yields the "adjusted niche earnings." The "adjusted non-niche earnings" is the same as

$$\text{EARN} - (B1 \times \text{NICHE} + B2 \times \text{NIED}).$$

The same equations were created from regressions for the reference group. Instead of being evaluated at reference group means, they were evaluated at comparison group means.

Note that Numbers 5–6 are estimates of the earnings of the average group member inside and outside the group's niches. Items 7–8 are estimates of the earnings of a worker in the reference group who has the same characteristics as the average member of the comparison group. Because niche (5) and non-niche (6) workers have the same characteristics, comparisons between the adjusted earnings figures give an estimate of real differences in returns to human capital inside and outside group niches. Also, because the group member and the worker in the reference group have the same characteristics (excepting those relating to immigration), comparisons between group members and reference group members inside niches and outside niches give an indication of whether discrimination against the group is greater inside or outside their niches. If the differences outside the niches (6–8) are greater than those within (5–7), then the group's niches do provide some protection against discrimination.

Though interpretation is offered in the text, further insight might be gained through detailed discussion of an example, in this case, the data for male African-Americans, presented in the third row of Table 4.2. The first column shows that, on average, those African-American men employed in African-American niches made 16 percent more than African-American men employed in industries that fell below niche levels (ratio of numbers 1 and 2). Since this first contrast presents an unadjusted ratio, part of the advantage may reflect the higher levels of skill held by men in the niche; while adjustment lowers the disparity, as seen in the second column, it shows that African-American men in the niche make more than comparable African-American men in industries of lower black density (ratio of numbers 5 and 6). Hence, I conclude that African-Americans are clustered in a favorable niche, comprised of industries that offer enhanced earnings potential.

A second issue concerns how well African-Americans are doing relative to native whites (or more precisely, non-Italian, non-Jewish, native whites, as noted above). The third column in Table 4.2 provides the raw comparison of African-Americans and native whites in the African-American niches; here, we see that the former earn almost three-quarters as much as the latter (ratio of numbers 1 and 3). The next column is similarly restricted to workers in the African-American niches but shows how well the average black worker does compared to native whites who possess the average characteristics of blacks (ratio of numbers 5 and 7). The fifth and sixth columns demonstrate the same set of contrasts for all those industries in which African-American employment does not reach niche levels (ratios of numbers 2 and 4, and 6 and 8, respectively). Since the adjustment process reduces the earnings gap by 21 percentage points outside the niche, but only 12 percentage points inside the niche, I conclude that discrimination has a smaller effect on industries in which African-Americans are concentrated at niche levels than on all other industries.

3. The literature on Jewish immigrants in the clothing industry is monumental. As of this writing, the latest major addition is Susan Glenn's *Daughters of the Shtetl* (Ithaca, N.Y.: Cornell University Press, 1990), which includes extended references to the historical literature. Nancy Green's forthcoming volume on immigrants in the garment industries of New York and Paris will probably be the definitive historical treatment; a small sample of that work appears as "Sweatshop Migrations: The Garment Industry between Home and Shop," in David Ward and Olivier Zunz, eds., *The Landscape of Modernity* (New York: Russell Sage Foundation, 1992), pp. 213–232. My earlier book, *Through the Eye of the Needle*, provides an account that links the earlier Jewish role in the industry to the experience of later minority and immigrant groups.

4. By 1900, one-quarter of New York's peddler's were Jews, a dominance that only increased with time, up to the 1930s. See Daniel Bluestone, " 'The Pushcart Evil,' " in Ward and Zunz, eds., *Landscape of Modernity* (see previous note), pp. 287–312. George H. Garvin, "Dry Goods" (Jews of New York, Works Progress Administration, Historical Records Survey—Federal Writers Project, box 3269, New York City Municipal Archives), estimates that in the 1930s, 90 percent of the roughly 25,000 workers employed in retail and wholesale "dry goods" establishments were Jews.

5. Deborah Dash Moore, *At Home in America: Second Generation New York Jews* (New York: Columbia University Press, 1981), pp. 44–50.

6. Heywood Broun and George Britt, *Christians Only: A Study in Prejudice* (New York: Vanguard Press, 1931), p. 224; Leonard Dinnerstein, *Anti-Semitism in America* (New York: Oxford University Press, 1994), p. 89.

7. Henry Feingold, *A Time for Searching: Entering the Mainstream, 1920–1945* (Baltimore: Johns Hopkins University Press, 1992), p. 147.

8. By 1940, white-collar jobs employed half of the second-generation Jews then working in the garment industry but only 21 percent of the foreign-born.

9. Dinnerstein, in *Anti-Semitism in America*, pp. 154–156, suggests a rapid decline in economic discrimination against New York's Jews in the years immediately following World War II. Nonetheless, a 1962 memorandum from the American Jewish Committee entitled "Employment and Housing Discrimination

against Jews" (files of the American Jewish Committee), reporting on a 1958 survey of 162 employment agencies in which 115 said that they would accept a job title for stenographers in which an employer specified that "white Protestants" were wanted, noted that some employment agencies still maintained elaborate codes to screen out Jewish job applicants.

10. In 1990, the seven remaining Jewish clusters in trade accounted for less than 6 percent of Jewish employment in Jewish niches.

11. John J. D'Alesandre, "Occupational Trends of Italians in New York City," *Italy-America Monthly*, 2, no. 2 (1935): 15.

12. Nettie McGill and Ellen Matthews, *The Youth of New York City* (New York: Macmillan, 1940), p. 45. The Welfare Council's study, a 1 percent sample of New York City youth aged 16–25, undertaken in 1935, found that 23.4 percent of Italian-born fathers worked in unskilled jobs, in contrast to 2.6 percent among the Jews.

13. Thomas Kessner, "Jobs, Ghettoes, and the Urban Economy, 1880–1915," *American Jewish History*, 71 (December 1981): 228–236; McGill and Matthews, *Youth of New York*, p. 45.

14. In 1940, 82 percent of adult, second-generation Italian New Yorkers reported schooling levels at the eighth grade or below—in contrast to 33 percent among their Jewish counterparts. At the other end of the educational spectrum, 20 percent of the Jews already reported some college or more, as against a scant 6 percent among the Italians. As to the causes of this educational disparity, Joel Perlmann's *Ethnic Differences* (New York: Cambridge University Press, 1988) remains the definitive account.

15. The Federal Writers Project book *The Italians of New York* (New York: Random House, 1938) provides a glimpse of the Italian business niche, resting on a heavy presence in the grocery trade and ice and coal dealing (p. 171).

16. Robert Orsi, *The Madonna of 115th Street* (New Haven: Yale University Press, 1985), p. 199.

17. Ronald Bayor, *Neighbors in Conflict: The Irish, Germans, Jews, and Italians of New York City, 1929–1941* (Baltimore: Johns Hopkins University Press, 1977), p. 21. A 1937 report entitled "The Industrial Classification of Jewish Gainful Workers in New York City," prepared by the Committee on Economic Adjustment, claimed that while Jews made up two-thirds of factory and retail store owners, they accounted for a quarter of factory workers and a third of store employees; both store and factory owners made heavy use of Italians (report in the files of the American Jewish Committee).

18. Joseph Anania, "Report on the Interdependence of Jews and Italians Living in New York City" (unpublished manuscript in the files of the American Jewish Committee, 1938), p. 22.

19. Italians were far more likely to work in higher-level jobs outside the niche, the reverse of the situation among Jews.

20. Richard Alba, *Italian Americans: Into the Twilight of Ethnicity* (Englewood Cliffs, N.J.: Prentice-Hall, 1985).

21. On black New Yorkers during the depression, see *Report of the New York State Temporary Commission on the Condition of the Urban Colored Population* (Albany: Temporary Commission, 1938); Larry Greene, "Harlem in the Great Depression, 1928–36" (Ph.D. diss., Columbia University, 1982); Cheryl Greenberg,

"Or Does It Explode?" Black Harlem in the Great Depression (New York: Oxford University Press, 1991).

22. "Three Thousand Negroes in N.Y. Post Office," *New York Age*, April 25, 1936.

23. New York State Commission against Discrimination, *Railroad Employment in New York and New Jersey* (New York.: Commission against Discrimination, n.d.); data calculated from tables 5a, 6a, pp. 25–26.

24. New York State Commission against Discrimination, *Apprentices, Skilled Craftsmen, and the Negro: An Analysis* (New York: Commission against Discrimination, 1960).

25. Ray Marshall and Vernon Briggs, *The Negro and Apprenticeship* (Baltimore: Johns Hopkins University Press, 1987).

26. Leon Fink and Brian Greenberg, *Upheaval in the Quiet Zone: A History of Hospital Workers' Union, Local 1199* (Urbana: University of Illinois Press, 1989), p. 8.

27. John S. Gambs, "Hospitals and the Unions," *Survey Graphic,* 26 (August 1937): 435–439.

28. Fink and Greenberg, *Upheaval in the Quiet Zone*, p. 8.

29. Judith Layzer, *Ethnic Survey of Hospital Employees: New Occupational Possibilities* New York: Office of the Mayor, 1970).

30. Peter Eisinger, "Local Civil Service Employment and Black Socio-economic Mobility," *Social Science Quarterly*, 67, no. 2 (1986): 171.

31. New York State Commission against Discrimination, "Employment in Department Stores: Complaints against Major New York Department Stores Received," mimeo, 1958 (Schomburg Library); Don O. Watkins and David McKinney, *A Study of Employment Patterns in the General Merchandise Group Retail Stores in New York City* (New York: City of New York Commission on Human Rights, 1966); Charles Perry, *The Negro in the Department Store Industry* (Philadelphia: Industrial Research Unit, Wharton School, 1971).

32. Bailey, *Immigrant and Native Workers*, p. 99.

33. Ibid., p. 117.

34. Glazer and Moynihan in *Beyond the Melting Pot*, and Thomas Sowell in "Three Black Histories" (in Thomas Sowell, ed., *Essays and Data on American Ethnic Groups* [Washington: Urban Institute, 1978], among other works, would fall into this camp.

35. Reynolds Farley and Walter Allen, *The Color Line and the Quality of Life in America* (New York: Russell Sage Foundation, 1987); Suzanne Model, "Caribbean Immigrants: A Black Success Story?" *International Migration Review*, 25, no. 2 (1991): 248–276.

36. Ira DeA. Reid, *The Negro Immigrant: His Background, Characteristics, and Social Adjustment, 1899–1937* (New York: AMS Press), 1939.

37. Ibid., p. 121.

38. See Philip Kasinitz, *Caribbean New Yorkers* (Ithaca, N.Y.: Cornell University Press, 1992), chap. 1; see also, Nancy Foner, "The Jamaicans: Race and Ethnicity among Migrants in New York City," in Nancy Foner, ed., *New Immigrants in New York* (New York: Columbia University Press, 1987), chap. 7.

39. Fink and Greenberg, *Upheaval in the Quiet Zone*, p. 8.

40. R. W. Palmer, "A Decade of West Indian Migration to the United States, 1962–1972: An Economic Analysis," *Social and Economic Studies*, 23 (1974): 576.

41. Shien-woo Kung, *Chinese in American Life* (Seattle: University of Washington Press, 1962), p. 185.

42. Jan Chien Lin, "Capital and Community in Urban Change: Chinatown, New York City," (Ph.D. diss., New School for Social Research, 1991), p. 138.

43. Shih-Shan Henry Tsai, *The Chinese Experience in America* (Bloomington: Indiana University Press, 1986), p. 148.

44. Albert Scardino, "Commercial Rents in Chinatown Soar as Hong Kong Exodus Grows," *New York Times*, December 25, 1986, p. A1.

45. Lin, "Capital and Community in Urban Change," p. 320.

46. Alejandro Portes and Min Zhou, "Gaining the Upper Hand: Old and New Perspectives in the Study of Ethnic Minorities," *Ethnic and Racial Studies*, 15 no. 4 (1992): 491–573.

47. Xiaolan Bao, " 'Holding Up More Than Half the Sky': A History of Women Garment Workers in New York's Chinatown, 1948–1991" (Ph.D. diss., New York University, 1991), pp. 38–39.

48. Lin, "Capital and Community in Urban Change," chap. 8.

49. A 1991 survey of members of the International Ladies' Garment Workers' Union found that 60 percent of the 1,162 Chinese respondents lived outside Manhattan; 40 percent lived in Brooklyn, mainly in the Sunset Park and Bensonhurst areas. (Garment Industry Development Corporation, "A Child Care Study of the New York City Garment Industry," November 1991, appendix D; private report prepared for the GIDC).

50. Louis Winnick, *New People in Old Neighborhoods* (New York: Russell Sage Foundation, 1990).

51. Roger Waldinger and Yenfen Tseng, "Divergent Diasporas," *Revue européene des migrations internationales*, 8, no. 3 (1992): 97–99.

52. Sherri Grasmuck and Patricia Pessar, *Between Two Islands: Dominican International Migration* (Berkeley: University of California Press, 1991), p. 103; see also Georges, *The Making of a Transnational Community*, pp. 37–43, 79–81.

53. Christopher Mitchell, "U.S. Foreign Policy and Dominican Migration to the United States," in Christopher Mitchell, ed., *Western Hemisphere Immigration and United States Foreign Policy* (University Park: Pennsylvania State University Press, 1992), pp. 89–124.

54. Georges, *The Making of a Transnational Community*, p. 81.

55. Glenn Hendricks, *Dominican Diaspora* (New York: Teachers College Press, 1974), p. 76.

56. Elaine Gale Wrong, *The Negro in the Apparel Industry* (Philadelphia: Industrial Research Unit, Wharton School, 1974), p. 97.

57. Luis Guarnizo, "One Country in Two: Dominican-Owned Firms in New York and in the Dominican Republic" (Ph.D. diss., Johns Hopkins University, 1992), p. 243.

58. Greta Gilbertson and Douglas Gurak, "Broadening the Enclave Debate: The Labor Market Experiences of Dominican and Colombian Men in New York," *Sociological Forum*, 8 (1993): 205–220.

59. For example, Alan Myerson's article in the *New York Times* explains how

Dominican supermarket owners thrive where "big chains won't go," January 7, 1992, p. D1.

60. Guarnizo, "One Country in Two," p. 112.

5. Who Gets the "Lousy" Jobs?

1. Edwin Fenton, *Immigrants and Unions: A Case Study* (New York: Arno, 1975); Mary Testa, "Anti-Semitism among Italian-Americans," *Equality*, July 1939, pp. 27–29; Joseph Anania, "Report on the Interdependence of Jews and Italians Living in New York City" (unpublished manuscript in the files of the American Jewish Committee, 1938), p. 22.

2. In 1900, 249 black women were employed as dressmakers in New York, but only 17 as "tailoresses," the category that designated clothing workers employed in the factory. On an index of representation, in which 1 equals a group's share of total employment, blacks stood at .6 among dressmakers and .03 among tailoresses. By contrast, the comparable figures for Russians (mainly Jews) were 8.04 and 7.94, respectively. Calculated from U.S. Bureau of the Census, *Occupations at the 1900 Census* (Washington, D.C.: Government Printing Office, 1904).

3. Benjamin Selekman, *The Clothing and Textile Industries of New York and Its Environs* (New York: Regional Plan Association, 1925), pp. 24–25, 58–60.

4. Irving R. Stuart, "A Study of Factors Associated with Intergroup Conflict in the Ladies' Garment Workers' Union" (Ph.D. diss., New York University, 1951).

5. Herbert Northrup, *Organized Labor and the Negro* (New York: Harper and Brothers, 1944).

6. Consumers' League, *A New Day for the Colored Woman Worker: A Study of Colored Women in Industry* (New York: Consumers' League, 1919).

7. Roy Helfgott, "Women's and Children's Apparel," in Max Hall, ed., *Made in New York*, Cambridge, Mass.: Harvard University Press, 1959), pp. 94–95.

8. Hasia R. Diner, *In the Almost Promised Land: American Jews and Blacks, 1915–1935* (Westport, Conn.: Greenwood Press, 1977), p. 212.

9. Walter Licht, *Getting Work: Philadelphia, 1840–1950* (Cambridge, Mass.: Harvard University Press, 1992).

10. Jack Hardy, *The Clothing Workers* (New York: International Press, 1935).

11. Stuart, "A Study of Factors."

12. Consumers' League, *A New Day*, p. 29.

13. Edith Kine, "The Garment Union Comes to the Negro Worker," *Opportunity*, April 1934, p. 108.

14. Stuart, "A Study of Factors," p. 182.

15. Case cited by Herbert Hill, "The Racial Practices of Organized Labor," in Julius Jacobson, ed., *The Negro and the American Labor Movement* (New York: Doubleday, 1968), p. 425. When questioned by a congressional subcommittee about the practices of the ILGWU's ethnic locals, Charles Zimmerman, then manager of Local 22, offered the following explanation:

Zimmerman: They [Italian dressmakers' Local 89] do not prohibit anybody to work in the shops together with Italians. They do not segregate Italian shops. They work together with all the workers. We have shops where there are Italians, Negroes. With 40 Italians, I think there are 2 Negroes. And the Negro lady is the chairlady in the shop.

Mr. Zelenko: Does she belong to 89?

Mr. Zimmerman: No. She is the chairlady of the shop.

Mr. Zelenko: If she is Italian, why can't she join 89.

Mr. Zimmerman: She is not Italian. She is Negro.

U.S. House Committee on Education and Labor, *Investigation of the Garment Industry*, hearings before the Ad hoc Committee on Investigation of the Garment Industry, 87th Congress, 2d sess., 1962, p. 95.

16. Will Herberg, "The Old-timers and the Newcomers, Ethnic Group Relations in a Needle Trades Union," *Journal of Social Issues*, 9 (1953): 12–19.

17. Sally Hillsman Baker and Bernard Levenson, "Job Opportunities of Black and White Working-Class Women," *Social Problems*, 22, no. 4 (1975): 522–553.

18. See the discussion in my article "Another Look at the International Ladies' Garment Workers' Union," in Ruth Milkman, ed., *Women, Work, and Protest* (London: Routledge, Kegan, and Paul, 1985), pp. 86–110.

19. Miriam Cohen, *Workshop to Office: Two Generations of Italian Women in New York City, 1900–1950* (Ithaca, N.Y.: Cornell University Press, 1992).

20. International Ladies' Garment Workers' Union, *Report of the General Executive Board to the 26th Convention, 1947*, pp. 88–89.

21. ILGWU, *Report of the General Executive Board to the 27th Convention, 1950*, p. 91.

22. Roy Helfgott, "Puerto Rican Integration in the Skirt Industry in New York City," in Aaron Antonovsky and Lewis Lorwin, eds., *Discrimination and Low Incomes* (New York: New York State International Committee on Low Incomes, 1959), pp. 257–258.

23. Peter Braestrup, "Life among City's Garment Workers," *New York Herald Tribune*, October 2, 1958, p. 13.

24. According to Peter Braestrup, blacks made up 65–70 percent of the members of the Dress Shipping Clerks' local as of 1958, with Puerto Ricans accounting for another 15–20 percent. "Color Still Bar to Skills, Union Office," *New York Herald Tribune*, October 6, 1958, p. 19.

25. ILGWU, *Report to the 26th Convention*, pp. 88–89.

26. Testimony of William Schwartz, manager-secretary, Local 60 and 60A, ILGWU, in House Committee, *Investigation of the Garment Industry*, p. 47.

27. Testimony of Moe Falikman, manager-secretary, Local 10, ILGWU, in House Committee, *Investigation of the Garment Industry*, p. 60.

28. ILGWU archives, Labor Management Documentation Center, Cornell University, Local 105 papers, box 3, file 9.

29. ILGWU archives, Labor Management Documentation Center, Cornell University, Zimmerman papers, box 26, file 9. While the numbers for black and Hispanic members reported above apply only to Local 22, the old Jewish dressmakers' local, the number for all dressmakers includes the members of Local 89 (which admitted only Italians). Membership figures come from ILGWU, *Report of General Executive Board to the 31st Convention, 1962*, p. 184.

30. ILGWU archives, Labor Management Documentation Center, Cornell University, Dubinsky papers, box 308, file 2.

31. While the ILGWU's ability to control the national market declined in the 1950s, it continued to control the local market until the late 1970s.

32. Herberg, "The Old-timers and the Newcomers," p. 15.

33. Helfgott, "Women's and Children's Apparel," p. 88.

34. Helfgott, "Puerto Rican Integration in the Skirt Industry," pp. 251–252.

35. Baker and Levenson, "Job Opportunities," p. 515.

36. Martin Segal, *Wages in the Metropolis* (Cambridge, Mass.: Harvard University Press, 1960), p. 129.

37. Peter Braestrup, "Color Still Ban to Skills, Union Office," *New York Herald Tribune*, October 6, 1958, p. 19.

38. Association of Catholic Trade Unionists (ACTU), *Spanish Speaking Workers and the Labor Movement* (New York: ACTU, 1957). From 1957 to 1959, the ACTU's monthly newspaper, *Labor Leader*, provided a running account of this wave of minority insurgency.

39. Peter Braestrup, "How the Unions Fail the Exploited," *New York Herald Tribune*, October 10, 1958, p. 20.

40. Peter Braestrup, "Life among the Garment Workers: ILGWU Sets Pace for Labor," *New York Herald Tribune*, October 7, 1958; "Puerto Ricans Rebel against Boss—and Union," *New York Herald Tribune*, October 8, 1958; "They Get Union Cake at Outings, But No Copies of Union Contracts," *New York Herald Tribune*, October 9, 1958.

41. Don Hogan and Peter Braestrup, "Dress Union Shares in Blame for Rackets," *New York Herald Tribune*, June 30, 1958, p. 1.

42. See Hill, "Racial Practices of Organized Labor," pp. 326–330; Wagner papers, box 217, New York City Municipal Archives.

43. Untitled memorandum, International Ladies' Garment Workers' Union and Amalgamated Clothing Workers of America, August 22, 1963, NAACP archives, Library of Congress, III, box 184, p. 3. This memorandum, written by the research directors of the two unions, begins by stating, "It is our considered judgment that the subsidized training of apparel workers under the Manpower Development and Training Act is unncessary and, in fact, contrary to the intent of the legislation." As the memo shows, both the ILGWU and the Amalgamated were responding with an eye toward the growth of nonunion firms in the South, where the plants tended to use unskilled workers for whom training costs were already low. See also Wrong, *The Negro in the Apparel Industry*, pp. 107–109.

44. Harry Fleischman, "Is the ILGWU Biased?" draft paper, ILGWU archives, Labor Management Documentation Center, Cornell University, Zimmerman papers, box 26, file 8; Fleischman, then director of national labor services for the American Jewish Committee, was a close ally and defender of the ILGWU in the controversy that pitted the union against the NAACP (described in the next paragraph).

45. Claude Brown, *Manchild in the Promised Land* (New York: New American Library, 1965), p. 298.

46. ILGWU archives, Labor Management Documentation Center, Cornell University, Falikman papers, box 8, file 2a. This file contains the union cards of Ernest Holmes.

47. Had the ILGWU leaders been less sensitive to criticism, and more astute as

to how such a controversy would play itself out in the public arena, the entire confrontation might have been averted. The State Commission against Discrimination issued its preliminary finding against the ILGWU based on testimony from only one person, Holmes, largely because ILGWU leaders refused to cooperate in any way. Once union leaders realized their error, they decided to provide the commission with evidence on the extent of minority membership in locals associated with the various trades, including the cutters. By this time, Holmes had already found a job and written the commission that he no longer wished to press his complaint, but the ILGWU sought vindication. For their part, NAACP leaders realized that they had few enough friends, and that they would do better to bring the controversy with their one-time ally to a quiet end. By 1963, Roy Wilkins was chastising Herbert Hill for continuing his crusade against the ILGWU; a year later, Wilkins assured ILGWU leaders that "I *do not* want things kept alive"; in 1965, the ILGWU donated $7,500 to the NAACP. NAACP archives, Library of Congress, III, box A184; IIIA, box 309; ILGWU archives, Labor Management Documentation Center, Cornell University, Dubinsky papers, box 308, file 2, box 375A, file 1.

48. See the controversy between Herbert Hill and Gus Tyler, then assistant president of the ILGWU, in Jacobson, *The Negro and the American Labor Movement*, pp. 286–379, and in Burton Hall, ed., *Autocracy and Insurgency in Organized Labor* (New Brunswick: Transaction, 1972), pp. 147–200. House Committee, *Investigation of the Garment Industry*, cited earlier, provides a further glimpse of the dispute. For a nuanced discussion, putting the controversy in a broader context, see Nancy Green, "Juifs et noirs aux états-unis: La rupture d'une 'alliance naturelle,' " *Annales*, March–April 1987, pp. 445–464.

49. "Core to Organize within ILGWU," *New York Times*, May 3, 1967, p. 26.

50. Herbert Koshetz, "Seventh Avenue Placing Help-wanted Ads," *New York Times*, July 27 1966, p. 49; Isadore Barmash, "Bustling Garment Industry Is Searching for Recruits," *New York Times*, August 14, 1967, section 3, p. 1.

51. Herbert Koshetz, "A Major Labor Shortage Squeezing New York Garment Center," *New York Times*, August 10, 1969.

52. Harlem Youth Opportunities, Inc., *Youth in the Ghetto: A Study of the Consequences of Powerlessness and a Blueprint for Change* (New York, 1964).

53. Wrong, *The Negro in the Apparel Industry*, p. 63.

54. Ibid., pp. 97–100.

55. "Jobs in U.S. Await 5,000 DP Tailors," *New York Times*, April 3, 1948, p. 12; "Jobs Are Offered for DP's in State," *New York Times*, July 29, 1948, p. 9.

56. *New York Times*, September 28, 1955, p. 26; October 29, 1955, p. 12.

57. Leonard Sloane, "U.S. Men's Wear Makers Are Going Abroad for Tailors," *New York Times*, April 17, 1966, section 3, p. 1.

58. Bernard Frieden and Lynn Sagalyn, *Downtown, Inc.* (Cambridge, Mass.: MIT Press, 1989).

59. Ibid.

60. New York State Commission against Discrimination, *Employment in the Hotel Industry* (New York: Commission against Discrimination, 1958), p. 11.

61. New York State Commission against Discrimination, *Hotel Industry*, p. 24.

62. Herman Bloch, "Discrimination against the Negro in Employment in New York, 1920–1963," *American Journal of Economics and Sociology*, 24, 4 (1965):

365–366, 373–375; U.S. House Committee on Education and Labor, *Investigation on Extension of Coverage to Laundry, Hotel, Restaurant, Bar, and Hospital Workers*, 87th Congress, 2d sess., 1962, pp. 22–29, 53–56.

63. New York State Commission against Discrimination, *Hotel Industry*, p. 14.

64. "Americana Picketed in Racial Protest," *New York Times*, February 8, 1964, p. 11; Damon Stetston, "Hotels and Labor Spur Integration," *New York Times*, October 15, 1964, p. 20.

65. Edward Koziara and Karen Koziara, *The Negro in the Hotel Industry* (Philadelphia: Industrial Relations Unit, Wharton School, 1967), pp. 15, 29.

66. Laventhol and Horvath, *U.S. Lodging Industry* (Philadelphia: Laventhol and Horvath, 1989), p. 5.

67. T. Lattin, "Human Resources Crisis Looming for Hotel Industry," *Hotel and Motel Management*, April 3, 1989, p. 30.

68. P. LaHue, "Employee Shortage Clouds Hospitality Hiring Practices," *Hotel and Motel Management*, November 2, 1987, p. 130.

69. Morris Horowitz, *The New York Hotel Industry: A Labor Relations Study* (Cambridge, Mass.: Harvard University Press, 1960).

70. See my article "Taking Care of the Guests: The Impact of Immigrants on Services—an Industry Case Study," *International Journal of Urban and Regional Research*, 16, no. 1 (1992); and Dorothy Sue Cobble and Michael Merrill, "Collective Bargaining in the Hospitality Industry," forthcoming in Paula Voos, ed., *Collective Bargaining in the Private Sector* (Madison, Wis.: Industrial Relations Research Association).

71. Wage data from the period 1947–1955 from Segal, *Wages in the Metropolis*, pp. 178–179.

6. Who Gets the Good Jobs?

1. Thomas Bailey, "Black Employment Opportunities," in Charles Brecher and Raymond Horton, eds., *Setting Municipal Priorities, 1990* (New York: New York University Press, 1989), pp. 80–117.

2. Census of Population, 1990, Public Use Microdata Sample.

3. Jonathan Leonard, "The Impact of Affirmative Action Regulation and Equal Employment Law on Black Employment," *Journal of Economic Perspectives*, 4, no. 4 (1990).

4. Philip Moss, "Employment Gains by Minorities, Women in Large City Government, 1976–83," *Monthly Labor Review*, 111 (1988); Gerald Jaynes and Robin Williams, eds., *A Common Destiny: Blacks and American Society* (Washington, D.C.: National Academy Press, 1989), pp. 241–244. Chapter 7 provides much greater detail on black employment in New York's municipal sector.

5. Robert Higgs, *Competition and Coercion: Blacks in the American Economy, 1865–1914* (New York: Cambridge University Press, 1977).

6. In 1970, when New York's construction sector employed 11,600 African-American men, the index of representation for native black men stood close to parity at .95. By 1990, there were only 7,200 native black men employed in construction, by which time the index had sunk to .72.

7. The basic references describing the industrial relations systems in construc-

tion and their relationship to the industry's characteristics are found in John T. Dunlop, "The Industrial Relations System in Construction," in Arnold Weber, ed., *The Structure of Collective Bargaining* (New York: Free Press, 1961); and D. Quinn Mills, *Industrial Relations in Construction* (Cambridge, Mass.: MIT Press, 1972). However, Mills and Dunlop are much more sympathetic to the organized interests in the industry than I am.

8. Business Roundtable, *More Construction for the Money*, a construction industry cost-effectiveness report (New York: Business Roundtable, 1983).

9. Howard Foster, "The Labor Market in Non-union Construction," *Industrial and Labor Relations Review*, 26 (1973): 1071–1985.

10. See Chapter 8 for further examples of this point.

11. See Mills, *Industrial Relations*, for a detailed description of training and labor utilization in the industry. Foster, "The Labor Market," describes problems in the open-shop sector resulting from the absence of these institutions.

12. Marshall and Briggs, *The Negro and Apprenticeship*, p.18; Marc Silver, *Under Construction: Work and Alienation in the Building Trades* (Albany: State University of New York Press, 1986), p. 111. Despite the high proportion of union workers who report having been taught by relatives, the proportion with fathers in the trade is likely to have declined since the 1960s as a result of the use of objective tests as one criteria for determining acceptance to apprenticeship programs.

13. Former apprentices made up only 40 percent of the 255 union members surveyed by Silver, but constituted 64 percent of the highly skilled workers; see Silver, *Under Construction*, p. 113.

14. Business Roundtable, *Training Problems in Open Shop Construction*, a construction industry cost-effectiveness report (New York: Business Roundtable, 1982); Mills, *Industrial Relations*. For reasons that will become clear below, apprenticeship programs are historically conservative in their estimates of the number of workers that the union sector can absorb; the industry's needs have almost always exceeded the number of new journeyworkers coming down the apprenticeship pipeline. Nevertheless, it does appear that the skill levels and earnings of journeyworkers who have graduated from apprentice programs exceed those of workers who enter journeyperson status directly. See William S. Franklin, "A Comparison of Formally and Informally Trained Journeymen in Construction," *Industrial and Labor Relations Review*, 26, no. 3 (1973): 1086–1095. Moreover, the apprenticeship is also a route to key worker or foreperson, which further embeds the apprenticeship system in the industry's informal training and recruitment system.

15. The contrast in training requirements between the armed forces and the apprenticeship programs suggests how inflated are the latter's skill requirements, a point to which I shall return in greater detail later. According to testimony provided by the director of training programs for the Office of the Assistant Secretary of Defense for Manpower Affairs: "military training programs for pipefitting and steamfitting were in the range of eighteen to nineteen weeks. The Navy Seabees train their pipefitters in a fourteen-week course. According to the testimony, a utility man in the Seabees could be qualified to work as a journeyman's partner on a construction site, installing pipe, and cutting, hanging, and screwing pipe—

in a fourteen-week period. After six months of practical experience he could work as an experienced journeyman." By contrast, the apprenticeship program in the steamfitters' union lasts five years. See William Gould, *Black Workers in White Unions: Job Discrimination in the United States* (Ithaca, N.Y.: Cornell University Press, 1977), p. 332.

16. Mills, *Industrial Relations*, pp. 171–172.

17. U.S. Department of Labor, Labor Management Services Administration, *Exclusive Union Work Referral Systems in the Building Trades* (Washington, D.C.: Government Printing Office, 1969).

18. Foster, "The Labor Market," p. 1072.

19. In New York, where unions entirely control public as well as commercial and industrial construction, the nonunion sector appears to offer blacks better employment opportunities, though more to the benefit of Caribbean immigrants than native blacks. Outside New York, where large nonunion concerns have experienced considerable growth, the situation looks quite different. Data for those nonunion firms that maintain employer-sponsored apprenticeship programs point to much lower levels of black participation. U.S. Department of Labor data for 1978, for example, show that minorities accounted for 21 percent of all apprentices in union programs, while they accounted for only 11 percent in nonunion programs. The same data also indicate that the highly skilled, mechanical trades were more segregated in the nonunion than in the union sector. Other sources support this conclusion. In 1974, black enrollment in apprenticeships in plumbing and the sheetmetal trades was, respectively, 18 and 20 percent in the union sector and 7 and 11 percent in the nonunion sector. Even Herbert Northrup, a strong supporter of the argument that the unions keep blacks out of the industry, acknowledges that serious problems for minority employment in the open-shop sector remain in the electrical, plumbing, and mechanical trades.

20. New York State Commission against Discrimination, *Apprentices, Skilled Craftsmen, and the Negro: An Analysis* (Albany: Commission against Discrimination, 1960); Northrup, *Organized Labor and the Negro*.

21. This description of the postwar situation relies on the discussion in Herman Bloch, *The Circle of Discrimination* (New York: New York University Press, 1969), pp. 118–126.

22. Marshall and Briggs, *The Negro and Apprenticeship*, pp. 51–54.

23. This paragraph draws on Herbert Hill's fascinating and detailed account, "The New York City Terminal Market Controversy: A Case Study of Race, Labor, and Power," *Humanities in Society*, 6, no. 4 (1984): 351–391.

24. New York State Commission against Discrimination. *Apprentices, Skilled Craftsmen, and the Negro*.

25. Marshall and Briggs, *The Negro and Apprenticeship*.

26. See Title 29 of the *Code of Federal Regulations*, part 30. The sponsors are the Joint (Management-Labor) Apprenticeship Committees.

27. This statement is based on an examination of a complete set of reports of the Labor Department's compliance reviews conducted over the past ten years, obtained through a Freedom of Information Act request initiated by the Legal Defense and Education Fund of the National Organization of Women and graciously made available to me by Alison Weatherfield, a staff lawyer with that organization.

28. Bailey, "Black Employment Opportunities," p. 99.

29. Testimony of Vergil Hodges, deputy commissioner, New York State Department of Labor, presented to the New York City Commission on Human Rights, *Hearings on the Construction Industry*, April 25, 1990, p. 1156.

30. *Expert Electric v. Levine*, 52 AD 2d 371, 384 NY X 2d 509 (3d dept. 1976).

31. Helen Neuborne, Sarah Burns, Alison Weatherfield, Sarah Starrett, and Lisa Morowitz, *Report and Recommendations of the NOW Legal Defense Fund to the New York City Commission on Human Rights and the New York City Offfice of Labor Services on Discrimination in the Construction Trades* (New York: NOW Legal Defense and Education Fund, 1990).

32. Testimony of Vergil Hodges, p. 1150.

33. This point was noted by the New York State Advisory Committee to the U.S. Commission on Civil Rights, mimeographed untitled report, 1963, p. 7.

34. U.S. House Committee on Appropriations, *Department of Labor, Health, Education, and Welfare, and Related Agencies: Appropriations for 1981, Part 1— Department of Labor* (Washington D.C.: Government Printing Office, 1980).

35. A detailed, essentially in-house account can be found in Robin Myers and Thomas R. Brooks, *Black Builders: A Job Program That Works—The Story of the Joint Apprenticeship Program of the Workers Defense League and the A. Philip Randolph Educational Fund* (New York: League for Industrial Democracy, n.d.). Much of the other literature cited in this chapter, e.g., Marshall and Briggs, *The Negro and Apprenticeship*, and Mills, *Industrial Relations*, also discusses the WDL program. In addition to these sources, the material in this paragraph and in the next draws on an interview I conducted on June 22, 1990, with Dennis Derryck, the program's former assistant director during the late 1960s.

36. This was the title of Rustin's celebrated article, published in *Commentary* in February 1965.

37. Dennis Derryck, *Improving the Retention Rate of Indentured Apprentices Placed by Apprenticeship Outreach Programs* (Waltham, Mass.: Heller School for Advanced Studies in Social Welfare, 1973).

38. R. B. Goldmann, "Black Builders: Report on the Workers Defense League— A. Philip Randolph Educational Fund's Joint Apprenticeship Program," unpublished report to the Ford Foundation, 1968.

39. Gerald Poyo, Karen Rowlett, and Sue Mutchler, "Combating Labor Market Underrepresentation through a Targeted Outreach Strategy: The Targeted Outreach Program," Working Paper, Center for the Study of Human Resources, University of Texas, Austin, 1981, p. 52.

40. See Joseph Goulden, *Meany* (New York: Atheneum, 1972).

41. Meany's father, Michael Meany, had been president of plumbers' Local 3, and the younger Meany retained his membership in the local until his death. Van Arsdale was an astute and powerful political operative, who had organized a special Unity Party to support Robert Wagner, Jr., in the 1961 mayoral race.

42. Meany supported his home local in this conflict, stating that it was official union policy to refuse to work with nonunion members. While the National Labor Relations Act allows unions in the construction industry to compel union membership seven days after employment (in contrast to the thirty-day period outside construction), it clearly forbids the closed shop. Thus, the stated policy of the

plumbers, reaffirmed by Meany, clearly violated the Taft-Hartley Act. See Gould, *Black Workers*, p. 294.

43. House Committee on Appropriations, *Appropriations for 1981*, p. 510.

44. Herbert Hill, "Labor Union Control of Job Training: A Critical Analysis of Apprenticeship Outreach Programs and the Hometown Plans," *Occasional Papers of the Institute for Urban Affairs and Research* (Howard University), 2, no. 1 (1974): 44. The characterization of the A. Philip Randolph Institute as an AFL-CIO front comes from Gould, *Black Workers*, p. 298. This characterization is entirely consistent with our knowledge based on personal observation and first-hand acquaintance with the formal and informal interpenetration of the AFL-CIO and the A. Philip Randolph Institute. The outreach programs served the contractors' interest in the same way, since contractors' associations also received money to run outreach programs. Thus, as Herbert Hill points out, the government was subsidizing the same contractors' associations and unions that it was suing for discrimination.

45. Poyo, Rowlett, and Mutchler, "Combating Labor Market Underrepresentation," p. 67.

46. In addition to the sources cited in the text, this section draws on interviews with James McNamara, March 21, June 21, July 13, 1990. McNamara, a former director of the Bureau of Labor Services under Mayor Lindsay and of the Office of Construction Industry Relations, under Mayor Koch, has been a key behind-the-scenes player in city policy-making and litigation for the past two decades.

47. An important selling point, emphasized by the building trades, was continuity of employment. Whereas minority trainees hired under the Philadelphia Plan would lose employment once the government-sponsored or subsidized project for which they had been hired was completed, the New York Plan provided an $80-a-week stipend for trainees to participate in classroom programs until a new job could be procured. Thomas P. Ronan, "Construction Men Sign Trainee Pact," *New York Times*, December 11, 1970.

48. The New York Plan was officially recognized by the Department of Labor and the federal compliance office as a hometown plan.

49. Gould, *Black Workers*, p. 312.

50. The four unions were Local 3, International Brotherhood of Electrical Workers, headed by Harry Van Arsdale, then also president of the New York City Central Labor Council; plumbers' Local 2; steamfitters' Local 638; and sheetmetal workers' Local 28. Emanuel Perlmutter, "Building Unions Defend Hiring Policy," *New York Times*, March 10, 1971.

51. *New York Times*, September 19, 1971.

52. *New York Times*, January 14, 1973.

53. *New York Times*, July 20, 1973. Since Lindsay's executive order mandating specific hiring goals was not to take effect until 1974, the controversy over the city's new plan became one of the first major crises facing the administration of Mayor Abraham Beame, who succeeded Lindsay in city hall in January 1974. Beame issued an executive order that set forth the same goals as Lindsay's; this revised plan went into effect on June 25, 1974. *New York Times*, April 23, 1974, p. 45; June 26, 1974, p. 47.

54. This position was a reward for Brennan's services in getting construction

workers employed on Wall Street to beat up antiwar protestors during protests following the U.S. invasion of Cambodia in 1970.

55. Federal Judge Morris Lasker first ruled that the city had the authority to impose fair employment rules more stringent than those approved by the state (*New York Times*, July 26, 1974); the next month, the city's regulations were declared invalid by the New York State Supreme Court (*New York Times*, August 8, 1974); finally, in November 1974, Judge Lasker reaffirmed his original ruling (*New York Times*, November 9, 1973).

56. *New York Times*, December 3, 1974, p. 20.

57. *New York Times*, May 12, 1976.

58. Electrical workers' Local 3, which the city sued in 1971 to enforce participation in the original New York Plan, consented to a separate training plan in which it would accept one hundred trainees with the goal of making them available for class A journeyperson status. However, the trainees were kept entirely distinct from the apprentices, instructed from obsolete textbooks, and taught a curriculum different from the one used for apprentices. Apprentices got a fifth year of classroom instruction essential for passing the union exam for class A status, which trainees did not receive. Rather than getting A cards after five years, trainees were put into the M, maintenance, division, which required another five to seven years before attaining full journeyworker status. Action begun in 1978 by the New York State Human Rights Commission on behalf of the trainees led to a 1982 finding, by the commission, that Local 3 was guilty of discrimination; this finding was upheld two years later in *Schuck v. SDHR et al.*, 102 AD 2d 673, 1984. As with the rest of our story, the six years required to pursue legal action against Local 3 is another case of the wheels of justice turning too slowly: by the time the court ruled in favor the trainees, the political support for the training program had already collapsed. In the meantime, many of the trainees who had originally been recruited into the program dropped out in disgust and frustration.

59. Testimony of Jim McNamara, New York City Bureau of Labor Service, presented to the New York City Commission on Human Rights, *Hearings on the Construction Industry*, April 24, 1990.

60. *Matter of Monarch Electrical Corporation v. Roberts*, 70 NY 2d 91, 517 NYS 2d 711 (1987). The court further noted that the State Labor Department "has been 'involved in' the trainee program in New York City, and has not challenged the use of 'trainees' on certain projects assisted by federal funds."

61. According to the City Human Rights Commission's 1993 report *Building Barriers: Discrimination in New York City's Construction Trades*, New York City has *never* denied a construction contract because of failure to comply with the city's nondiscrimination policy (p. 338).

62. Interview with James Dooley, executive secretary, and Claudius Johnson, director, New York Plan for Training, Inc., April 22, 1988.

63. New York City, Office of Construction Industry Relations, *Problems of Discrimination and Extortion in the Building Trades* (New York: Office of Construction Industry Relations, Mayor's Office, 1982), p. 6.

64. The Sheetmetal Workers' International Union was formed in 1888, under a constitution that provided for the establishment of "white local unions" and relegated blacks to membership in subordinate locals. Local 28 was established in

1913 as a "white local union." Racial restrictions were formally deleted from the International Constitution in 1948.

65. Local 28 had offered journeyworkers' examinations in 1968 and 1969 as a result of arbitration proceedings initiated by the Contractors' Association to force Local 28 to increase its manpower. Only 24 of the 330 individuals, all of them white, passed the first examination and were admitted to the union.

66. This paragraph is based on *Sheet Metal Workers v. EEOC*, 92 L Ed 2d 344, *U.S. Supreme Court Reports*, 1986, pp. 357–365.

67. Interview with David Raff, special master of Local 28 Sheetmetal Workers' Apprenticeship Program, and Rob McGonaghy, director of Local 28 Membership Assistance Program, March 13, 1991.

68. Interview with David Raff and Rob McGonaghy, March 8, 1988, March 10, 1988; for further details, see Thomas Bailey and Roger Waldinger, "Access and Opportunity: Developing a Skilled Construction Labor Force in the Port Authority Region," report prepared for the Office of Business and Job Opportunity of the Port Authority of New York and New Jersey, January 1989, pp. 51–57, 68–69.

69. Bonacich, "A Theory of Ethnic Antagonism."

70. Wilson, *Declining Significance*, p. 110.

71. Bonacich, "Advanced Capitalism and Black/White Relations," p. 48.

72. *New York Times*, June 25, 1978, p. 35; June 27, 1978, section 2, p. 3.

73. Joint Industry Board of the Electrical Industry, unpublished data.

74. Louis E. Harris and Bert Swanson, *Black-Jewish Relations in New York City* (New York: Praeger, 1970), p. 162.

75. *New York Times*, April 23, 1974, p. 45.

76. Committee on Economic Adjustment, "The Industrial Classification of Jewish Gainful Workers in New York City," 1937 (in the files of the American Jewish Committee).

77. Jeffrey Gurock, *When Harlem Was Jewish* (New York: Columbia University Press, 1979), pp. 66–67.

78. George H. Garvin, "House Painting and Decorating," Jews of New York, Works Progress Administration, Historical Records Survey—Federal Writers Project, box 3629, New York City Municipal Archives.

79. Moore, *At Home in America*, pp. 44–50.

80. Marshall and Briggs, *The Negro and Apprenticeship*, pp. 38–39.

81. Marshall and Briggs also contended that blacks were less disposed, for cultural and historical reasons, toward skilled manual jobs than whites (*The Negro and Apprenticeship*, p. 39). Whereas I have little basis, either empirical or intuitive, for judging this claim, it does appear that the apprenticeship programs have greater success in attracting whites with at least some college education than they do in attracting comparably educated blacks.

82. Bailey and Waldinger, "Access and Opportunity," pp. 30–38, 44–48.

83. Corcoran, *Irish Illegals*, p. 57.

84. John Calagione, "Working in Time: Music and Power on the Job in New York City," in John Calagione, Doris Francis, and Daniel Nugent, eds., *Workers' Experessions: Beyond Accommodation and Resistance* (Binghampton: State University of New York Press, 1992), chap. 2.

7. The Ethnic Politics of Municipal Jobs

1. Calculated from Census of Population, 1990, U.S. summary volume, table 47.

2. Norman Fainstein and Susan Fainstein, "Urban Regimes and Black Citizens: The Economic and Social Impacts of Black Political Incorporation in U.S. Cities," *International Journal of Urban and Regional Research*, forthcoming, 1996.

3. Terry Nichols Clark, "The Irish Ethic and the Spirit of Patronage," *Ethnicity*, 2 (1975): 129–166.

4. Stephen Erie, *Rainbow's End* (Berkeley: University of California Press, 1985).

5. Peter Eisinger, "Affirmative Action in Municipal Employment: The Impact of Black Political Power," *American Political Science Review*, 76, no. 2 (1982): 380–392.

6. Martin Shefter, *Political Crisis, Fiscal Crisis* (New York: Basic Books, 1985).

7. Wilbur Rich, *The Politics of Urban Personnel Policy: Reformers, Politicians, and Bureaucrats* (Port Washington, N.Y.: Kennikat Press, 1982), p. 22.

8. Morton Keller, *Affairs of State* (Cambridge, Mass.: Harvard University Press, 1977), p. 239.

9. Charles Garrett, *The LaGuardia Years: Machine and Reform in New York City* (New Brunswick, N.J.: Rutgers University Press, 1961).

10. O. Glenn Stahl, "Training Career Civil Servants for the City of New York" (Ph.D. diss., New York University, 1936).

11. Wallace Sayre and Herbert Kaufman, *Governing New York City* (New York: Norton, 1960).

12. Citizens Budget Commission, *Civil Service in the City of New York* (New York: Budget Commission, 1938).

13. Robert Fogelson, *Big-City Police* (Cambridge, Mass.: Harvard University Press, 1977).

14. Calculated from U.S. Bureau of the Census, *Census of Occupations at the 1900 Census*, pp. 634–637.

15. Erie, *Rainbow's End*, p. 88.

16. Ibid., p. 89.

17. Burton Hendricks, "The Jewish Invasion of New York," *McClure's*, March 1913, pp. 138–141; cited in Irving Howe, *World of Our Fathers* (New York: Harcourt Brace Jovanovich, 1976), p. 166.

18. Nancy Rapoport, "Employment Criteria in the New York City Civil Service: A History" (M.A. thesis, Graduate School of Public Administration, New York University, 1971); Stahl, "Training Career Civil Servants"; Wallace Sayre and Milton Mandell, *Education and the Civil Service in New York City* (Washington, D.C.: U.S. Department of the Interior, Office of Education, bulletin 1937, no. 20, 1938).

19. Calculated from reports of the Civil Service Commission.

20. Norman Thomas and Paul Blanshard, *What's the Matter with New York* (New York: Macmillan, 1932).

21. Moore, *At Home in America*, p. 100. In a more recent book on New York City's schoolteachers, Ruth Jacknow Markowitz reports that the Board of Exam-

iners was first officially charged with anti-Jewish bias in 1931 (*My Daughter, the Teacher* [New Brunswick, N.J.: Rutgers University Press, 1993], p. 81).

22. Henry Feingold, *A Time for Searching: Entering the Mainstream* (Baltimore: Johns Hopkins University Press, 1992), p. 200.

23. Bayor, *Neighbors in Conflict.*

24. Sayre and Kaufman, *Governing New York*, p. 305.

25. Data on positions and classifications from reports of the Civil Service Commission.

26. City of New York, Civil Service Commission, *Merit System Advancing: 55th Annual Report* (New York: Civil Service Commission, 1938), p. 8.

27. City of New York, Civil Service Commission, *Merit System Advancing: 56th Annual Report* (New York: Civil Service Commission, 1940).

28. Rapoport, "Employment Criteria"; Sayre and Mandell, *Education and the Civil Service in New York.*

29. Rebecca Rankin, *New York Advancing* (New York: Municipal Reference Library, 1945).

30. Stahl, "Training Career Civil Servants."

31. Budget Commission, *Civil Service in the City*, p. 23.

32. City of New York, Municipal Civil Service Commission, *Merit System Advancing: 54th Annual Report* (New York: Civil Service Commission, 1937), p. 35.

33. Rapoport, "Employment Criteria," p. 28.

34. Sayre and Mandell, *Education and the Civil Service in New York.*

35. Data on applications for new positions and for promotions from annual reports of the Civil Service Commission.

36. Civil Service Commission, *Merit System Advancing: 54th Annual Report*, p. 13.

37. Civil Service Commission, *Merit System Advancing: 56th Annual Report*, p. 32.

38. Ibid., p. 9.

39. City of New York, Municipal Civil Service Commission, *Civil Service Gains: 52d Annual Report* (New York: Civil Service Commission, 1935), p. 23.

40. Bayor, *Neighbors in Conflict.*

41. Markowitz, *My Daughter, the Teacher*, p. 155.

42. Richard Herrnstein et al., "New York City Police Department Class of 1940: A Preliminary Report," unpublished manuscript, Department of Psychology, Harvard University, n.d.

43. Arthur Niederhoffer, *Behind the Shield* (Garden City, N.Y.: Doubleday, 1967), p. 74.

44. Interview with Louis Weiser, director, Council of Jewish Civil Servants, April 25, 1991.

45. "Secret Reds to Be Put over New York Police!" *Social Justice*, September 11, 1939; "Is There an OGPU in New York?" *Social Justice*, September 18, 1939.

46. Shefter, *Political Crisis, Fiscal Crisis.*

47. Sayre and Kaufman, *Governing New York*, p. 385.

48. Mayor's Committee on Management Survey, *Modern Management for the City of New York* (New York: n.p, 1952), p. 177.

49. David Rogers, *110 Livingston Street: Politics and Bureaucracy in the New York City School System* (New York: Vintage, 1967), p. 161.

50. But white ethnic competition did not disappear. To take one example, Jewish defense organizations immediately went into high gear in the mid-1950s when the New York Children's Court sought to appoint probation officers by religion in proportion to the religious composition of the children under probation—a policy that would have sharply diminished employment opportunities for Jews. (News release of the American Jewish Committee, "AJC Urges Disapproval of Religious Quotas in Appointment of Children's Court Probation Officers," January 1, 1955, files of the American Jewish Committee.)

51. David Stanley, *Managing Local Government under Union Pressure* (Washington, D.C.: Brookings Institution, 1972), p. 41.

52. City of New York, Department of Personnel, "The Policies, Activities, and Accomplishments of the Civil Service Commission and the Department of Personnel," four-year report, 1966–1969, to Mayor John V. Lindsay, unpublished, 1970, p. 26.

53. Solomon Hoberman, "Personnel Management and Labor Relations in New York City: Summary of Findings and Recommendations," in State Charter Revision Commission, *Personnel Reforms for New York City* (New York: Revision Commission, 1974), p. 9.

54. David Stanley and associates, *Professional Personnel for the City of New York* (Washington, D.C.: Brookings Institution, 1963).

55. City of New York, Personnel Council, *Adapting the Civil Service System to Changing Times and Needs* (New York: Personnel Council, 1972).

56. John R. Morse, "Strategies for Job Mobility of Minority Workers: A Study of Mobility among Unionized Civil Service Municipal Employees in New York City" (Ph.D. diss., New York University, 1974).

57. Peter Allan, "The Executive in New York City Government" (Ph.D. diss., New York University Graduate School of Business Administration, 1969).

58. Raymond Horton, *Municipal Labor Relations in New York City: Lessons of the Lindsay-Wagner Years* (New York: Praeger, 1972); Stanley, *Managing Local Government under Union Pressure*.

59. Stanley and associates, *Professional Personnel for the City of New York*, p. 95.

60. E. S. Savas and Sigmund G. Ginsburg, "The Civil Service: A Meritless System?" *Public Interest*, 32 (1973): 70–85.

61. Stanley and associates, *Professional Personnel for the City of New York*, p. 101.

62. Mary White Ovington, *Half a Man* (New York: Longman's Green, 1911).

63. Colored Citizens' Non-Partisan Committee for the Re-election of Mayor Walker, "New York City and the Colored Citizen," LaGuardia papers, box 3530, New York Municipal Archives, n.d. (1930?).

64. Greene, "Harlem in the Depression," p. 115.

65. *New York Post*, January 21, 1936. See Schomburg Center Clipping File (microfiche), 004, 843.

66. "Negro Fire Captain on Promotion List," *New York Times*, July 28, 1938.

67. Edwin Lewinson, *Black Politics in New York City* (New York: Twayne, 1974); Greenberg, *"Or Does it Explode?"*

68. State of New York, "Report of the New York State Temporary Commission on the Condition of the Urban Colored Population," legislative document no. 63, 1938, p. 33.

69. City of New York, Mayor's Commission on Conditions in Harlem, "The Negro in Harlem: A Report on Social and Economic Conditions Responsible for the Outbreak of March 19, 1935," LaGuardia papers, box 3529, New York City Municipal Archives.

70. City of New York, Mayor's Commission on Conditions in Harlem, "Hearings: Employment Discrimination in Harlem," LaGuardia papers, box 3770, New York City Municipal Archives.

71. Josh Freeman, *In Transit: The Transport Workers Union in New York City, 1933–1966* (New York: Oxford University Press, 1989), p. 29.

72. NAACP archives, Library of Congress, III, box A341.

73. Freeman, *In Transit*, p. 154.

74. Calculated from the Census of Population, 1940, Public Use Microdata Samples.

75. Ira Katznelson, *Black Men, White Cities* (New York: Oxford University Press, 1973), p. 82.

76. State of New York, "The Condition of the Urban Colored Population," p. 34.

77. National Urban League files, Library of Congress, Part I, IV A, box 6.

78. Anna Arnold Hedgeman, *The Trumpet Sounds: A Memoir of Negro Leadership* (New York: Holt Rinehart and Winston, 1964), pp. 71–74.

79. City of New York, LaGuardia papers, box 3769, New York City Municipal Archives.

80. Memorandum for conference with fire commissioner; report of conference, in NAACP archives, Library of Congress, II B, box 65.

81. Charles V. Hamilton, *Adam Clayton Powell: The Political Biography of an American Dilemma* (New York: Atheneum, 1991).

82. Wallace Sayre, "The Triumph of Technique over Purpose," *Public Administration Review*, 8 (1948).

83. Stanley and associates, *Professional Personnel for the City of New York*.

84. Peter Kihss, "High School Diploma Is Dropped as a Requirement for Some Civil Service Jobs in City," *New York Times*, March 18, 1968.

85. "Poverty Workers Sue City on Tests," *New York Times*, April 17 1968, p. 44.

86. Stanley, *Managing Local Government under Union Pressure*.

87. Horton, *Municipal Labor Relations in New York City*.

88. Mark Haskell, *The New Careers Concept* (New York: Praeger, 1969).

89. Stanley, *Managing Local Government under Union Pressure*.

90. Morse, "Strategies for Job Mobility of Minority Workers."

91. Union views as summarized in a 1967 memorandum prepared for Mayor Lindsay; see Rapoport, "Employment Criteria," pp. 98–99.

92. Marilyn Gittell, "Public Employment and the Public Service," in Alan Gartner et al., eds., *Public Service Employment: An Analysis of Its History, Problems, and Prospects* (New York: Praeger, 1973), pp. 121–142.

93. Emanuel Perlmutter, "State High Court Quashes Model Cities Job Project," *New York Times*, July 4, 1973, p. 1.

94. "Gentle Touch Has Turned Tough School," *New York World Telegram*, February 1951, Schomburg Clipping File, 004, 843; Hope McLeod, "Close-Up: Education," *New York Post*, November 1, 1965, Schomburg Clipping File, 004, 843.

95. M. S. Handler, "Black Principal Named in Bronx," *New York Times*, October 12, 1969.

96. Diane Ravitch, *The Great School Wars* (New York: Basic Books, 1975).

97. Harris and Swanson, *Black-Jewish Relations in New York City*, p. 132.

98. NAACP Legal Defense Fund, press release, "LDF Charges Bias in Licensing of School Supervisory Personnel," September 24, 1970; American Jewish Congress, untitled press release, September 16, 1971; NAACP Legal Defense Fund, press release, "LDF Defends Lower Court Victory over 'Insider' New York City Principals' Examination," February 14, 1972; in Schomburg Clipping File, 004, 058.

99. Peter Kihss, "Anti-Defamation Unit Charges Bias in Selection of Principals," *New York Times*, July 17, 1974.

100. Shefter, *Political Crisis, Fiscal Crisis*.

101. Marilyn Gittell, "New York City," in S. A. Levitan and R. Taggart, eds., *Emergency Employment Act: The PEP Generation* (Salt Lake City: Olympus, 1974), pp. 201–220.

102. Mary McCormick, "Labor Relations," in Charles Brecher and Raymond Horton, eds., *Setting Municipal Priorities: New York and the American Experience* (New York: New York University Press, 1985), pp. 302–330.

103. John Mollenkopf, *Phoenix from the Ashes* (Princeton, N.J.: Princeton University Press, 1992).

104. Walter Stafford with Edwin Die, *Employment Segmentation in New York City Municipal Agencies* (New York: CSS Institute for Community Empowerment, 1989).

105. City of New York, Mayor's Commission on Black New Yorkers, *Report* (New York: Commission on Black New Yorkers, 1987), p. 99.

106. City of New York, Citywide Equal Employment Opportunity Committee, *Equal Employment Opportunity in New York City Government, 1977–1987* (New York: Citywide Committee, 1988), p. 58.

107. Data from unpublished EEOC reports; see Table 7.1.

108. City of New York, Mayor's Advisory Committee for Police Management and Personnel Policy, *Final Report: Recommendations*, vol. 1 (New York: Mayor's Committee, 1987).

109. Raymond Horton, "Human Resources," in Charles Brecher and Raymond Horton, eds., *Setting Municipal Priorities: New York and the American Experience* (New York: New York University Press, 1985), p. 193.

110. State of New York, Commission on Government Integrity, *"Playing Ball" with City Hall: A Case Study of Political Patronage in New York City* (New York: Commission on Government Integrity, 1989), p. 73.

111. New York City Department of Personnel, "Annual Report to the New York State Civil Service Commission," 1979–1989, unpublished; memorandum from Douglas White, director of the Department of Personnel, to Mayor David Dinkins, "Quarterly Report on Provisionals," December 31, 1990.

112. Stanley and associates, *Professional Personnel for the City of New York.*

113. Horton, "Human Resources."

114. Charles Brecher and Raymond Horton with Robert A. Cropf and Dean Michael Mead, *Power Failure: New York City Politics and Policy since 1960* (New York: Oxford University Press, 1993), p. 249.

115. Brecher and Horton, *Power Failure,* p. 259.

116. Calculated from Citywide Equal Employment Opportunity Committee, *Equal Employment Opportunity,* p. 6.

117. *New York Times,* September 12, 1991, B: 2, 1.

118. *New York Times,* October 8, 1991, B: 1, 2; on the *Forward*'s reaction, see Benjamin Ginsberg, *The Fatal Embrace: Jews and the State* (Chicago: University of Chicago Press, 1993).

119. Miriam Lee Kaprow, "Magical Work: Firefighters in New York," *Human Organization,* 50, no. 1 (1991): 97–103.

120. Edith Lynton, *Entry Level Training in the New York City Uniformed Services* (Albany: Center for Women in Government, State University of Albany, 1987), p. 98.

121. Center for Social Policy and Practice in the Workplace, *Gender Integration in the Fire Department of the City of New York* (New York: Columbia University School of Social Work, 1989), p. 40; Brecher and Horton, *Power Failure,* p. 259.

122. The tendency for police officers, observed by Lynton in the study quoted above, to transfer into the Fire Department appears to be long-standing. For evidence from an earlier period, see Bernard Cohen and Jan M. Chaiken, *New York City's Police: The Background and Performance of the Class of '57* (New York: New York City Rand Institute, 1973).

123. According to my informants in the Department of Personnel, efforts were made to broad-band scores and thereby avoid strict rank-order selection. However, even with broad-banding, "the gap between whites and minorities [remained] so large that it was unbridgeable."

124. Robert Gearty, "Fire Dept. Flunks Test on Minority Recruiting: New Class 96% White," *Daily News,* May 6, 1993.

125. This paragraph draws on unpublished data provided by the New York City Department of Personnel.

126. Ellen Tumposky, "Firefighters Test Defended: Better Shot for Minorities, Women," *Daily News,* April 17, 1992.

127. Vincent Lee and Dick Sheridan, "Fire Exam Blasted," *Daily News,* April 16, 1992; *New York Times,* April 17, 1992, B: 1, 6.

128. Whites composed 82 percent of the 1992 applicants and almost certainly a higher proportion of those who actually took the test.

129. "Welfare Unit Claims Negro Hiring Record," *New York Times,* February 16, 1950.

130. NAACP archives, Library of Congress, III, box A341.

131. Stephen Jaekel, "Provisional Rolls Climb to 42,000," *Chief-Leader,* April 13, 1990, p. 1.

132. William Murphy, "A City Test Few Will Fail," *Daily News,* December 3, 1992.

133. Richard Steier, "City Big Axed Job List as 'Too White and Male': Union," *New York Post,* May 13, 1992.

134. *New York Times*, June 8, 1993, B: 1, 6.

135. Mayor's Commission on Hispanic Concerns, *Report* (New York: Commission on Hispanic Concerns, 1986), p. 109.

136. David E. Pitt, "Racial Tensions Work in Three Ways Now," *New York Times*, February 19, 1989, D: 6, 4.

137. Angelo Falcon, "The Puerto Rican Experience in New York City under Mayor-Elect David Dinkins," in Institute for Puerto Rican Policy, *The Dinkins Administration and the Puerto Rican Community* (New York: Institute for Puerto Rican Policy, 1990), pp. 15–16.

138. A report prepared by the Institute for Puerto Rican Policy called *The Impact of the Giuliani Budget Cuts on the Latino Community* notes, among other things, "a *disturbing* level of *extreme* over-representation . . . for certain jobs groups for White[s] and Blacks" (Institute for Puerto Rican Policy, 1994, p. 3; italics added).

139. The official did not get the figures quite right: 101,201 people applied to take the sanworkers test, but "only" 71,007 actually took it. The previous test, conducted in 1983, produced a list with almost 45,000 names, enough to supply the city with 84 candidates for each actual opening. See Brecher and Horton, *Power Failure*, p. 260.

140. Brecher and Horton, *Power Failure*, p. 42.

141. Work force totals for 1989 and 1993 from Citizens Budget Commission, "Political Leadership in the Two New Yorks," (June 1993), pp. 6, 19; 1975 work force total from Brecher and Horton, *Power Failure*, p. 36.

142. Andy Logan, "Around New York," *New Yorker*, September 23, 1991, p. 104.

143. Falcon, "The Puerto Rican Experience in New York," p. 14.

8. Small Business

1. Glazer and Moynihan, *Beyond the Melting Pot*, pp. 31–34.

2. Ivan Light, *Ethnic Enterprise in America* (Berkeley: University of California Press, 1972).

3. Ivan Light and Edna Bonacich, *Ethnic Entrepreneurs: Koreans in Los Angeles, 1965–1983* (Berkeley: University of California Press, 1988).

4. Thomas Bailey and Roger Waldinger, "Primary, Secondary, and Enclave Labor Markets: A Training Systems Approach," *American Sociological Review*, 56, no. 4 (August 1991): 432–445.

5. Alejandro Portes and Julia Sensenbrenner, "Embeddedness and Immigration: Notes on the Social Determination of Embeddedness," *American Journal of Sociology*, 98, no. 6: (1993): 1320–1351.

6. Herbert Gans, *The Urban Villagers* (New York: Free Press, 1962).

7. Annelise Orleck, "The Soviet Jews: Life in Brighton Beach, Brooklyn," in Nancy Foner, ed., *New Immigrants in New York* (New York: Columbia University Press, 1987), pp. 279–280.

8. Kasinitz, *Caribbean New Yorkers*, p. 69.

9. Michael Massing, "Crack's Destructrive Spring across America," *New York Times*, October, 1, 1989.

10. See Waldinger, Aldrich, Ward, and associates, *Ethnic Entrepreneurs*, chap. 2.

11. For research on ecological succession and its impact on the makeup of the local small-business population, see Howard Aldrich and Albert J. Reiss, Jr., "Con-

tinuities in the Study of Ecological Succession: Changes in the Race Composition of Neighborhoods and Their Businesses," *American Journal of Sociology*, 81, no. 4 (1976): 846–866; Howard Aldrich, Catherine Zimmer, and David McEvoy, "Continuities in the Study of Ecological Succession: Asian Businesses in Three English Cities," *Social Forces*, 67, no. 4 (1989): 920–943.

12. Roger Waldinger, "Structural Opportunity or Ethnic Advantage? Immigrant Business Development in New York," *International Migration Review*, 23, no. 1 (1989): 48–72.

13. Illsoo Kim, *The New Urban Immigrants* (Princeton, N.J.: Princeton University Press, 1981), p. 111.

14. Kim, *The New Urban Immigrants*; Pyong Gap Min, *Ethnic Business Enterprise: Korean Small Business in Atlanta* (New York: Center for Migration Studies, 1988); Pyong Gap Min, "Cultural and Economic Boundaries of Korean Ethnicity: A Comparative Analysis," *Ethnic and Racial Studies*, 14 (1991): 225–241.

15. Peter Kwong, *The New Chinatown* (New York: Hill and Wang, 1987), p. 32.

16. This history of Chinatown's early garment industry comes from Xiaolan Bao's dissertation, "Holding Up More Than Half the Sky," p. 28, where the author cites a Chinese-language book by Guo Zhengzhi, *The Vicissitude of a Chinatown: A History of New York's Chinatown* (Hong Kong: Buo Yi Press, 1985).

17. S. W. Kung, *Chinese in American Life* (Seattle: University of Washington Press, 1962), p. 185.

18. Waldinger, *Through the Eye of the Needle*, p. 117.

19. Abeles, Haeckel, Schwartz, and Silverblatt (consulting firm), *The Chinatown Garment Industry Study* (New York: Local 23-25, International Ladies' Garment Workers' Union, and New York Skirt and Sportswear Association, 1983); Waldinger and Tseng, "Divergent Diasporas," pp. 93–95.

20. Bao, "Holding Up More Than Half the Sky," p. 75.

21. Min Zhou, *Chinatown: The Socio-economic Potential of an Ethnic Enclave* (Philadelphia: Temple University Press, 1991), p. 246.

22. Timothy Bates, "The Minority Share of Small Business Generally and Construction Specifically," report to the Regional Alliance for Small Contractors, New School for Social Research, 1992.

23. Data calculated from the Census of Population, 1990, Public Use Microdata Sample.

24. See chap. 1 in Waldinger, Aldrich, Ward, and associates, *Ethnic Entrepreneurs*.

25. I am indebted to Carmenza Gallo's paper "The Construction Industry in New York City: Immigrants and Black Entrepreneurs," unpublished manuscript, Conservation of Human Resources, Columbia University, 1983, for this point.

26. See Robert Glover, *Minority Enterprise in Construction* (New York: Praeger, 1977), pp. 57–59. Gallo reports similar findings in "Construction Industry," p. 27.

27. Calculated from the Census of Population, 1990, Public Use Microdata Samples.

28. Arthur Stinchcombe, "Social Structure and the Invention of Organizational Forms," in Tom Burns, ed., *Industrial Man* (Baltimore: Penguin, 1969), p. 160.

29. Glover, *Minority Enterprise in Construction*.

30. Gallo similarly found that contractors doing larger commercial and indus-

trial work selected on the basis of "previous experience and an established relationship, because, as one electrician commented, the bidding process is ultimately costly and does not guarantee good work. Therefore, whenever possible, the contractor would invite a restricted number of potential subcontractors to bid. For a subcontractor, in turn, it is enough to know three or four contractors; a reasonable estimate, backed up by previous performance, keeps him in business" (Gallo, "Construction Industry," p. 29).

31. Pyong Gap Min, "Ethnic Business, Intergroup Conflict, and Ethnic Solidarity," unpublished manuscript, 1993, pp. 109–117 (forthcoming, University of California Press).

32. Pyong Gap Min, "Cultural and Economic Boundaries of Korean Ethnicity: A Comparative Analysis," *Ethnic and Racial Studies*, 14 (1991): 225–241; Roger Waldinger, "When the Melting Pot Boils Over: The Irish, Jews, African-Americans, and Koreans of New York," in Michael Peter Smith and Joe Feagin, eds., *The Bubbling Cauldron: The New Political Sociology of Race and Ethnicity in America* (Minneapolis: University of Minnesota Press, 1995).

33. Kim, *The New Urban Immigrants*, p. 113.

Appendix 1

1. Introduced by Edgar S. Dunn in 1960 (see "A Statistical and Analytical Technique for Regional Analysis," *Papers and Proceedings of the Regional Science Association*, 6 [1960]: 98–112), shift-share analysis is a commonly used tool for analyzing economic change by industrial sector in a region, state, or locality. Though there are now numerous variants of Dunn's original formulation (for example, Francisco Arcelus, "An Extension of Shift-Share Analysis," *Growth and Change*, 15, no. 1 [1984]: 3–8; K. C. Bishop and C. E. Simpson, "Components of Change Analysis: Problems of Alternative Approaches to Industrial Structure," *Regional Studies*, 6, no. 1 [1972]: 59–68), shift-share analysis typically decomposes employment change in a region into three components: a national growth effect, an industrial mix effect, and a competitive effect. My interest, of course, concerns the employment change undergone by an ethnic group *within* a region (in this case, New York City). Hence, in my analysis, ethnic groups substitute for regions; my "growth effect" corresponds to the standard "national growth effect," with the exception that I use New York City, and not the nation, as a baseline; likewise, my "industrial effect" corresponds to the standard "industrial mix effect." However, I break the competitive effect down into two components: the "population effect" and the "shift"; the reasons for doing so are indicated in the text. For a review and critique of my approach, see Richard Barff and Mark Ellis, "Immigrants and the Changing Racial/Ethnic Division of Labor in New York City, 1970–1990," *Urban Geography*, forthcoming, 1996; I am grateful to Barff and Ellis for clarifying aspects of shift-share analysis, in both the conventional and the less conventional form, in which it appears here.

Index